America's
TEST KITCHEN

MENU
COOKBOOK

KITCHEN-TESTED MENUS FOR FOOLPROOF DINNER PARTIES

51 Menus for Every Occasion

Plus Strategies that Guarantee Less Stress and Better Food

By the Editors at America's Test Kitchen

Photography by Carl Tremblay, Keller + Keller, and Daniel J. van Ackere

Copyright © 2011 by the Editors at America's Test Kitchen

America's Test Kitchen
17 Station Street, Brookline, MA 02445

Library of Congress Cataloging-in-Publication Data

The America's Test Kitchen menu cookbook : kitchen-tested menus for foolproof dinner parties : 51 menus for every occasion plus strategies that guarantee less stress and better food / by the editors at America's Test Kitchen ; photography by Carl Tremblay, Keller + Keller, and Daniel J. van Ackere. -- 1st ed.
      p. cm.
Includes index.
ISBN 978-1-933615-90-5
1. Menus. 2. Dinners and dining. 3. Cooking, American. 4. Cookbooks. I. Tremblay, Carl. II. Van Ackere, Daniel. III. America's Test Kitchen (Firm) IV. Keller + Keller.
TX731.A633 2011
641.5973--dc23
                2011026475

Manufactured in the United States of America
10 9 8 7 6 5 4 3 2 1

Distributed by America's Test Kitchen
17 Station Street, Brookline, MA 02445

EDITORIAL DIRECTOR: Jack Bishop
EXECUTIVE EDITOR: Elizabeth Carduff
EXECUTIVE FOOD EDITOR: Julia Collin Davison
SENIOR EDITOR: Suzannah McFerran
ASSOCIATE EDITOR: Adelaide Parker
TEST COOKS: Rebecca Morris, Christie Morrison
PHOTOSHOOT KITCHEN TEAM:
    ASSOCIATE EDITORS: Chris O'Connor, Yvonne Ruperti
    ASSISTANT TEST COOKS: Daniel Cellucci, Danielle DeSiato-Hallman,
    and Kate Williams
EDITORIAL ASSISTANT: Alyssa King
DESIGN DIRECTOR: Amy Klee
ART DIRECTOR: Greg Galvan
ASSOCIATE ART DIRECTOR: Matthew Warnick
PHOTOGRAPHY: Carl Tremblay
STAFF PHOTOGRAPHER: Daniel J. van Ackere
ADDITIONAL PHOTOGRAPHY: Keller + Keller
FOOD STYLING: Marie Piraino and Mary Jane Sawyer
ILLUSTRATOR: John Burgoyne
PRODUCTION DIRECTOR: Guy Rochford
SENIOR PRODUCTION MANAGER: Jessica Quirk
SENIOR PROJECT MANAGER: Alice Carpenter
PRODUCTION AND TRAFFIC COORDINATOR: Kate Hux
ASSET AND WORKFLOW MANAGER: Andrew Mannone
PRODUCTION AND IMAGING SPECIALISTS: Judy Blomquist, Heather Dube,
and Lauren Pettapiece
COPYEDITOR: Cheryl Redmond
PROOFREADER: Debra Hudak
INDEXER: Elizabeth Parson

PICTURED ON FRONT OF JACKET: Individual Hot Fudge Pudding Cakes (page 149)
PICTURED OPPOSITE TITLE PAGE: Japanese Salmon Dinner (page 187)
PICTURED ON BACK OF JACKET: Easy and Elegant Cornish Game Hen Dinner
(page 211), Tapas Party (page 73), Big Game Day Party (page 271), and Classic Beef
Tenderloin Dinner (page 49)

ALSO BY THE EDITORS
AT AMERICA'S TEST KITCHEN

The Cook's Illustrated Cookbook

The America's Test Kitchen
Healthy Family Cookbook

The America's Test Kitchen
Family Baking Book

The America's Test Kitchen
Family Cookbook

The Complete America's Test Kitchen
TV Show Cookbook

Slow Cooker Revolution

The Best Simple Recipes

AMERICA'S TEST KITCHEN ANNUALS:

The Best of America's Test Kitchen
(2007–2012 Editions)

Cooking for Two
(2009–2011 Editions)

Light & Healthy
(2010 and 2011 Editions)

THE COOK'S COUNTRY SERIES:

From Our Grandmothers' Kitchens

Cook's Country Blue Ribbon Desserts

Cook's Country Best Potluck Recipes

Cook's Country Best Lost Suppers

Cook's Country Best Grilling Recipes

The Cook's Country Cookbook

America's Best Lost Recipes

THE BEST RECIPE SERIES:

The New Best Recipe

The Best One-Dish Suppers

Soups, Stews & Chilis

More Best Recipes

The Best Skillet Recipes

The Best Slow & Easy Recipes

The Best Chicken Recipes

The Best International Recipe

The Best Make-Ahead Recipe

The Best 30-Minute Recipe

The Best Light Recipe

The Cook's Illustrated Guide to
Grilling & Barbecue

Best American Side Dishes

Cover & Bake

Steaks, Chops, Roasts & Ribs

Baking Illustrated

For a complete listing of all our books
or to order any of our books, visit us at
http://www.cooksillustrated.com
http://www.americastestkitchen.com
or call 800-611-0759

TABLE OF CONTENTS

Spring

≤ 18 ≥

Summer

≤ 78 ≥

Fall

⋦ 136 ⋧

Winter

⋦ 192 ⋧

Celebrations
and Holidays

⋦ 250 ⋧

WELCOME TO
AMERICA'S TEST KITCHEN

This book has been tested, written, and edited by the folks at America's Test Kitchen, a very real 2,500-square-foot kitchen located just outside of Boston. It is the home of *Cook's Illustrated* magazine and *Cook's Country* magazine and is the Monday-through-Friday destination for more than three dozen test cooks, editors, food scientists, tasters, and cookware specialists. Our mission is to test recipes over and over again until we understand how and why they work and until we arrive at the "best" version.

We start the process of testing a recipe with a complete lack of conviction, which means that we accept no claim, no theory, no technique, and no recipe at face value. We simply assemble as many variations as possible, test a half-dozen of the most promising, and taste the results blind. We then construct our own hybrid recipe and continue to test it, varying ingredients, techniques, and cooking times until we reach a consensus. The result, we hope, is the best version of a particular recipe, but we realize that only you can be the final judge of our success (or failure). As we like to say in the test kitchen, "We make the mistakes, so you don't have to."

All of this would not be possible without a belief that good cooking, much like good music, is indeed based on a foundation of objective technique. Some people like spicy foods and others don't, but there is a right way to sauté, there is a best way to cook a pot roast, and there are measurable scientific principles involved in producing perfectly beaten, stable egg whites. This is our ultimate goal: to investigate the fundamental principles of cooking so that you become a better cook. It is as simple as that.

You can watch us work (in our actual test kitchen) by tuning in to *America's Test Kitchen* (www.americastestkitchentv.com) or *Cook's Country from America's Test Kitchen* (www.cookscountrytv.com) on public television, or by subscribing to *Cook's Illustrated* magazine (www.cooksillustrated.com) or *Cook's Country* magazine (www.cookscountry.com). We welcome you into our kitchen, where you can stand by our side as we test our way to the "best" recipes in America.

PREFACE

The Vermonters I grew up with had no problem planning menus because every midday dinner was about the same: meat, potatoes, biscuits or bread, a vegetable, and milk from the cow out back. Dessert was a sugar or molasses cookie or, occasionally, since the town baker, Marie, didn't take to pie-making, a slice of apple or lemon meringue pie. Any culture that depends on the availability of simple, local ingredients has few panic attacks when it comes to menu planning—one eats what is in season along with a store of preserved foods from the cellar, including potatoes, apples, brined pork, dried meats, succotash, and the like.

That lack of choice offers simplicity but most of us would be hard pressed to consume such a restrictive diet. That reminds me of a story about a frugal farmer, a train, and a pig. An elderly farmer, known far and wide for his parsimony, stopped at the Sanbornton Bridge ticket office in New Hampshire.

"How much to Littleton?" he asked the ticket agent.

"Two dollars."

The farmer said nothing for a bit. "Well then, how much for a cow?"

"Three dollars."

"A pig?"

"One dollar."

"Book me as a pig," said the old-timer promptly.

I do know something about cooking but I was not blessed with the ability to quickly pair recipes and create menus that one can actually execute without a ton of last-minute work and which don't offer such a strange combination of tastes and textures that one wonders, halfway through dinner, "What was I thinking?" The menu cookbooks that I have consulted over the years tend to fall into the trap of trying to impress company to a fault, turning dinner into a feat of culinary Olympics, or they offer such a strange set of options you would think the menus had been prepared for a movie set or perhaps the Broadway stage. And don't even get me started about clever "event" menus with silly names.

That's a long introduction to a simple premise—*The America's Test Kitchen Menu Cookbook*. These are practical menus (we know, since we prepared each menu in its entirety to make absolutely sure that each and every one is practical and appealing) composed of the sorts of recipes that real cooks want to make at home. They don't just look good on paper; they work in the kitchen and the dining room as well.

We start off with a few quick ideas for last-minute appetizers (I love the Easy Melted Brie with Honey and Herbs), easy sides (Broiled Asparagus with Lemon and Roasted Baby Carrots with Browned Butter are my favorites), no-prep salad dressings (how about a Parmesan Vinaigrette?), and easy ice cream desserts (Chocolate Ice Cream with Amaretto and Espresso is a winner). We have assembled our favorite quick tips and also put together an entertaining troubleshooting guide that includes one of my favorite tips: If you slice into a roast and the meat is too rare, place the slices on a wire rack over a rimmed baking sheet and broil, covered with pieces of lettuce so that the meat gently steams without overcooking. We have also worked hard on an emergency substitution chart that tells you how to make substitutes for sour cream, brown sugar, confectioners' sugar, half-and-half, unsweetened chocolate, and wine, among many others.

At the heart of *The America's Test Kitchen Menu Cookbook* are, of course, the menus, more than 50 kitchen-tested groups of recipes with all the logistic nightmares solved. We explain what can be done the day before including brining, salting, marinating, and baking. We provide the total preparation time for each recipe and explain which recipes can be cooked together. We also make sure that there is a minimum amount of last-minute preparation and cooking, the death knell of most badly organized dinner parties. We do expect to enjoy our guests! Some of my favorite menus include Rustic Tuscan Supper featuring Hearty Tuscan Bean Stew and Skillet-Roasted Apples with Caramel Sauce for dessert. I also serve the Farmhouse Chicken Dinner, which features Honeyed Goat Cheese with Spiced Walnuts and Figs, Rustic Breaded Chicken with Brussels Sprouts, Herbed Barley Pilaf, and Autumn Pear Crumble. Another favorite is the Elegant Salmon Dinner, which starts off with Rustic Caramelized Onion Tart, offers Israeli Couscous with Caramelized Fennel and Spinach as a side, and then ends with Goat Cheese and Lemon Cheesecake. Or you could make something even simpler, a One-Pot Bolognese dinner, or a real make-ahead staple with a taste of France, Beef Stew Provençal. We've also come up with some new recipes for special-occasion entertaining, including Easy Mushroom Pâté, BLT Canapés, Cheddar and Apple Panini Bites, Skillet Caramelized Pears with Blue Cheese, Stuffed Mushrooms with Boursin and Prosciutto, as well as simple Ham and Cheese Palmiers.

Of course, if you are confident in your menu-creating skills, you can mix and match among the 250 recipes in this book or simply leave off a first course, remove a dessert, or swap out something simpler for something more elegant. No problem. But it's nice to have a starting point, a fresh idea, a new combination of flavors and textures for the next time you decide to give a Sunday supper or a holiday dinner party. We've done the work for you.

As I have said, I find menus thoroughly confusing and that, of course, reminds me of one last story about a student who was equally bewildered. An admiral was visiting a naval officer's training school in England and asked one of the students to chart his whereabouts, a fun exercise to break the ice. After a long while, the student handed him the result of his calculations. The admiral looked at it and immediately took off his hat.

"Why did you do that?" the student asked.

"Well, this chart shows that we are in Westminster Abbey and, if that's the case, I certainly should remove my hat!"

Enjoy the menus and your next dinner party.

Cordially,

CHRISTOPHER KIMBALL
Founder and Editor,
Cook's Illustrated and *Cook's Country*
Host, *America's Test Kitchen* and
Cook's Country from America's Test Kitchen

THE WELL-STOCKED KITCHEN

When you're putting on a dinner party, you're cooking larger batches of food and very likely more courses at once than you'd ever make on a weeknight. You need everything to go smoothly. And having exactly the right equipment can make a big difference. The list here represents the cookware and tools that are absolutely essential when entertaining—of course this isn't a comprehensive list of everything we expect you to have in your kitchen, but rather key items along with the brands that won our extensive testings.

Food Processor

We can't imagine putting on a dinner party without a food processor in our kitchen. We make pizza dough in it, shred cheese, make pie dough, make relishes and pestos, slice potatoes thinly for a gratin, and much, much more. We even make some simple cake batters right in the food processor. So given all this piece of equipment can do, don't cheap out when you buy one. We've found time and again that the cheapest models aren't sturdy and can't perform the most basic tasks efficiently. Our winner is the **KitchenAid KFP750 12-Cup Food Processor**, which is powerful, simple to operate, and offers ample capacity in an intuitive, compact design. It excelled at every task we threw its way, from grinding bread crumbs and nuts to cutting cold butter into flour for pie dough. While it's not a bargain—it costs $199—it's an investment that will last a long time and ensure entertaining success.

Stand Mixer

Just like a good food processor, a stand mixer is a kitchen workhorse and a must-have—and useful for more than just desserts. This piece of equipment can mix, whip, beat, or knead anything you throw its way. Look for a stand mixer that operates using planetary action—meaning the bowl is stationary and a single mixing arm moves around the bowl, rather than the beaters being stationary and the bowl moving—as it will be less likely to get stuck on stiff doughs and batters. Also, the bowl shouldn't be deep and gigantic, or small batches of dough won't get mixed properly and scraping down the side of the bowl will lead to dirty sleeves; one that's squat and holds 5 to 6 quarts works better. The **Cuisinart 5.5-Quart Stand Mixer** ($299) has a powerful motor that excelled at all tasks, including kneading heavy bread. For a best buy, we like the **KitchenAid Classic Plus Stand Mixer**, which is $100 cheaper.

Dutch Oven

Our kitchen would stop running without a Dutch oven. And we could not entertain without it. The best choice for soups, a Dutch oven is also ideal for frying, stewing, braising, steaming, and boiling and it is built for both oven and stovetop use (many of our stews go from stovetop to the oven for more even cooking). When you're cooking for a crowd, you absolutely need a good Dutch oven that is between 6 and 8 quarts in capacity. We like a Dutch oven that is roughly twice as wide as it is tall. The bottom should be thick—so that it maintains moderate heat and prevents food from scorching—and the lid should fit tightly to prevent excessive moisture loss. We recommend the **Le Creuset 7¼-Quart Round French Oven** ($269), which we consider to be the "gold standard" of Dutch ovens. For a more affordable option, but still an impressive piece of equipment, we like the **Tramontina 6½-Quart Cast-Iron Dutch Oven**, which costs just $49 and performed nearly as well as the more expensive models.

Skillets

It pays to invest in a good 12-inch traditional skillet and a 12-inch nonstick skillet. While it is handy to have smaller versions of these skillets as well, you'll definitely need the larger sizes for family-size meals and for entertaining. A traditional skillet allows food to stick, for the development of fond (the crusty brown bits that contribute flavor), which can be used to make pan sauces; this skillet is ideal for cooking steaks, chicken, and pork. A nonstick skillet is great for delicate, quick-cooking food like fish or eggs—but don't spend big bucks on one since the coating can wear off within a few years. For both skillets, look for a comfortable, ovensafe handle and a wide, roomy cooking surface. We've found the sturdy, durable **All-Clad Stainless 12-Inch Fry Pan** ($119) offers stellar cooking performance. For nonstick skillets, we like the **T-Fal Professional Total Nonstick 12½-Inch Fry Pan** ($34.99).

Saucepans

Saucepans are just the right size and shape for a thousand and one common kitchen tasks. They are easy to maneuver and stay out of your way on a crowded cooktop. We think every kitchen should be equipped with two saucepans: one with a capacity of 3 to 4 quarts and a second 2-quart nonstick saucepan. Larger saucepans are great for sauces and vegetables, but the smaller saucepans can be used for cooking foods that stick easily and are great for making rice. Be sure your saucepans have tight-fitting lids. There is nothing worse than trying to make rice or another side dish with a leaky lid. Also, a comfortable, stay-cool handle is a must given that you need to hold the pot to fully incorporate ingredients and also to scrape them out. Our longtime favorite large saucepan is the **All-Clad Stainless 4-Quart Saucepan** ($194.99); for a small saucepan, we recommend the **Calphalon Contemporary Nonstick 2½-Quart Shallow Saucepan** ($39.95).

Roasting Pan

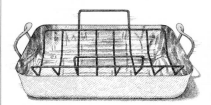

Sure you need one for roasting the big bird at Thanksgiving or the ham at Easter, but this kitchen essential comes in handy year-round. For instance, when making a big batch of beef stew to serve a crowd, we use a roasting pan since a double batch won't fit in a Dutch oven. Even for cooking a pork loin roast and vegetables for company, no other pan is large enough with tall sides to protect the meat from overcooking. And some desserts in this book, like our Individual Flans and Goat Cheese and Lemon Cheesecake, need to cook in a water bath—which is where the roasting pan comes in handy. Just don't buy a nonstick pan; the dark finish camouflages the crusty brown bits you need to make gravy for roasted meats. We like the **Calphalon Contemporary Stainless Roasting Pan with Rack** ($129.99). Its upright, riveted handles make it easy to move this pan in and out of the oven, and it comes with its own sturdy rack.

Rimmed Baking Sheets and Cooling Racks

We use rimmed baking sheets (18 by 13 inches) for everything from roasting vegetables and meat and baking cookies to, yes, baking the occasional sheet cake. Fitted with the right-size wire cooling rack, this versatile pan can stand in for a roasting pan. We think it pays to have two rimmed baking sheets on hand as they are serious multitaskers. We recommend the **Wear-Ever Half Size Heavy Duty Sheet Pan (13 Gauge) by Vollrath (formerly Lincoln Foodservice; model 5314)** ($19).

Cooling racks are also incredibly useful; we recommend you also have two for cooling baked goods and elevating roasted meats above the baking sheet, and keeping breaded foods crisp. It also makes a handy drying rack for wine glasses when entertaining and your dishwasher is full. Our winner is the **CIA Bakeware 12 by 17-Inch Cooling Rack** ($16). It has an extra brace—great for supporting a roast.

Salad Spinner

A good salad spinner makes quick work of drying greens for a crowd, and you can use it to rinse and dry other fruits and vegetables as well. Our favorite spinner is the **OXO Good Grips Salad Spinner** ($29.99), which has a top-mounted pump that locks into place for easy storage. Plus the bowl can double as a serving bowl.

Knives

Your knives get a workout when cooking for company given the amount of vegetable and other prep work that is usually involved, so it pays to have good sharp knives on hand. But contrary to what most retailers would have you believe, you don't need a knife block with a dozen knives. You just need a few high-quality knives. First, you need a good chef's knife with an 8-inch blade. This kitchen workhorse can be used for any cutting task. The **Victorinox Fibrox 8-Inch Chef's Knife (formerly Victorinox Forschner)** is a premium-quality knife—at the bargain price of $29.95. For jobs requiring more accuracy like deveining shrimp or cutting citrus segments, we reach for a paring knife with a 3 to 3½-inch blade; we like the especially nimble and razor-sharp **Wüsthof Classic 3½-Inch Paring Knife with PEtec** (which stands for "Precision Edge Technology"; $39.95). A serrated knife will glide through crusty breads and tomato skins while a slicing knife will produce thin, uniform slices of meat. The **Wüsthof Classic 10-Inch Bread Knife** ($89.95) has a long blade with deeply tapered, pointed serrations, perfect for sawing through crusty baguettes. The **Victorinox Fibrox 12-inch Granton Edge Slicing Knife** ($49.95) has a razor-sharp blade long and wide enough to draw through a large roast in one stroke. Invest in each of these and you will be all set to tackle any kitchen task requiring a knife.

Tart Pan

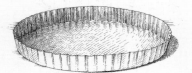

There's nothing worse than a tart crust crumbling as you attempt to liberate it from the pan—especially when you have a table full of friends and family waiting. That's why we like a tinned steel pan with a removable bottom; it will effortlessly release your Lemon Tart every time. And the steel will ensure the crust is evenly browned, too. Because tart dough tends to be so rich, a nonstick coating is unnecessary. The blackened steel tart pans absorb heat and encourage browning, so if you're using one of these pans, we recommend that you reduce the oven temperature by 25 degrees. The **Kaiser Tinplate 9-Inch Quiche Pan with Removable Bottom** ($12) is our top-rated model. If you bake a lot, it's useful to have pans in multiple sizes—note that some of our larger tarts require an 11-inch tart pan.

Springform Pan

When you are cooking for company, you will undoubtedly want to make a cheesecake, flourless chocolate cake, or some other dessert (like our Mexican Ice Cream Cake) that requires a springform pan. These come in several sizes but the most versatile size and the one we call for the most is a 9-inch springform pan. In addition to a smooth-working buckle, we found the most crucial feature on a reliable springform pan to be its ability to resist leakage—either batter out or water in (for those cakes that are baked in a water bath). We like **Frieling's Handle-It 9-Inch Glass Bottom Springform Pan** ($49.99), which has helper handles and a tempered-glass bottom that makes it easy to monitor browning on crusts and cakes.

Knife Sharpener

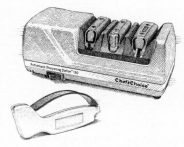

Your beef tenderloin might be perfectly cooked, but if you don't have a sharp knife to slice it with, it won't matter much—no one's going to be impressed by messy, nicked shreds of beef. That's why we suggest having a knife sharpener on hand. Even the most expensive, well-made knives lose their sharpness quickly when used regularly. And if you entertain frequently, it can happen that much faster. When it comes to knife sharpeners, you have a choice between manual and electric—and there's a big price differential. Our winning electric model is the **Chef'sChoice Model 130 Professional Sharpening Station** and it costs about $150. The sharpening material used is diamond, and there are spring-loaded blade guides to make sharpening foolproof. For a manual sharpener, we like the **AccuSharp Knife and Tool Sharpener**, which is just $12 and is the size of a stapler—perfect for easy storage.

Garlic Press

Mincing garlic can be a sticky and stinky job—and when you're making an Italian dinner for a crowd, chances are you've got a pile of garlic to prep, which is also time-consuming. Having a garlic press makes this job much easier and quicker. A good press has a large chamber to hold multiple cloves of garlic. Our favorite press is the **Kuhn Rikon Easy-Squeeze Garlic Press** ($20), which has a comfortable handle.

Oven Thermometer

Most ovens are inaccurate, at least by a few degrees, which is why it's important to have an oven thermometer. Even if your oven is slightly off, that can make all the difference between a moist, tender, impressive roast and one that's dried out, chewy, and disappointing. It doesn't make sense not to have an oven thermometer—they don't cost a lot, and a good one can literally save your dinner (plus everything else you cook or bake). Our favorite model is the **Cooper-Atkins Oven Thermometer** ($5.95), which is accurate and easy to hang from or prop up on oven racks. Plus, it has a display that remains clear and readable, even after lots of time spent in a hot oven.

Graters

It pays to have both a sturdy box grater (for shredding cheese) and a rasp grater, which is not only useful for grating Parmesan but makes quick work of grating ginger, nutmeg, and citrus zest. The **OXO Good Grips Box Grater** ($17.95) has sharp teeth and a container that attaches to the bottom to collect whatever you're grating, making for easy cleanup. For a rasp-style grater, we keep the test kitchen stocked with the super-sharp **Microplane Classic 40020 Zester/Grater** ($14.95).

Instant-Read Thermometer

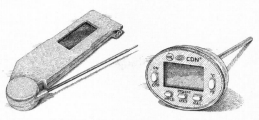

We rely on an instant-read thermometer to take a quick temperature and help us determine when foods are properly cooked or have reached a certain stage in the cooking process. We think that this thermometer, coupled with knowledge of how temperatures relate to desired doneness (see page 13), will ensure success in the kitchen—whether you are an experienced cook or just starting out. There is nothing worse when cooking for company than worrying about whether your pork loin or expensive beef roast is perfectly cooked and tender or overdone and dried out. Look for a digital model that has a long stem (to reach the center of large roasts). We like the **ThermoWorks Splash-Proof Super-Fast Thermapen** ($96), which takes readings in just seconds. But if its price tag is too high, we have a best buy recommendation in the **CDN ProAccurate Quick-Read Thermometer**, which is just $16.95.

Kitchen Timers

In cooking, timing is everything. And when you're preparing a multicourse meal, minutes matter even more—which is why a good timer is essential. In the test kitchen, we like multitask timers that are easy to use and read. We use the **Polder 3-in-1 Clock, Timer, and Stopwatch** ($12) in the test kitchen; it has a lengthy time range (great for long braises and slow roasts) and the ability to count up after an alarm has gone off. But it has the capacity to time just one item. When cooking for a crowd, we prefer the **5 in 1 DoneRight Kitchen Timer** ($24.95). This clever stove-shaped device has four individual timers in the position of each burner, as well as one for the oven, so you can easily keep track of all the components of your dinner.

Kitchen Tongs and Rubber Spatula

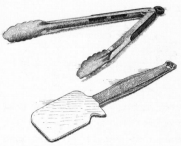

Both tongs and a spatula function as an extension of your hands and are seldom out of reach in our kitchens. We use kitchen tongs for turning meat and vegetables in a skillet, reaching into the oven to turn food on a baking sheet, and much more. So that you always have a clean pair of tongs handy, buy at least two. A heatproof rubber spatula is equally essential. It is great for stirring sauces on the stovetop as well as mixing batters and scraping out bowls. For tongs, our top-rated brand is the **OXO Good Grips 12-inch Locking Tongs** ($12.95), which are long enough to keep our hands out of the heat when reaching into a steaming hot pot or the oven. For a spatula, we like the **Rubbermaid Professional 13½-inch High Heat Scraper** ($18.99), which is heatproof and has a wide blade for efficient scraping.

THE TEST KITCHEN'S FAVORITE QUICK TIPS

A few small kitchen tricks can make all the difference when cooking for a crowd. Not only can a few saved minutes here and there really add up, but being well-organized will relieve a lot of stress. Over the years, we've come across thousands of kitchen tips and tricks, but have narrowed the list down here to just a few of our most useful favorites that are perfect when entertaining.

Making the Prep Even Easier

Once you've settled on your menu, it's the prep work that can seem overwhelming. With a few tips and tricks under your belt, like the fastest, easiest way to chop an onion, you'll be able to move through all these tasks with ease. Here are our best Test Kitchen Quick Tips for stress-free cooking.

Sharpening a Knife

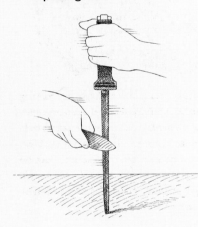

The duller the blade of a knife, the more force it takes to do the job—and the easier it is for the blade to stop and miss the mark, quickly sending the knife toward your hand. With a sharp knife, the blade does the work—and the razorlike edge is far less likely to slip. Using a sharpening steel (as pictured above) will help hone a slightly dulled blade edge, but it can't resharpen a very dull blade. If your knife is very dull, you'll need to sharpen it either by sending it to a professional, or using an electric or manual sharpener.

Keeping Your Cutting Board Stable

Having a stable, steady place to do all your chopping is essential. Laying your cutting board on the counter often isn't good enough; your board will be rocking and sliding all over before you know it. To anchor your board firmly to the counter, place a wet sheet of paper towel underneath the board. Not only will it prevent the board from slipping as you chop, but you can then use the wet towel to clean up the counter when you're done.

Removing Garlic Skin

Forget trying to painstakingly peel skin off garlic. Crush the clove with the side of a chef's knife. The skin will loosen for easy removal.

Hand Deodorizer

After working with pungent ingredients, such as garlic and onions, lemon juice can help to wash away any lingering odors. When the odor is too strong for citrus, try washing your hands with a couple tablespoons of mouthwash. Any inexpensive brand will do the job.

Chopping an Onion Finely

When cooking multiple courses for a crowd, you'll no doubt wind up chopping lots of onions. Here's how to make quick work of them. Also, if you find your eyes tearing up terribly, stick your head in the freezer; the cool air will quickly relieve the burning sensation. Mincing a shallot is the same process as mincing an onion, but on a much smaller scale using a paring knife.

I. Using a chef's knife, halve the onion pole to pole. Lop off the tops of the each half, leaving the root end intact, and peel the onion.

2. Make horizontal cuts, starting with the heel of the blade and carefully pulling the knife toward you, without cutting through the root end.

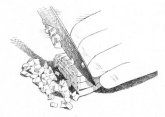

3. Using the tip of the knife, take several vertical cuts, dragging the knife toward you.

4. Slice across the lengthwise cuts, using your knuckles as a guide for the knife while holding the onion with your fingertips.

Washing Fruit and Vegetables

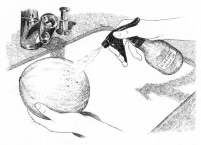

Forget buying expensive fruit and vegetables washes. A mixture of 3 parts water and 1 part white vinegar works just as well and will remove up to 98 percent of surface bacteria. You can put this water-vinegar mixture into either a bowl or fill up a spray bottle. After washing the fruit or vegetable with the mixture, simply rinse it under cold tap water and pat dry.

Washing Raspberries

Raspberries are much more delicate than other types of fruit and berries and they require special washing instructions. To wash raspberries, fill a bowl with 3 parts cold water and 1 part white vinegar. Add the berries, and gently toss them with your hands to rinse. To dry them, simply spread them out over a paper towel–lined plate in a single layer. Also, be sure to wash them right before you need to use them; once washed, the raspberries will disintegrate quickly.

Shredding Soft Cheese

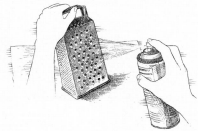

Semisoft cheese, such as mozzarella, can make a smeary mess when grating it on a box grater, and clog the holes. To prevent this, spray the box grater lightly with vegetable oil spray before grating the cheese. The spray will keep the cheese from sticking to the grater.

An Extra-Large Trivet

Finding a place to put a large, hot roasting pan that you've just pulled out of the oven can be hard, especially since most trivets are far too small. To solve this problem, we place an overturned baking sheet on the counter and use it as safe, sturdy resting place for either a hot roasting pan or Dutch oven.

Storing Salad Greens

After washing and drying lettuce, loosely roll the leaves inside paper towels and store in a zipper-lock bag. Leave the bag slightly open to allow some airflow.

Clever Serving Tricks

Once all the food is cooked and ready to go, getting it to the table hot and looking good is the next hurdle. Here are some clever tricks we've learned that make the dinner service go more smoothly.

Reheating Before Serving

Lots of the recipes in this book come with make-ahead instructions to help minimize the last-minute work before your guests arrive. To make it easier to remember the finishing instructions, consider writing them on a sticky-note and sticking it right onto the dish itself.

Label Your Dishes

Though it sounds a little silly, we think labeling your serving platters and pulling out serving utensils in advance is time well spent. Not only does it prevent you from having to dig deep into a closet or basement for all your dishes at the last minute, but it makes it easy for others to help you.

Warming Your Plates

Warmed plates or bowls are particularly nice when serving soups, stews, or pasta dishes in cold-weather months. Of course you can stack them on a clean cookie sheet and warm them in a low oven. If, however, your oven is in use, consider using the drying cycle on the dishwasher to warm them up.

Easier Bread Slicing

Slicing a loaf of rustic bread freshly heated in the oven can be a hot and messy proposition: It's hard to get a hold on the bread, and the crumbs tend to spray everywhere. Avoid this by cutting slices of bread about ¾ of the way down to the bottom crust before crisping the loaf in the oven. Then, because the loaf is still intact, it is easy to transfer to a serving basket, and the slices can be torn apart at the table with minimal mess.

Making Chocolate Shavings

Chocolate shavings are an easy way to garnish many desserts from cakes, tarts, and chocolate mousse to a simple bowl of ice cream. To make chocolate shavings, warm a block of bittersweet or semisweet chocolate by sweeping a hair dryer over it, taking care not to melt the chocolate; hard, cold chocolate will crumble rather than curl. Holding a paring knife at a 45-degree angle against the warmed chocolate, carefully scrape it towards you to make long, elegant chocolate curls. A vegetable peeler will also work.

Keeping The Cake Plate Clean

To keep the rim of a cake plate clean when icing a cake, lay strips of parchment over the edges of the platter, then place the cake on top and decorate the cake as desired. Remove the parchment before serving.

Drip-Free Ladling

Fill the ladle three-quarters full, then double-dip the bottom of the ladle into the soup again before lifting it out of the pot. The tension on the surface of the soup will grab any drips hanging off the bottom of the ladle and pull them back into the pot.

Cleaning Up the Mess

There is no way around it. Parties make a mess and at the end of the night (or maybe the next morning) you'll have to clean it up. Here are our favorite cleaning and organizing tips that not only help you make cleanup a snap, but help you put things away in an organized fashion so that you're ready for your next party.

Extra Drying Room

Everyone dreads the huge pile of dishes that pile up after a dinner party and quickly fill the dishwasher and drying rack. When this happens, pull out a clean cooling rack and place it over a dish towel to help with drying rack overflow.

Wine Glass Buffer Zone

Washing fragile glassware by hand is the best way to stave off breakage—unless it slips from your grasp and crashes into the sink. Lining a portion of the sink with a rubber shelf liner helps make the sink a breakage free zone.

Smarter Knife Cleaning

Scrub pads work well to remove gunk from knife blades but eventually damage the finish. To keep knives shiny, use a wine cork instead. Simply rub the cork over the knife to remove residue, then wash the knife in hot, soapy water with a soft sponge.

Don't Forget to Wash the Sink

Believe or not, washing the sink is as important as washing your dishes. The sink, including the faucet handle, can harbor lots of dirt and bacteria that is then quickly and easily spread around your kitchen. Hot soapy water is amazingly effective at eliminating bacteria, but for added insurance, clean these areas frequently with a solution of 1 tablespoon bleach to 1 quart water.

Wrap Your Plates and Platters

Extra plates and platters for company are usually stored in closets or the basement when not in use where they tend to collect dust. To help keep them clean between uses (and save you from having to wash them both before and after the party), wrap them tightly in plastic wrap after they've been cleaned and dried.

Cleaning Sponges

If your sponge isn't clean, you can wind up spreading dirt and bacteria onto everything it touches. We tested a variety of sponge sanitizing methods—microwaving, freezing, bleaching, boiling, dishwashing— then had the sponges tested in a lab to determine which method worked best. Boiling the sponges in boiling water for 5 minutes was the most effective.

Removing Wax from a Tablecloth

Trying to get melted wax out of your favorite tablecloth can be a real chore, if not a little nerve-racking especially if the cloth is an heirloom. We've found the easiest way to do this is to first place an ice cube on the wax to freeze it, then scrape off as much as you can with the edge of a credit card (a knife may cut the fabric). Then drape the tablecloth over an ironing board, place a single layer of clean paper towel on top of and underneath the waxy spot, and heat through with a medium-hot iron; the heat from the iron will remelt the wax, which will be absorbed by the paper towel.

THE ENTERTAINING TROUBLESHOOTING GUIDE

No one wants to find themselves standing in the kitchen faced with a cooking problem—like knowing whether your roast is perfectly cooked or dealing with a sauce that's too salty—while guests are lingering in the other room. Here are some tips to help you avoid or overcome the most common kitchen calamities.

If You Have a Big, Greasy Spill

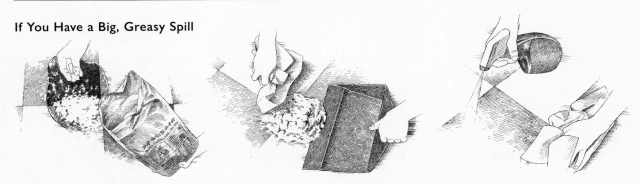

Whether you've dropped a bottle of oil or dribbled some grease from the roasting pan onto the floor, a greasy spill is both tedious to clean up and dangerous if not done well. Rather than trying to wipe up the mess with numerous rolls of paper towels, which will spread the grease around and making a bigger mess, try this solution. Sprinkle a thick layer of flour over the grease spill, and let it absorb for a couple of minutes. The greasy flour can then be easily swept up and the floor cleaned quickly with window cleaner.

If the Food Tastes Too Salty, Too Sweet, or Too Spicy

Most mild cases of over-seasoning can be easily fixed by adding an ingredient from the opposite end of the flavor spectrum; see the chart below for suggestions. Severe cases of over-seasoning, however, may require that you dilute the dish with additional water or low-sodium broth, then rebuild the flavor by adding more aromatics along with the opposite seasonings. (By the way, adding a cooked potato to an over-seasoned dish is useless.)

IF YOUR FOOD IS . . .	ADD . . .	SUCH AS . . .
Too salty	An acid or sweetener	Lemon juice, lime juice, or vinegar; Sugar, honey, maple syrup, or fruit jam
Too sweet	An acid or seasonings	Lemon juice, lime juice, or vinegar; Chopped fresh herbs or a dash of cayenne; Or, for sweet dishes, liqueur or instant espresso
Too spicy or acidic	A fat or sweetener	Butter, olive oil, heavy cream, cheese, or sour cream; Sugar, honey, maple syrup, or fruit jam

If the Pan Is on Fire

It happens to the best of us. The fat in the pan splatters, catches the edge of the flame, and suddenly your whole pan is on fire. The solution is to act fast and put a metal lid or baking sheet over the pan, then turn off all the burners. Salt or baking soda will also help to put out the fire if handy. If the fire seems to grow quickly, however, don't hesitate to get everyone out the house and call the fire department. Also, be sure to stock your kitchen with a portable ABC-type fire extinguisher.

If You Get Multiple Temperature Readings with the Thermometer

Using an instant-read thermometer is the best way to tell when your meat is perfectly cooked. But what if your thermometer gives you multiple readings? The solution is make sure your readings are from the very center of the meat, and then use the lowest reading as your guide. If there are bones in the meat, take the temperature close to, but not touching, the bone. And remember, the temperature of the meat will continue to climb 5 to 10 degrees as it rests.

TYPE OF MEAT	COOK UNTIL IT REGISTERS
Beef, Veal, and Lamb	
Rare	115°–120°
Medium-Rare	120°–125°
Medium	130°–135°
Well-Done	150°–155°
Pork	140°–145°
Chicken and Turkey (white meat)	160°–165°
Chicken and Turkey (dark meat)	175°

If Food Sticks to the Pan

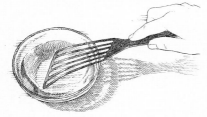

Food that initially sticks to the pan usually releases on its own after a crust begins to form. As long as the food is not burning, wait a minute or two and then try again. For stubbornly stuck pieces of meat or fish, dip a thin, flexible spatula into cold water and slide the inverted spatula blade underneath the food.

If Food Won't Simmer Slowly

Many side dishes (like polenta and rice), sauces, and stews should be cooked over very low flames to prevent burning, overreducing, or bubbling over. Yet many stovetops simply don't go low enough. To solve this problem, improvise a flame tamer out of a thick ring of aluminum foil. Set the foil ring on the burner, then place the pot on top.

If the Roast Is Undercooked

You've roasted, rested, and sliced up the meat, only to find it much too rare. Obviously, you need to return the meat to the oven to finish cooking, but the trick here is to prevent the meat from drying out and turning gray. Our solution is to place the slices of meat on a wire rack set in a rimmed baking sheet, top with pieces of lettuce, and finish the cooking under the broiler. The meat will gently steam under the lettuce, without drying out.

Fixing Thin Soups or Sauces

To fix thin watery soups and sauces, you have several options. Simmering the dish further on the stovetop will work, but it can also overcook vegetables and intensify unwanted flavors. Adding an actual thickener, such as cold butter, cornstarch, or bread, is often a better solution.

ADD BUTTER: Whisking in cold pieces of butter before serving adds both richness and body.

ADD CORNSTARCH: A cornstarch slurry (cornstarch mixed with cold water) can be whisked to any sauce, soup, or stew, then brought to a quick simmer to activate the cornstarch and thicken the dish. Mixing the cornstarch with water is crucial to preventing lumps.

ADD BREAD: To thicken soups, soak a piece of crustless bread in some of the soup liquid until soggy, then puree in a blender, adding more of the liquid as needed, until smooth. Add the puree to the soup as needed to thicken.

Fixing Thick Soups or Sauces

For a sauce or soup that's too thick, gradually stir in hot water or broth (or whatever liquid seems appropriate), until the desired consistency is reached.

EMERGENCY SUBSTITUTIONS

It's the 11th hour, you're making dessert, and you realize your eggs are extra-large, not large, and you have skim milk, not whole milk, in your fridge. Don't panic. We've been there ourselves, so we tested scores of published ingredient substitutions to figure out which ones work under what circumstances and which ones simply don't cut it. There's a lot to organize when planning a dinner party, and we know that all too often, an ingredient or two you needed just might not have made it into your cart. If you find yourself without any of the ingredients below (and no time to run to the store), we bet you have one of our recommended substitutions on hand. Problem solved.

TO REPLACE	AMOUNT	SUBSTITUTE
Whole Milk	1 cup	⅝ cup skim milk + ⅜ cup half-and-half OR ⅔ cup 1% milk + ⅓ cup half-and-half OR ¾ cup 2% milk + ¼ cup half-and-half OR ⅞ cup skim milk + ⅛ cup heavy cream
Half-and-Half	1 cup	¾ cup whole milk + ¼ cup heavy cream OR ⅔ cup skim or lowfat milk + ⅓ cup heavy cream
Heavy Cream	1 cup	1 cup evaporated milk *Not suitable for whipping or baking, but fine for soups and sauces.*

Eggs	LARGE	JUMBO	EXTRA-LARGE	MEDIUM	
	1	1	1	1	*For half of an egg, whisk the yolk and white together and use half of the liquid.*
	2	1½	2	2	
	3	2½	2½	3½	
	4	3	3½	4½	
	5	4	4	6	
	6	5	5	7	

TO REPLACE	AMOUNT	SUBSTITUTE
Buttermilk	1 cup	1 cup milk + 1 tablespoon lemon juice or white vinegar *Let stand to thicken, about 10 minutes. Not suitable for raw applications, such as a buttermilk dressing.*
Sour Cream	1 cup	1 cup whole-milk plain yogurt *Nonfat and low-fat yogurts are too lean to replace sour cream.*
Plain Yogurt	1 cup	1 cup sour cream
Cake Flour	1 cup	⅞ cup all-purpose flour + 2 tablespoons cornstarch
Bread Flour	1 cup	1 cup all-purpose flour *Bread and pizza crusts may bake up with slightly less chew.*
Baking Powder	1 teaspoon	¼ teaspoon baking soda + ½ teaspoon cream of tartar *Use right away.*
Light Brown Sugar	1 cup	1 cup granulated sugar + 1 tablespoon molasses *Pulse the molasses in a food processor along with the sugar or simply add it along with the other wet ingredients.*
Dark Brown Sugar	1 cup	1 cup granulated sugar + 2 tablespoons molasses
Confectioners' Sugar	1 cup	1 cup granulated sugar + 1 teaspoon cornstarch, ground in a blender (not a food processor) *Works well for dusting over cakes, less so in frostings and glazes.*
Table Salt	1 tablespoon	1½ tablespoons Morton Kosher Salt or fleur de sel OR 2 tablespoons Diamond Crystal Kosher Salt or Maldon Sea Salt *Not recommended for use in baking recipes.*
Fresh Herbs	1 tablespoon	1 teaspoon dried herbs
Wine	½ cup	½ cup broth + 1 teaspoon wine vinegar (added just before serving) OR ½ cup broth + 1 teaspoon lemon juice (added just before serving) *Vermouth makes an acceptable substitute for white wine.*
Unsweetened Chocolate	1 ounce	3 tablespoons cocoa powder + 1 tablespoon vegetable oil OR 1½ ounces bittersweet or semisweet chocolate (remove 1 tablespoon sugar from the recipe)
Bittersweet or Semisweet Chocolate	1 ounce	⅔ ounce unsweetened chocolate + 2 teaspoons sugar *Works well with fudgy brownies. Do not use in a custard or cake.*

11ᵀᴴ HOUR RECIPES

What skill separates an experienced host from a novice party thrower? Knowing how to make things work when well-made plans start to fall through. Did unexpected guests show up? (Just bulk up the appetizers and portion the dinner plates smaller.) Did the cake slip off its plate and crash to the floor? (Comb through the liquor cabinet for something flavorful and pour it over ice cream with some toasted nuts.) Or are you just feeling like you need an easier option for an appetizer or dessert? Here is a collection of some of our favorite easy appetizers, side dishes, salads, and desserts to help you pull through any dinner party in style. You'll also find many easy alternatives throughout the book—just look for the Even Easier feature.

Five Last-Minute Appetizers

You need to have appetizers when throwing a party. Not only is it a nice way to welcome your guests, but it also buys you some valuable time to either finish making dinner or keep folks happily occupied while waiting for late-comers. And though there is no shame in serving a nice piece of cheese alongside some good crackers or bread, it's nearly as easy to kick things up a notch. Each of these recipes will serve eight.

Easy Melted Brie with Honey and Herbs

Using a serrated knife, carefully slice the rind off the top of an 8-ounce wheel of firm Brie cheese; leave the rind on the sides and bottom. Place the Brie cut side up on a microwave-safe serving platter. Drizzle 2 tablespoons honey over the Brie and sprinkle with ½ teaspoon minced fresh thyme or rosemary. Microwave the cheese until it is warm and begins to bubble, 1 to 2 minutes. Serve with crackers or a thinly sliced baguette.

Boursin–Cheddar Cheese Spread

Process a softened 5.2-ounce package of Boursin Garlic and Fine Herbs cheese with 1 cup shredded extra-sharp cheddar cheese, 2 tablespoons mayonnaise, ½ tablespoon Worcestershire sauce, and a pinch cayenne pepper in a food processor until smooth, scraping down the sides as needed, about 1 minute. Transfer the cheese mixture to a serving bowl, sprinkle with 2 tablespoons minced chives, and serve with crackers or a thinly sliced baguette.

Sun-Dried Tomato Tapenade with Farmer's Cheese

Pulse 1 cup oil-packed sun-dried tomatoes, rinsed and patted dry, with ¼ cup extra-virgin olive oil in a food processor until finely chopped, about 25 pulses; transfer to a small serving bowl. Pulse 1 cup pitted kalamata olives, ¼ cup coarsely chopped parsley, and 1 tablespoon rinsed capers in a food processor until finely chopped, about 10 pulses; stir into the chopped tomatoes. Season with salt and pepper to taste and serve with 8 ounces farmer's cheese (or goat cheese) and crackers or a thinly sliced baguette.

Baked Goat Cheese with Olive Oil and Herbs

Heat the oven to 400 degrees. Using dental floss, slice a chilled 12-ounce log of goat cheese into ⅓-inch-thick rounds. Shingle the cheese into a small casserole dish or shallow ovensafe bowl. Combine ⅓ cup olive oil, 2 teaspoons honey, ½ teaspoon grated orange or lemon zest, ½ teaspoon dried herbes de Provence, ¼ teaspoon salt, ⅛ teaspoon pepper, and ⅛ teaspoon red pepper flakes in a small bowl, then pour the mixture over the cheese. Bake the cheese until the oil is bubbling and the cheese begins to brown around the edges, 10 to 15 minutes. Serve warm with crackers or a thinly sliced baguette.

Cheddar and Chutney Canapés with Walnut Bread

Cut 1 loaf artisanal-style walnut bread (or similar fruit or nut bread) into canapé-size pieces (about 3 inches). Slice 8 ounces high-quality farmhouse cheddar into similar-size pieces. Spread ½ cup apple chutney (or apple butter) over one side of the bread, top with the cheddar, and serve.

Six Easy Sides

Unlike appetizers or desserts, which can be easily bought or assembled at the last minute, vegetable side dishes just don't work that way. So what do you do if you're feeling overwhelmed and short on time? Here are our top six side dishes that require little (if any) prep work and go with almost everything. All of these recipes serve eight.

Boiled Red Potatoes with Butter and Herbs

We prefer to use small red potatoes, measuring 1 to 2 inches in diameter, in this recipe. If using large potatoes, halve or quarter the potatoes and adjust the cooking time as needed.

Cover 4 pounds small red potatoes (about 24 potatoes) by 1 inch water in a large pot and bring to a boil over high heat. Reduce to a simmer and cook until the potatoes are tender, 20 to 25 minutes. Drain the potatoes well, then toss gently with 4 tablespoons unsalted butter in a large bowl until the butter melts. Season with salt and pepper to taste, sprinkle with 2 tablespoons minced fresh chives, tarragon, or parsley, and serve.

Broiled Asparagus with Lemon

Do not use pencil-thin asparagus here. For quick asparagus trimming, cut off all of the tough ends at once while the bunch is still banded together.

Adjust an oven rack 3 inches from the broiler element and heat the broiler. Toss 3 pounds trimmed asparagus with 1 tablespoon extra-virgin olive oil and season with salt and pepper to taste. Lay the asparagus, in the same direction, on a rimmed baking sheet. Broil, shuffling the asparagus from top to bottom every few minutes, until the spears are tender and the tips begin to brown, 5 to 10 minutes. Squeeze ½ lemon over the spears and serve.

Buttery Green Beans with Almonds

Haricots verts can be substituted for the green beans and fresh sage can be substituted for the thyme. Also, consider swapping chopped toasted walnuts or hazelnuts for the almonds.

Bring 6 quarts water to a boil in a large pot over high heat. Stir in 2 pounds trimmed green beans and 1 tablespoon salt and cook until the beans are crisp-tender, 2 to 5 minutes. Drain the beans and return to the pot. Add 3 tablespoons unsalted butter and ⅓ cup toasted sliced almonds, and toss to coat. Cover and let sit off the heat until the butter has melted, about 2 minutes. Season with salt and pepper to taste and serve.

Walk-Away Herbed White Rice

Be sure to cover the water when bringing it to a boil. Our favorite brand of long-grain white rice is Lundberg Organic.

Adjust an oven rack to the middle position and heat the oven to 375 degrees. Spread 2½ cups long-grain white rice, rinsed, into a 13 by 9-inch baking dish. Combine 3¾ cups water and 1 teaspoon salt in a large saucepan, cover, and bring to a brief boil over high heat. Immediately pour the boiling water over the rice and cover the baking dish tightly with a double layer of aluminum foil. Bake the rice until it is tender and no water remains, 30 to 40 minutes. Remove the dish from the oven, uncover, and fluff the rice with a fork, scraping up any rice that has stuck to the bottom. Re-cover the dish with foil and let the rice stand for 10 minutes. Stir in 2 tablespoons minced fresh parsley, basil, chives, cilantro, dill, or tarragon and season with salt and pepper to taste.

Sautéed Buttery Peas

Melt 2 tablespoons unsalted butter in a 12-inch nonstick skillet over medium-high heat. Add 1 minced shallot and 1 minced garlic clove and cook until shallot is softened, about 2 minutes. Stir in ¾ cup heavy cream and 2 teaspoons sugar and simmer until thickened, about 5 minutes. Stir in 1½ pounds frozen peas (not thawed), cover, and cook until the peas are heated through, about 5 minutes. Off the heat, stir in 1 tablespoon minced fresh tarragon and season with salt and pepper to taste.

Roasted Baby Carrots with Browned Butter

Adjust an oven rack to the middle position and heat the oven to 475 degrees. Toss 2 pounds baby carrots, thoroughly dried, with 2 tablespoons olive oil and ½ teaspoon salt and spread into a single layer over a broiler-pan bottom. Roast the carrots for 12 minutes. Shake the pan and continue to roast the carrots, shaking the pan occasionally, until the carrots are lightly browned and tender, about 8 minutes longer. Meanwhile, cook 3 tablespoons unsalted butter in a small saucepan over medium heat, swirling occasionally, until browned, 1 to 2 minutes. Toss the roasted carrots with the browned butter and serve.

Five No-Prep Salad Dressings

You'll find lots of great salad ideas throughout this book; however, many of them require a little work, like segmenting fruit or chopping up vegetables. If you're feeling rushed, make a simple salad and use one of these no-prep dressings. Each of these dressings makes the perfect amount for 12 ounces of mesclun greens, which serves eight.

Feta and Buttermilk Dressing

Whisk ¾ cup crumbled feta, ⅓ cup buttermilk, ⅓ cup mayonnaise, ¼ teaspoon pepper, ¼ teaspoon garlic powder, and ¼ teaspoon ground coriander together.

Parmesan Vinaigrette

Whisk ¾ cup grated Parmesan cheese, ½ cup extra-virgin olive oil, 2 tablespoons white wine vinegar or rice vinegar, ½ teaspoon sugar, ¼ teaspoon garlic powder, ¼ teaspoon salt, ¼ teaspoon pepper, ¼ teaspoon dried oregano or rosemary, and ⅛ teaspoon red pepper flakes together.

Fruity Balsamic Vinaigrette

Whisk ½ cup extra-virgin olive oil, 3 tablespoons fruit jam, 2 tablespoons balsamic vinegar, ¼ teaspoon salt, and ⅛ teaspoon pepper together.

Dijon-Honey Dressing

Whisk ½ cup extra-virgin olive oil, 2 tablespoons white wine vinegar, 2 tablespoons honey, 1 tablespoon Dijon mustard, ¼ teaspoon salt, ⅛ teaspoon pepper, and ⅛ teaspoon red pepper flakes together.

Orange-Sesame Vinaigrette

Whisk ⅓ cup vegetable oil, 2½ tablespoons rice wine vinegar, 2 tablespoons toasted sesame oil, 2 tablespoons orange juice, 1 tablespoon honey, ½ teaspoon ground ginger, and ½ teaspoon salt together.

Five Easy Ice Cream Desserts

Ice cream is the ultimate dessert for company: The trick, however, is figuring out how to gussy up a simple bowl of ice cream so it seems elegant. Here are some of our favorite ideas (you'll find others throughout the book); each of the recipes below serves eight generously.

Vanilla Ice Cream with Guinness and Grated Chocolate

Portion 4 pints (½ gallon) vanilla ice cream into individual bowls. Drizzle with 1½ cups Guinness and sprinkle with ¼ cup grated chocolate. Serve with your favorite crisp chocolate cookie.

Chocolate Ice Cream with Amaretto and Espresso

Portion 4 pints (½ gallon) chocolate ice cream into individual bowls. Drizzle with ½ cup amaretto liqueur (or any other nut-flavored liqueur). Sprinkle with 2 teaspoons instant espresso powder, followed by ½ cup toasted sliced almonds. Serve with biscotti.

Raspberry Sorbet with Prosecco and Fresh Berries

Portion 4 pints (½ gallon) raspberry sorbet into individual bowls. Drizzle with 2 cups prosecco (or other sparkling wine) and sprinkle with 3 cups fresh raspberries and/or sliced strawberries. Serve with almond thins (such as Jules Destrooper Almond Thins).

Butter-Pecan Ice Cream with Maple and Bourbon

Portion 4 pints (½ gallon) butter-pecan ice cream into individual bowls. Drizzle with ½ cup bourbon and ¼ cup maple syrup. Sprinkle with ½ cup chopped toasted pecans. Serve with delicate tuile cookies (such as Pepperidge Farm Pirouette Rolled Wafers).

Lime Sorbet with Rum and Mint

Portion 4 pints (½ gallon) lime sorbet into individual bowls. Drizzle with ½ cup light rum and sprinkle with 2 tablespoons chopped fresh mint. Serve with delicate gingersnaps (such as Anna's Ginger Thins).

Rack of Lamb Dinner, page 43

Tapas Party, page 73

Dressing Up Chicken, page 55

Shrimp Dinner with Greek Flavors, page 27

SPRING

Elegant Salmon Dinner 21

Rustic Caramelized Onion Tart with Goat Cheese
Oven-Roasted Salmon Fillets with Almond Vinaigrette
Israeli Couscous with Caramelized Fennel and Spinach
Goat Cheese and Lemon Cheesecake with Hazelnut Crust

Shrimp Dinner with Greek Flavors 27

Artichoke-Lemon Hummus
Greek-Style Shrimp with Tomatoes and Feta
Lemon-Scented Rice Pilaf
Mâche and Mint Salad with Cucumbers
Vanilla Ice Cream with Homemade Salted Pistachio Brittle

Farmers' Market Vegetarian Dinner 31

Bruschetta with Artichoke Hearts and Parmesan
Spring Vegetable Pasta
Baked Goat Cheese Salad with Pecans and Radishes
Vanilla Bean Panna Cotta with Strawberry Coulis

Rustic Pork Stew Dinner 37

Rosemary and Garlic White Bean Dip
Pork Stew with Fennel, Leeks, and Prunes
Buttered Egg Noodles
Roasted Beet and Carrot Salad with Watercress
French Silk Chocolate Pie

Rack of Lamb Dinner 43

Roasted Red Pepper and Walnut Dip
Roasted Racks of Lamb with Mint Relish
Broiled Asparagus with Lemon
Couscous with Lemon, Scallions, and Feta
Rustic Walnut Tart with Bourbon Whipped Cream

Classic Beef Tenderloin Dinner 49

Goat Cheese with Caramelized Onion Jam
Roast Beef Tenderloin with Persillade Relish
Arugula and Tomato Salad with Balsamic Vinaigrette
Potato and Fennel Gratin
Lemon Tart

Dressing Up Chicken 55

Smoked Salmon with Herbed Crème Fraîche
    and Potato Chips
Lemony Goat Cheese–Stuffed Chicken Breasts
Easy Green Beans with Porcini Butter
Wild Rice Pilaf with Almonds and Dried Apricots
Berry Fools

A Taste of Spain 61

Marinated Feta and Green Olives
Spanish Shellfish Stew
Spinach Salad with Sherry Vinaigrette
Individual Flans

Casual Pan-Latin Supper 67

Roasted Tomatillo Salsa
Chicken and Avocado Arepas
Black Bean Chili
Tres Leches Cake

Tapas Party 73

Sangría
Spanish Tortilla with Garlic Mayonnaise
Sizzling Garlic Shrimp
Spanish Cheese and Meat Board
Cocktail Meatballs in Tomato-Saffron Sauce
Marinated Cauliflower and Chickpea Salad
Dulce de Leche Sandwich Cookies

Elegant Salmon Dinner

THE GAME PLAN
⤞

ONE DAY AHEAD...

MAKE CHEESECAKE: 2¼ hours
(plus 10 hours for cooling)
CARAMELIZE ONIONS FOR TART: 30 minutes

ON THE DAY OF...

MAKE COUSCOUS: 1¼ hours
MAKE ONION TART: 1¼ hours
MAKE ALMOND VINAIGRETTE: 15 minutes
ROAST SALMON: 30 minutes

ELEGANT SALMON DINNER

⤐ *Serves 8* ⤏

Rustic Caramelized Onion Tart with Goat Cheese
Oven-Roasted Salmon Fillets with Almond Vinaigrette
Israeli Couscous with Caramelized Fennel and Spinach
Goat Cheese and Lemon Cheesecake with Hazelnut Crust

Oven-Roasted Salmon Fillets with Almond Vinaigrette

The consistency of the vinaigrette should be thick and clingy. It is important to keep the salmon skin on during cooking; however, you can remove it before serving if desired.

ALMOND VINAIGRETTE

½	cup whole almonds, toasted (see page 29)
1	shallot, minced
3	tablespoons white wine vinegar
4	teaspoons honey
2	teaspoons Dijon mustard
⅔	cup extra-virgin olive oil
3	tablespoons water, plus extra as needed
2	tablespoons minced fresh tarragon
	Salt and pepper

SALMON

2	(2-pound) skin-on salmon fillets, about 1½ inches thick
4	teaspoons olive oil
	Salt and pepper

1. FOR THE ALMOND VINAIGRETTE: Place almonds in zipper-lock bag and pound with rolling pin until coarsely crushed. Whisk crushed almonds, shallot, vinegar, honey, and mustard in medium bowl. Whisking constantly, drizzle in olive oil. Whisk in water and tarragon and season with salt and pepper to taste. (Makes 1½ cups.)

2. FOR THE SALMON: Use sharp knife to remove any whitish fat from belly of salmon and cut each fillet into 4 equal pieces. Using sharp (or serrated) knife, cut 4 shallow slashes, about 1 inch apart, through skin of each fillet (do not cut into flesh). Pat salmon dry with paper towels and rub with oil. (Prepped salmon can be refrigerated for up to 24 hours before cooking.) *continued* ➤

continued ➤

> ☑ **WHY THIS RECIPE WORKS**
> The key to perfectly roasted salmon is to preheat a baking sheet in a very hot oven, then lay the fish on the hot pan and reduce the oven to a gentle 275 degrees to cook. The initial blast of high heat firms the exterior of the salmon and helps to render some of the excess fat. The fish then gently cooks as the oven temperature slowly drops, keeping the meat moist and succulent. To help the fat render, we cut several slits in the skin. For evenly cooked salmon, be sure to cut the pieces the same size; we found it easiest to buy a large piece of salmon and cut the fillets ourselves.

PREPARING SALMON FOR ROASTING

Using a sharp knife, trim away the whitish, fatty portion of the belly at an angle. Cut each salmon fillet into four evenly sized pieces. Make four or five shallow slashes along the skin side of each piece of fish, being careful not to cut into the flesh.

3. Adjust oven rack to lowest position, place rimmed baking sheet on rack, and heat oven to 500 degrees. Season salmon with salt and pepper. Reduce oven temperature to 275 degrees and remove hot baking sheet. Carefully lay salmon, skin side down, on hot sheet. Roast until center is still translucent when checked with tip of paring knife and registers 125 degrees (for medium-rare), 9 to 13 minutes.

4. Transfer fillets to individual plates or platter, spoon vinaigrette over top, and serve.

Israeli Couscous with Caramelized Fennel and Spinach

WHY THIS RECIPE WORKS Baby spinach and thinly sliced fennel elevate Israeli couscous to a party-worthy side. Since Israeli couscous is larger than traditional couscous, it requires a slightly different cooking technique. Whereas traditional couscous can simply be soaked in boiling water to rehydrate and turn tender, the larger grains of the Israeli couscous require actual boiling (much like pasta) in order to turn tender.

Do not substitute regular couscous in this dish. Serve with lemon wedges.

3   cups Israeli couscous
      Salt and pepper
¼   cup extra-virgin olive oil
5   fennel bulbs, stalks discarded, bulbs
      halved, cored, and sliced thin
1   onion, halved and sliced ¼ inch thick
3   garlic cloves, minced
¾   teaspoon grated lemon zest plus
      2 tablespoons juice
7   ounces baby spinach (7 cups)
⅓   cup minced fresh chives

1. Bring 4 quarts water to boil in Dutch oven. Stir in couscous and 1 tablespoon salt and cook until tender, about 5 minutes. Drain couscous, transfer to large bowl, and cover to keep warm. Wipe pot dry.

2. Heat 3 tablespoons oil in now-empty pot over medium-low heat until shimmering. Add fennel, onion, and ½ teaspoon salt, cover, and cook, stirring occasionally, until vegetables have softened and released their liquid, about 15 minutes. Uncover, increase heat to medium-high, and continue to cook, stirring often, until lightly browned and liquid has evaporated, 20 to 25 minutes.

3. Stir in garlic and lemon zest and cook until fragrant, about 1 minute. Off heat, stir in spinach, cover, and let sit until spinach wilts, about 2 minutes. Stir in couscous, lemon juice, chives, and remaining 1 tablespoon oil. Season with salt and pepper to taste. (Couscous can be held at room temperature for up to 2 hours; if desired, reheat in microwave before serving.) Serve warm or at room temperature.

PREPARING FENNEL

Cut off the stalks and feathery fronds. (The fronds can be minced and used for a garnish, if desired.) Trim a very thin slice from the base, remove any tough or blemished outer layers, and cut the bulb in half through the base. Use a small, sharp knife to remove the pyramid-shaped core. Slice each bulb half into thin strips. If necessary, the strips can then be chopped or cut into smaller pieces.

Rustic Caramelized Onion Tart with Goat Cheese

You can substitute ½ pound store-bought pizza dough or pizza dough from your favorite local pizzeria here. All-purpose flour can be substituted for the bread flour in the pizza dough, but the resulting crust will be a little less crisp and chewy. If desired, you can slow down the dough's rising time by letting it rise in the refrigerator for 8 to 16 hours in step 2; let the refrigerated dough soften at room temperature for 30 minutes before using.

✔ **WHY THIS RECIPE WORKS**
Topped with caramelized onions, scallions, fresh herbs, and goat cheese, this rustic tart is a winning appetizer that is easy to make—especially if you rely on store-bought pizza dough. Make sure your oven is really hot (500 degrees) as this is crucial for a crisp crust. Also, we found it best to use just a small amount of very flavorful toppings to prevent the thin dough from being weighed down.

PIZZA DOUGH

1–1¼	cups (5½ to 6¾ ounces) bread flour
¾	teaspoon instant or rapid-rise yeast
½	teaspoon salt
2	teaspoons olive oil
7	tablespoons warm water

TART

¼	cup extra-virgin olive oil
1	pound onions, halved and sliced ¼ inch thick
1¼	teaspoons minced fresh thyme
½	teaspoon brown sugar
	Salt and pepper
4	ounces goat cheese, crumbled (1 cup)
2	tablespoons minced fresh parsley, scallion, basil, dill, or tarragon

1. FOR THE PIZZA DOUGH: Pulse 1 cup flour, yeast, and salt together in food processor (fitted with dough blade if possible) to combine. With processor running, pour in oil, then water and process until rough ball forms, 20 to 30 seconds. Let dough rest for 2 minutes, and then process for 30 seconds longer.

2. Turn dough onto lightly floured counter and knead by hand to form smooth, round ball, about 5 minutes, adding remaining ¼ cup flour, 1 tablespoon at a time, to prevent dough from sticking to counter. Place dough in lightly greased bowl, cover tightly with greased plastic wrap, and let rise in warm place until doubled in size, 1 to 1½ hours. (Risen dough can be frozen for up to 1 month; let thaw on counter for several hours before using.)

3. FOR THE TART: Heat 1 tablespoon oil in 12-inch nonstick skillet over medium-low heat until shimmering. Add onions, 1 teaspoon thyme, brown sugar, and ¼ teaspoon salt, cover, and cook, stirring occasionally, until onions have softened and released their liquid, about 10 minutes. Uncover, increase heat to medium-high, and continue to cook, stirring often, until onions are deeply browned, 10 to 15 minutes. (Onions can be refrigerated for up to 3 days.)

4. Adjust oven rack to lowest position and heat oven to 500 degrees. Brush rimmed baking sheet with 1 tablespoon oil. Turn dough out onto lightly floured counter. Press and roll dough into 14 by 8-inch oval. Transfer dough to prepared baking sheet, reshape as needed, and gently dimple with fingertips.

5. Brush dough with remaining 2 tablespoons oil and season with pepper. Scatter caramelized onions, goat cheese, and remaining ¼ teaspoon thyme evenly over dough, leaving ½-inch border around edge. (Assembled tart can be held at room temperature for up to 4 hours before baking.)

6. Bake until tart is deep golden brown, 8 to 12 minutes, rotating baking sheet halfway through baking. Sprinkle with parsley, cut into 16 equal pieces, and serve warm.

Goat Cheese and Lemon Cheesecake with Hazelnut Crust

✔ WHY THIS RECIPE WORKS The beauty of this show-stopping dessert is that, while the recipe takes several hours from start to finish, the actual preparation is simple, and baking and cooling proceed practically unattended. We love the tanginess the goat cheese adds to this cheesecake, and the easy lemon curd complements the cheesecake perfectly, adding a bright burst of lemony flavor.

This cheesecake is baked in a hot water bath. To prevent water from leaking into the cake during baking, be sure to wrap your springform pan tightly in a double layer of heavy-duty aluminum foil. Running a knife around the edge of the cake as it cools will help prevent cracks from forming and helps the cake release from the pan more easily when serving. Note that this cheesecake will serve 12 to 14; leftovers will keep for several days.

HAZELNUT CRUST
- ⅓ cup hazelnuts, toasted (see page 29) and skinned
- 3 tablespoons sugar
- 3 ounces Nabisco Barnum's Animals Crackers or Social Tea Biscuits
- 3 tablespoons unsalted butter, melted and cooled

CHEESECAKE
- 1¼ cups (8¾ ounces) sugar
- 1 tablespoon grated lemon zest plus ¼ cup juice (2 lemons)
- 1 pound cream cheese, cut into 1-inch pieces and softened
- 8 ounces goat cheese, cut into 1-inch pieces and softened
- 4 large eggs, room temperature
- 2 teaspoons vanilla extract
- ¼ teaspoon salt
- ½ cup heavy cream

LEMON CURD
- ⅓ cup lemon juice (2 lemons)
- 2 large eggs plus 1 large yolk
- ½ cup (3½ ounces) sugar
- 2 tablespoons unsalted butter, cut into ½-inch cubes and chilled
- 1 tablespoon heavy cream
- ¼ teaspoon vanilla extract
  Pinch salt

1. FOR THE HAZELNUT CRUST: Adjust oven rack to lower-middle position and heat oven to 325 degrees. Process hazelnuts and sugar in food processor until finely ground, about 30 seconds. Add crackers and process until finely ground, about 30 seconds. While pulsing processor, add butter in slow, steady stream until mixture is evenly moistened and resembles wet sand, about 10 pulses.

2. Sprinkle mixture into 9-inch spring-form pan and press firmly into even, compact

SKINNING HAZELNUTS

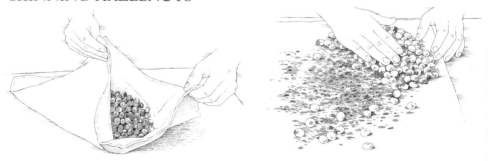

Place warm toasted hazelnuts inside a large clean towel and gently rub the nuts against one another to scrape off the skins. It's fine if a few patches of skin remain. Carefully open the towel, lay it flat, and gently roll the cleaned nuts away from the skins.

layer with bottom of dry measuring cup. Use back of spoon to press and smooth edges. Bake until fragrant and beginning to brown, 10 to 15 minutes. Let crust cool to room temperature, about 30 minutes. When cool, wrap outside of pan with two 18-inch square pieces heavy-duty foil and set inside roasting pan.

3. FOR THE CHEESECAKE: While crust is cooling, process ¼ cup sugar and lemon zest in food processor until sugar is very yellow, about 15 seconds. Transfer lemon sugar to bowl and stir in remaining 1 cup sugar.

4. Using stand mixer fitted with paddle, beat cream cheese and goat cheese on low speed to break up pieces, about 5 seconds. With mixer running, add sugar mixture in slow, steady stream. Increase speed to medium and continue to beat until mixture is creamy and smooth, about 3 minutes, scraping down bowl as needed. Reduce speed to medium-low and add eggs, 2 at a time, until incorporated, scraping down bowl after each addition. Add lemon juice, vanilla, and salt and beat until just incorporated, about 5 seconds. Add heavy cream and beat until just incorporated, about 5 seconds.

5. Give batter final stir by hand, then pour into prepared springform pan. Fill roasting pan with enough hot tap water to come halfway up sides of springform pan. Bake until center jiggles slightly, sides just start to puff, surface is no longer shiny, and center of cake registers 150 degrees, 55 to 60 minutes.

6. Turn off oven, prop open oven door with wooden spoon, and let cake sit in water bath for 1 hour longer. Transfer springform pan, without foil, to wire rack and let cool to room temperature, about 2 hours, running paring knife around edge of cake every hour. Wrap tightly in plastic wrap and refrigerate until cold, about 3 hours.

7. FOR THE LEMON CURD: While cheesecake bakes, heat lemon juice in small saucepan over medium heat until hot but not boiling. Whisk whole eggs and egg yolk in medium bowl, then gradually whisk in sugar. Whisking constantly, slowly pour

hot lemon juice into egg mixture. Return mixture to saucepan and cook, stirring constantly, until mixture is thick enough to cling to spoon and registers 170 degrees, about 3 minutes. Immediately remove from heat and stir in butter until incorporated. Stir in cream, vanilla, and salt. Strain through fine-mesh strainer into small bowl. Cover surface of curd directly with plastic wrap and refrigerate until needed.

8. When cheesecake is cold, spread lemon curd evenly over top while still in pan. Cover tightly with plastic wrap and refrigerate until set, about 4 hours. (Lemon cheesecake can be refrigerated, covered, for up to 1 day.) To serve, remove sides of springform pan and cut cake into wedges.

EVEN EASIER ➤ Don't have time to make cheesecake? Consider serving vanilla ice cream topped with warm lemon curd (our top-rated brand is Wilkin and Sons Tiptree).

Shrimp Dinner with Greek Flavors

THE GAME PLAN

ONE DAY AHEAD...

MAKE HUMMUS: 25 minutes

MAKE BRITTLE: 35 minutes (plus 30 minutes for cooling)

ON THE DAY OF...

MAKE SHRIMP: 1¼ hours

MAKE RICE: 50 minutes

MAKE SALAD: 20 minutes

SHRIMP DINNER WITH GREEK FLAVORS

⇀ Serves 8 ↽

Artichoke-Lemon Hummus ↭ Greek-Style Shrimp with Tomatoes and Feta
Lemon-Scented Rice Pilaf ↭ Mâche and Mint Salad with Cucumbers
Vanilla Ice Cream with Homemade Salted Pistachio Brittle

Greek-Style Shrimp with Tomatoes and Feta

You can either leave the shrimp tails on for a more attractive presentation or remove them for easier eating. Jumbo shrimp (16 to 20 per pound) are great in this dish if you can find them; if using jumbo shrimp, add 2 minutes to the cooking time in step 4. If you can't find ouzo or Pernod, substitute vodka mixed with 3 tablespoons of anise seeds.

6	tablespoons extra-virgin olive oil
5	tablespoons ouzo or Pernod
8	garlic cloves, minced
1½	teaspoons grated lemon zest
	Salt and pepper
2½	pounds extra-large shrimp (21 to 25 per pound), peeled and deveined (see page 304)
1	onion, chopped fine
1	red bell pepper, stemmed, seeded, and cut into ½-inch pieces
1	green bell pepper, stemmed, seeded, and cut into ½-inch pieces
½	teaspoon red pepper flakes
1	(28-ounce) can diced tomatoes, drained with ½ cup juice reserved
1	(14.5-ounce) can diced tomatoes, drained
⅓	cup dry white wine
3	tablespoons minced fresh parsley
10	ounces feta cheese, crumbled (2½ cups)
3	tablespoons chopped fresh dill

1. Mix 2 tablespoons oil, 2 tablespoons ouzo, 1 tablespoon minced garlic, lemon zest, ¼ teaspoon salt, and ⅛ teaspoon pepper in large bowl. Add shrimp, toss to coat, and let marinate for at least 15 minutes and up to 1 hour.

2. Heat 3 tablespoons oil in Dutch oven over medium heat until shimmering. Add onion, bell peppers, and ¼ teaspoon salt, cover, and cook until vegetables release their moisture, 3 to 5 minutes. Uncover and continue to cook, stirring occasionally, until moisture evaporates and vegetables are softened, about 5 minutes.

3. Stir in pepper flakes and remaining minced garlic and cook until fragrant, about 1 minute. Stir in tomatoes and reserved juice, wine, and remaining 3 tablespoons ouzo. Bring to simmer and cook, stirring occasionally, until flavors meld and sauce is slightly thickened (sauce should not be completely dry), 5 to 8 minutes. (Sauce can be removed from heat, covered, and set aside for up to 1½ hours; return to simmer and stir in water as needed to adjust consistency.)

4. Reduce heat to medium-low. Stir in parsley and shrimp with any accumulated liquid. Cover and simmer gently, stirring occasionally and adjusting heat as needed to maintain bare simmer, until shrimp are opaque throughout, 6 to 9 minutes. Off heat, sprinkle with feta, drizzle with remaining 1 tablespoon oil, and sprinkle with dill. Serve immediately.

✔ **WHY THIS RECIPE WORKS**
This easy but company-worthy Greek dish features shrimp simmered in a sweet-tart tomato sauce with a sprinkling of feta cheese for tangy contrast. Using extra-large (or jumbo) shrimp not only makes for an impressive-looking dinner but also cuts down on prep time since these larger shrimp are easier to prep (and harder to overcook). To give the shrimp an authentic kick of Greek flavor, we marinated them in a mixture of garlic, olive oil, lemon zest, and ouzo (a lightly sweet, anise-based Greek liqueur) before cooking.

Artichoke-Lemon Hummus

WHY THIS RECIPE WORKS
Homemade hummus tastes far better than anything you can buy at the store. And we love this fresh-tasting and lemony variation with artichokes. To prevent homemade hummus from having a grainy consistency, however, we found it important to emulsify the liquids and oil into the chickpeas using a food processor. Don't rush the processing time, or the hummus won't have a silky smooth texture.

We prefer Pastene brand canned chickpeas and Joyva or Krinos tahini. Serve with Garlic Toasts (page 62), pita chips, or a thinly sliced baguette.

¼	teaspoon grated lemon zest plus ¼ cup juice (2 lemons)
¼	cup water, plus extra as needed
6	tablespoons tahini
2	tablespoons extra-virgin olive oil, plus extra for drizzling
1	(14-ounce) can artichoke hearts, rinsed and patted dry
1	(15-ounce) can chickpeas, rinsed
1	small garlic clove, minced
½	teaspoon salt
	Pinch cayenne
2	teaspoons minced fresh parsley or mint

1. Combine lemon juice and water in small liquid measuring cup. In separate small liquid measuring cup, whisk tahini and oil.

2. Process ¾ cup artichoke hearts, chickpeas, garlic, salt, lemon zest, and cayenne in food processor until almost fully ground, about 15 seconds; scrape down bowl. With processor running, add lemon juice mixture in steady stream. Scrape down bowl and process for 1 minute longer. With processor running, add tahini mixture in steady stream. Continue to process until hummus is smooth and creamy, about 15 seconds longer.

3. Transfer hummus to serving bowl and let sit at room temperature until flavors meld, about 30 minutes. Chop remaining artichoke hearts for garnish. (Hummus and artichoke garnish can be refrigerated, separately, for up to 2 days. Makes 2 cups.)

4. Before serving, season hummus with salt to taste and stir in extra water as needed to adjust consistency. Sprinkle with chopped artichokes and parsley, drizzle with extra olive oil to taste, and serve.

Lemon-Scented Rice Pilaf

WHY THIS RECIPE WORKS
Lightly toasting the rice and using chicken broth gives this pilaf a deeper, heartier flavor that stands up nicely to the somewhat spicy shrimp. Using just 1½ parts broth to 1 part rice and letting the rice steam off the heat for the final 10 minutes ensures that the entire pot of rice is perfectly cooked through, from top to bottom. We chose to skip the traditional method of rinsing the raw rice before cooking because we liked how the extra starch made the rice a little sticky and easier to eat with the shrimp.

We prefer basmati rice here as it is slightly more fragrant than long-grain white rice.

4	tablespoons unsalted butter
1	onion, chopped fine
	Salt
2½	cups basmati or long-grain white rice
3	garlic cloves, minced
1	bay leaf
3¾	cups low-sodium chicken broth
3	(2-inch) strips lemon zest plus 1 tablespoon juice
¼	cup minced fresh parsley or mint

1. Melt butter in large saucepan over medium-high heat. Add onion and ½ teaspoon salt and cook until just softened, about 3 minutes. Stir in rice and cook, stirring often, until fragrant and edges begin to turn translucent, about 2 minutes. Stir in garlic and bay leaf and cook until fragrant, about 30 seconds.

2. Stir in broth and zest and bring to boil. Cover, reduce heat to low, and cook until liquid is absorbed and rice is tender, about 20 minutes. Remove from heat and let stand, covered, for 10 minutes. Discard bay leaf and fluff rice with fork. Fold in lemon juice and parsley, season with salt to taste, and serve.

MAKING STRIPS OF ZEST

Use a vegetable peeler to remove long, wide strips of zest from lemons and oranges avoiding the bitter white pith.

Mâche and Mint Salad with Cucumbers

Mâche is a baby lettuce with sweet, nutty flavor. It is a very delicate green, so be sure to handle it gently and make sure it is dried thoroughly before tossing with the vinaigrette. If you can't find mâche, substitute either baby spinach or baby mesclun greens.

1	tablespoon lemon juice
1	tablespoon minced fresh parsley
1	tablespoon capers, rinsed and minced
1	teaspoon minced fresh thyme
1	garlic clove, minced
¼	teaspoon salt
¼	teaspoon pepper
¼	cup extra-virgin olive oil
12	ounces mâche (12 cups)
½	cup chopped fresh mint
1	cucumber, sliced thin
⅓	cup pine nuts, toasted

Whisk lemon juice, parsley, capers, thyme, garlic, salt, and pepper in small bowl. Whisking constantly, drizzle in oil. In large bowl, gently toss mâche with mint, cucumber, and pine nuts. Just before serving, whisk dressing to re-emulsify, then drizzle over salad and toss gently to coat.

TOASTING NUTS AND SEEDS

Toasting nuts and seeds maximizes their flavor, and takes only a few minutes. To toast a small amount (less than 1 cup) of nuts or seeds, put them in a dry skillet over medium heat. Shake the skillet occasionally to prevent scorching and toast until they are lightly browned and fragrant, 3 to 8 minutes. Watch the nuts closely because they can go from golden to burnt very quickly. To toast a large quantity of nuts, spread the nuts onto a rimmed baking sheet and toast in a 350-degree oven, stirring occasionally, until lightly browned and fragrant, 5 to 10 minutes.

✔ **WHY THIS RECIPE WORKS**
The assertively flavored Greek-style shrimp dinner cries out for a simple and cooling salad, and this one fits the bill perfectly without being at all boring. The combination of delicate mâche and thinly sliced cucumber tastes great, and the mint and pine nuts are in keeping with the menu's Mediterranean theme. The capers are unexpected but give this salad added personality.

Vanilla Ice Cream with Homemade Salted Pistachio Brittle

If you don't have a nonstick baking sheet, line a regular rimmed baking sheet with aluminum foil and spray generously with vegetable oil spray. Don't let the caramel get too dark in step 1, because it will continue to darken as it cools. It should be the color of bourbon. Our favorite brand of vanilla ice cream is Ben and Jerry's.

1½	cups (10½ ounces) sugar
¾	cup corn syrup
⅓	cup water
3	tablespoons unsalted butter
1	teaspoon baking soda
1¾	cups salted shelled pistachios (7¾ ounces)
3	tablespoons sesame seeds, toasted
	Coarse ground sea salt or kosher salt
4	pints (½ gallon) vanilla ice cream

1. Set nonstick rimmed baking sheet on counter. Lightly grease offset spatula. Combine sugar, corn syrup, water, and butter in large saucepan. Bring to boil over high heat and cook, stirring occasionally, until mixture is light amber in color and registers 350 degrees, 12 to 14 minutes.

2. Working quickly, remove from heat and carefully stir in baking soda (mixture will foam slightly). Stir in pistachios and sesame seeds, then immediately pour mixture onto sheet and spread into even, ¼-inch-thick layer with greased spatula. (Mixture may not cover entire sheet.) Sprinkle lightly with salt while brittle is hot.

3. Let brittle cool completely, about 30 minutes, then break into 2-inch shards. (Brittle can be stored at room temperature for up to 1 month.) To serve, portion ice cream into individual bowls and garnish with brittle.

✔ **WHY THIS RECIPE WORKS**
It's hard to imagine a better ending to this menu than creamy vanilla ice cream and dark and salty homemade brittle. We took the brittle up a notch by using pistachios and sesame seeds instead of the usual peanuts. Adding corn syrup and baking soda to the brittle helped ensure that it would break apart easily (and kept it from being tooth-breakingly hard). A sprinkling of coarse salt is the finishing touch.

Farmers' Market Vegetarian Dinner

THE GAME PLAN

ONE DAY AHEAD...

MAKE PANNA COTTA: 35 minutes
(plus 24 hours for chilling)

MAKE STRAWBERRY COULIS: 15 minutes

MAKE GOAT CHEESE ROUNDS: 25 minutes
(plus 3 hours for chilling)

ON THE DAY OF...

MAKE BRUSCHETTA: 25 minutes

MAKE PASTA: 1½ hours

MAKE SALAD: 15 minutes (includes 10 minutes
for baking goat cheese)

FARMERS' MARKET VEGETARIAN DINNER

⇥ Serves 8 ⇤

Bruschetta with Artichoke Hearts and Parmesan

Spring Vegetable Pasta ⇚ Baked Goat Cheese Salad with Pecans and Radishes

Vanilla Bean Panna Cotta with Strawberry Coulis

Spring Vegetable Pasta

Campanelle is our pasta of choice for this dish, although both farfalle and penne are acceptable substitutes. You will need at least a 6-quart Dutch oven for this recipe.

2½	pounds leeks, white and light green parts halved lengthwise, sliced ½ inch thick, and washed thoroughly; dark green parts chopped coarse, washed thoroughly, and reserved separately (see page 37)
1½	pounds asparagus, trimmed (see page 45), tough ends reserved and chopped coarse; spears sliced ½ inch thick on bias
3	cups frozen peas, thawed
6	garlic cloves, minced
6	cups vegetable broth
1½	cups water, plus extra as needed
9	tablespoons extra-virgin olive oil
	Salt and pepper
¼	teaspoon red pepper flakes
1½	pounds campanelle
1½	cups dry white wine
3	tablespoons minced fresh mint
3	tablespoons minced fresh chives
¾	teaspoon grated lemon zest plus 3 tablespoons juice
1½	ounces Parmesan cheese, grated (¾ cup), plus extra for serving

1. Place dark green leek parts, asparagus ends, 1½ cups peas, half of garlic, vegetable broth, and water in large saucepan. Bring to simmer and cook gently for 10 minutes. Strain through fine-mesh strainer into 8-cup liquid measuring cup, pressing on solids to extract as much liquid as possible. (You should have 8 cups broth; add water as needed to measure 8 cups. Broth can be refrigerated for up to 1 day.) Return broth to saucepan, cover, and keep warm over low heat.

2. Meanwhile, heat 3 tablespoons oil in Dutch oven over medium heat until shimmering. Add white and light green leek parts and pinch salt, cover, and cook, stirring occasionally, until leeks begin to brown, about 5 minutes. Stir in asparagus and cook until asparagus is crisp-tender, 4 to 6 minutes. Stir in remaining garlic, pepper flakes, and pinch pepper and cook until fragrant, about 30 seconds. Stir in remaining 1½ cups peas and cook for 1 minute. Transfer vegetables to plate. Wipe pot dry.

3. Heat remaining 6 tablespoons oil in now-empty pot over *continued* ➤

continued ➤

✔ WHY THIS RECIPE WORKS

This spring vegetable pasta dish takes the fast lane to the ultimate marriage of pasta, sauce, and spring vegetables. We cooked the pasta right in the sauce (much like a risotto). Not only is this method a little simpler, but the sauce flavors the pasta and the pasta starch helps thicken the broth into a creamy sauce without using cream or butter, which would overpower the delicate flavors of the vegetables. Doctoring store-bought vegetable broth with extra flavor by using the vegetable trimmings is crucial for a fresh-tasting sauce.

medium heat until shimmering. Add pasta and cook, stirring often, until just beginning to brown, 5 to 7 minutes. Stir in wine and cook, stirring constantly, until absorbed, about 2 minutes.

4. Add warm broth, increase heat to medium-high, and bring to boil. Cook, stirring frequently, until most of liquid is absorbed and pasta is al dente, 12 to 14 minutes. Meanwhile, combine mint, chives, and lemon zest in bowl.

5. Off heat, stir in cooked vegetables, half of mint mixture, lemon juice, and Parmesan. Season with salt and pepper to taste. Serve, passing Parmesan and remaining herb mixture separately.

Bruschetta with Artichoke Hearts and Parmesan

Toast the bread just before serving to help preserve its warm, crunchy texture.

✔ **WHY THIS RECIPE WORKS**
There's a whole lot more to bruschetta than chopped tomatoes and basil, and once you try this artichoke version—thick slabs of crusty toasted bread piled high with a flavorful pureed artichoke mixture and topped with shavings of Parmesan—you'll never go back to the old standby. Pureeing canned artichoke hearts, which we prefer to their marinated cousins, with lemon juice, garlic, and basil not only makes a flavorful mixture but also makes a paste that stays on the bread (and doesn't fall on your shirt).

TOPPING
1 (14-ounce) can artichoke hearts, rinsed and patted dry
2 tablespoons extra-virgin olive oil, plus extra for serving
2 tablespoons chopped fresh basil
2 teaspoons lemon juice
1 garlic clove, minced
¼ teaspoon salt
¼ teaspoon pepper
2 ounces Parmesan cheese, 1 ounce grated (½ cup) and 1 ounce shaved

TOASTED BREAD
1 (10 by 5-inch) loaf thick-crusted country bread, ends trimmed, sliced crosswise into ¾-inch-thick pieces
1 garlic clove, peeled
¼ cup extra-virgin olive oil
Salt and pepper

1. FOR THE TOPPING: Pulse artichoke hearts, oil, basil, lemon juice, garlic, salt, and pepper in food processor to coarse puree, about 6 pulses, scraping down bowl as needed. Add grated Parmesan and pulse to combine, about 2 pulses. (Topping can be refrigerated for up to 2 days.)

2. FOR THE TOASTED BREAD: Adjust oven rack 4 inches from broiler element and heat broiler. Place bread on aluminum foil–lined baking sheet and broil until deep golden on both sides, 1 to 2 minutes per side. Lightly rub 1 side of bread with garlic clove, brush with olive oil, and season with salt. Spread artichoke mixture over toasts and top with Parmesan shavings. Season with pepper to taste, drizzle with olive oil, and serve. (Makes 10 bruschetta.)

SHAVING CHEESE

To achieve paper-thin slices of Parmesan or Manchego cheese for garnishing, run a vegetable peeler over the block of cheese. Use a light touch for thin shavings.

Baked Goat Cheese Salad with Pecans and Radishes

You can substitute walnuts, pistachios, or almonds for the pecans. Don't skimp on the goat cheese chilling time (in both steps 1 and 2) or the cheese will be very hard to work with.

GOAT CHEESE
- 1½ cups pecans (6 ounces)
- 12 ounces goat cheese, softened
- 2 tablespoons chopped fresh chives
- 1 teaspoon minced fresh thyme
- 2 large eggs
- Vegetable oil spray

VINAIGRETTE AND SALAD
- 5 teaspoons red wine vinegar
- 2 teaspoons Dijon mustard
- 1 small shallot, minced
- ⅛ teaspoon salt
- Pinch pepper
- ¼ cup extra-virgin olive oil
- 12 cups mesclun greens (12 ounces)
- 4 radishes, trimmed and sliced thin

1. FOR THE GOAT CHEESE: Pulse pecans in food processor until finely chopped, about 15 pulses; transfer to bowl. Process goat cheese, chives, and thyme in food processor until smooth, about 30 seconds. Refrigerate cheese mixture in covered bowl until firm, about 1 hour.

2. Roll chilled cheese mixture into eight 1¾-inch balls (generous 2 tablespoons each). Beat eggs in medium bowl. Dip each cheese ball into eggs, then roll in chopped nuts, pressing gently to adhere. Arrange balls, 2 inches apart, on baking sheet and press into ¾-inch-thick rounds with greased bottom of dry measuring cup. Cover with plastic wrap and freeze until completely firm, at least 2 hours and up to 1 week.

3. FOR THE VINAIGRETTE AND SALAD: Whisk vinegar, mustard, shallot, salt, and pepper in small bowl. Whisking constantly, drizzle in oil. In large bowl, gently toss mesclun greens with radishes.

4. Adjust oven rack to top position and heat oven to 475 degrees. Unwrap cheese and coat lightly with oil spray. Bake until nuts are golden brown and cheese is warmed through, 7 to 10 minutes. Whisk vinaigrette to re-emulsify, then drizzle over greens and toss gently to coat. Divide salad among 8 individual plates, top with warm goat cheese, and serve immediately.

EVEN EASIER ⟿ Don't have time to make baked goat cheese? Simply toss 1 cup crumbled goat cheese and ½ cup coarsely chopped toasted pecans with the salad and vinaigrette before serving.

WHY THIS RECIPE WORKS

Baked goat cheese salads are as popular today as they were when Alice Waters brought them into the limelight in the early 1970s, but most people only enjoy them in restaurants. We think they are a great accompaniment to our vegetarian pasta dinner, and the goat cheese rounds can be prepared the day before and baked at the last minute, making this a great recipe when entertaining. Coating the cheese rounds in ground nuts instead of the usual bread crumbs added a big boost of flavor, which our tasters loved. We also found that giving the cheese a whirl in the food processor allowed us to incorporate fresh herbs into the cheese. Baking the rounds in a blazing hot oven for just 7 to 10 minutes ensured a crunchy coating and a smooth, but not melted, interior. To avoid runny cheese rounds, be sure to freeze the rounds until completely firm (at least 2 hours) before baking.

Vanilla Bean Panna Cotta with Strawberry Coulis

For same-day panna cotta, increase the amount of gelatin to 2¾ teaspoons and reduce the chilling time to 4 hours in step 4. Do not substitute low-fat or nonfat milk here. Two teaspoons of vanilla extract can be substituted for the vanilla bean. Eight 4- or 6-ounce ramekins can be substituted for the wine glasses. Garnish with sliced strawberries if desired.

PANNA COTTA

1	cup whole milk
2½	teaspoons unflavored gelatin
½	vanilla bean
3	cups heavy cream
6	tablespoons sugar
	Pinch salt

STRAWBERRY COULIS

12	ounces fresh strawberries, hulled and sliced, or frozen strawberries, thawed and sliced (2½ cups)
5–7	tablespoons sugar
¼	cup water, plus extra as needed
⅛	teaspoon salt
2	teaspoons lemon juice

1. FOR THE PANNA COTTA: Pour milk into medium saucepan, sprinkle gelatin evenly over top, and let sit for 10 minutes. Cut vanilla bean in half lengthwise, then, using tip of paring knife, scrape out seeds. Combine vanilla seeds, vanilla pod, and cream in 4-cup liquid measuring cup. Set 8 wine glasses on baking sheet. Make ice bath in very large bowl.

2. Heat milk mixture over high heat, stirring constantly, until gelatin dissolves and mixture registers 135 degrees, about 1½ minutes. Off heat, stir in sugar and salt until dissolved, about 1 minute. Stirring constantly, slowly add cream mixture.

3. Transfer mixture to medium bowl and set in ice bath. Let mixture chill, stirring frequently, until it has thickened to consistency of eggnog and registers 50 degrees, about 10 minutes.

4. Strain mixture through fine-mesh strainer into pitcher, then pour evenly into wine glasses. Cover glasses with plastic wrap and refrigerate until set and chilled, at least 24 hours and up to 5 days.

5. FOR THE STRAWBERRY COULIS: Simmer berries, 5 tablespoons sugar, water, and salt in medium saucepan over medium heat, stirring occasionally, until sugar is dissolved and berries are heated through, 1 to 3 minutes.

6. Transfer mixture to blender and puree until smooth, about 20 seconds. Strain mixture through fine-mesh strainer into bowl, pressing on solids to extract as much puree as possible. Stir in lemon juice and season with remaining sugar to taste. (Coulis can be refrigerated for up to 4 days; stir in extra water as needed to adjust consistency.)

7. To serve, unwrap panna cotta, and spoon 2 to 3 tablespoon coulis over top.

REMOVING SEEDS FROM A VANILLA BEAN

Use a small sharp knife to cut the vanilla bean in half lengthwise. Place the knife at one end of one bean half and press down to flatten the bean as you move the knife away from you and catch the seeds on the edge of the blade. Add the seeds as well as the pods to the liquid ingredients.

Rustic Pork Stew Dinner

THE GAME PLAN

ONE DAY AHEAD...

MAKE BEAN DIP: 10 minutes

MAKE PORK STEW: 3¼ hours

MAKE PIE: 1¼ hours (plus 6 hours for baking, cooling, and chilling)

ON THE DAY OF...

MAKE GARLIC TOASTS FOR DIP: 10 minutes

MAKE SALAD: 1¼ hours (plus 30 minutes for cooling)

FINISH PORK STEW: 45 minutes

MAKE EGG NOODLES: 30 minutes

Pork Stew with Fennel, Leeks, and Prunes

Boneless pork butt roast is often labeled Boston butt in the supermarket. While 1¼ cups of brandy may seem like a lot, we recommend using an inexpensive brand and not skimping on the amount—it provides just the right balance of flavors. You will need at least a 6-quart Dutch oven for this recipe. Be sure to stir the stew gently once the pork is cooked, especially if reheating, or the pork will break apart into shreds.

✔ **WHY THIS RECIPE WORKS**
This elegantly flavored pork stew with brandy and prunes is a rich-tasting and impressive entrée. Pork butt (or pork shoulder) is by far the best choice for this recipe and produces the most flavorful and tender pieces of stew meat. For big batches of stew like this, it is only necessary to brown half the meat to ensure enough flavorful fond (browned bits) in the pot upon which to build a rich foundation for the stew. To ensure that the meat cooked through evenly and that the bottom of the pot didn't scorch during the several hours of simmering time, we found it best to cook the stew gently in a 325-degree oven rather than on the stovetop.

6	pounds boneless pork butt roast, pulled apart at seams, trimmed, and cut into 1½-inch pieces
	Salt and pepper
3	tablespoons vegetable oil
2	leeks, white and light green parts only, halved lengthwise, sliced ¼ inch thick, and washed thoroughly
5	garlic cloves, minced
¼	cup all-purpose flour
1¼	cups brandy
5	cups low-sodium chicken broth
2	bay leaves
2	fennel bulbs, stalks discarded, bulbs halved, cored, and sliced into ½-inch-thick strips (see page 22)

1½	pounds carrots, peeled and cut into 1-inch pieces
1½	cups heavy cream
1½	cups prunes, halved
3	tablespoons minced fresh tarragon
3	tablespoons minced fresh parsley
2	tablespoons lemon juice

1. Adjust oven rack to lower-middle position and heat oven to 325 degrees. Pat pork dry with paper towel and season with salt and pepper. Heat 2 tablespoons oil in Dutch oven over medium-high heat until just smoking. Working in 2 batches, brown half of pork on all sides, about 8 minutes per batch; transfer to bowl. *continued* ➤

PREPARING LEEKS

Trim the roots and the dark green leaves; these leaves are often discarded, but can be used to reinforce the flavor of store-bought broth as in the Spring Vegetable Pasta recipe on page 31. Slice the trimmed leek in half lengthwise, then cut into pieces as directed in the recipe. Wash the cut leeks thoroughly to remove dirt and sand.

2. Heat remaining 1 tablespoon oil in now-empty pot over medium heat until shimmering. Add leeks and 1 teaspoon salt and cook, stirring often, until wilted and lightly browned, 5 to 7 minutes. Stir in garlic and cook until fragrant, about 30 seconds. Stir in flour and cook, stirring constantly, until golden, about 1 minute.

3. Slowly whisk in brandy, scraping up browned bits. Gradually whisk in broth until smooth and bring to simmer. Stir in browned pork with any accumulated juices, remaining raw pork, and bay leaves and return to simmer. Cover, place pot in oven, and cook for 1 hour.

4. Stir in fennel and carrots and continue to cook, covered, until meat is just tender, about 45 minutes. Remove and discard bay leaves. (Stew can be cooled and refrigerated for up to 2 days. Discard hardened fat from surface and gently reheat over medium-low heat, about 30 minutes.)

5. Gently stir in cream and prunes, cover, and let sit for 5 minutes. Stir in tarragon, parsley, and lemon juice. Season with salt and pepper to taste and serve.

Rosemary and Garlic White Bean Dip

WHY THIS RECIPE WORKS For a white bean dip to really stand out as terrific, it needs to have both a little texture and a lot of flavor. Rather than process all of the beans into a smooth puree, we reserved a handful of beans and pulsed them in at the end for an appealingly chunky texture. To give these otherwise bland beans some flavor, we used a heavy hand with raw garlic, rosemary, and lemon juice.

The brand of canned white beans you use here will make a difference; our favorite brand is Progresso. Crackers, pita chips, or thinly sliced baguette can be substituted for the Garlic Toasts if desired.

2	(15-ounce) cans cannellini beans, rinsed
½	cup extra-virgin olive oil
¼	cup water, plus extra as needed
2	tablespoons lemon juice
2	garlic cloves, minced
½	teaspoon chopped fresh rosemary
	Salt and pepper
1	recipe Garlic Toasts (page 62)

1. Process two-thirds of beans, 6 tablespoons oil, water, lemon juice, garlic, and rosemary in food processor until smooth, about 10 seconds; scrape down bowl. Add remaining beans and pulse to incorporate (do not puree smooth), about 5 pulses. Season with salt and pepper to taste.

2. Transfer to serving bowl and let sit at room temperature until flavors meld, about 30 minutes. (Dip can be refrigerated for up to 2 days; bring to room temperature and stir in extra water as needed to adjust consistency. Makes 2 cups.) Before serving, make small well in center of dip and pour remaining 2 tablespoons oil into well. Serve with Garlic Toasts.

Buttered Egg Noodles

WHY THIS RECIPE WORKS When you have a real showstopper of a stew, we like to pair it with a simple side dish, such as boiled egg noodles. Be sure to use a large pot of boiling, salted water or you'll risk unevenly cooked noodles.

Egg noodles are available in a wide variety of sizes; be sure to use wide noodles here because their larger size is better suited to accompany the stew.

1	pound wide egg noodles
	Salt and pepper
4	tablespoons unsalted butter

Bring 4 quarts water to boil in large pot. Add noodles and 1 tablespoon salt and cook until tender, 6 to 8 minutes. Drain noodles and return to pot. Stir in butter, season with salt and pepper to taste, and serve.

Roasted Beet and Carrot Salad with Watercress

If using a dark-colored nonstick baking sheet for the carrots, line the pan with aluminum foil to prevent scorching.

2 pounds beets, trimmed
6 tablespoons extra-virgin olive oil
  Salt and pepper
½ teaspoon sugar
2 pounds carrots, peeled and sliced ¼ inch thick on bias
¼ cup white wine vinegar
1 shallot, minced
1 teaspoon honey
12 ounces watercress (12 cups)

1. Adjust oven racks to lowest and middle positions. Place large rimmed baking sheet on lowest rack and heat oven to 450 degrees.

2. In large bowl, toss beets with 2 tablespoons oil, ½ teaspoon salt, ¼ teaspoon pepper, and ¼ teaspoon sugar. Wrap beets individually in aluminum foil and place on second baking sheet. In now-empty bowl, toss carrots with 2 tablespoons oil, ½ teaspoon salt, ½ teaspoon pepper, and remaining ¼ teaspoon sugar.

3. Working quickly, spread carrots out over hot baking sheet. Place baking sheet with beets on middle rack. Roast carrots until tender and well browned on one side, 20 to 25 minutes, and beets until tender, 35 to 45 minutes.

4. While vegetables roast, whisk vinegar, shallot, honey, ½ teaspoon salt, and ¼ teaspoon pepper in now-empty bowl. Whisking constantly, drizzle in remaining 2 tablespoons oil.

5. When carrots are cooked, transfer to bowl with vinaigrette. When beets are cooked, unwrap, rub off skins, using paper towels, and slice into ½-inch-thick wedges. Add beets to bowl with carrots. Toss vegetables gently to coat with vinaigrette and let cool for 30 minutes. (Dressed vegetables can be held at room temperature for up to 4 hours.)

6. Just before serving, add watercress to bowl of roasted vegetables, season with salt and pepper to taste, and gently toss.

REMOVING BEET SKINS

To remove the skin from a cooked beet, cradle it inside several layers of paper towels and gently rub off the skins.

✔ WHY THIS RECIPE WORKS
An interesting and hearty salad is a great way to round out this rustic, French-inspired menu. Beets and carrots are a winning combination here, and roasting them brings out their earthy sweetness. We tossed them with the vinaigrette while they were still hot, which allowed them to absorb more flavor. To make this a true salad—rather than dressed roasted vegetables—we added crisp, peppery watercress.

French Silk Chocolate Pie

You will need an electric hand-held mixer to make this pie. Our favorite brand of bittersweet chocolate is Ghirardelli 60 percent Cacao Bittersweet Chocolate; it can be found in most supermarkets. For more information on making a pie shell, see page 325. Serve with lightly sweetened whipped cream and shaved chocolate if desired.

CRUST

1¼	cups (6¼ ounces) all-purpose flour
1	tablespoon sugar
½	teaspoon salt
3	tablespoons vegetable shortening, cut into ½-inch pieces and chilled
5	tablespoons unsalted butter, cut into ¼-inch pieces and chilled
4–6	tablespoons ice water

FILLING

1	cup heavy cream, chilled
3	large eggs
¾	cup (5¼ ounces) sugar
2	tablespoons water
8	ounces bittersweet chocolate, melted and cooled
1	tablespoon vanilla extract
8	tablespoons unsalted butter, cut into ½-inch pieces and softened

1. FOR THE CRUST: Process flour, sugar, and salt together in food processor until combined, about 10 seconds. Scatter shortening over top and process until mixture resembles coarse cornmeal, about 10 seconds. Scatter butter pieces over top and pulse mixture until it resembles coarse crumbs, about 10 pulses. Transfer mixture to medium bowl.

2. Sprinkle 4 tablespoons ice water over mixture. Stir and press dough together, using stiff rubber spatula, until dough sticks together. If dough does not come together, stir in remaining water, 1 tablespoon at a time, until it does. Turn dough onto sheet of plastic wrap and flatten into 4-inch disk. Wrap dough tightly in plastic wrap and refrigerate for at least 1 hour and up to 2 days.

3. Let chilled dough soften slightly at room temperature, about 10 minutes. Roll dough into 12-inch circle on lightly floured counter. Roll dough loosely around rolling pin, then unroll over 9-inch pie plate. Ease dough into plate by gently lifting edges. Trim dough to overhang plate by ½ inch. Fold overhanging dough underneath itself to be flush with rim of plate, and crimp edge. Cover loosely with plastic wrap and refrigerate for at least 20 minutes and up to 1 day.

4. Adjust oven rack to middle position and heat oven to 375 degrees. Line chilled crust with aluminum foil and fill with pie weights. Bake until crust looks dry and is light in color, 25 to 30 minutes. Remove weights and foil and continue to bake crust until deep golden brown, 10 to 12 minutes longer. Transfer crust to wire rack and let cool to room temperature, about 1 hour.

5. FOR THE FILLING: Using electric hand-held mixer, whip cream on medium-low speed until foamy, about 1 minute. Increase speed to high and whip until stiff peaks form, 1 to 3 minutes. Cover and refrigerate.

6. Combine eggs, sugar, and water in large heatproof bowl set over medium saucepan filled with ½ inch barely simmering water (don't let bowl touch water). Using electric hand-held mixer, beat mixture on medium speed until thickened and registers 160 degrees, 7 to 10 minutes. Remove bowl from heat and continue to beat mixture until fluffy and cooled to room temperature, about 8 minutes.

7. Beat in chocolate and vanilla until incorporated. Beat in butter, a few pieces at a time, until well combined. Using spatula, fold in whipped cream until no streaks remain. Scrape filling into cooled pie crust and refrigerate until set, at least 3 hours and up to 24 hours. Serve.

✔ **WHY THIS RECIPE WORKS**
Don't let the name fool you. French silk pie was actually "born" in America, having been created by Betty Cooper in 1951 for the third annual Pillsbury Bake-Off. Bringing this classic into the 21st century, however, took a little work. We ditched the raw eggs in the original custard for a quick cooked custard, swapped whipped cream for some of the butter for a more satiny texture, and boosted the chocolate flavor by stirring in a hefty dose of melted bittersweet chocolate.

Rack of Lamb Dinner

THE GAME PLAN

ONE DAY AHEAD...

MAKE RED PEPPER DIP: 50 minutes
(plus 30 minutes for chilling)

MAKE TART: 40 minutes
(plus 3¾ hours for baking and cooling)

ON THE DAY OF...

MAKE MINT RELISH: 15 minutes

ROAST LAMB: 1 hour (plus 10 minutes for resting)

MAKE COUSCOUS: 45 minutes

MAKE ASPARAGUS: 20 minutes

MAKE WHIPPED CREAM FOR TART: 5 minutes

RACK OF LAMB DINNER

≯ Serves 8 ≮

Roasted Red Pepper and Walnut Dip

Roasted Racks of Lamb with Mint Relish ≯ Broiled Asparagus with Lemon

Couscous with Lemon, Scallions, and Feta ≯ Rustic Walnut Tart

Roasted Racks of Lamb with Mint Relish

We prefer the milder taste and larger size of American lamb for this recipe. If using imported lamb, note that the racks will probably be smaller and will therefore cook through more quickly. Often, the racks of lamb you buy at the store have already been frenched (cleaned of excess fat and meat), but inevitably, they will still need some cleaning up. For the relish, consider using a food processor to mince the parsley and mint.

MINT RELISH

¾ cup minced fresh parsley

¾ cup minced fresh mint

¾ cup extra-virgin olive oil

⅓ cup red wine vinegar

3 tablespoons water

1 shallot, minced

5 garlic cloves, minced

2½ teaspoons sugar

1½ teaspoons salt

LAMB

4 (1¼- to 1½-pound) racks of lamb, 8 to 9 ribs each, trimmed
Salt and pepper

2 tablespoons vegetable oil

1. FOR THE MINT RELISH: Combine all ingredients in bowl. Let sit at room temperature until needed. (Makes 1½ cups.)

2. FOR THE LAMB: Line large roasting pan with aluminum foil. Adjust oven rack to lower-middle position, place prepared pan on rack, and heat oven to 425 degrees.

3. Pat lamb dry with paper towels and season with salt and pepper. Heat 1 tablespoon oil in 12-inch skillet over medium-high heat until just smoking. Place 2 racks in skillet, fat side down with ribs facing outward, and cook until well browned, about 5 minutes.

4. Using tongs, stand racks up in skillet, leaning them against each *continued* ➤

TRIMMING A LAMB RACK

Using a sharp boning or paring knife, trim the fat that covers the loin, leaving the strip of fat that separates the loin and small eye of meat directly above it. Make a straight cut along the top side of the bones, an inch up from the small eye of meat. Remove any fat above this line and scrape any remaining meat or fat from the exposed bones.

other, and brown bottoms, about 2 minutes; transfer to large platter. Repeat with remaining 1 tablespoon oil and remaining 2 lamb racks; transfer to platter. (Seared lamb can be held at room temperature for up to 1 hour before finishing in the oven.)

5. Transfer lamb racks to hot pan in oven and roast until lamb registers about 125 degrees (for medium-rare), 12 to 15 minutes. Transfer lamb to carving board, tent loosely with foil, and let rest for 5 to 10 minutes. Cut lamb racks into individual chops by slicing between each rib and serve with mint relish.

Roasted Red Pepper and Walnut Dip

You can substitute 4 large jarred roasted red peppers (about 9 ounces), thoroughly rinsed and dried, for the fresh bell peppers and skip steps 1 through 3. Pomegranate molasses can be found in Middle Eastern markets as well as in the international foods aisle of many supermarkets; if you cannot find it, substitute 3 tablespoons lemon juice, 1 tablespoon mild molasses, and 1 teaspoon honey. Serve with pita chips or fresh pita bread cut into wedges.

♂ **WHY THIS RECIPE WORKS**
Also known as *muhammara*, this dip made from roasted red peppers, walnuts, and pomegranate molasses is popular throughout the eastern Mediterranean. In Arabic, the word *muhammara* means "brick colored," which is the exact hue of the spread. Of course freshly roasted peppers taste best here, but jarred peppers make for a decent substitute in a pinch. We also found that crumbled wheat crackers added both flavor and substance to the dip and prevented it from having a watery texture. Lastly, we noted that the flavors needed time to meld—at least 30 minutes—before serving.

4   large red bell peppers
1   cup walnuts, toasted (see page 29)
¼   cup coarsely ground plain wheat crackers, such as Carr's Whole Wheat
3   tablespoons pomegranate molasses
2   tablespoons extra-virgin olive oil
¾   teaspoon salt
½   teaspoon ground cumin
¼   teaspoon cayenne pepper
2   tablespoons minced fresh parsley or cilantro

1. Adjust oven rack 3 inches from broiler element and heat broiler. (If necessary, set upside-down rimmed baking sheet on oven rack to get close to broiler element.) Line rimmed baking sheet with aluminum foil.

2. Cut tops and bottoms off peppers and remove stems from tops. Remove seeds and cores from peppers. Slice each pepper through 1 side, press flat, and trim away remaining white ribs. Lay flattened peppers, pepper tops, and pepper bottoms on prepared baking sheet. Broil until pepper skin is charred and puffed but flesh is still firm, 6 to 10 minutes, rotating baking sheet halfway through broiling.

3. Transfer broiled peppers to bowl, cover with plastic wrap, and let steam until skins peel off easily, 10 to 15 minutes. Peel and discard skin using paring knife. Chop roasted peppers coarse.

4. Pulse roasted peppers with walnuts, crackers, pomegranate molasses, oil, salt, cumin, and cayenne in food processor until smooth, about 10 pulses. Transfer to serving bowl, cover, and refrigerate until flavors meld, at least 30 minutes and up to 2 days. Sprinkle with parsley before serving. (Makes 2 cups.)

ROASTING BELL PEPPERS

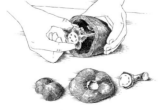  

Cut off the tops and bottoms of the peppers and remove the stems from the tops. Remove the seeds and cores from the peppers. Slice each pepper through one side, press flat, and trim away the remaining white ribs. Lay the flattened peppers, pepper tops, and pepper bottoms on a foil-lined baking sheet and broil until the skin is charred and puffed but the flesh is still firm, 6 to 10 minutes, rotating the baking sheet halfway through broiling.

Broiled Asparagus with Lemon

Avoid pencil-thin asparagus when using this cooking method, as it has a tendency to cook unevenly.

3 pounds asparagus, trimmed
1 tablespoon olive oil
  Salt and pepper
½ lemon

1. Adjust oven rack 3 inches from broiler element and heat broiler. (If necessary, set upside-down rimmed baking sheet on oven rack to get close to broiler element.) Toss asparagus with oil, season with salt and pepper, and arrange spears in same direction on large rimmed baking sheet.

2. Broil, shuffling asparagus from top to bottom every few minutes, until spears are tender and tips begin to brown, 5 to 10 minutes. Squeeze lemon over spears and serve immediately.

TRIMMING ASPARAGUS

Holding the asparagus about halfway down the stalk, bend it until the hard, woody end snaps off. Using this piece of asparagus as a guide, trim the remaining asparagus to the same length with a knife. The hard, woody ends of the asparagus are often discarded, but can be used to reinforce the flavor of store-bought broth as in the Spring Vegetable Pasta recipe on page 31.

Couscous with Lemon, Scallions, and Feta

For an accurate measurement of boiling water, bring a full kettle of water to a boil, then measure out the desired amount. This dish can be served warm or at room temperature.

2¼ cups couscous
5 tablespoons olive oil
1 onion, chopped fine
4 garlic cloves, minced
¼ teaspoon cayenne pepper
3 cups boiling water
  Salt and pepper
2 teaspoons grated lemon zest plus ¼ cup juice (2 lemons)
8 ounces feta cheese, crumbled (2 cups)
½ cup pine nuts, toasted (see page 29)
12 scallions, sliced thin
½ cup chopped fresh mint

1. Toast couscous with 2 tablespoons olive oil in 12-inch skillet over medium heat, stirring occasionally, until lightly browned, 3 to 5 minutes; transfer to large bowl.

2. Heat 1 tablespoon oil in now-empty skillet over medium-high heat until shimmering. Add onion and cook until softened, about 5 minutes. Stir in garlic and cayenne and cook until fragrant, about 30 seconds. Transfer to bowl with couscous. Stir boiling water and ¾ teaspoon salt into couscous, cover tightly with plastic wrap, and let sit until couscous is tender, about 12 minutes.

3. Fluff couscous with fork, breaking up any clumps. Combine remaining 2 tablespoons oil, lemon zest and juice in small bowl. Add lemon mixture, feta, pine nuts, and scallions to couscous and gently toss to incorporate. Season with salt and pepper to taste. (Couscous can sit at room temperature for up to 2 hours and be refrigerated for up to 1 day. If refrigerated, bring to room temperature or microwave, covered, until hot, 3 to 5 minutes.) Before serving, fold in mint.

Rustic Walnut Tart with Bourbon Whipped Cream

✔ WHY THIS RECIPE WORKS
This elegant nut tart is the perfect ending to a rack of lamb dinner. As a bonus, it's very easy to prepare, with a press-in crust you can make in a food processor and a very simple filling. To boost the flavor of the crust, we added nuts and brown sugar. For the filling, we used a pecan pie base but swapped in walnuts, reduced the amount of sugar, and added a hefty amount of vanilla as well as a hit of bourbon (or rum). The liquor cuts through the sweetness and intensifies the flavor of the nuts.

Pecans can be substituted for the walnuts if desired. If you don't have a tart pan, you can substitute an 8-inch square or 9-inch round cake pan (greased and lined with parchment); press the crust only over the bottom of the pan (do not press up the sides), and bake as directed.

CRUST
- 1 cup (5 ounces) all-purpose flour
- ⅓ cup packed (2⅓ ounces) light brown sugar
- ¼ cup walnuts, toasted (see page 29) and chopped coarse
- 1 teaspoon salt
- ¼ teaspoon baking powder
- 6 tablespoons unsalted butter, cut into ½-inch pieces and chilled

FILLING
- ½ cup packed (3½ ounces) light brown sugar
- ⅓ cup light corn syrup
- 4 tablespoons unsalted butter, melted and cooled
- 1 tablespoon bourbon or dark rum
- 2 teaspoons vanilla extract
- ½ teaspoon salt
- 1 large egg
- 1¾ cups walnuts (7 ounces), chopped coarse

WHIPPED CREAM
- 1 cup heavy cream, chilled
- ¼ cup bourbon or dark rum (optional)
- 1 tablespoon granulated sugar
- ¼ teaspoon vanilla extract
- Pinch salt

1. FOR THE CRUST: Grease 9-inch tart pan with removable bottom. Process flour, sugar, walnuts, salt, and baking powder in food processor until combined, about 5 pulses. Sprinkle butter over top and pulse until mixture is pale yellow and resembles coarse cornmeal, about 8 pulses.

2. Sprinkle mixture into prepared pan. Press crumbs firmly into an even layer over pan bottom and up sides using bottom of dry measuring cup. Set tart pan on large plate, cover with plastic wrap, and freeze for at least 30 minutes and up to 1 week.

3. Adjust oven rack to middle position and heat oven to 350 degrees. Set tart pan on baking sheet. Press double layer aluminum foil into frozen tart shell and over edges of pan and fill with pie weights. Bake until tart shell is golden brown and set, about 30 minutes, rotating sheet halfway through baking. Let tart shell cool slightly while making filling.

4. FOR THE FILLING: Whisk sugar, corn syrup, butter, bourbon, vanilla, and salt in large bowl until sugar dissolves. Whisk in egg until combined. Pour filling evenly into tart shell and sprinkle with walnuts. Bake until filling is set and walnuts begin to brown, 30 to 40 minutes, rotating baking sheet halfway through baking. Let tart cool completely, about 2 hours. (Tart can be refrigerated for up 2 days; bring to room temperature before serving.)

5. FOR THE WHIPPED CREAM: Using stand mixer fitted with whisk, whip cream, bourbon, if using, sugar, vanilla, and salt on medium-low speed until foamy, about 1 minute. Increase speed to high and whip until soft peaks form, 1 to 3 minutes. (Whipped cream can be refrigerated for up to 8 hours; rewhisk briefly before serving.)

6. To serve, remove outer ring from tart pan, slide thin metal spatula between tart and tart pan bottom, and carefully slide tart onto serving platter or cutting board. Slice tart into pieces and serve with whipped cream.

Classic Beef Tenderloin Dinner

THE GAME PLAN

ONE DAY AHEAD...

MAKE ONION JAM: 1 hour

MAKE POTATO GRATIN: 40 minutes
(plus 2½ hours for baking and cooling)

MAKE TART DOUGH: 15 minutes
(plus 1 hour for chilling)

MAKE PERSILLADE RELISH: 15 minutes

ON THE DAY OF...

MAKE LEMON TART: 40 minutes
(plus 3 hours for baking and cooling)

MAKE BEEF TENDERLOIN: 1¼ hours
(plus 30 minutes for resting)

FINISH POTATO GRATIN: 1½ hours

MAKE SALAD: 20 minutes

CLASSIC BEEF TENDERLOIN DINNER

⊱ *Serves 8* ⊰

Goat Cheese with Caramelized Onion Jam

Roast Beef Tenderloin with Persillade Relish ⟿ Arugula and Tomato Salad

Potato and Fennel Gratin ⟿ Lemon Tart

Roast Beef Tenderloin with Persillade Relish

A peeled beef tenderloin will be slightly more expensive, but will require very little trimming. Note that an unpeeled tenderloin will weigh 6 pounds or more. For the relish, consider using a food processor to mince the parsley.

RELISH

- ¾ cup minced fresh parsley
- ½ cup extra-virgin olive oil
- 6 tablespoons minced cornichons plus 1 teaspoon cornichon juice
- ¼ cup capers, rinsed and chopped coarse
- 2 scallions, minced
- 1 teaspoon sugar
  Salt and pepper

TENDERLOIN

- 1 (4½- to 5-pound) whole peeled beef tenderloin, trimmed, tail end tucked under, and tied at 1½-inch intervals
- 2 tablespoons olive oil
  Salt and pepper

1. FOR THE RELISH: Combine all ingredients in bowl and season with salt and pepper to taste. Let sit at room temperature until needed. (Relish can be refrigerated for up to 1 day; bring to room temperature before serving. Makes 1¼ cups.)

2. FOR THE TENDERLOIN: Adjust oven rack to upper-middle position and heat oven to 425 degrees. Line rimmed baking sheet with aluminum foil and top with wire rack. Pat tenderloin dry with paper towels, coat with oil, and season with salt and pepper. Lay tenderloin on prepared rack. (Prepped tenderloin can be held at room temperature for up to 1 hour before roasting.)

3. Roast until tenderloin registers 120 to 125 degrees (for medium-rare), 45 to 60 minutes. Tent tenderloin loosely with foil and let rest for 30 minutes. Transfer roast to carving board and remove twine. Slice meat into 1-inch-thick pieces and serve with relish.

✔ WHY THIS RECIPE WORKS

For parties, few cuts top beef tenderloin. This elegant roast cooks quickly, serves a crowd, and its rich, buttery slices are fork-tender. It does have one liability, though—because it is lean and has a long, narrow shape, it can be easily overcooked. After much testing, we found that a hot oven (425 degrees) delivered the rich, roasted flavor this cut really needs, producing perfectly rosy meat with an appealing crust. Tying the roast and tucking the tail end under ensured even cooking. This roast needs company, and our simple but pungent parsley relish with capers and cornichons is just the ticket.

TYING A BEEF TENDERLOIN

To ensure that the tenderloin roasts more evenly, fold 6 inches of the thin tip end under the roast. Using 12-inch lengths of kitchen twine, tie the roast securely every 1½ inches.

Goat Cheese with Caramelized Onion Jam

✔ **WHY THIS RECIPE WORKS**
The key to a great onion jam is making perfectly caramelized onions. Starting out over high heat helped the onions to release their moisture and natural sugars, which jump-starts the caramelizing process. Once the onions had released their moisture, we then turned down the heat and let the sugars brown and the onions soften. We love the depth of flavor ruby port adds to this jam.

Use an inexpensive ruby port here. This jam also tastes terrific with many other types of cheese, including two test kitchen favorites, farmhouse cheddar and Robiola (a creamy Italian soft-ripened cheese). Serve with Garlic Toasts (page 62) or crackers.

1   tablespoon unsalted butter
1   tablespoon vegetable oil
2   pounds onions, halved and sliced ¼ inch thick
1   teaspoon light brown sugar
      Salt and pepper
1   teaspoon minced fresh thyme
½   cup ruby port
1   (10-ounce) log goat cheese

1. Melt butter and oil in 12-inch non-stick skillet over high heat. Add onions, sugar, and ½ teaspoon salt and cook until onions begin to soften and release some moisture, about 5 minutes. Reduce heat to medium and cook, stirring often, until onions are deeply browned and slightly sticky, about 40 minutes. (Reduce heat if onions begin to sizzle or scorch. Increase heat if onions are not browning after 15 to 20 minutes.)

2. Stir in thyme and cook until fragrant, about 30 seconds. Stir in port and cook until it reduces to glaze, 4 to 6 minutes. Season with salt and pepper to taste. (Jam can be refrigerated for up to 7 days; bring to room temperature and stir in water as needed to adjust consistency. Makes 1 cup.) Transfer jam to serving bowl with spoon or spreader, and serve alongside cheese.

Arugula and Tomato Salad with Balsamic Vinaigrette

✔ **WHY THIS RECIPE WORKS**
When you're serving an expensive cut of meat like beef tenderloin, you don't want it upstaged by a fussy salad but you want something colorful and bright-tasting. This salad, with its zesty balsamic vinaigrette, pungent arugula, and halved cherry tomatoes, comes together quickly and looks and tastes great.

We like the slightly bitter flavor of arugula with this menu; however, baby spinach or baby mesclun greens can be substituted.

3   tablespoons balsamic vinegar
1   shallot, minced
1   teaspoon minced fresh thyme
1   small garlic clove, minced
½   teaspoon salt
¼   teaspoon pepper
¾   cup extra-virgin olive oil
12   ounces baby arugula (12 cups)
1½   pounds cherry or grape tomatoes, halved

Whisk vinegar, shallot, thyme, garlic, salt, and pepper in small bowl. Whisking constantly, drizzle in olive oil. In large bowl, gently toss arugula with tomatoes. Just before serving, whisk dressing to re-emulsify, then drizzle over salad and toss gently to coat.

Potato and Fennel Gratin

Slicing the potatoes ⅛ inch thick is crucial for the success of this dish; use a mandoline, a V-slicer, or a food processor fitted with a ⅛-inch-thick slicing blade. Prep and assemble all of the gratin ingredients before slicing the potatoes or they will turn brown. Do not store the sliced potatoes in water to prevent browning or the gratin will be watery. This gratin needs to be cooked in advance, then reheated quickly before serving while the tenderloin rests.

2½   pounds russet potatoes, peeled and sliced ⅛ inch thick
1   large fennel bulb, stalks discarded, bulb halved, cored, and sliced thin (see page 22)
2   tablespoons unsalted butter
2   shallots, minced
1½   teaspoons salt
3   garlic cloves, minced
2   teaspoons minced fresh thyme
¼   teaspoon fennel seeds, crushed
¼   teaspoon pepper
⅛   teaspoon ground nutmeg
⅛   teaspoon cayenne pepper
1   tablespoon all-purpose flour
1½   cups heavy cream
3   ounces Gruyère or Parmesan cheese, grated (1½ cups)

1. Adjust oven rack to middle position and heat oven to 350 degrees. Thoroughly grease shallow 2- or 3-quart casserole dish. Place potatoes and fennel in very large bowl.

2. Melt butter in small saucepan over medium heat. Add shallots and salt and cook until softened, about 2 minutes. Stir in garlic, thyme, fennel seeds, pepper, nutmeg, and cayenne and cook until fragrant, about 30 seconds. Stir in flour and cook for 1 minute. Whisk in cream, bring to simmer, and cook until thickened, about 2 minutes.

3. Pour sauce over potatoes and fennel and toss to coat. Transfer mixture to prepared dish and gently pack into even layer, removing any air pockets. Cover dish with aluminum foil and bake until potatoes are tender and fork inserted in center meets little resistance, about 1¾ hours, rotating dish halfway through baking.

4. Transfer gratin to wire rack, remove foil, and let cool until just warm, about 45 minutes. (Gratin can be wrapped tightly and refrigerated for up to 2 days; let sit at room temperature for 1 hour before continuing.)

5. As soon as tenderloin is removed from oven, adjust oven rack to middle position and heat to 450 degrees. Sprinkle Gruyère evenly over top of casserole. Bake, uncovered, until cheese is golden brown and sauce is bubbling around edges, 15 to 20 minutes. Cool for 10 minutes before serving.

Lemon Tart

✔ WHY THIS RECIPE WORKS
There is nothing like the near-transcendent simplicity of a lemon tart to top off a great but undeniably heavy meal of roast beef and cheesy potato gratin. But despite its apparent simplicity, there is much that can go wrong with a lemon tart. It can slip over the edge of sweet into cloying; its tartness can grab at your throat; it can be gluey or eggy or, even worse, metallic-tasting. After testing many ratios of sugar, lemon juice, and egg in the filling, we finally landed the right combination for creamy, perfectly balanced, sweet yet tart lemon curd. Cooking the curd to just 170 degrees before cooling it down again with cold cream is crucial for a smooth, silky texture.

When buying lemons, look for ones that feel heavy for their size and give a little when squeezed; very hard lemons will yield little juice. The tart shell needs to be warm when adding the filling; for more information on making a tart shell, see page 262. If desired, dust with confectioners' sugar before serving.

CRUST
1	large egg yolk
1	tablespoon heavy cream
½	teaspoon vanilla extract
1¼	cups (6¼ ounces) all-purpose flour
⅔	cup (2⅔ ounces) confectioners' sugar
¼	teaspoon salt
8	tablespoons unsalted butter, cut into ¼-inch pieces and chilled

FILLING
2	large eggs plus 7 large yolks
1	cup (7 ounces) granulated sugar
¼	cup grated lemon zest plus ⅔ cup juice (4 lemons)
	Pinch salt
4	tablespoons unsalted butter, cut into 4 pieces
3	tablespoons heavy cream, chilled

1. FOR THE CRUST: Whisk egg yolk, cream, and vanilla in bowl. Process flour, sugar, and salt in food processor until combined, about 5 seconds. Scatter butter over top and pulse until mixture resembles coarse cornmeal, about 15 pulses. With processor running, add egg mixture and continue to process until dough just comes together around processor blade, about 12 seconds.

2. Turn dough onto sheet of plastic wrap and flatten into 6-inch disk. Wrap dough tightly in plastic and refrigerate for at least 1 hour and up to 2 days.

3. Let chilled dough soften slightly at room temperature, about 10 minutes. Roll dough out to 11-inch circle on lightly floured counter. Roll dough loosely around rolling pin, then unroll over 9-inch tart pan

with removable bottom. Fit dough into tart pan, pressing it firmly into pan corners and fluted edge. Trim excess dough hanging over edge of pan and use trimmings to patch weak spots. Set tart pan on large plate, cover with plastic, and freeze for at least 30 minutes and up to 1 week.

4. Adjust oven rack to middle position and heat oven to 375 degrees. Set tart pan on baking sheet. Press double layer of aluminum foil into tart shell and over edges of pan, then fill with pie weights. Bake until tart shell is golden brown and set, about 30 minutes, rotating baking sheet halfway through baking. Carefully remove weights and foil and continue to bake until crust is fully baked and golden, 5 to 10 minutes. Let tart shell cool slightly on baking sheet while making filling.

5. FOR THE FILLING: Whisk eggs and egg yolks in medium saucepan. Whisk in sugar until combined, then whisk in lemon zest, lemon juice, and salt. Add butter and cook over medium-low heat, stirring constantly, until mixture thickens slightly and registers 170 degrees, about 5 minutes. Immediately strain mixture through fine-mesh strainer into medium bowl. Stir in cream.

6. Pour filling into warm tart shell. Bake until filling is shiny, opaque, and center jiggles slightly when shaken, 10 to 15 minutes.

7. Let tart cool completely on baking sheet, about 1½ hours. (Cooled tart can be held at room temperature for 8 hours.) To serve, remove outer metal ring of tart pan, slide thin metal spatula between tart and tart pan bottom, and carefully slide tart onto serving platter.

Dressing Up Chicken

THE GAME PLAN
➤

ONE DAY AHEAD...

COOK RICE FOR PILAF: 1¼ hours

STUFF CHICKEN BREASTS: 25 minutes

MAKE PORCINI BUTTER: 10 minutes

ON THE DAY OF...

MAKE BERRY FOOLS: 1 hour (plus 2 hours for chilling)

MAKE HERBED CRÈME FRAÎCHE FOR APPETIZER: 15 minutes (plus 30 minutes for chilling)

ASSEMBLE APPETIZER: 5 minutes

BAKE CHICKEN: 35 minutes (plus 10 minutes for resting)

FINISH GREEN BEANS: 25 minutes

FINISH RICE PILAF: 20 minutes

DRESSING UP CHICKEN

↣ Serves 8 ↢

Smoked Salmon with Herbed Crème Fraîche and Potato Chips

Lemony Goat Cheese–Stuffed Chicken Breasts

Easy Green Beans with Porcini Butter

Wild Rice Pilaf with Almonds and Dried Apricots ↣ Berry Fools

Lemony Goat Cheese–Stuffed Chicken Breasts

It is important to buy similarly sized chicken breasts that have the skin still attached and intact; otherwise, the stuffing will leak out. Serve with lemon wedges.

6	ounces goat cheese, softened
4	ounces cream cheese, softened
4	teaspoons minced fresh thyme
1	garlic clove, minced
½	teaspoon grated lemon zest
	Salt and pepper
8	(12-ounce) bone-in split chicken breasts, trimmed
1	tablespoon olive oil

1. Adjust oven racks to lowest and middle positions and heat oven to 450 degrees. Mix goat cheese, cream cheese, thyme, garlic, lemon zest, ¼ teaspoon salt, and ¼ teaspoon pepper in bowl. (Mixture can be refrigerated for up to 2 days.)

2. Pat chicken dry with paper towels and season with salt and pepper. Use fingers to gently loosen center portion of skin covering each breast. Place about 1½ tablespoons filling under skin in center of each breast. (Stuffed chicken can be refrigerated for up to 1 day.)

3. Line 2 rimmed baking sheets with aluminum foil and top with wire racks. Place chicken breasts, skin side up, on racks. Brush tops with oil. Bake until chicken registers 160 degrees, 30 to 35 minutes, switching and rotating baking sheets halfway through baking. Let rest for 5 to 10 minutes before serving.

✔ **WHY THIS RECIPE WORKS** Stuffed chicken breasts can be a truly impressive, albeit labor-intensive, entrée for company—one that usually involves butterflying, pounding, stuffing, and rolling boneless chicken breasts. Yearning for an easier, more foolproof, but no less impressive option, we turned to bone-in split breasts. Using the skin to help keep the filling in place during cooking, we "stuffed" the chicken with a flavorful goat cheese and herb mixture.

FILLING STUFFED CHICKEN BREASTS

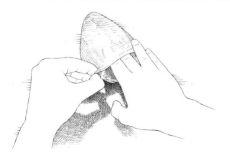 

Using your fingers, gently loosen the center portion of the skin covering each breast, making a pocket for the filling. Using your fingers or a small spoon, place about 1½ tablespoons of filling under the loosened skin, directly on the meat in the center of each breast half. Gently press on the skin to distribute the filling over the meat.

Smoked Salmon with Herbed Crème Fraîche and Potato Chips

✓ **WHY THIS RECIPE WORKS**
Good smoked salmon needs little embellishment to elevate it to appetizer status. Here we stuck with the classic flavor combination of salmon, crème fraîche, dill, and chives and kept things extremely easy and contemporary.

We prefer using kettle-cooked potato chips (we like Lay's Kettle Cooked Original) because they are sturdier than average and will support the weight of the toppings. Feel free to arrange the salmon strips in a pile on the platter or fold them in half and arrange them in rows.

- 4 ounces cream cheese
- 1 cup crème fraîche
- 3 tablespoons minced fresh dill
- 2 tablespoons minced fresh chives
- 2 teaspoons grated lemon zest plus 1 tablespoon juice
  Salt and pepper
- 12 ounces thinly sliced smoked salmon, cut into 1½-inch pieces
- 1 bag kettle-cooked potato chips

Microwave cream cheese in bowl until very soft, 20 to 25 seconds. Whisk in crème fraîche, dill, chives, lemon zest, and lemon juice. Season with salt and pepper to taste. Cover and refrigerate until flavors meld, at least 30 minutes and up to 2 days. Transfer dip to serving bowl with spoon or spreader and serve alongside salmon and potato chips.

Easy Green Beans with Porcini Butter

✓ **WHY THIS RECIPE WORKS**
Green beans make a great last-minute side dish but need a little dressing up for special occasions. Here, a simple porcini butter gives them some pizzazz and can be made ahead and just tossed into the pot with the cooked and drained green beans.

Don't skimp on the amount of water when boiling the beans or they will not cook evenly.

- ½ ounce dried porcini mushrooms, rinsed
- 4 tablespoons unsalted butter, softened
- 1 shallot, minced
- 1 teaspoon minced fresh thyme
  Salt and pepper
- 2 pounds green beans, trimmed

1. Microwave ½ cup water and porcini in covered bowl until steaming, about 1 minute. Let stand until softened, about 5 minutes. Drain porcini through fine-mesh strainer, discard liquid, and mince mushrooms. Mash porcini, butter, shallot, thyme, ½ teaspoon salt, and ¼ teaspoon pepper together in bowl. (Butter can be refrigerated for up to 1 week.)

2. Bring 6 quarts water to boil in large pot over high heat. Stir in green beans and 1 tablespoon salt and cook until crisp-tender, 4 to 8 minutes. Drain beans and return to pot. Add porcini butter, cover, and let sit off heat until butter has melted, about 2 minutes. Toss beans gently to coat and serve.

Wild Rice Pilaf with Almonds and Dried Apricots

Wild rice goes from tough to pasty in a flash, so begin testing the rice at the 35-minute mark and drain it as soon as it is tender.

- 2 cups low-sodium chicken broth
- 2 bay leaves
- 1 cup wild rice, rinsed
- 3 tablespoons extra-virgin olive oil
- 1 onion, chopped fine
  Salt and pepper
- 1½ cups long-grain white rice, rinsed
- 2¼ cups plus 1 tablespoon water
- ¾ cup dried apricots, chopped fine
- ¾ cup sliced almonds, toasted (see page 29)
- ¼ cup minced fresh cilantro
- 2 scallions, sliced thin
- 1 teaspoon lime juice

1. Bring broth and bay leaves to boil in medium saucepan over high heat. Stir in wild rice and bring to simmer. Reduce heat to low, cover, and continue to simmer until rice is tender, 35 to 40 minutes. Drain rice, discarding bay leaves. Return rice to saucepan and cover to keep warm.

2. Meanwhile, heat 2 tablespoons oil in large saucepan over medium heat until shimmering. Add onion and ½ teaspoon salt and cook until softened, 5 to 7 minutes. Stir in white rice and cook until edges of grains begin to turn translucent, about 3 minutes.

3. Stir in 2¼ cups water and bring to simmer. Reduce heat to low, cover, and continue to simmer until rice is tender and water is absorbed, 16 to 18 minutes. Off heat, lay a clean folded dish towel underneath lid and let rice sit for 10 minutes. Fluff rice with fork.

4. Combine cooked wild rice and white rice in large bowl. (Rice mixture can be refrigerated for up to 1 day. Reheat in microwave, covered, until hot, 2 to 4 minutes.)

5. Microwave apricots and remaining 1 tablespoon water in covered bowl until hot, about 30 seconds. Fold apricots, almonds, cilantro, scallions, lime juice, and remaining 1 tablespoon oil into rice. Season with salt and pepper to taste and serve.

CHOPPING DRIED FRUIT

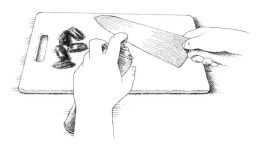

Dried fruit, especially apricots (or dates), very often sticks to the knife when you try to chop it. To avoid this problem, coat the blade with a thin film of vegetable cooking spray just before you begin chopping any dried fruit. The chopped fruit won't cling to the blade, and the knife will stay relatively clean.

♥ WHY THIS RECIPE WORKS
Wild rice is a welcome change of pace from a standard white rice side dish, especially when serving company. However, wild rice can be an overpowering and temperamental ingredient. The most foolproof method we found for cooking wild rice is to simmer it gently in a flavorful liquid, and taste it often; it can go from tough to overcooked in mere minutes. To help temper its strong, grassy flavor, we tossed it with cooked long-grain white rice and lots of aromatics. The best part about wild rice pilaf is that it can easily be made ahead of time and reheats like a dream in the microwave before serving.

Berry Fools

Blueberries or blackberries can be substituted for the raspberries; don't substitute frozen fruit here. We like the granular texture and nutty flavor of Carr's Whole Wheat Crackers, but graham crackers or gingersnaps will also work.

2½	pounds strawberries, hulled (5 cups)
15	ounces raspberries (3 cups)
1	cup (7 ounces) sugar
1	tablespoon unflavored gelatin
1¼	cups heavy cream, chilled
⅓	cup sour cream
¾	teaspoon vanilla extract
4	Carr's Whole Wheat Crackers, crushed fine (¼ cup)
8	sprigs fresh mint (optional)

1. Process half of strawberries, half of raspberries, and ¾ cup sugar in food processor until mixture is completely smooth, about 1 minute. Strain puree through fine-mesh strainer into 4-cup liquid measuring cup (you should have 3 cups puree; discard extra).

2. Transfer ¾ cup puree to small bowl, sprinkle gelatin evenly over top, then stir to incorporate; let stand for 5 minutes. Heat remaining 2¼ cups puree in small saucepan over medium heat until it begins to bubble, 4 to 6 minutes. Off heat, stir in gelatin mixture until dissolved. Transfer mixture to bowl, cover, and refrigerate until cold, at least 2 hours and up to 24 hours.

3. Meanwhile, chop remaining strawberries into ¼-inch pieces. Toss strawberries, remaining raspberries, and 2 tablespoons sugar in bowl and let sit for 1 hour.

4. Using stand mixer fitted with whisk, whip cream, sour cream, vanilla, and remaining 2 tablespoons sugar on medium-low speed until foamy, about 1 minute. Increase speed to high and whip until stiff peaks form, 1 to 3 minutes. Transfer ⅓ cup whipped-cream mixture to bowl; set aside. Leave remaining whipped-cream mixture in stand mixer.

5. Using hand whisk, whisk chilled berry puree briskly to remove any lumps. With stand mixer running on medium speed, slowly add two-thirds of puree to remaining whipped-cream mixture and mix until incorporated, about 15 seconds. Using spatula, gently fold in remaining berry puree, leaving streaks.

6. Drain chopped berries through fine-mesh strainer. Divide two-thirds of chopped berries evenly among 8 tall parfait or sundae glasses. Divide cream–berry puree mixture evenly among glasses, followed by remaining chopped berries. Top each glass with reserved whipped cream. (Parfaits can be refrigerated for up to 1 hour.) Just before serving, sprinkle with crushed crackers and garnish with mint sprigs, if using.

A Taste of Spain

THE GAME PLAN

ONE DAY AHEAD...

MAKE MARINATED FETA AND OLIVES: 20 minutes
(plus 1½ hours for marinating)

MAKE FLANS: 45 minutes
(plus 4¼ hours for baking and cooling)

ON THE DAY OF...

MAKE SHELLFISH STEW: 2 hours

MAKE GARLIC TOASTS: 10 minutes

MAKE SALAD: 20 minutes

A TASTE OF SPAIN

⤜ Serves 8 ⤛

Marinated Feta and Green Olives

Spanish Shellfish Stew ⤜ Spinach Salad with Sherry Vinaigrette

Individual Flans

Spanish Shellfish Stew

You will need at least a 6-quart Dutch oven for this recipe. We like Sauvignon Blanc or any non-oaky Chardonnay in this recipe. Avoid large clams, which will not only take up more room in the pot, but will exude more liquid than desired, diluting the broth. The cooking time of the scallops will depend on their size; we used extra-large scallops (about 2 inches in diameter and 1 inch thick), but if your scallops are smaller, they will cook more quickly and should be added to the pot with the shrimp.

PICADA

- ⅓ cup slivered almonds
- 3 slices hearty white sandwich bread, torn into quarters
- 3 tablespoons extra-virgin olive oil
- ⅛ teaspoon salt
  Pinch pepper

STEW

- 6 tablespoons olive oil
- 1½ pounds extra-large shrimp (21 to 25 per pound), peeled and deveined (see page 304), shells reserved
- 3 cups dry white wine, plus extra as needed
- 2 onions, chopped fine
- 2 red bell peppers, stemmed, seeded, and chopped fine
  Salt and pepper
- 6 garlic cloves, minced
- 2 teaspoons paprika
- ½ teaspoon saffron threads, crumbled
- ¼ teaspoon red pepper flakes
- 3 bay leaves
- 2 tablespoons brandy

- 2 (28-ounce) cans whole tomatoes, drained with juice reserved, chopped coarse
- 3 pounds littleneck clams, scrubbed
- 1 pound mussels, scrubbed and debearded (see page 246)
- 1½ pounds extra-large sea scallops, tendons removed
- 2 tablespoons minced fresh parsley
- 2 teaspoons lemon juice, plus extra as needed
- 1 recipe Garlic Toasts (page 62)

1. FOR THE PICADA: Adjust oven rack to middle position and heat oven to 375 degrees. Pulse almonds in food processor to fine crumbs, about 20 pulses. Add bread, olive oil, salt, and pepper and pulse to coarse crumbs, about 10 pulses. Spread mixture evenly over rimmed baking sheet and toast, stirring often, until golden brown, about 15 minutes; let cool.

2. FOR THE STEW: Heat 2 tablespoons oil in medium saucepan over medium heat until shimmering. Add *continued* ➤

> **WHY THIS RECIPE WORKS**
> Known as *zarzuela* in Spain, this beautiful stew is chock-full of shrimp, scallops, clams, and mussels in a fragrant tomato-based broth seasoned with saffron and paprika. The stew is thickened with a *picada*, a flavorful mixture of ground almonds, bread crumbs, and olive oil. In order to give the broth some real flavor without having to make a time-consuming fish stock, we used the shrimp shells. Sautéing the shells before steeping them in wine brought out and deepened their flavor.

salt and cook, stirring often, until onion is softened and lightly browned, 12 to 15 minutes. Stir in garlic, paprika, saffron, pepper flakes, and bay leaves and cook until fragrant, about 30 seconds. Stir in brandy and simmer for 30 seconds. Stir in tomatoes and reserved juice and cook until slightly thickened, 5 to 7 minutes.

4. Strain wine mixture into Dutch oven through fine-mesh strainer, pressing on shrimp shells to extract as much liquid as possible; discard shells. Continue to simmer sauce until flavors meld, 3 to 5 minutes. (Sauce can be refrigerated for up to 1 day; return to simmer and add wine as needed to adjust consistency.)

5. Increase heat to medium high. Add clams, cover, and cook, stirring occasionally, until first few clams begin to open, about 5 minutes. Add mussels and scallops, cover, and continue to cook until most clams have opened, about 3 minutes longer. Add shrimp, cover, and continue to cook until shrimp are opaque throughout and clams and mussels have opened, about 2 minutes longer.

6. Remove and discard bay leaves and any mussels or clams that have not opened. Using slotted spoon, portion seafood into warmed individual serving bowls. Stir picada, parsley, and lemon juice into broth and season with salt, pepper, and lemon juice to taste. Ladle broth over seafood and serve immediately with Garlic Toasts.

reserved shrimp shells and cook until pink, about 5 minutes. Off heat, stir in wine, cover, and let steep until ready to use.

3. Heat remaining ¼ cup oil in Dutch oven over medium heat until shimmering. Add onions, bell peppers, and ½ teaspoon

Garlic Toasts

✓ **WHY THIS RECIPE WORKS** The trick to making good garlic toasts (or crostini) is to rub raw garlic over one side of the bread after it has been toasted and is still slightly warm. The rough texture of the toasted bread acts like sandpaper on the garlic to release its flavor, while the warmth helps to bloom its fragrance.

We like to use a baguette for these because its narrow shape makes perfectly sized toasts. Baguettes are sold in a variety of lengths; obviously, longer or shorter baguettes will produce more or fewer toasts.

1 (12-inch) baguette, ends trimmed, sliced ½ inch thick on bias
2 garlic cloves, peeled
  Extra-virgin olive oil
  Salt and pepper

Adjust oven rack 6 inches from broiler element and heat broiler. Spread bread out over rimmed baking sheet and broil until golden brown on both sides, about 2 minutes per side. While warm, rub one side of each toast briefly with garlic. Drizzle toasts lightly with oil and season with salt and pepper to taste. (Makes 20 toasts.)

Marinated Feta and Green Olives

Be sure to buy a block of feta, not crumbled feta, for this recipe. Our preferred brand of feta cheese is Mt. Vikos Traditional. Serve with extra Garlic Toasts (page 62), pita chips, or warm pita bread.

1¼ cups extra-virgin olive oil
1 tablespoon minced fresh oregano
2 garlic cloves, sliced thin
1½ teaspoons grated orange zest
1 teaspoon cumin seeds, toasted (see page 29)
¼ teaspoon red pepper flakes
12 ounces feta cheese, cut into ½-inch cubes (2 cups)
1½ cups pitted green olives, chopped coarse

Heat 1 cup oil, oregano, garlic, zest, cumin, and pepper flakes in small saucepan over low heat until garlic is softened, about 10 minutes. Off heat, gently stir in feta and olives. Cover and let sit until mixture reaches room temperature, about 1½ hours. Stir in remaining ¼ cup oil and serve. (Marinated olives and feta can be refrigerated for up to 1 week; bring to room temperature before serving.)

✔ WHY THIS RECIPE WORKS
Here we combine marinated feta and olives—perfect for the start of this Spanish menu. In order to bloom the flavors of the marinade and have them readily absorbed by the feta and olives, we found it important to heat the marinade gently on the stovetop. Adding more olive oil to the mixture after it has cooled freshens the flavors of the marinade—perfect for dipping with bread.

Spinach Salad with Sherry Vinaigrette

We prefer the flavor of sherry vinegar in this salad; however, red wine vinegar can be substituted.

5 teaspoons sherry vinegar
1 shallot, minced
1 teaspoon Dijon mustard
¼ teaspoon salt
¼ teaspoon pepper
¼ cup extra-virgin olive oil
12 ounces baby spinach (12 cups)
1 red bell pepper, stemmed, seeded, and cut into 1-inch-long matchsticks
⅓ cup sliced almonds, toasted (see page 29)
2 ounces Manchego or Parmesan cheese, shaved (see page 32)

Whisk vinegar, shallot, mustard, salt, and pepper in small bowl. Whisking constantly, drizzle in olive oil. In large bowl, gently toss spinach with bell pepper and almonds. Just before serving, whisk dressing to re-emulsify, then drizzle over salad and toss gently to coat. Garnish individual portions with Manchego.

✔ WHY THIS RECIPE WORKS
Manchego cheese, almonds, and sherry are some of the hallmarks of Spanish cuisine, and they inspired this bright spinach salad with red bell pepper matchsticks and a sherry vinaigrette.

Individual Flans

We prefer to use 2 percent low-fat fat milk in this recipe, although any type of milk (even skim) can be used, resulting in varying degrees of richness. Be very careful when working with the hot caramel in step 1. Cleaning ramekins with caramel stuck in the bottom can be a chore; to help dissolve the caramel, fill the ramekins with boiling water and let sit.

¾	cup (5¼ ounces) sugar
3	tablespoons water
3	large eggs plus 5 large yolks
¼	teaspoon grated lemon zest
2¼	cups 2 percent low-fat milk
2	cups sweetened condensed milk

1. Adjust oven rack to middle position and heat oven to 350 degrees. Place dish towel in bottom of large roasting pan and place eight 6-ounce ramekins on towel. Bring sugar and water to boil in small saucepan, swirling pan gently, until sugar dissolves, about 3 minutes. Reduce to simmer and cook, gently swirling pan occasionally, until caramel has deep mahogany color, 7 to 10 minutes. Carefully pour caramel into ramekins and let cool slightly until hardened.

2. Bring full kettle of water to boil. Meanwhile, whisk whole eggs and egg yolks in medium bowl, about 1 minute. Whisk in zest, milk, and sweetened condensed milk until well combined. Transfer mixture to 8-cup liquid measuring cup, then pour mixture evenly into ramekins on top of hardened caramel.

3. Gently place roasting pan in oven. Being careful not to splash water inside ramekins, pour boiling water into roasting pan until it reaches halfway up side of ramekins. Bake until center of custards are set and register 180 to 185 degrees, 30 to 45 minutes.

4. Carefully remove roasting pan from oven. Carefully transfer ramekins to wire rack and let cool to room temperature, about 1½ hours. When cool, wrap ramekins with plastic wrap and refrigerate until well chilled, at least 2 hours and up to 24 hours.

5. To serve, run knife around edge of ramekins to loosen custard. Place inverted serving plate over top of each ramekin and, holding ramekin and plate together firmly, gently flip custard onto plate. Drizzle any extra caramel sauce left in ramekin over top (some caramel will remain stuck in ramekin).

EVEN EASIER ⤙ Don't have time to make flan? Consider serving vanilla ice cream topped with warm caramel sauce and a few flakes of sea salt (or fleur de sel).

MAKING CARAMEL FOR FLAN

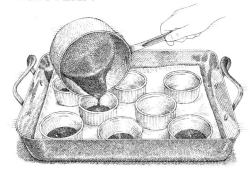

Caramel is extremely hot and can cause serious burns, so care should be taken during this step. Before making the caramel, ready the water bath by placing a dish towel in the bottom of a large roasting pan. Place eight 6-ounce ramekins in the roasting pan, about 1 inch apart. Once the caramel is ready, slowly pour the caramel into the ramekins, being careful not to splash.

✔ **WHY THIS RECIPE WORKS**
Flan is a deceptively simple classic Spanish dessert. Made with just a few ingredients that are readily available (sugar, eggs, and milk), it is similar in construction and flavor to other baked custards, but has a slightly lighter texture and is highlighted by a dark, rich caramel sauce. The biggest surprise we stumbled across during our testing was that low-fat milk actually tasted better than whole milk. It not only produced a lighter, cleaner-tasting custard, but pairing the low-fat milk with condensed milk helped to give the custard a rich but not overpowering creamy texture.

Casual
Pan-Latin Supper

THE GAME PLAN

⤙

ONE DAY AHEAD...

MAKE CAKE: 1 hour (plus 4¼ hours
for baking and cooling)

MAKE CHILI: 4½ hours

MAKE AREPAS: 25 minutes

ON THE DAY OF...

MAKE SALSA: 35 minutes

BAKE AND FILL AREPAS: 25 minutes

REHEAT CHILI: 30 minutes

Chicken and Avocado Arepas

Masarepa, a precooked corn flour that is also called *harina precocida* and *masa al instante*, is available in specialty Latin markets, or the Latin American aisle at supermarkets. While we had the best results with masarepa, we found that white cornmeal can be substituted. To save time, consider using a rotisserie chicken for the filling; one chicken will yield more than enough meat for the filling.

CORN CAKES

2	cups (10 ounces) masarepa blanca
1	teaspoon salt
1	teaspoon baking powder
2½	cups warm water
¼	cup vegetable oil

FILLING

1½	cups cooked chicken, shredded into bite-size pieces
2	avocados, pitted and cut into ½-inch pieces (see page 121)
2	tablespoons minced fresh cilantro
3	scallions, sliced thin
2	tablespoons lime juice
½	teaspoon chili powder
	Salt and pepper

1. FOR THE CORN CAKES: Whisk masarepa, salt, and baking powder in medium bowl. Gradually stir in water to form dough. Shape dough into eight 3-inch patties (arepas), about ½ inch thick.

2. Heat 2 tablespoons oil in 12-inch nonstick skillet over medium-high heat until shimmering. Lay 4 arepas in skillet and cook until golden on both sides, about 2 minutes per side; transfer to parchment paper–lined baking sheet. Repeat with remaining 2 tablespoons oil and remaining 4 arepas; transfer to baking sheet. (Arepas can be refrigerated for up to 3 days and frozen up to 1 month. If frozen, increase baking time to 20 minutes in step 4.)

3. FOR THE FILLING: Mix all ingredients together and season with salt *continued* ➤

WHY THIS RECIPE WORKS

Arepas are a type of corn cake (popular in Venezuela and Colombia) with a subtle corn flavor and a firm polenta-like texture. In Venezuela, the arepas are split open and stuffed with a filling—anything from meat and cheese to eggs, corn, beans, and even fish—much like a sandwich. We found this filling with shredded chicken and avocados especially appealing. To make the arepas, we like to use a combination of masarepa, water, salt, and a little baking powder (which is untraditional) for lightness. Arepas are traditionally cooked on a griddle or deep-fried, but we found it easiest to brown them in a skillet, then finish baking them through in the oven.

COOKING CHICKEN FOR FILLING

Pat 12 ounces boneless, skinless chicken breasts dry with paper towels and season with salt and pepper. Heat 1 tablespoon vegetable oil in 12-inch nonstick skillet over medium-high heat until just smoking. Add chicken and cook until browned on 1 side, about 3 minutes. Flip chicken over, add ½ cup water, and cover. Reduce heat to medium and continue to cook until thickest part of chicken registers 160 to 165 degrees, 5 to 7 minutes longer. Transfer chicken to carving board, cool slightly, then shred into bite-size pieces. (Makes 1½ cups. For 1 cup of shredded meat, use 8 ounces chicken.)

and pepper to taste. (Filling can be refrigerated for up to 6 hours.)

4. Adjust oven rack to middle position and heat oven to 400 degrees. Bake arepas until they sound hollow when tapped on bottom, about 10 minutes. Split hot arepas open using paring knife (like an English muffin) and stuff each with generous 2 tablespoons of filling. Serve warm.

Roasted Tomatillo Salsa

☑ **WHY THIS RECIPE WORKS**
Broiling the tomatillos chars their skin and softens their flesh for a deep, rich-tasting salsa. Traditionally, this charring is done on the stovetop in a dry pan reserved solely for this purpose, but we prefer to use the oven rather than sacrifice any of our good skillets. For more flavor, we broiled a jalapeño and onion alongside the tomatillos, then simply pulsed them all together in a food processor to make the salsa.

Canned tomatillos cannot be substituted in this recipe. Adding the minced jalapeño seeds will make the salsa spicier. Serve with tortilla chips.

2 pounds fresh tomatillos, husked and washed
1 small onion, chopped coarse
1 jalapeño chile, stemmed, halved, and seeds reserved
2 garlic cloves, peeled
2 teaspoons olive oil
1 cup fresh cilantro leaves
2 tablespoons lime juice
Salt

1. Adjust oven rack 6 inches from broiler element and heat broiler. Toss tomatillos, onion, jalapeño, and garlic with oil and spread out over aluminum foil–lined rimmed baking sheet. Broil, shaking pan occasionally, until vegetables are well charred, about 15 minutes.

2. Let broiled vegetables cool for 5 minutes, then transfer to food processor. Add cilantro, lime juice, and ½ teaspoon salt and process until coarsely chopped, about 10 pulses. Transfer to serving bowl and season with minced jalapeño seeds and salt to taste. Serve. (Salsa can be refrigerated for up to 2 days. Makes 3 cups.)

SEEDING JALAPEÑOS

Using a knife to remove the seeds and ribs from a jalapeño takes a very steady hand. Fortunately, there is a safer alternative. Cut the chile in half lengthwise with a knife. Starting opposite the stem end, run the edge of a small melon baller scoop down the inside of the chile, scraping up seeds and ribs. Cut off the core with the scoop.

Black Bean Chili

You will need at least a 6-quart Dutch oven for this recipe. This chili is fairly spicy; to make it milder, reduce the amount of chipotle. Be sure to stir the chili gently once the beans are cooked to keep from mashing them. Serve with lime wedges, sour cream, shredded cheddar or Monterey Jack cheese, chopped tomatoes, and/or minced onion.

I	pound white mushrooms, trimmed
4	teaspoons mustard seeds
I	tablespoon cumin seeds
8	slices bacon, chopped fine
2	onions, chopped fine
9	garlic cloves, minced
4	teaspoons minced canned chipotle chile in adobo sauce
¼	cup chili powder
5	cups water, plus extra as needed
4	cups low-sodium chicken broth
1½	pounds dried black beans (3¾ cups), picked over and rinsed
4	teaspoons light brown sugar
⅛	teaspoon baking soda
2	bay leaves
I	(28-ounce) can crushed tomatoes
I	(14.5-ounce) can diced tomatoes
3	red bell peppers, stemmed, seeded, and cut into ½-inch pieces
¾	cup chopped fresh cilantro
	Salt and pepper

1. Adjust oven rack to lower-middle position and heat oven to 325 degrees. Pulse mushrooms in food processor until coarsely chopped, about 10 pulses.

2. Toast mustard seeds and cumin seeds in Dutch oven over medium-low heat, stirring constantly, until fragrant, about 1 minute. Add bacon and cook until fully rendered and crisp, 10 to 15 minutes. Stir in onions and processed mushrooms, cover, and cook until vegetables release their liquid, about 5 minutes. Uncover and continue to cook until vegetables are dry and brown, about 10 minutes.

3. Stir in garlic and chipotle and cook until fragrant, about 30 seconds. Stir in chili powder and cook, stirring constantly, until fragrant, about 1 minute (do not let it burn). Stir in water, broth, beans, sugar, baking soda, and bay leaves and bring to simmer, skimming as needed. Cover, place pot in oven, and cook for 1½ hours.

4. Stir in crushed tomatoes, diced tomatoes, and bell peppers. Cover and continue to cook in oven until beans are fully tender, about 1½ hours longer. (If chili begins to stick to pot bottom or look too thick, stir in extra water as needed.)

5. Remove pot from oven and remove and discard bay leaves. (Chili can be refrigerated for up to 2 days; reheat over medium-low heat and stir in extra water as needed to adjust consistency.) Stir in cilantro, season with salt and pepper to taste, and serve.

✓ WHY THIS RECIPE WORKS

This is the ultimate black bean chili—chunky, colorful, and packed with deep flavor. A combination of crushed and diced tomatoes gives the chili its texture, and lots of aromatics, including bacon, cumin seeds, chipotle, and of course, chili powder, gives it a flavorful kick. Finally, we found that white mushrooms added a meaty flavor to the chili without overpowering the flavor of the black beans. And the mustard seeds? They added a surprising pungency, which tasters loved.

Tres Leches Cake

WHY THIS RECIPE WORKS

A great *tres leches* cake—a spongecake soaked with a mixture of "three milks" (heavy cream, evaporated milk, and sweetened condensed milk)—should be moist but not mushy. Most recipes for spongecake use just egg whites. Since we needed to make our cake sturdy enough to handle the milk mixture, we used whipped whole eggs. Although some tres leches cake recipes use equal amounts of evaporated milk, sweetened condensed milk, and cream, we found that cutting back on the cream produced a thicker mixture that didn't oversaturate the cake. Finally, letting the cake sit and soak for at least 3 hours is crucial for a moist, but not wet, cake.

The cake will become more moist and dense as it sits in the refrigerator in steps 5 and 6.

MILK MIXTURE

- 1 (14-ounce) can sweetened condensed milk
- 1 (12-ounce) can evaporated milk
- 1 cup heavy cream
- 1 teaspoon vanilla extract

CAKE

- 2 cups (10 ounces) all-purpose flour
- 2 teaspoons baking powder
- 1 teaspoon salt
- ½ teaspoon ground cinnamon
- 8 tablespoons unsalted butter
- 1 cup whole milk
- 4 large eggs, room temperature
- 2 cups (14 ounces) sugar
- 2 teaspoons vanilla extract

FROSTING

- 1 cup heavy cream, chilled
- 3 tablespoons corn syrup
- 1 teaspoon vanilla extract

1. FOR THE MILK MIXTURE: Microwave condensed milk in large covered bowl on low power, stirring every 3 to 5 minutes, until slightly darkened and thickened, 9 to 15 minutes. Slowly whisk in evaporated milk, cream, and vanilla and let cool to room temperature.

2. FOR THE CAKE: Adjust oven rack to middle position and heat oven to 325 degrees. Grease and flour 13 by 9-inch baking pan. Whisk flour, baking powder, salt, and cinnamon in bowl. Melt butter and milk in small saucepan over low heat; remove from heat.

3. Using stand mixer fitted with whisk, whip eggs for 30 seconds. Slowly add sugar until incorporated, about 1 minute. Increase speed to medium-high and continue to whip mixture until very thick and glossy, 5 to 7 minutes.

4. Reduce mixer speed to low and slowly add melted butter mixture and vanilla. Add flour mixture in 3 additions, scraping down bowl as necessary. Increase speed to medium and whip batter until fully incorporated, about 30 seconds. Give batter final stir by hand. Scrape batter evenly into prepared pan and bake until toothpick inserted in center comes out clean, 30 to 45 minutes.

5. Let cake cool for 10 minutes. Using skewer, poke holes at ½-inch intervals in top of cake. Slowly pour cooled milk mixture over cake. Let cake sit for 15 minutes, then refrigerate uncovered for 3 to 24 hours.

6. FOR THE FROSTING: Using stand mixer fitted with whisk, whip cream, corn syrup, and vanilla on medium-low speed until foamy, about 1 minute. Increase speed to high and whip until soft peaks form, 1 to 3 minutes. Spread whipped cream over top of cake and serve. (Frosted cake can be refrigerated for up to 3 days.)

EVEN EASIER ⋐➤ Don't have time to make Tres Leches Cake? Consider drizzling slices of pound cake with warm dulce de leche and topping it with slightly sweetened (or rum-flavored) whipped cream. (You can make your own dulce de leche following the instructions in Dulce de Leche Sandwich Cookies on page 77, or buy it at a Latin market or in the Latin section of the supermarket.)

Tapas Party

THE GAME PLAN

TAPAS PARTY

⤝ *Serves 8* ⤞

Sangría ⤞ Spanish Tortilla with Garlic Mayonnaise ⤞ Sizzling Garlic Shrimp
Spanish Cheese and Meat Board ⤞ Cocktail Meatballs in Tomato-Saffron Sauce
Marinated Cauliflower and Chickpea Salad
Dulce de Leche Sandwich Cookies

Spanish Tortilla with Garlic Mayonnaise

When making this mayonnaise, we like to whisk in the extra-virgin olive oil by hand to protect its delicate flavor.

GARLIC MAYONNAISE

2 large egg yolks
2 teaspoons Dijon mustard
2 teaspoons lemon juice
1 garlic clove, minced
¾ cup vegetable oil
1 tablespoon water
½ teaspoon salt
¼ teaspoon pepper
¼ cup extra-virgin olive oil

TORTILLA

1½ pounds Yukon Gold potatoes, peeled, quartered lengthwise, and sliced crosswise ⅛ inch thick
1 small onion, halved and sliced thin
6 tablespoons plus 1 teaspoon extra-virgin olive oil

Salt and pepper

8 large eggs
½ cup jarred roasted red peppers, rinsed, patted dry, and cut into ½-inch pieces
½ cup frozen peas, thawed

1. FOR THE GARLIC MAYONNAISE: Process egg yolks, mustard, lemon juice, and garlic in food processor until combined, about 10 seconds. With processor running, slowly drizzle in vegetable oil, about 1 minute. Transfer mixture to medium bowl and whisk in water, salt, and pepper. Whisking constantly, slowly drizzle in olive oil. (Mayonnaise can be refrigerated for up to 4 days. Makes 1¼ cups.) *continued* ➤

✓ **WHY THIS RECIPE WORKS**
This savory, velvety potato and egg cake is perhaps Spain's most recognizable tapa. Served with a garlicky mayonnaise, it is irresistible. Parcooking the potatoes before combining them with the eggs and other flavorings was crucial, and easily done in a covered skillet. Flipping the tortilla over halfway through cooking ensured that it was cooked through evenly on both sides. Traditional recipes instruct to "flip" the tortilla up in the air, but we found using two plates to flip it over to be much more foolproof.

MAKING SPANISH TORTILLA

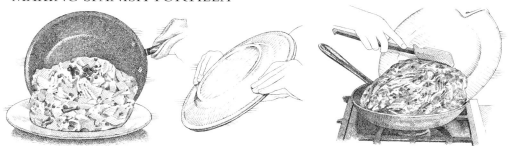

After browning the first side, loosen the tortilla with a rubber spatula and slide onto a large plate. Place a second plate face down over the tortilla; invert browned side up on the second plate. Slide the tortilla back into the pan, browned side up, and tuck the edges into the pan with the rubber spatula.

2. FOR THE TORTILLA: Toss potatoes, onion, ¼ cup oil, ½ teaspoon salt, and ¼ teaspoon pepper in large bowl. Heat 2 tablespoons oil in 10-inch nonstick skillet over medium-high heat until shimmering. Add potato mixture and reduce heat to medium-low. Cover and cook, stirring occasionally, until potatoes are tender, 22 to 28 minutes.

3. In now-empty bowl, whisk eggs with ½ teaspoon salt. Fold in hot potatoes, roasted red peppers, and peas.

4. Heat remaining 1 teaspoon oil in now-empty skillet over medium-high heat until just smoking. Add egg-potato mixture and cook, shaking pan and folding mixture constantly, for 15 seconds. Smooth top of mixture and reduce heat to medium. Cover

and cook, gently shaking pan every 30 seconds, until bottom is golden brown and top is lightly set, about 2 minutes.

5. Using rubber spatula, loosen tortilla from pan. Shake pan gently until tortilla slides around freely, then slide tortilla onto large plate. Invert tortilla onto second large plate, then slide back into skillet, browned side up. Tuck in tortilla edges and continue to cook over medium heat, gently shaking often, until second side is golden brown, about 2 minutes.

6. Slide tortilla onto cutting board and let cool for 15 minutes. (Tortilla can be held at room temperature for up to 4 hours.) Cut into wedges or squares and serve warm or at room temperature.

Sizzling Garlic Shrimp

✓ **WHY THIS RECIPE WORKS** Sizzling garlic shrimp—*gambas al ajillo*—is a classic tapas dish. The trick to making it is to infuse the oil with lots of garlic flavor, and not overcook the shrimp. For a well-rounded and inescapable garlic flavor, we added it in three ways: as minced cloves in the shrimp marinade, as smashed whole cloves to infuse the cooking oil, and as slices added right into the dish during cooking. To prevent the shrimp from overcooking, we cooked them gently over medium-low heat.

You can substitute ¼ teaspoon paprika for the dried chile if necessary. For a true sizzling effect, transfer the cooked shrimp mixture to an 8-inch cast-iron skillet that has been heated for 2 minutes over medium-high heat just before serving. Serve with crusty bread for dipping in the richly flavored olive oil.

1	pound large shrimp (31 to 40 per pound), peeled, deveined (see page 304), and tails removed
14	garlic cloves, peeled, 2 cloves minced and 12 cloves left whole
½	cup olive oil
¼	teaspoon salt
1	bay leaf
1	(2-inch) piece mild dried chile, such as New Mexican, roughly broken with seeds
1½	teaspoons sherry vinegar
1	tablespoon minced fresh parsley

1. Toss shrimp with minced garlic, 2 tablespoons oil, and salt in bowl and let marinate at room temperature for at least 30 minutes and up to 1 hour.

2. Meanwhile, using flat side of chef's knife, smash 4 garlic cloves. Heat smashed garlic and remaining 6 tablespoons oil in 12-inch skillet over medium-low heat,

stirring occasionally, until garlic is light golden brown, 4 to 7 minutes. Let oil cool to room temperature. Using slotted spoon, remove and discard smashed garlic.

3. Thinly slice remaining 8 garlic cloves. Return skillet with cooled oil to low heat and add sliced garlic, bay leaf, and chile. Cook, stirring occasionally, until garlic is tender but not browned, 4 to 7 minutes. (If garlic has not begun to sizzle after 3 minutes, increase heat to medium-low.)

4. Increase heat to medium-low and add shrimp with marinade. Cook, without stirring, until oil starts to gently bubble, about 2 minutes. Using tongs, flip shrimp and continue to cook until almost cooked through, about 2 minutes. Increase heat to high and add sherry vinegar and parsley. Cook, stirring constantly, until shrimp are cooked through and oil is bubbling vigorously, 15 to 20 seconds. Remove and discard bay leaf. Serve immediately.

Spanish Cheese and Meat Board

We chose to highlight Spanish cheeses and ham here, but feel free to substitute other types of cheese and cured meat as desired. Also, consider adding fresh or dried fruit, such as figs, grapes, sliced oranges, apricots, or pitted dates.

10	ounces Cabrales cheese, room temperature
10	ounces Manchego cheese, room temperature
8	ounces quince paste, room temperature
8	ounces Marcona almonds

8	ounces thinly sliced Serrano ham
1	large baguette, sliced ½ inch thick on bias

Arrange all ingredients attractively on large serving platter or cutting board and serve.

✔ **WHY THIS RECIPE WORKS**
An interesting selection of cheeses, meats, nuts, fruit, and other accompaniments is what is important to note here. Also, a nice cheese board like this is an incredibly easy way to round out this tapas "dinner" without having to do much work.

Cocktail Meatballs in Tomato-Saffron Sauce

We like to use a nonstick skillet in this recipe because it prevents the tender meatballs from sticking to the pan and breaking apart. Serve with toothpicks or cocktail forks.

MEATBALLS

2	slices hearty white sandwich bread, torn into small pieces
⅓	cup whole milk
8	ounces 85 percent lean ground beef
8	ounces ground pork
¼	cup grated Manchego or Parmesan cheese
2	tablespoons minced fresh parsley
1	large egg yolk
1	garlic clove, minced
¾	teaspoon salt
⅛	teaspoon pepper
2	tablespoons olive oil

SAUCE

1	small onion, chopped fine
1	small tomato, cored, seeded, and chopped medium
¼	teaspoon saffron threads, crumbled
¼	teaspoon paprika
1	cup low-sodium chicken broth
½	cup dry white wine
1	tablespoon minced fresh parsley
1	tablespoon finely chopped almonds
2	garlic cloves, minced
⅛	teaspoon salt
	Pinch pepper

1. FOR THE MEATBALLS: In large bowl, mash bread and milk together to form smooth paste. Add ground beef, ground pork, Manchego, parsley, egg yolk, garlic, salt, and pepper and mix with hands until uniform. Shape into forty 1-inch round meatballs, about 1 tablespoon each. (Meatballs can be refrigerated for up to 2 days.)

2. Heat oil in 12-inch nonstick skillet over medium-high heat until shimmering. Add half of meatballs and brown on all sides, 8 to 10 minutes; transfer to paper towel–lined plate. Repeat with remaining meatballs; transfer to plate.

3. FOR THE SAUCE: Discard all but 1 tablespoon fat left in skillet. Add onion and cook over medium heat, scraping up browned bits, until very soft and lightly browned, 6 to 9 minutes. Stir in tomato, saffron, and paprika and cook for 1 minute. Stir in broth and wine. (Sauce can be held in skillet for up to 2 hours; return to simmer and add water as needed to adjust consistency.)

4. Carefully add meatballs to skillet, cover, and simmer until just cooked through, about 10 minutes. Combine parsley, almonds, garlic, salt, and pepper in bowl. Gently stir parsley mixture into skillet. Transfer meatballs and sauce to serving dish and serve.

✔ **WHY THIS RECIPE WORKS**
These Spanish-style meatballs put the usual potluck meatballs to shame. The meatballs themselves are rich-tasting and packed with flavor, not to mention that they are swimming in a saffron-infused sauce. For super-tender meatballs that don't fall apart, it's important to use a panade (a mixture of bread and milk) along with a combination of ground beef and pork. Browning the meatballs before making the sauce helps build flavor and keep the meatballs intact during simmering. Raw garlic and chopped almonds add classic flavor to this dish and help to thicken the sauce before serving.

Marinated Cauliflower and Chickpea Salad

Make sure to use a small sprig of rosemary or its flavor will be overpowering and medicinal. This dish can be served cold or at room temperature.

1 head cauliflower (2 pounds), cored and cut into 1-inch florets
Salt and pepper
½ cup hot water
¼ teaspoon saffron threads, crumbled
¾ cup extra-virgin olive oil
10 garlic cloves, peeled and smashed
3 tablespoons sugar
1 tablespoon smoked paprika
1 (3-inch) sprig rosemary
¼ cup sherry vinegar
1 (15-ounce) can chickpeas, rinsed
1 lemon, sliced thin
2 tablespoons minced fresh parsley (optional)

1. Bring 2 quarts water to boil in large saucepan. Add cauliflower and 1 tablespoon salt and cook until cauliflower begins to soften, about 3 minutes. Drain cauliflower and transfer to paper towel–lined baking sheet.

2. Combine hot water and saffron in bowl. Heat oil and garlic in small saucepan over medium-low heat until garlic is fragrant and beginning to sizzle but not browned, 4 to 6 minutes. Stir in sugar, paprika, and rosemary and cook until fragrant, about 30 seconds. Stir in saffron mixture, vinegar, 2 teaspoons salt, and ¼ teaspoon pepper.

3. In large bowl, toss cauliflower, chickpeas, and lemon with hot saffron marinade until well coated. Transfer mixture to gallon-sized zipper-lock bag. Refrigerate for 4 hours and up to 3 days, flipping bag occasionally. To serve, transfer to serving bowl with slotted spoon. Remove and discard rosemary and sprinkle with parsley, if using. (Makes about 6 cups.)

Sangría

The longer sangría sits before drinking (up to 24 hours), the more smooth and mellow it will taste. We tried several inexpensive fruity, medium-bodied red wines and tasters thought most of them performed well in this recipe; we found Merlot to be an especially good choice.

4 large juice oranges
2 large lemons
½ cup sugar
2 (750-ml) bottles inexpensive Merlot, chilled
½ cup triple sec

1. Slice 2 oranges and lemons. Combine sliced fruit and sugar in large punch bowl (or 2 pitchers) and mash gently with wooden spoon to release some juice and dissolve sugar, about 1 minute (do not crush fruit completely).

2. Juice remaining 2 oranges, discarding spent fruit. Add fresh squeezed juice, wine, and triple sec to bowl. Cover and refrigerate until flavors meld, at least 2 hours and up to 24 hours. Before serving, add 12 to 16 ice cubes and stir briskly to distribute settled fruit and pulp.

Dulce de Leche Sandwich Cookies

Be sure to use a heavy-bottomed saucepan when making the dulce de leche in step 1. You can substitute ¾ cup store-bought dulce de leche if desired; look for it in the international foods aisle of the supermarket or in a Latin market. If the cookie dough becomes too soft when slicing the cookies, return it to the refrigerator until firm. Dipping the cookies in chocolate is optional but a nice touch if you have the time.

DULCE DE LECHE

4	cups whole milk
1	cup (7 ounces) granulated sugar
½	teaspoon vanilla extract
½	teaspoon salt
½	teaspoon baking soda

COOKIES

1	cup plus 2 tablespoons (5⅔ ounces) all-purpose flour
¼	teaspoon salt
8	tablespoons unsalted butter, softened
⅓	cup (2⅓ ounces) granulated sugar
¼	cup (1 ounce) confectioners' sugar
1	large egg yolk
1	teaspoon vanilla extract
5	ounces bittersweet chocolate, finely chopped (optional)

1. FOR THE DULCE DE LECHE: Whisk milk, sugar, vanilla, salt, and baking soda in large saucepan to dissolve sugar. Bring to simmer over medium heat (mixture will foam up). Simmer gently, stirring and skimming foam, until dark caramel in color and measures ¾ cup, 2½ to 3 hours. Strain through fine-mesh strainer and let cool. (Dulce de leche can be refrigerated for up to 1 month; bring to room temperature before using.)

2. FOR THE COOKIES: Whisk flour and salt in bowl. Using stand mixer fitted with paddle, beat butter, granulated sugar, and confectioners' sugar until pale and fluffy, about 3 minutes. Add egg yolk and vanilla and beat until combined, about 30 seconds.

Reduce speed to low and slowly add flour mixture until combined, about 30 seconds. Give batter final stir by hand.

3. Transfer dough to clean counter. Roll into 1½-inch-thick log, about 11 inches long. Wrap dough tightly in plastic wrap and refrigerate until firm, about 2 hours. (Dough can be refrigerated for up to 3 days and frozen for up to 1 month; if frozen, let thaw completely before using.)

4. Adjust oven racks to upper-middle and lower-middle positions and heat oven to 325 degrees. Line 2 baking sheets with parchment paper. Slice dough into ⅛-inch-thick rounds and place ¾ inch apart on prepared baking sheets.

5. Bake cookies until edges begin to brown, 12 to 15 minutes, switching and rotating baking sheets halfway through baking. Cool cookies on baking sheets for 5 minutes. Transfer cookies to wire rack and cool completely, about 1 hour. (Cookies can be stored at room temperature for up to 2 days.)

6. To make cookie sandwiches, spread 1 teaspoon dulce de leche between 2 cookies. If desired, microwave chocolate in small bowl on 50 percent power, stirring occasionally, until melted, 2 to 4 minutes. Dip half of each cookie into melted chocolate and transfer to parchment-lined baking sheet. Refrigerate chocolate-dipped cookies until chocolate is set, about 15 minutes, before serving. (Filled cookies can be held at room temperature for up to 1 day. Makes 32 cookies.)

✔ WHY THIS RECIPE WORKS

Dulce de leche is a milk-based caramel sauce and spread used throughout Latin America, although similar sauces can be found under a wide variety of different names all over the world. We found lots of recipes for making dulce de leche. Some simmered milk in the oven until it caramelized, while others cooked it on the stovetop. Several recipes have you submerge and boil a can of condensed milk, which did indeed work, but we found it slightly scary. After testing a variety of cooking methods, we found that simmering on the stovetop worked best because it was easiest to watch and stir. We flavored the milk with sugar, vanilla, and salt, and also added some baking soda (which is common) to hasten the browning and ensure a smooth texture.

Eastern Shore Crab and Corn Cake Supper, page 85

Southern Fried Chicken Dinner, page 95

Grilled Shrimp Dinner, page 131

Middle Eastern Shish Kebab Dinner, page 125

→ SUMMER ←

Dinner from the Garden 81

Zucchini Fritters with Cucumber-Yogurt Sauce
Spaghetti with Roasted Cherry Tomatoes, Olives, Capers,
   and Pine Nuts
Tricolor Salad with Balsamic Vinaigrette
Nectarines and Berries in Prosecco

Eastern Shore Crab
and Corn Cake Supper 85

Chilled Tomato Soup with Homemade Cheese Straws
Maryland Crab and Corn Cakes with Rémoulade Sauce
Summer Vegetable Chopped Salad
Fresh Berry Gratins

Easy Halibut Dinner 91

Goat Cheese with Pink Peppercorns and Herbs
Pan-Roasted Halibut with Chermoula
Fingerling Potato and Arugula Salad
Easy Berry Cake with Lemon Whipped Cream

Southern Fried Chicken Dinner 95

BLT Canapés with Basil Mayonnaise
Batter-Fried Chicken
Edamame Succotash with Jalapeños and Cilantro
Creamy Buttermilk Coleslaw
Peach Shortcakes

Mexican Fiesta 101

Easy Mini Chicken Empanadas
Spicy Shredded Pork Tostadas
Jícama and Red Cabbage Slaw
Mexican Ice Cream Torte

Mediterranean Flank Steak Supper 107

Farmer's Cheese with Homemade Tomato Jam
Grilled Flank Steak with Grilled Vegetables and Salsa Verde
Orzo with Lemon, Basil, and Feta
Free-Form Nectarine-Raspberry Tarts

Easy Grilled Chicken Dinner 113

Eggplant Caviar
Easy Garlic Flatbreads
Grilled Lemon Chicken Breasts
Green Bean and Potato Salad with Cilantro Dressing
Pistachio-Raspberry Buckles

Fajitas and 'Ritas 119

Margaritas
Fresh Tomato Salsa and Guacamole
Grilled Chicken Fajitas
Easy Boiled Corn with Lime Butter
Key Lime Pie

Middle Eastern
Shish Kebab Dinner 125

Spicy Whipped Feta
Lamb Shish Kebabs with Garlicky Yogurt Sauce
Persian Rice Salad with Dates and Pistachios
Moroccan Carrot Salad
Pistachio-Lemon Ice Cream Sandwiches

Grilled Shrimp Dinner 131

Tomato and Mozzarella Tart
Grilled Shrimp Skewers with Lemon-Garlic Sauce
Couscous with Carrots and Chickpeas
Zucchini Ribbons with Shaved Parmesan
Glazed Lemon Pound Cake with Strawberries
   and Whipped Cream

Dinner
from the
Garden

THE GAME PLAN

ON THE DAY OF...

MAKE ZUCCHINI FRITTERS AND YOGURT SAUCE:
1 hour (plus 1 hour for chilling)

**MAKE SPAGHETTI WITH ROASTED CHERRY
TOMATOES:** 1¼ hours

MAKE SALAD: 15 minutes

MAKE NECTARINES AND BERRIES IN PROSECCO:
20 minutes (plus 1 hour for chilling)

DINNER FROM THE GARDEN

➤ *Serves 8* ➤

Zucchini Fritters with Cucumber-Yogurt Sauce
Spaghetti with Roasted Cherry Tomatoes, Olives, Capers, and Pine Nuts
Tricolor Salad with Balsamic Vinaigrette ➤ Nectarines and Berries in Prosecco

Spaghetti with Roasted Cherry Tomatoes, Olives, Capers, and Pine Nuts

We prefer to serve spaghetti with this sauce; however, linguine and vermicelli also work well. Our preferred brand of spaghetti is Ronzoni.

4	pounds cherry tomatoes, halved
7	tablespoons olive oil
⅓	cup capers, rinsed
4	garlic cloves, sliced thin
4½	teaspoons sugar
½	teaspoon red pepper flakes
	Salt and pepper
1½	pounds spaghetti
3	ounces Pecorino Romano, grated (1½ cups)
⅓	cup pitted kalamata olives, chopped coarse
¼	cup chopped fresh oregano
⅓	cup pine nuts, toasted (see page 29)

1. Adjust oven racks to upper-middle and lower-middle positions and heat oven to 425 degrees. Gently toss tomatoes with 5 tablespoons oil, capers, garlic, sugar, pepper flakes, ½ teaspoon salt, and ¼ teaspoon pepper in bowl. Spread evenly over 2 rimmed baking sheets and roast until tomato skins are slightly shriveled, but tomatoes still retain their shape, 35 to 40 minutes, switching and rotating baking sheets halfway through baking. (Tomatoes can be transferred to bowl, covered, and held at room temperature for up to 3 hours. Before continuing with step 3, add 1 tablespoon water, cover, and microwave until hot, 1 to 2 minutes.)

2. Meanwhile, bring 6 quarts water to boil in large pot. Add pasta and 1½ tablespoons salt and cook, stirring often, until al dente. Reserve ½ cup pasta cooking water, then drain pasta and return it to pot.

3. Scrape warm tomato mixture into pot of pasta. Add ½ cup Pecorino, olives, oregano, and remaining 2 tablespoons oil, and toss to combine. Add reserved cooking water as needed to adjust sauce consistency. Serve, sprinkling individual portions with remaining 1 cup Pecorino and pine nuts.

✔ **WHY THIS RECIPE WORKS**
In the summer months, we prefer a pasta dish that is light and fresh, and this easy recipe fits the bill perfectly. Packed with roasted and slightly caramelized cherry tomatoes, along with garlic, capers, and olives, this fragrant dish is colorful and bright-tasting. The trick is to roast the tomatoes on two baking sheets with some sugar, which helps caramelize them. The hot oven drives off excess liquid and concentrates the flavor of the tomatoes in just 35 minutes. Chopped olives, oregano, Pecorino, and pine nuts are mixed in just before serving for a dish that tastes like summer in a bowl.

Zucchini Fritters with Cucumber-Yogurt Sauce

☑ WHY THIS RECIPE WORKS
These crisp and lightly fried zucchini fritters, served with a tangy cucumber-yogurt sauce, are the perfect start to a summer dinner party. The key to these fritters is to draw out the excess moisture from the zucchini; we found that ten minutes of salting and draining plus some serious squeezing in paper towels eliminated enough liquid to produce crisp fritters. We used eggs and flour to bind the fritters while scallions and dill enhanced the fresh garden flavor; the fritters really hit their stride though when we stirred in crumbled feta: now every bite was laced with a pocket of tangy, salty cheese. For a finishing touch, we whipped up a cool and creamy tzatziki (yogurt and cucumber) sauce to serve alongside.

Be sure to squeeze the zucchini until it is completely dry or the fritters will be soggy and fall apart in the skillet. These fritters are great warm or at room temperature.

SAUCE

- 1 cup whole-milk Greek yogurt
- 2 tablespoons extra-virgin olive oil
- 2 tablespoons minced fresh mint and/or dill
- 1 small garlic clove, minced
- 1 cucumber, peeled, halved lengthwise, seeded (see page 89), and shredded
  Salt and pepper

FRITTERS

- 1½ pounds zucchini, shredded
  Salt and pepper
- 12 ounces feta cheese, crumbled (3 cups)
- 3 large eggs, lightly beaten
- 3 scallions, minced
- 3 tablespoons minced fresh dill
- 2 garlic cloves, minced
- ⅓ cup all-purpose flour
- 9 tablespoons olive oil
  Lemon wedges

1. FOR THE SAUCE: Whisk yogurt, oil, mint, and garlic together in bowl. Stir in cucumber and season with salt and pepper to taste. Cover and refrigerate until chilled, at least 1 hour and up to 2 days.

2. FOR THE FRITTERS: Adjust oven rack to middle position and heat oven to 200 degrees. Toss zucchini with 1 teaspoon salt and let drain in fine-mesh strainer for 10 minutes. Press zucchini dry thoroughly between several layers of paper towels. Combine dried zucchini, feta, eggs, scallions, dill, garlic, and ¼ teaspoon pepper in bowl. Sprinkle flour over mixture and stir to incorporate.

SHREDDING ZUCCHINI

Shred trimmed zucchini on the large holes of a box grater or in a food processor fitted with a shredding disk. After salting and draining the zucchini, wrap it in several layers of paper towels or a clean dish towel and squeeze out excess liquid until it's dry.

3. Heat 3 tablespoons oil in 12-inch nonstick skillet over medium heat until shimmering. Drop 2-tablespoon-size portions of batter into pan, then use back of spoon to press batter into 2-inch-wide fritters (you should fit about 6 fritters in pan at a time). Fry until golden brown on both sides, 2 to 3 minutes per side. Transfer fritters to paper towel–lined baking sheet and keep warm in oven.

4. Discard oil and wipe out now-empty skillet with paper towels. Repeat with remaining 6 tablespoons oil and remaining batter in 2 batches; discard oil and wipe out pan between batches. Serve warm or at room temperature with sauce and lemon wedges.

Tricolor Salad with Balsamic Vinaigrette

Toss the dressing with the greens just before serving. Our favorite balsamic vinegar is Lucini Gran Riserva Balsamico.

7	teaspoons balsamic vinegar
2	teaspoons red wine vinegar
	Salt and pepper
6	tablespoons extra-virgin olive oil
5	ounces baby arugula (5 cups)
1	head radicchio (10 ounces), cut into 1-inch pieces
2	heads Belgian endive (8 ounces), cut into 2-inch pieces

Whisk balsamic vinegar, red wine vinegar, ¼ teaspoon salt, and ⅛ teaspoon pepper in small bowl. Whisking constantly, drizzle in oil. In large bowl, toss arugula with radicchio and endive. Just before serving, whisk dressing to re-emulsify, then drizzle over salad and toss gently to coat.

✔ WHY THIS RECIPE WORKS

This mixed salad refreshes the palate with its clean and robust flavor. And its simple dressing strikes a balance between rich, fruity olive oil and bright, tangy vinegar. Most vinaigrette recipes contain only extra-virgin olive oil, red wine vinegar, and salt, but we liked the sweet, complex addition of balsamic vinegar as well.

Nectarines and Berries in Prosecco

Sliced peaches, sliced plums, peeled and sliced kiwi, and melon cut into bite-size chunks can also be used in this recipe. Just make sure you have about 3½ pounds of fruit in total. Serve with biscotti and/or sorbet.

1½	pounds nectarines, pitted and cut into ¼-inch-thick wedges
1	pound strawberries, hulled and quartered (3 cups)
10	ounces raspberries (2 cups)
5	ounces blackberries (1 cup)
½	cup sugar, plus extra as needed
2	tablespoons orange liqueur, such as Grand Marnier or triple sec
¼	teaspoon grated lemon zest
1½	cups chilled prosecco or other young, fruity sparkling white wine
2	tablespoons chopped fresh mint

Gently toss nectarines, strawberries, raspberries, blackberries, sugar, orange liqueur, and lemon zest together in large serving bowl. Refrigerate for at least 1 hour and up to 8 hours. Just before serving, pour prosecco over fruit, season with extra sugar to taste, and stir in mint.

✔ WHY THIS RECIPE WORKS

For a refreshing conclusion to a summer meal, we tossed a combination of nectarines, strawberries, raspberries, and blackberries with some sugar and allowed the mixture to macerate until the fruit softened and released some of its juice. Orange liqueur added some fire as well as some nice citrus notes. Then we poured chilled prosecco over the macerated fruit for a harmonious blend of fruit and fizz.

Eastern Shore Crab and Corn Cake Supper

THE GAME PLAN

◄▸

ONE DAY AHEAD...

MAKE TOMATO SOUP: 35 minutes
(plus 3 hours for draining and chilling)

MAKE CHEESE STRAWS: 15 minutes
(plus 20 minutes for baking and cooling)

MAKE RÉMOULADE SAUCE: 10 minutes

ON THE DAY OF...

MAKE BERRY GRATINS: 15 minutes
(plus 25 minutes for baking and cooling)

MAKE CRAB CAKES: 40 minutes (plus 1 hour for chilling)

MAKE CHOPPED SALAD: 25 minutes
(plus 15 minutes for draining)

EASTERN SHORE
CRAB AND CORN CAKE SUPPER

~ *Serves 8* ~

Chilled Tomato Soup with Homemade Cheese Straws
Maryland Crab and Corn Cakes with Rémoulade Sauce
Summer Vegetable Chopped Salad ⟿ Fresh Berry Gratins

Maryland Crab and Corn Cakes with Rémoulade Sauce

The flavor and texture of these crab cakes obviously depends on the type of crabmeat you buy; we strongly prefer to use fresh jumbo lump crabmeat. Like tartar sauce, rémoulade sauce is a classic complement to seafood dishes. You can substitute 1 tablespoon chopped bread-and-butter pickles for the sweet pickle relish.

RÉMOULADE SAUCE

- 1 cup mayonnaise
- 1 tablespoon sweet pickle relish
- 2 teaspoons hot sauce
- 2 teaspoons lemon juice
- 2 teaspoons minced fresh parsley
- 1 teaspoon capers, rinsed
- 1 teaspoon Dijon mustard
- 1 garlic clove, minced
  Salt and pepper

CRAB AND CORN CAKES

- 28 saltines
- 2 pounds lump crabmeat, picked over for shells
- 2 ears corn, kernels cut from cob (see page 97)
- 6 scallions, minced
- ½ cup mayonnaise
- 6 tablespoons unsalted butter, 4 tablespoons melted and 2 tablespoons softened
- 2 large egg yolks
- 2 tablespoons Dijon mustard
- 4 teaspoons hot sauce
- 2 teaspoons Old Bay seasoning
  Lemon wedges

1. FOR THE RÉMOULADE SAUCE: Pulse all ingredients in food processor until well combined but not smooth, about 10 pulses. Season with salt and pepper to taste. Transfer to serving bowl. (Rémoulade sauce can be refrigerated for up to 3 days.)

2. FOR THE CRAB AND CORN CAKES: Process saltines in food processor until finely ground, about 20 seconds. Dry crabmeat well with paper towels. Using rubber spatula, gently combine crabmeat, ½ cup ground saltines, corn, scallions, mayonnaise, melted butter, egg yolks, mustard, hot sauce, and Old Bay in large bowl.

3. Divide mixture into 8 portions (¾ cup each) and shape into tight, mounded cakes that measure roughly 3 inches wide and 1½ inches thick. Press top of each cake in remaining ground saltine crumbs. Transfer crab cakes, crumb side down, *continued* ➤

✔ WHY THIS RECIPE WORKS

We wanted to combine two of our favorite summer pleasures by incorporating corn into a crab cake packed with sweet crabmeat, the barest breading, and just enough binder to hold the cake together. After forming the cakes, a short chill in the fridge allowed them to set up and the crumbs to absorb moisture. The fact that they can stay in the fridge for up to 8 hours at this point makes them convenient, but our real fuss-reducing breakthrough was to forgo messy pan-frying for broiling. Broiled in one batch on a baking sheet, the crab cakes required no flipping to brown the other side, so they remained intact and moist with a flavorful, golden crust. (Dunking one side of each crab cake in extra saltine crumbs prevents the bottom from becoming soggy.)

to large platter, cover, and refrigerate for at least 1 hour and up to 8 hours.

4. Adjust oven rack 8 inches from broiler element and heat broiler. Grease rimmed baking sheet with softened butter. Transfer crab cakes to prepared baking sheet, crumb side down. Broil until crab cakes are golden brown, 12 to 15 minutes. Let crab cakes rest for 2 minutes, then serve with lemon wedges.

Chilled Tomato Soup

✔ **WHY THIS RECIPE WORKS**
A chilled tomato soup is a refreshing start to a summer dinner, but only if it shines with bright tomato flavor. Since a tomato's flavor is built up in its cells, we reasoned the key to improving the taste of an inferior supermarket tomato would be to burst those cells. We turned to salting to coax flavor from the tomatoes: Sure enough, an hour of salting gave the tomatoes a deep, full flavor. A slice of bread provided body and "creaminess" without the dulling effect of dairy, while processing the soup in a blender first, then straining it through a fine-mesh strainer produced an emulsified, smooth texture.

Be sure to use juicy, ripe tomatoes for this soup. Depending on the flavor of the tomatoes, you may need to season the soup with extra sugar and/or vinegar before serving. For ideal flavor, allow the soup to sit in the refrigerator overnight before serving. Serve with Homemade Cheese Straws (page 88).

3½ pounds tomatoes, cored and chopped coarse
    Salt and pepper
 1 shallot, peeled and halved
 1 garlic clove, peeled and quartered
 1 teaspoon sugar, plus extra as needed
 1 slice hearty white sandwich bread, crust removed, bread cut into 1-inch pieces
 5 tablespoons olive oil, plus extra for serving
 1 teaspoon sherry vinegar, plus extra as needed
 2 tablespoons minced fresh basil
 1 tablespoon minced fresh mint

1. Toss tomatoes with ½ teaspoon salt and let drain through fine-mesh strainer, set over bowl to reserve drained liquid, for 1 hour. Toss drained tomatoes with shallot, garlic, and sugar in separate bowl. Add bread to drained tomato liquid, let soak for 1 minute, then stir into tomatoes.

2. Transfer half of mixture to blender and process for 30 seconds. With blender running, slowly drizzle in 3 tablespoons oil until completely smooth, about 2 minutes. Strain through fine-mesh strainer into large bowl, using rubber spatula to help pass soup through strainer. Repeat with remaining mixture and remaining 2 tablespoons olive oil; strain into bowl.

3. Stir in vinegar and season with salt and pepper to taste. Cover and refrigerate until chilled and flavors have melded, at least 2 hours and up to 2 days.

4. Before serving, season with salt, pepper, extra sugar, and extra vinegar to taste. Stir in 1 tablespoon basil and mint. Garnish individual bowls with remaining 1 tablespoon basil, and drizzle lightly with olive oil.

Homemade Cheese Straws

To thaw frozen puff pastry, allow it to sit either in the refrigerator for 24 hours or on the counter for 30 to 60 minutes.

1   (9½ by 9-inch) sheet frozen puff pastry, thawed
2   ounces Parmesan or Asiago cheese, grated (1 cup)
1   tablespoon minced fresh parsley
¼   teaspoon salt
⅛   teaspoon pepper

1. Adjust oven rack to middle position and heat oven to 425 degrees. Line rimmed baking sheet with parchment paper.

2. Lay puff pastry on sheet of parchment paper and sprinkle with Parmesan, parsley, salt, and pepper. Top with another sheet of parchment. Using rolling pin, press cheese into dough, then roll dough into 10-inch square.

3. Remove top layer of parchment and cut dough into thirteen ¾-inch-wide strips with sharp knife (or pizza cutter). Gently twist each strip of dough and lay on prepared baking sheet, about ½ inch apart. (Cheese straws can be frozen for up to 1 month; do not thaw before continuing with step 4.)

4. Bake until straws are fully puffed and golden brown, 10 to 15 minutes. Let cool for 5 minutes before serving. (Cheese straws can be held at room temperature for up to 24 hours.)

SHAPING CHEESE STRAWS

Holding 1 strip of dough at each end, gently twist the dough in opposite directions into a corkscrew shape and transfer to a parchment-lined baking sheet. Repeat with the remaining pieces of dough, spacing the strips about ½ inch apart.

Summer Vegetable Chopped Salad

Letting the vegetables marinate in the vinaigrette for a few minutes before adding the lettuce intensifies their flavor greatly. Be sure to add the lettuce just before serving, however, or it will turn soggy.

3   cucumbers, peeled, halved lengthwise, seeded (see page 89), and cut into ½-inch pieces (3 cups)
1½ pounds cherry tomatoes, quartered Salt and pepper
1   yellow bell pepper, stemmed, seeded, and cut into ½-inch pieces
1   small red onion, chopped fine
8   ounces radishes, trimmed and sliced thin
¾   cup chopped fresh parsley
¼   cup red wine vinegar
1   garlic clove, minced
¼   cup extra-virgin olive oil
1   romaine lettuce heart (6 ounces), cut into 1-inch pieces

1. Toss cucumbers and tomatoes with 1 teaspoon salt and let drain in colander for 15 minutes. In large bowl, combine drained cucumbers and tomatoes, bell pepper, onion, radishes, and parsley. (Bowl of vegetables can be refrigerated for up to 4 hours before continuing with step 3.)

2. Whisk vinegar, garlic, ¼ teaspoon salt, and ⅛ teaspoon pepper in small bowl. Whisking constantly, drizzle in oil.

3. Just before serving, whisk dressing to re-emulsify, then drizzle over vegetable mixture and toss gently to coat. Let vegetables absorb dressing for at least 5 minutes and up to 20 minutes. Add romaine, gently toss to combine, and serve.

SEEDING A CUCUMBER

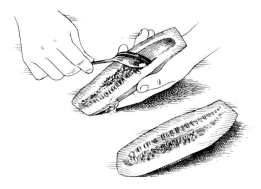

Peel each cucumber and halve lengthwise. Use a small spoon to remove the seeds and surrounding liquid from each cucumber half.

Fresh Berry Gratins

Though a mixture of berries is a wonderful combination, we also like adding sliced peaches or nectarines when in season. Just make sure you have about 2 pounds of fruit in total. Serve with whipped cream or vanilla ice cream.

- 3 croissants, torn into quarters
- 2 tablespoons unsalted butter, softened
- ⅓ cup packed (2⅓ ounces) brown sugar Pinch ground cinnamon
- 2 pounds mixed raspberries, blueberries, blackberries, and/or quartered strawberries (about 6 cups)
- 4½ teaspoons granulated sugar
- 4½ teaspoons kirsch or other eau de vie (optional) Pinch salt

1. Pulse croissants, butter, sugar, and cinnamon in food processor until mixture resembles coarse crumbs, about 10 pulses. (Crumbs can be held at room temperature for up to 8 hours.)

2. Gently toss fruit with sugar, kirsch, if using, and salt in bowl. Divide mixture evenly among eight 6-ounce ramekins. Place ramekins on rimmed baking sheet and sprinkle crumbs evenly over top. (Gratins can be held at room temperature for up to 4 hours before baking.)

3. Bake gratins until crumbs are deep golden brown and fruit is hot, 15 to 20 minutes. Cool for 5 minutes before serving.

✔ WHY THIS RECIPE WORKS

Quicker and dressier than a crisp, a gratin is a layer of fresh fruit piled into a shallow baking dish, dressed up with crumbs. The topping browns and the fruit is warmed just enough to release a bit of juice. We wanted to find the quickest, easiest route to this pleasing dessert. For the topping, we borrowed a page from the French, grinding croissants with brown sugar, cinnamon, and butter in the food processor. In addition to being ridiculously easy, the croissant topping was ridiculously good.

Easy Halibut Dinner

THE GAME PLAN

ON THE DAY OF...

MAKE CAKE: 35 minutes (plus 1¼ hours for baking and cooling)

MAKE GOAT CHEESE APPETIZER: 10 minutes

MAKE SALAD: 50 minutes (plus 1 hour for draining and cooling)

MAKE HALIBUT AND CHERMOULA: 45 minutes

EASY HALIBUT DINNER

➤ *Serves 8* ◄

Goat Cheese with Pink Peppercorns and Herbs

Pan-Roasted Halibut with Chermoula ➤ Fingerling Potato and Arugula Salad

Easy Berry Cake with Lemon Whipped Cream

Pan-Roasted Halibut with Chermoula

Thick white fish fillets with a meaty texture, like cod, sea bass, or red snapper, can be substituted for the halibut. Depending on the thickness of the fish fillets, they may cook at different rates; be prepared to remove the fillets from the oven, one at a time, as they finish cooking.

CHERMOULA

1¼	cups fresh cilantro leaves
¼	cup fresh parsley leaves
⅔	cup extra-virgin olive oil
2	tablespoons lemon juice
3	garlic cloves, minced
1	teaspoon ground cumin
1	teaspoon paprika
¼	teaspoon cayenne pepper
¼	teaspoon salt
	Pinch sugar

HALIBUT

8	(6- to 8-ounce) skinless halibut fillets, 1 to 1½ inches thick
	Salt and pepper
1	teaspoon sugar
2	tablespoons vegetable oil

1. FOR THE CHERMOULA: Process all ingredients in food processor until smooth, about 20 seconds, stopping to scrape down bowl as needed. Transfer to serving bowl. (Chermoula can be refrigerated for up to 2 days; bring to room temperature before serving.)

2. FOR THE HALIBUT: Adjust oven rack to middle position and heat oven to 425 degrees. Spray rimmed baking sheet with vegetable oil spray.

3. Pat fish dry with paper towels and season with salt and pepper. Sprinkle sugar evenly over 1 side of each fillet. Heat 1 tablespoon oil in 12-inch nonstick skillet over high heat until just smoking. Place half of fillets in skillet, sugared side down, and press down lightly to ensure even contact with pan. Cook until browned, 1 to 1½ minutes. Using 2 spatulas, transfer fish to prepared baking sheet, browned side facing up.

4. Wipe out now-empty skillet with paper towels. Heat remaining 1 tablespoon oil over high heat until just smoking and repeat with remaining fish fillets. Transfer to baking sheet. (Browned fillets can be held at room temperature for up to 30 minutes before continuing with step 5.)

5. Roast fillets until fish flakes apart when gently prodded with paring knife and registers 140 degrees, 7 to 10 minutes. Transfer fish to serving plates and spoon some chermoula over top. Serve, passing remaining chermoula separately.

✔ **WHY THIS RECIPE WORKS**

Chermoula, a fragrant, pungent Moroccan sauce made with cilantro, lemon, and garlic, pairs perfectly with fish and is a natural fit for a bright summer menu. To keep things simple, we chose to pan-roast the fish: searing the exterior of the fish in a skillet on the stovetop, then transferring the fish to the oven to gently finish cooking. Working in two batches, we seared half the fillets on one side in the skillet, then transferred them (seared side up) to a large baking sheet. Once both batches were browned, the fish could be finished together on the baking sheet in the oven. To accelerate the browning of the crust, we rubbed a little sugar on the fish before searing, which greatly boosted the color and flavor of the fish.

Goat Cheese with Pink Peppercorns and Herbs

✔ **WHY THIS RECIPE WORKS**
Goat cheese is often sold rolled in herbs or ash, which always seems more appealing than the naked log. But why not make your own rub? We started with a base of bright, eye-catching cracked pink peppercorns. Despite being unrelated to the black peppercorn, pink peppercorn has some of the familiar pungency of its namesake, but with a much more delicate, fruity, almost floral flavor. An equal amount of fresh minced thyme and a teaspoon of toasted fennel seeds round out the flavor and texture of the rub.

To crush fennel seeds and pink peppercorns, place in a zipper-lock bag and, using a rolling pin or heavy skillet, crush mixture to desired size. Serve with Garlic Toasts (page 62), crackers, or a thinly sliced baguette.

4 teaspoons whole pink peppercorns, crushed coarse
4 teaspoons minced fresh thyme
1 teaspoon fennel seeds, toasted (see page 29) and crushed
1 (10-ounce) log goat cheese, well chilled
¼ cup extra-virgin olive oil

Combine peppercorns, thyme, and fennel in shallow dish. Roll goat cheese log in peppercorn mixture to coat thoroughly, pressing gently to help it adhere. Transfer cheese to serving plate, sprinkle with any remaining herb mixture, and drizzle with olive oil. (Cheese can be held at room temperature for up to 4 hours.)

Fingerling Potato and Arugula Salad

✔ **WHY THIS RECIPE WORKS**
Looking for a side dish to pair with the halibut, we settled on a combination of tender potatoes, baby greens, and a lively vinaigrette for a hearty, fresh-tasting salad. Tasters unanimously sang the praises of fingerling potatoes here and felt that the distinctly elongated, narrow shape of this small potato elevated the dish to company-worthy status. We found it best to slice the fingerlings and boil them in salted water, as roasting muddied the clean flavor we were after.

Dressing the potatoes while still warm helps them to absorb flavor. To avoid wilting the arugula, make sure to cool the potatoes completely, and toss the salad with the dressing just before serving.

5 tablespoons white wine vinegar
1 shallot, minced
1 tablespoon minced fresh thyme
1 teaspoon Dijon mustard
   Salt and pepper
⅔ cup extra-virgin olive oil
3 pounds fingerling potatoes, sliced ¼ inch thick
12 ounces cherry tomatoes, quartered
6 ounces baby arugula (6 cups)

1. Whisk vinegar, shallot, thyme, mustard, ¼ teaspoon salt, and ⅛ teaspoon pepper together in small bowl. Whisking constantly, drizzle in oil.

2. Place potatoes and 2 tablespoons salt in Dutch oven and add cold water to cover by 1 inch. Bring to a boil. Reduce to gentle simmer and cook until potatoes are tender but not falling apart, about 8 minutes. Drain potatoes and spread evenly over 2 rimmed baking sheets.

3. Whisk dressing to re-emulsify, then drizzle ¾ cup dressing over warm potatoes. Let potatoes cool completely, about 30 minutes. (Cooled potatoes can be refrigerated for up to 1 day; bring to room temperature before continuing with step 4.)

4. Toss tomatoes with ½ teaspoon salt and let drain in colander for 30 minutes. Combine potatoes and drained tomatoes in large bowl. Just before serving, add arugula to bowl. Whisk remaining dressing to re-emulsify, then drizzle over salad and toss gently to coat.

Easy Berry Cake with Lemon Whipped Cream

This simple cake tastes best when a combination of berries is used. Be sure to use fresh, not frozen, berries here.

CAKE

1½	cups (7½ ounces) all-purpose flour
1½	teaspoons baking powder
½	teaspoon salt
8	tablespoons unsalted butter, softened
¾	cup (5¼ ounces) sugar, plus 2 tablespoons
2	large eggs plus 1 large white, room temperature
1	teaspoon vanilla extract
⅓	cup whole milk, room temperature
10	ounces mixed raspberries, blueberries, and/or blackberries (2 cups)

WHIPPED CREAM

1	cup heavy cream, chilled
1½	tablespoons sugar
1	teaspoon grated lemon zest plus 1 teaspoon juice

1. FOR THE CAKE: Adjust oven rack to middle position and heat oven to 350 degrees. Grease 9-inch springform pan. Whisk flour, baking powder, and salt in bowl.

2. Using stand mixer fitted with paddle, beat butter and ¾ cup sugar until pale and fluffy, about 3 minutes. Add whole eggs and egg white, 1 at a time, and beat until combined. Beat in vanilla until incorporated.

3. Add flour mixture in 3 additions, alternating with 2 additions of milk, scraping down bowl as needed. Give batter final stir by hand. Gently fold in berries.

4. Scrape batter into prepared pan, smooth top, and gently tap pan on counter to release air bubbles. Sprinkle remaining 2 tablespoons sugar evenly over top. Bake until top is lightly golden and toothpick inserted in center comes out clean, 35 to 45 minutes, rotating pan halfway through baking. Let cake cool in pan for at least 30 minutes and up to 8 hours.

5. FOR THE WHIPPED CREAM: Using stand mixer fitted with whisk, whip cream, sugar, lemon zest, and lemon juice together on medium-low speed until foamy, about 1 minute. Increase speed to high and whip until soft peaks form, 1 to 3 minutes. (Whipped cream can be refrigerated for up to 8 hours; rewhisk briefly before serving.)

6. Run paring knife around edge of cake, remove sides of springform pan, and carefully slide cake onto platter. Serve warm or at room temperature with whipped cream.

Southern Fried Chicken Dinner

THE GAME PLAN

ONE DAY AHEAD...

MAKE BATTER-FRIED CHICKEN: 1½ hours (plus 30 minutes for brining)

MAKE COLESLAW: 20 minutes (plus 1½ hours for salting and chilling)

ON THE DAY OF...

MAKE PEACH SHORTCAKES: 45 minutes (plus 1 hour for baking and cooling)

MAKE BLT CANAPÉS: 50 minutes

MAKE SUCCOTASH: 45 minutes

SOUTHERN
FRIED CHICKEN DINNER

⇀ *Serves 8* ⇀

BLT Canapés with Basil Mayonnaise ⇝ Batter-Fried Chicken
Edamame Succotash with Jalapeños and Cilantro
Creamy Buttermilk Coleslaw ⇝ Peach Shortcakes

Batter-Fried Chicken

You will need at least a 6-quart Dutch oven for this recipe. If using kosher chicken, do not brine and instead season with salt in step 4 after patting the chicken dry. To ensure even cooking, breasts should be halved crosswise and leg quarters separated into thighs and drumsticks. This also allows each serving to include both white and dark meat.

½	cup sugar
	Salt and pepper
5	(10- to 12-ounce) bone-in split chicken breasts, trimmed (see page 113) and cut in half
5	(6-ounce) bone-in chicken thighs, trimmed
5	(6-ounce) bone-in chicken drumsticks
1	cup all-purpose flour
1	cup cornstarch
2	teaspoons baking powder
1	teaspoon paprika
½	teaspoon cayenne pepper
1¾	cups cold water
3	quarts peanut or vegetable oil

1. Dissolve sugar and ½ cup salt in 2 quarts cold water in large container. Submerge chicken in brine, cover, and refrigerate for 30 to 60 minutes.

2. Meanwhile, whisk flour, cornstarch, baking powder, paprika, cayenne, 5 teaspoons pepper, and 1 teaspoon salt together in large bowl. Whisk in water until smooth. Refrigerate until needed (but no longer than 1 hour).

3. Adjust oven rack to middle position and heat oven to 200 degrees. Heat oil in large Dutch oven over medium-high heat until it registers 350 degrees. Set wire rack in rimmed baking sheet.

4. Remove chicken from brine and pat dry with paper towels. Whisk batter to recombine. Add one-third of chicken to batter and coat thoroughly. Using tongs, remove chicken from batter 1 piece at a time, allowing excess batter to drip back into bowl, and add to hot oil.

5. Fry chicken, stirring occasionally and adjusting heat as necessary to maintain oil temperature between 300 and 325 degrees, until chicken is deep golden brown, breasts register 160 to 165 degrees, and thighs and drumsticks register 175 degrees, 12 to 15 minutes. Transfer chicken to prepared baking sheet and keep warm in oven.

6. Return oil to 350 degrees and repeat with remaining chicken and batter in 2 batches, transferring batches to oven to keep warm. Serve. (Fried chicken can be cooled slightly then refrigerated up to 24 hours; reheat on wire rack in 400-degree oven until crisp and hot, 10 to 15 minutes.)

✔ WHY THIS RECIPE WORKS

Perfectly fried chicken is an unbeatable crowd-pleaser, but most recipes disappoint with bland meat and soggy coating that fall far short of the ideal. The old-fashioned method of dipping chicken in a batter (not unlike pancake batter) before frying promises a delicate, crunchy coating and is easier than the typical messy flour-egg-flour preparation. To foolproof and modernize this unusual technique, we start by brining chicken pieces to ensure moist and seasoned meat. We found that using equal parts cornstarch and flour in the batter produced an ultra-crisp crust on the chicken while baking powder added lift and lightness without doughiness. Black pepper, paprika, and cayenne give the batter simple but unambiguous flavor. Best of all, this chicken can be re-crisped to its original glory in a hot oven even a full day after frying.

BLT Canapés with Basil Mayonnaise

Our preferred brand of bacon is Farmland Hickory Smoked Bacon.

WHY THIS RECIPE WORKS
The B also stands for "basil" in these elegant but playful bite-size appetizers: a bright, basil mayonnaise infused with a spritz of lemon and garlic elevates the much-loved but pedestrian sandwich to dinner party appetizer. We kept the prep easy, pureeing lots of fresh basil leaves with store-bought mayonnaise for the spread and cooking the bacon in the oven, which is less messy and more hands-off than in a skillet. The toast rounds are made by punching rounds from regular store-bought bread with a biscuit cutter and then toasting them in one batch in the oven. Even in summer, supermarket tomatoes can be unreliable, but cherry tomatoes are always sweet, and scaled perfectly for a pint-size appetizer.

2 cups fresh basil leaves, plus ¼ cup chopped fresh basil
⅔ cup mayonnaise
4 teaspoons lemon juice
2 garlic cloves, minced
Salt and pepper
11 slices hearty white sandwich bread
Vegetable oil spray
11 slices bacon
6 ounces cherry tomatoes, sliced ⅓ inch thick

1. Process 2 cups basil leaves, mayonnaise, lemon juice, garlic, and ¼ teaspoon salt in food processor until smooth, about 1 minute, scraping down bowl as needed. Transfer to bowl and season with salt to taste. (Mayonnaise can be refrigerated for up to 4 days.)

2. Adjust oven rack 6 inches from broiler element and heat broiler. Using 2-inch round biscuit cutter, cut rounds out of sliced bread, avoiding crust (about 3 rounds per slice); discard scraps or save for another use. Spray both sides of bread rounds with vegetable oil spray and lay on rimmed baking sheet. Broil until golden brown on both sides, about 5 minutes, flipping bread over halfway through broiling. Let cool. (Toasts can be held at room temperature for up to 6 hours.)

3. Adjust oven rack to middle position and heat oven to 400 degrees. Lay bacon in single layer on rimmed baking sheet. Roast until crisp and brown, 10 to 12 minutes, rotating baking sheet halfway through cooking. Transfer bacon to paper towel–lined plate and let cool. Break each bacon slice evenly into 3 short pieces.

4. Season tomatoes with salt and pepper. Spread ¾ teaspoon basil mayonnaise over top of each toast, then top with 1 piece bacon and 1 slice tomato. Sprinkle with chopped basil and serve. (Canapés can be held at room temperature for up to 2 hours. Makes 33 canapés.)

EVEN EASIER ⇝ Don't have time to make canapés? Consider making a simple dip using the same flavors. Mix 1¼ cups sour cream, ¾ cup mayonnaise, ½ cup chopped fresh basil, ⅓ cup finely chopped oil-packed sun-dried tomatoes, and 4 slices cooked, crumbled bacon together in a serving bowl. Season with salt and pepper to taste. Serve with potato chips or tortilla chips.

Edamame Succotash with Jalapeños and Cilantro

We far prefer the texture and flavor of fresh corn in this dish; don't substitute frozen corn. To make this dish spicier, add the reserved chile seeds.

WHY THIS RECIPE WORKS
For a modern twist on old-school succotash we substituted shelled edamame for the usual lima beans and punched up the flavors with bright jalapeños and cilantro. We found frozen edamame were fine in this dish, but bland frozen corn was no match for the sweetness and crunch of fresh corn.

8 ears corn, husks and silk removed
8 tablespoons unsalted butter
1 onion, chopped fine
2 red bell peppers, stemmed, seeded, and cut into ½-inch pieces
1 pound shelled frozen edamame, thawed (4 cups)

Salt and pepper
4 garlic cloves, minced
2 jalapeño chiles, stemmed, seeds reserved, and minced
Pinch cayenne pepper
½ cup minced fresh cilantro

1. Cut kernels from cobs into large bowl. Using back of butter knife, scrape pulp from cobs into same bowl.

2. Melt 3 tablespoons butter in 12-inch nonstick skillet over medium-high heat. Add onion, bell peppers, edamame, 1 teaspoon salt, and ¼ teaspoon pepper. Cook until vegetables are tender, 10 to 12 minutes. Stir in garlic, jalapeños, and cayenne and cook until fragrant, about 1 minute. Transfer vegetables to large bowl and cover to keep warm.

3. Melt remaining 5 tablespoons butter in now-empty skillet over medium-high heat. Stir in corn kernels and pulp and ¼ teaspoon salt. Cook until corn is tender, 6 to 8 minutes.

4. Transfer corn to bowl with edamame and stir in cilantro. Season with salt and pepper to taste and serve. (Succotash can be held at room temperature for up to 1 hour; microwave, covered, until hot, 3 to 5 minutes before serving.)

REMOVING CORN FROM THE COB

Standing the corn upright inside a large bowl, carefully cut the kernels from the cobs, using a paring knife. Before discarding the cobs, use the back of a butter knife to scrape out the remaining pulp.

Creamy Buttermilk Coleslaw

Salting the cabbage rids it of excess moisture and prevents a watery coleslaw.

1	head green cabbage (2 pounds), cored and sliced thin (12 cups) (see page 103)
2	carrots, peeled and shredded
	Salt and pepper
⅔	cup buttermilk
½	cup mayonnaise
¼	cup sour cream
8	scallions, minced
2	tablespoons sugar
1	teaspoon Dijon mustard

1. Toss shredded cabbage and carrots with 1 teaspoon salt and let drain in colander until wilted, about 1 hour. Rinse cabbage and carrots under cold water, drain, and dry well with paper towels. Transfer to large bowl. (Prepped cabbage can be refrigerated in zipper-lock bag for up to 24 hours.)

2. Whisk buttermilk, mayonnaise, sour cream, scallions, sugar, mustard, and ¼ teaspoon pepper together in bowl. Add buttermilk mixture to cabbage and toss to combine. Cover and refrigerate until chilled, at least 30 minutes and up to 1 day. Season with salt and pepper to taste before serving.

✔ WHY THIS RECIPE WORKS
A few tricks make this classic side dish foolproof. First, we salted the shredded cabbage to remove excess water before dressing it. After some experimentation, we found that adding a little mayonnaise and sour cream to the dressing served to thicken and add body. The addition of shredded carrots and chopped scallions keeps this dish bright and fresh despite the richness of the dairy.

Peach Shortcakes

✔ **WHY THIS RECIPE WORKS**

We love a good peach pie or peach crisp, but juicy, sweet peaches picked at the height of summer don't need all that sugar and spice. Enter the peach shortcake: Mounds of freshly whipped cream and a barely sweetened, tender biscuit make an ideal showcase for fragrant summer peaches. Most recipes for peach shortcake simply call for replacing the usual strawberries with peaches, but strawberries release more liquid than peaches during maceration (the step of tossing the fruit with sugar to draw out juices). The key to our peach filling, ironically, turned out to be a little cooking: We microwaved a few thinly sliced peaches with peach schnapps (which contributes a sweet, fruity background without being overly assertive) until completely tender, then mashed these cooked peaches to create a peach jam to be added to the rest of the (uncooked) peaches. This technique was so successful that should you find yourself with only mealy supermarket peaches, you'll still be able to turn out great peach shortcakes.

This recipe works well with any peaches, regardless of their ripeness. If your peaches are firm, you should be able to peel them with a sharp vegetable peeler. If they are too soft to withstand the pressure of a peeler, you'll need to blanch them in a pot of simmering water for 15 seconds and then shock them in a bowl of ice water before peeling. Orange juice or orange liqueur can be used in place of the peach schnapps. Note that this recipe yields 9 biscuits—they can be crumbly and hard to slice perfectly so it's handy to have an extra one.

BISCUITS

- 3 cups (15 ounces) all-purpose flour
- 3 tablespoons sugar
- 1 tablespoon baking powder
- 1 teaspoon salt
- 1 cup buttermilk, chilled
- 1 large egg
- 12 tablespoons unsalted butter, melted and hot

PEACHES AND CREAM

- 3 pounds peaches, peeled, pitted, and cut into ¼-inch-thick wedges
- 11 tablespoons sugar
- 3 tablespoons peach schnapps
- 1 cup heavy cream, chilled
- 1 teaspoon vanilla extract

1. FOR THE BISCUITS: Adjust oven rack to middle position and heat oven to 475 degrees. Line rimmed baking sheet with parchment paper. Whisk flour, 1½ tablespoons sugar, baking powder, and salt together in large bowl. In medium bowl, whisk chilled buttermilk and egg together, then whisk in hot melted butter and let form into small clumps.

2. Stir clumpy buttermilk mixture into flour mixture until dough comes together, then continue to stir dough vigorously for 30 seconds. Using greased ⅓ cup dry measure, portion dough into 9 mounds on prepared baking sheet, spaced 1½ inches apart. (If dough sticks to cup, use small spoon to pull it free). Sprinkle with remaining 1½ tablespoons sugar.

3. Bake biscuits until golden and crisp, about 15 minutes. Transfer biscuits to wire rack and let cool for 15 minutes. (Biscuits can be stored at room temperature for up to 24 hours; if desired, refresh in 300-degree oven for 10 minutes before serving.)

4. FOR THE PEACHES AND CREAM: Gently toss three-quarters of peaches with 6 tablespoons sugar in large bowl and let sit for 30 minutes. Toss remaining peaches with 3 tablespoons sugar and schnapps in medium bowl and microwave, stirring occasionally, until bubbling, 1 to 2 minutes. Using potato masher, crush hot peaches to coarse pulp, then let sit for 30 minutes. (Peaches can be held at room temperature for up to 4 hours.)

5. Using stand mixer fitted with whisk, whip cream, remaining 2 tablespoons sugar, and vanilla on medium-low speed until foamy, about 1 minute. Increase speed to high and whip until soft peaks form, 1 to 3 minutes. (Whipped cream can be refrigerated for up to 8 hours; rewhisk briefly before serving.)

6. To serve, split each biscuit in half and place bottoms on individual serving plates. Spoon some crushed peach mixture over each bottom, followed by peach slices with some of juice. Top with whipped cream, and cap with biscuit top.

Mexican Fiesta

THE GAME PLAN

≈

ONE DAY AHEAD...

MAKE ICE CREAM TORTE: 50 minutes
(plus 9 hours for chilling)

FRY TORTILLAS FOR TOSTADAS: 45 minutes

MAKE PORK FOR TOSTADAS: 3 hours

ON THE DAY OF...

MAKE JÍCAMA AND CABBAGE SLAW: 25 minutes
(plus 1½ hours for salting and chilling)

MAKE EMPANADAS: 50 minutes (plus 35 minutes
for baking and cooling)

REHEAT AND ASSEMBLE TOSTADAS: 15 minutes

FINISH ICE CREAM TORTE: 10 minutes

MEXICAN FIESTA

➤ Serves 8 ◄

Easy Mini Chicken Empanadas

Spicy Shredded Pork Tostadas ✎ Jícama and Red Cabbage Slaw

Mexican Ice Cream Torte

Spicy Shredded Pork Tostadas

Once trimmed, the pork should weigh about 3 pounds. We prefer the complex and smoky flavor of ground chipotle powder, but 1½ tablespoons minced canned chipotle chile can be substituted. This dish is spicy; use less chipotle powder to make it milder. Ready-made tostada shells can be substituted for the fried corn tortillas in step 5; our favorite brand of ready-made tostadas is Mission.

SHREDDED PORK

4	pounds boneless pork butt roast, pulled apart at seams, trimmed, and cut into 1-inch pieces
4	onions, 2 onions quartered and 2 onions chopped fine
7	garlic cloves, peeled, 4 cloves smashed and 3 cloves minced
6	sprigs fresh thyme
	Salt
9	cups water
2	tablespoons olive oil
1	teaspoon dried oregano
1½	tablespoons ground chipotle powder
2	(14.5-ounce) cans tomato sauce
2	bay leaves

TOSTADAS

24	(6-inch) corn tortillas
1¼	cups vegetable oil
	Salt

GARNISHES

Queso fresco or feta cheese
Fresh cilantro leaves
Sour cream
Diced avocado (see page 121)
Lime wedges

1. FOR THE SHREDDED PORK: Bring pork, quartered onions, smashed garlic, thyme, 1½ teaspoons salt, and water to simmer in large Dutch-oven over medium-high heat, skimming off any foam that rises to surface. Reduce heat to medium-low, partially cover, and cook until pork is tender, 1¼ to 1½ hours.

2. Reserve 2 cups cooking liquid, then drain pork, discarding onions, garlic, and thyme. Off heat, return pork to pot and, using potato masher, mash until shredded into rough ½-inch pieces.

3. Heat olive oil in 12-inch nonstick skillet over medium-high heat until shimmering. Add chopped onions and oregano and cook until onions are softened, 5 to 7 minutes. Add half of shredded pork and cook, stirring often, until pork is well browned and crisp, 7 to 10 minutes. Stir in minced garlic and chipotle powder and cook until fragrant, about 30 seconds.

4. Return browned pork mixture to pot with remaining pork. Stir in reserved cooking liquid, tomato sauce, and bay leaves. Bring to simmer and cook until nearly all liquid is evaporated, 15 to 20 minutes. Off heat, remove and discard bay *continued* ➤

leaves and season with salt to taste. (Pork can be refrigerated for up to 2 days; microwave, covered, until hot, 3 to 5 minutes before serving.)

5. FOR THE TOSTADAS: Line rimmed baking sheet with several layers of paper towels. Heat ¾ cup vegetable oil in 8-inch skillet over medium heat to 350 degrees. Meanwhile, poke center of each tortilla 3 or 4 times with fork (to prevent puffing during frying). Fry tortillas, 1 at a time while holding them flat with metal potato masher, until crisp and lightly browned, about 1 minute. Replenish oil in skillet as needed with remaining ½ cup oil. Transfer to prepared baking sheet and season with salt. (Tostadas can be stored at room temperature for up to 1 day.)

6. To serve, spoon small amount of hot shredded pork onto center of each tostada and top with cheese, cilantro, sour cream, and avocado. Serve with lime wedges.

Easy Mini Chicken Empanadas

✔ **WHY THIS RECIPE WORKS**
Authentic empanada recipes are a labor of love. Our pint-size appetizer versions streamline the process by starting with store-bought pie dough, and they can be assembled ahead of time and baked just before serving. The shredded chicken filling requires no cooking (save poaching the chicken, which can be done ahead of time); instead it's constructed with flavorful ingredients that don't need a lot of coaxing, like sharp cheddar cheese, lime juice, cilantro, chipotle, and chopped green olives. We used the food processor to make a vibrant salsa that comes together in minutes.

To make this sauce spicier, add the reserved chile seeds to the sauce. Our favorite brand of store-bought pie dough is Pillsbury Just Unroll! Pie Crusts; you will need 2 boxes of pie dough for this recipe.

SALSA
- 1 small onion, quartered
- 1 green bell pepper, stemmed, seeded, and quartered
- 1 jalapeño chile, stemmed, seeds reserved, and minced
- 2 tablespoons fresh cilantro leaves
- ½ teaspoon salt
- 2 tomatoes, cored and chopped coarse
- ⅓ cup white wine vinegar
- 3 tablespoons extra-virgin olive oil

EMPANADAS
- 1 cup cooked chicken, shredded fine (see page 67)
- ½ cup pitted green olives, chopped fine
- 4 ounces sharp cheddar cheese, shredded (1 cup)

- ¼ cup minced fresh cilantro
- 2 teaspoons lime juice
- 1 teaspoon minced canned chipotle chile in adobo sauce
  Salt and pepper
- 4 (9-inch) rounds pie dough

1. FOR THE SALSA: Pulse onion, bell pepper, jalapeño, cilantro, and salt in food processor until minced, about 10 pulses, scraping down sides of bowl as needed. Add tomatoes and pulse until coarsely chopped, about 2 pulses. Transfer to serving bowl and stir in vinegar and oil. Let sit at room temperature until flavors meld, about 30 minutes. (Sauce can be refrigerated for up to 2 days; bring to room temperature before serving.)

MAKING MINI EMPANADAS

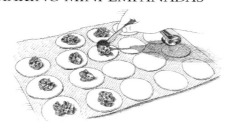 

Place about 2 teaspoons of the filling in the center of each dough round and moisten the edge of the dough round with water, using either your finger or a pastry brush. Fold the dough in half over the filling, making a half-moon shape. Pinch the seam along the edge to close. Using a dinner fork, crimp the sealed edge to secure.

2. FOR THE EMPANADAS: Combine chicken, olives, cheese, cilantro, lime juice, and chipotle in bowl. Season with salt and pepper to taste. Cover and refrigerate until needed and up to 2 days.

3. Line rimmed baking sheet with parchment paper. Using 3½-inch biscuit cutter, cut rounds out of pie crusts (6 rounds per crust); discard dough scraps.

4. Working with half of dough at a time, place 2 teaspoons chicken filling in center of each dough round. Moisten edge of dough with water, then fold dough over filling into half-moon shape. Pinch edges together to seal, then crimp with fork to secure. Arrange on prepared baking sheet, cover with plastic wrap, and refrigerate until baking time and up to 3 days.

5. Adjust oven rack to middle position and heat oven to 425 degrees. Bake empanadas until golden, 23 to 28 minutes, rotating baking sheet halfway through baking. Let cool for 5 minutes, then serve with salsa. (Makes 24 empanadas.)

Jícama and Red Cabbage Slaw

To make this dish spicier, add the reserved chile seeds to the dressing. To shred the carrots and jícama, use either the large holes of a box grater or the shredding disk of a food processor.

½	head red cabbage (1 pound), cored and sliced thin (6 cups)
2	carrots, peeled and shredded
	Salt and pepper
1	pound jícama, peeled and shredded
½	cup minced fresh cilantro
½	cup lime juice (4 limes)
¼	cup sugar
1	jalapeño chile, stemmed, seeds reserved, and minced
1	small garlic clove, minced
¼	teaspoon ground cumin
½	cup olive oil

1. Toss cabbage and carrots with 1 teaspoon salt and let drain in colander until wilted, about 1 hour. Rinse cabbage and carrots under cold water, drain, and dry well with paper towels. (Prepped cabbage can be refrigerated in a zipper-lock bag for up to 24 hours.)

2. In large bowl, combine cabbage-carrot mixture, jícama, and cilantro. In small bowl, whisk lime juice, sugar, jalapeño, garlic, cumin, and ¼ teaspoon salt together. Whisking constantly, drizzle in oil. Drizzle dressing over cabbage mixture and toss gently to coat. Cover and refrigerate until chilled, at least 30 minutes and up to 1 day. Season with salt and pepper to taste before serving.

✔ WHY THIS RECIPE WORKS

This tangy Latin take on coleslaw pairs red cabbage with jícama, a tuberous root vegetable with a crisp, crunchy texture and a taste that lies somewhere between an apple and a potato. As we'd learned in the past, salting the cabbage to rid it of excess moisture is key to preventing weepy, watery slaw. Lime juice, balanced by some sugar, and olive oil form the base of the bright and tart dressing. Jalapeño, minced cilantro, garlic, and cumin round out the flavor, and shredded carrot makes the salad pop.

SHREDDING CABBAGE

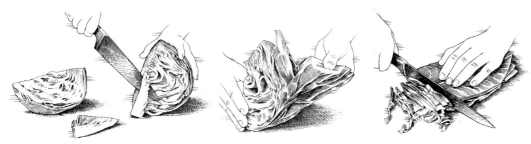

Cut the cabbage into quarters and cut away the hard piece of core attached to each quarter. Separate the cored cabbage into stacks of leaves that flatten when pressed lightly. Use a chef's knife to cut each stack diagonally (this ensures long pieces) into thin shreds. (Or roll the stacked leaves crosswise to fit them into the feed tube of a food processor fitted with the shredding disk.)

Mexican Ice Cream Torte

For clean and easy serving, dip the knife in hot water between slices when cutting up the cake. You may have a few leftover almonds after decorating the cake in step 5; having a few extra almonds makes decorating the sides of the cake a little easier.

25	Oreo cookies, broken into rough pieces
3	tablespoons unsalted butter, melted and cooled
I	pint chocolate ice cream
I	pint coffee ice cream
I	pint vanilla ice cream
I	teaspoon ground cinnamon
I ½	cups sliced almonds (5¼ ounces), toasted (see page 29)

1. Adjust oven rack to middle position and heat oven to 325 degrees. Process Oreos in food processor until finely and evenly ground, about 30 seconds. With processor running, add butter and continue to process until mixture resembles wet sand (you should have about 2 cups).

2. Transfer ⅔ cup crumbs to 9-inch springform pan, press firmly into even, compact layer with bottom of dry measuring cup. Use back of teaspoon to press and smooth edges. Bake until crust is fragrant and set, 5 to 10 minutes. Let crust cool to room temperature, about 30 minutes.

3. Scoop chocolate ice cream into large bowl, and mix with stiff rubber spatula or wooden spoon until softened and smooth. Spread ice cream evenly over crust. Sprinkle with ⅔ cup Oreo crumbs and pack lightly.

Cover with plastic wrap and freeze until ice cream is just firm, about 30 minutes. Repeat with coffee ice cream and remaining ⅔ cup Oreo crumbs; freeze for 30 minutes longer.

4. Scoop vanilla ice cream into large bowl, sprinkle with cinnamon, and mix until softened and smooth. Spread evenly into pan, smoothing top with offset spatula. Wrap pan tightly with plastic and freeze until firm, at least 8 hours and up to 1 week.

5. To serve, hold paring knife under hot tap water for 10 seconds to heat it, then run around edge of pan to loosen cake. Remove sides of springform pan. Slide thin metal spatula between crust and pan bottom to loosen, then slide cake onto serving platter. Press handfuls of almonds gently onto sides of cake, then sprinkle single layer of almonds evenly over top. Serve immediately.

EVEN EASIER ➻ Don't have time to make an ice cream torte? Combine ½ cup toasted chopped almonds, ¼ cup grated bittersweet chocolate, I tablespoon instant espresso powder, and I teaspoon cinnamon in a small bowl. Portion 4 quarts (½ gallon) vanilla ice cream into individual serving bowls, sprinkle with the almond mixture, and drizzle lightly with a coffee liquor (such as Tia Maria or Kahlúa). Serve with delicate chocolate cookies (such as Nabisco Famous Chocolate Wafers).

MAKING A CRUMB CRUST

 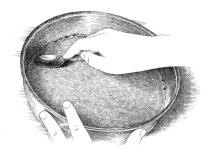

Use the bottom of a ramekin, I-cup measuring cup, or drinking glass to press the crumbs into the bottom of a springform pan. Press the crumbs as far as possible into the edge of the pan. Use a teaspoon to neatly press the crumbs into the edge of the pan to create a clean edge.

Mediterranean Flank Steak Supper

THE GAME PLAN

ONE DAY AHEAD...

MAKE TOMATO JAM: 1 hour

MAKE SALSA VERDE: 15 minutes

MAKE ORZO: 20 minutes

ON THE DAY OF...

MAKE FREE-FORM TARTS: 1 hour (plus 3 hours for chilling and baking)

GRILL FLANK STEAK AND VEGETABLES: 1 hour (plus 30 minutes for heating grill)

MEDITERRANEAN FLANK STEAK SUPPER

Serves 8

Farmer's Cheese with Homemade Tomato Jam

Grilled Flank Steak with Grilled Vegetables and Salsa Verde

Orzo with Lemon, Basil, and Feta ❧ Free-Form Nectarine-Raspberry Tarts

Grilled Flank Steak with Grilled Vegetables and Salsa Verde

You will need four 14-inch metal skewers for this recipe. When cooking the vegetables in step 4, be ready to pull them off the grill in stages as they finish cooking. When cutting the grilled vegetables for serving in step 5, we found they look nicest when cut into rustic 2- to 3-inch pieces.

2	large red onions, sliced into ½-inch-thick rings
12	ounces cherry tomatoes
3	zucchini, sliced lengthwise into ¾-inch-thick planks
2	pounds eggplant, sliced lengthwise into ¾-inch-thick planks
½	cup olive oil
	Salt and pepper
4½	pounds flank steak, trimmed
1	recipe Salsa Verde (page 108)

1. Thread onion rounds from side to side onto 2 metal skewers. Thread cherry tomatoes onto 2 more skewers. Brush onions, tomatoes, zucchini, and eggplant evenly with oil and season with salt and pepper. Pat steak dry with paper towels and season with salt and pepper.

2A. FOR A CHARCOAL GRILL: Open bottom grill vent completely. Light large chimney starter filled with charcoal briquettes (6 quarts). When top coals are partially covered with ash, pour evenly over grill. Set cooking grate in place, cover, and open lid vent completely. Heat grill until hot, about 5 minutes.

2B. FOR A GAS GRILL: Turn all burners to high, cover, and heat grill until hot, about 15 minutes. Leave all burners on high.

3. Clean and oil cooking grate. Place steak and onion skewers on grill. Cook (covered if using gas), flipping as needed, until steak is well browned on both sides and registers 120 to 125 degrees *continued* ➤

SLICING FLANK STEAK ON THE BIAS

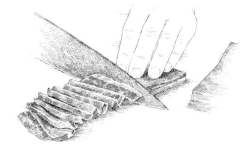

Once the steak has rested, slice the meat across the grain into thin pieces.

(for medium-rare) and onions are spottily charred and tender, 7 to 12 minutes. Transfer steak to carving board, tent loosely with aluminum foil, and let rest for 5 to 10 minutes. Transfer onions to large bowl and cover to keep warm.

4. Place tomatoes skewers, zucchini, and eggplant on grill and cook (covered if using gas) until vegetables are tender and well browned, 10 to 15 minutes, turning as needed.

Transfer vegetables to bowl with onions.

5. Cut onions, zucchini, and eggplant into attractive, 2- to 3-inch pieces and remove cherry tomatoes from skewers. Arrange vegetables on serving platter and season with salt and pepper to taste. Slice steak on bias, against grain, and arrange on separate platter. Drizzle steak with some of salsa verde. Serve, passing remaining salsa verde separately.

Salsa Verde

✓ **WHY THIS RECIPE WORKS** Though made from simple ingredients like parsley, olive oil, garlic, and vinegar, brilliant green salsa verde brings a bracing piquancy to grilled dishes. Our version of this all-purpose Italian green sauce swaps out vinegar for less-harsh lemon juice, which accents the fresh, clean flavor of the parsley and ensures a balanced but bold-flavored sauce. For a thick, uniform texture (and an easy method), we used the food processor to puree chunks of bread with lemon juice and oil. Once we had a smooth base, we rounded out the sauce with parsley, capers, garlic, and anchovies for a touch of complexity (but not fishiness).

Two slices of sandwich bread pureed into the sauce keeps the flavors balanced and gives the sauce body. Toasting the bread rids it of excess moisture that might otherwise make for a gummy sauce.

2	slices hearty white sandwich bread
1	cup extra-virgin olive oil
¼	cup lemon juice (2 lemons)
4	cups fresh parsley leaves
4	anchovy fillets, rinsed
¼	cup capers, rinsed
2	garlic cloves, minced
¼	teaspoon salt

1. Toast bread in toaster at lowest setting until surface is dry but not browned, about 15 seconds. Remove crust and cut bread into rough ½-inch pieces.

2. Process bread pieces, oil, and lemon juice in food processor until smooth, about 10 seconds. Add parsley, anchovies, capers, garlic, and salt and pulse until mixture is finely chopped (mixture should not be smooth), about 5 pulses, scraping down bowl as needed. Transfer mixture to bowl and serve. (Sauce can be refrigerated for up to 2 days; bring to room temperature before serving.)

Farmer's Cheese with Homemade Tomato Jam

If you can't find farmer's cheese, goat cheese works well, too. Fish sauce can be found in most supermarkets in the international foods aisle alongside other Thai and Vietnamese ingredients. If you want the jam to be spicier, add the reserved chile seeds. Serve with Garlic Toasts (page 62), thinly sliced baguette, or crackers.

2	pounds plum tomatoes, cored and chopped
1¼	cups sugar
¾	cup red wine vinegar
¼	cup fish sauce
6	garlic cloves, minced
1	large jalapeño chile, stemmed, seeds reserved, and minced
1	tablespoon grated fresh ginger
2	star anise pods
8	ounces farmer's cheese

1. Combine all ingredients except cheese in 12-inch skillet and bring to boil. Reduce to simmer and cook until mixture begins to thicken, 25 to 30 minutes. Remove and discard star anise. Mash mixture with potato masher until relatively smooth, then continue to simmer until spatula leaves trail through jam, 5 to 10 minutes longer.

2. Transfer jam to bowl and let cool to room temperature. (Jam can be refrigerated for up to 7 days; bring to room temperature before serving.) Transfer jam to serving bowl with spoon or spreader, and serve alongside farmer's cheese. (Makes 2 cups.)

✔ WHY THIS RECIPE WORKS

Make this spicy and fragrant jam once and it will become your favorite condiment. After a little experimenting, we discovered a few additions that boosted this jam from good to eye-widening: grated ginger and star anise added spice and aromatic complexity. But it was an unlikely ingredient—fish sauce, which is high in glutamates (the amino acids responsible for "meaty" flavor)—that made the jam explode with savory depth (without tasting fishy).

Orzo with Lemon, Basil, and Feta

Rinsing the pasta under cold water will halt the cooking process and keep the orzo from sticking together.

1	pound orzo
	Salt and pepper
3	tablespoons extra-virgin olive oil
2	teaspoons grated lemon zest plus 2 tablespoons juice
2	garlic cloves, minced
8	ounces feta cheese, crumbled (2 cups)
½	cup chopped fresh basil

Bring 4 quarts water to boil in large pot. Add orzo and 1 tablespoon salt and cook, stirring often, until tender. Drain orzo and rinse under cold water. Transfer orzo to large bowl and toss with oil, lemon zest and juice, and garlic. Fold in feta and season with salt and pepper to taste. (Orzo can be refrigerated for up to 2 days; bring to room temperature before serving.) Fold in basil and serve.

✔ WHY THIS RECIPE WORKS

To produce separate, distinct pieces of orzo, we cooked the orzo in abundant boiling water then rinsed it in cold water to prevent sticking. So that it would play well with the steak, vegetables, and a bracing salsa verde, we kept the flavor bright but uncomplicated with lemon, garlic, feta cheese, and plenty of chopped basil.

Free-Form Nectarine-Raspberry Tarts

WHY THIS RECIPE WORKS Few things are better than a summer fruit pie, but that takes time and skill. A free-form tart—a single layer of buttery pie dough folded up around fresh fruit—is an easier alternative that produces both crust and fruit with half the work of a regular pie. For the tart dough, we use a high proportion of butter to flour, which provides the most buttery flavor and tender texture without compromising the structure. Shaping the dough into two 9-inch tarts yields plenty for company and is easier to work with than one huge tart or eight individual tarts. The filling is a combination of slightly tart raspberries and sweet nectarines tossed with sugar, lemon juice, and cinnamon, plus cornstarch to absorb the fruits' exuded juices that would otherwise leak and cause the crust to be soggy. We brushed the tarts with egg wash before baking for an attractive sheen.

To ensure a flaky crust, keep the tart dough chilled until just before you are ready to use it; you will need to let it soften at room temperature briefly before rolling it out. Serve with vanilla ice cream or whipped cream.

DOUGH
- 3 cups (15 ounces) all-purpose flour
- 1 teaspoon salt
- 20 tablespoons unsalted butter (2½ sticks), cut into ¼-inch pieces and chilled
- ½–¾ cups ice water

FRUIT FILLING
- 2 pounds nectarines, pitted and cut into ½-inch-thick wedges
- 10 ounces raspberries (2 cups)
- 1 cup plus 1 tablespoon sugar
- 2 tablespoons lemon juice
- 4 teaspoons cornstarch
- ¼ teaspoon ground cinnamon

- 1 egg, lightly beaten
- 1 tablespoon sugar

1. FOR THE DOUGH: Process flour and salt together in food processor until combined, about 2 seconds. Scatter butter pieces over top and pulse until mixture resembles coarse cornmeal, about 15 pulses. Transfer to large bowl and, using rubber spatula, mix in water, 1 tablespoon at a time, until dough comes together and forms a ball.

2. Divide dough into 2 even pieces and shape each into 6-inch disk. Wrap disks tightly in plastic wrap and refrigerate for at least 1 hour and up to 2 days.

3. Let chilled dough soften slightly at room temperature, about 10 minutes. Working with 1 piece of dough at a time, roll out to 12-inch circle between 2 large sheets of floured parchment paper. Slide dough, still between parchment, onto separate rimmed baking sheets. Refrigerate until firm, about 20 minutes.

4. FOR THE FRUIT FILLING: Adjust oven racks to upper-middle and lower-middle positions and heat oven to 375 degrees. Toss all ingredients together in bowl.

5. Working with 1 piece of dough at a time, remove top sheet of parchment. Mound half of fruit in center of dough, leaving 3-inch border of dough around edge. Fold edge of dough up over filling, using underlying parchment to help lift and pleat dough. Brush dough with beaten egg and sprinkle with sugar.

6. Bake tarts until crust is golden and fruit is tender, about 1 hour, switching and rotating baking sheets halfway through baking.

7. Let tarts cool slightly on baking sheets for 10 minutes, then use parchment paper to gently transfer tarts to wire racks. Use metal spatula to loosen tarts from parchment and remove. Let tarts cool on rack until juices have thickened, at least 25 minutes and up to 6 hours. Serve warm or at room temperature.

EVEN EASIER ⇻ Don't have time to make free-form tarts? Melt 1 tablespoon unsalted butter in medium saucepan over medium heat. Stir in ¾ teaspoon ground cardamom and cook until fragrant, about 30 seconds. Stir in 1 cup peach preserves and let melt. Stir in 2 pounds frozen peaches and cook, stirring often, until hot and fragrant, about 15 minutes. Off heat, stir in 2 tablespoons lemon juice and let mixture cool slightly. Portion 4 quarts (½ gallon) vanilla ice cream into individual serving bowls, top with peach mixture, and sprinkle with 2 cups fresh raspberries. Serve with delicate gingersnap cookies (such as Anna's Ginger Thins).

MAKING A FREE-FORM TART

Place half the fruit in the center of one piece of dough, leaving a 3-inch border around the fruit. Fold the dough border up over the filling, using the underlying parchment to lift and pleat the dough to fit snugly.

Easy Grilled Chicken Dinner

THE GAME PLAN
❧

ONE DAY AHEAD...

MAKE EGGPLANT CAVIAR: 35 minutes
(plus 2½ hours for draining, roasting, and chilling)

MAKE GREEN BEAN AND POTATO SALAD:
1¼ hours (plus 30 minutes for cooling)

ON THE DAY OF...

MAKE PISTACHIO-RASPBERRY BUCKLES: 25 minutes
(plus 40 minutes for baking and cooling)

MAKE FLATBREADS: 25 minutes
(plus 15 minutes for baking)

GRILL CHICKEN BREASTS: 1½ hours
(plus 1 hour for marinating and heating grill)

EASY GRILLED CHICKEN DINNER

⇀ Serves 8 ↽

Eggplant Caviar ⇌ Easy Garlic Flatbreads ⇌ Grilled Lemon Chicken Breasts

Green Bean and Potato Salad with Cilantro Dressing

Pistachio-Raspberry Buckles

Grilled Lemon Chicken Breasts

You may not need to squeeze all the grilled lemons in step 5 to obtain ⅓ cup of lemon juice. Cut any unsqueezed lemons into wedges for serving.

- 2 teaspoons grated lemon zest, plus 5 lemons, halved
  Salt and pepper
- 8 (10-ounce) bone-in split chicken breasts, trimmed
- 1 (13 by 9-inch) disposable aluminum roasting pan (if using charcoal)
- 2 tablespoons minced fresh parsley
- 2 teaspoons Dijon mustard
- 1 garlic clove, minced to paste (see page 256)
- 1 teaspoon sugar
- ⅔ cup extra-virgin olive oil

1. Combine lemon zest, 2 teaspoons salt, and 1 teaspoon pepper in bowl. Using your fingers, gently loosen center portion of skin covering each chicken breast, and rub zest mixture evenly underneath skin. Transfer chicken to wire rack set in rimmed baking sheet and let sit for 30 minutes. (Chicken can be covered and refrigerated for up to 24 hours.) Before grilling, pat chicken dry with paper towels and season with salt and pepper.

2A. FOR A CHARCOAL GRILL: Open bottom grill vent halfway and place roasting pan in center of grill. Light large chimney starter filled with charcoal briquettes (6 quarts). When top coals are partially covered with ash, pour into 2 even piles on either side of roasting pan. Set cooking grate in place, cover, and open lid vent halfway. Heat grill until hot, about 5 minutes.

2B. FOR A GAS GRILL: Turn all burners to high, cover, and heat grill until hot, about 15 minutes. Turn all burners to medium-low. (Adjust burners as needed to maintain grill temperature around 350 degrees.)

3. Clean and oil cooking grate. Place lemon halves, cut side down, on grill (over coals if using charcoal). *continued* ➤

TRIMMING SPLIT CHICKEN BREASTS

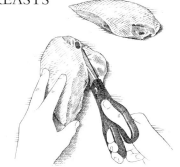

Split chicken breasts often contain a rib section along one side that should be trimmed away with kitchen shears. There is no meat in the section, and trimming it away makes the chicken smaller and easier to maneuver.

♥ WHY THIS RECIPE WORKS

For this recipe we wanted moist, perfectly grilled chicken with lemon flavor straight to the bone. We started with bone-in breasts and cooked them over an aluminum pan in the center of the grill (with coals piled on either side). The pan catches the slowly rendering fat, preventing it from dripping on the coals and starting fires that char the chicken's exterior and dry out the interior. A final sear directly over the dying coals at the end of cooking crisps and browns the skin nicely, without risk of flare-ups. To get lemon flavor that penetrates the surface, we rubbed lemon zest, salt, and pepper under the skin directly on the meat before cooking. For an additional dose of lemon flavor, we caramelized lemon halves over the grill—which concentrated their flavor and tempered their acidity—and then we made a bright sauce from their juice.

Place chicken breasts, skin side down, on grill (over roasting pan if using charcoal). Cover and cook until lemons are deep brown, about 5 minutes; transfer to bowl. Continue to cook chicken, covered, until skin is crisp and golden and chicken registers 150 degrees, 15 to 25 minutes longer.

4. Turn all burners to medium-high if using gas, or slide chicken over coals if using charcoal. Continue to cook (covered if using gas), turning as needed, until chicken is well browned on both sides and registers 160 degrees, 5 to 15 minutes.

5. Transfer chicken to platter, tent loosely with aluminum foil, and let rest for 5 to 10 minutes. Meanwhile, squeeze ⅓ cup juice from grilled lemons into bowl. Stir in parsley, mustard, garlic, sugar, ½ teaspoon salt, and ½ teaspoon pepper. Whisking constantly, drizzle in olive oil. Drizzle chicken with some of vinaigrette, and serve, passing remaining vinaigrette separately.

Eggplant Caviar

✔ **WHY THIS RECIPE WORKS**
Also known as "poor man's caviar," this Russian spread gets its name from the eggplant seeds that make it resemble actual caviar. We wanted smooth and silky eggplant caviar, with balanced acidity and the subtle earthy flavor of eggplant at the fore. We tried roasting, broiling, and sautéing both diced and whole eggplants. In the end, after much experimenting, we concluded that halving the eggplants lengthwise, scoring the cut sides of the flesh, and roasting them cut side down on a baking sheet not only allowed the eggplant to caramelize lightly, which contributed to the flavor, but also released moisture, thereby concentrating flavor.

Make sure you cook the onions until completely softened; otherwise they will give the caviar an unpleasant crunchy texture and raw onion taste. Serve with Easy Garlic Flatbreads (page 115).

2 pounds eggplant, halved lengthwise, flesh scored about 1 inch deep
½ cup extra-virgin olive oil
Salt and pepper
1 small onion, chopped fine
4 garlic cloves, minced
2 teaspoons tomato paste
2 tablespoons lemon juice
1 tablespoon minced fresh dill

1. Adjust oven rack to middle position and heat oven to 400 degrees. Line rimmed baking sheet with aluminum foil. Drizzle cut sides of eggplant with ¼ cup oil and season with salt and pepper.

2. Lay eggplant, cut side down, on prepared baking sheet and roast until eggplant is very soft, skin is shriveled and shrunken, and knife piercing flesh meets no resistance, about 1 hour. Let eggplant cool, about 5 minutes.

3. Set small colander over bowl. Scoop hot eggplant pulp out of skins into colander; discard skins. Scrape up any eggplant that has stuck to foil and add to colander. Let pulp drain for 30 minutes. Transfer eggplant pulp to cutting board and chop coarse; transfer to bowl.

4. Meanwhile, heat 2 tablespoons oil in 10-inch nonstick skillet over medium heat until shimmering. Add onion and

SCORING EGGPLANT

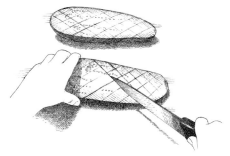

Using the tip of a chef's knife, score the cut side of each eggplant half in a 1-inch diamond pattern, about 1 inch deep.

cook until softened, 5 to 7 minutes. Stir in garlic and cook until fragrant, about 30 seconds. Stir in tomato paste and cook until mixture deepens slightly in color, about 3 minutes. Stir in chopped eggplant and cook until warmed through, about 2 minutes longer.

5. Transfer eggplant mixture to serving bowl. Stir in remaining 2 tablespoons oil, lemon juice, and dill. Season with salt and pepper to taste. Cover and refrigerate until chilled, at least 1 hour and up to 2 days. (Makes 2 cups.)

EVEN EASIER ↢ Don't have time to make Eggplant Caviar? Mix 16 ounces store-bought baba ghanoush (or roasted eggplant hummus) with ¼ cup extra-virgin olive oil, 2 tablespoons minced fresh dill, 2 minced scallions, 1 teaspoon lemon juice, and ½ teaspoon smoked paprika in serving bowl. Serve with pita chips or crackers.

Easy Garlic Flatbreads

You can use homemade pizza dough, store-bought pizza dough, or pizza dough bought from your favorite local pizzeria.

⅔ cup plus 2 tablespoons extra-virgin olive oil
6 garlic cloves, minced
Pinch red pepper flakes (optional)
Salt and pepper
2 pounds pizza dough

1. Adjust oven racks to upper-middle and lower-middle positions, place rimmed baking sheet on each rack, and heat oven to 500 degrees. Meanwhile, cook ⅔ cup oil, garlic, and pepper flakes, if using, in small saucepan over medium heat, stirring occasionally, until garlic begins to sizzle, 2 to 3 minutes; transfer to small bowl.

2. Divide dough into 2 even pieces. Working with 1 piece of dough a time, lay on lightly floured counter and stretch, roll, and shape dough into 16 by 12-inch rectangle.

3. Remove hot baking sheets from oven and brush with remaining 2 tablespoons oil. Carefully lay dough onto hot baking sheets, brush with garlic oil mixture, and season with salt and pepper. Bake until golden brown, 10 to 12 minutes, switching and rotating baking sheets halfway through baking. Let flatbreads cool slightly, then cut each into 16 pieces. Serve warm or at room temperature.

TO MAKE YOUR OWN PIZZA DOUGH

Pulse 4 cups bread flour, 2¼ teaspoons instant or rapid-rise yeast, and 1½ teaspoons salt together in food processor to combine. With processor running, pour in 2 tablespoons olive oil, then 1½ cups warm water (about 110 degrees) and process until rough ball forms, 20 to 30 seconds. Let dough rest for 2 minutes, then process for 30 seconds longer. Turn dough onto lightly floured counter and knead into smooth, round ball, about 5 minutes. Place in lightly greased bowl, cover with greased plastic wrap, and let rise in warm place until doubled in size, 1 to 1½ hours. (Risen dough can be frozen for up to 1 month; thaw on counter before using. Makes 2 pounds.)

❤ **WHY THIS RECIPE WORKS**
Our easy version employs the convenience of store-bought pizza dough flavored generously with olive oil infused with plenty of garlic and a pinch of red pepper flakes. To replicate the roaring hot brick ovens typically used to cook flatbreads, we preheated large rimmed baking sheets in a 500-degree oven. Working quickly, we brushed the hot baking sheets with some olive oil, added the dough, then coated the top with plenty more oil before returning the sheets to the oven. This method ensured that the bread would be well seasoned top to bottom, with a crisp crust and chewy interior.

Green Bean and Potato Salad with Cilantro Dressing

✔ **WHY THIS RECIPE WORKS**
We wanted to develop a recipe for bright green crisp-tender green beans and tender potatoes coated with a cilantro dressing that balanced herbal flavor with richness from olive oil and nuts. A generous amount of cilantro (stems and leaves) was necessary to make the amount of sauce we needed, and a food processor made quick work of it. We enriched the dressing with walnuts, which we toasted to enhance their flavor. The potatoes and green beans required separate treatment—we sliced and boiled the potatoes, then brushed them with some of the sauce while still hot so they could absorb maximum flavor. The green beans were blanched in boiling salted water until crisp-tender then shocked in ice water to halt the cooking.

We prefer the mild flavor of regular olive oil in this sauce compared to the stronger flavor of extra-virgin olive oil. Don't worry about patting the beans dry with towels before tossing them with the sauce; any water that clings to the beans helps to thin out the dressing.

½ cup walnuts
4 garlic cloves, unpeeled
5 cups fresh cilantro leaves and stems, trimmed (4 bunches)
¾ cup olive oil
¼ cup water
2 tablespoons lemon juice
2 scallions, sliced thin
    Salt and pepper
2 pounds red potatoes, sliced ½ inch thick
2 pounds green beans, trimmed and cut into 2-inch lengths

1. Toast walnuts in small heavy skillet over medium heat, stirring frequently, until just golden and fragrant, about 5 minutes; transfer to bowl. Add garlic to now-empty skillet and toast over medium heat, shaking pan occasionally, until fragrant and color deepens slightly, about 7 minutes. Let garlic cool slightly, then peel and chop.

2. Process toasted walnuts, garlic, cilantro, oil, water, lemon juice, scallions, ½ teaspoon salt, and ⅛ teaspoon pepper in food processor until smooth, stopping to scrape down sides of bowl as needed, about 1 minute.

Transfer to bowl and season with salt and pepper to taste. (Sauce can be refrigerated for up to 2 days.)

3. Place potatoes and 1 tablespoon salt in large saucepan, and add cold water to cover by 1 inch. Bring to boil. Reduce to gentle simmer and cook until potatoes are tender but not falling apart, about 10 minutes. Drain potatoes and spread evenly over rimmed baking sheet. Drizzle ½ cilantro sauce over potatoes and let cool to room temperature, about 30 minutes.

4. Meanwhile, bring 4 quarts water to boil in large Dutch oven over high heat. Fill large bowl with ice water. Add 1 tablespoon salt and green beans to boiling water and cook until crisp-tender, about 5 minutes. Transfer beans to ice water using large slotted spoon, and let sit until chilled, about 2 minutes.

5. Drain beans well, discarding any ice. Toss beans with remaining cilantro sauce in large bowl. Gently fold in potatoes, season with salt and pepper to taste, and serve. (Salad can be refrigerated for up to 1 day; bring to room temperature before serving.)

Pistachio-Raspberry Buckles

Do not substitute frozen berries here. The buckles can be served in their ramekins or you can run a paring knife around the edges of the ramekins and flip the buckles out onto individual plates (flip them right side up again before serving). Serve with vanilla ice cream or whipped cream.

1	cup (7 ounces) sugar
¾	cup pistachios, toasted (see page 29) and chopped coarse
5	tablespoons unsalted butter, softened
¼	teaspoon salt
½	cup heavy cream
3	large eggs
1½	teaspoons vanilla extract
1	cup (5 ounces) all-purpose flour
¾	teaspoon baking powder
20	ounces raspberries (4 cups)

1. Adjust oven rack to middle position and heat oven to 375 degrees. Grease eight 6-ounce ramekins and place on rimmed baking sheet.

2. Process sugar, ½ cup pistachios, butter, and salt together in food processor until finely ground, 10 to 15 seconds. With processor running, add cream, eggs, and vanilla and continue to process until smooth, about 5 seconds.

3. Add flour and baking powder and pulse until just incorporated, about 5 pulses. Transfer batter to large bowl and gently fold in raspberries. Spoon batter into prepared ramekins and sprinkle with remaining ¼ cup pistachios. (Buckles can be wrapped tightly in plastic wrap and refrigerated for up to 1 day.)

4. Bake until buckles are golden and begin to pull away from sides of ramekins, 25 to 30 minutes, rotating baking sheet halfway through baking. Let cool on wire rack for 10 minutes before serving. Serve warm or at room temperature. (Buckles can be held at room temperature for up to 6 hours; if desired, microwave until warm, 1 to 2 minutes before serving.)

✔ WHY THIS RECIPE WORKS
We gave this homey dessert a modern spin by baking it in individual ramekins and infusing the batter with ground pistachios. And it can be made in a food processor which makes it a snap to make. After spooning the batter into greased ramekins, we sprinkled the cakes with more chopped pistachios for crunch.

Fajitas and 'Ritas

THE GAME PLAN
>⤜

ONE DAY AHEAD...

MAKE KEY LIME PIE: 30 minutes
(plus 4¾ hours for baking and cooling)

MAKE MARGARITAS: 15 minutes
(plus 4 hours for chilling)

ON THE DAY OF...

MAKE SALSA: 15 minutes (plus 30 minutes for draining)

MAKE GUACAMOLE: 15 minutes

MAKE CHICKEN FAJITAS: 1¼ hours (plus 45 minutes
for marinating and heating grill)

MAKE CORN: 30 minutes

FAJITAS AND 'RITAS

⇝ *Serves 8* ⇜

Margaritas ⇝ Fresh Tomato Salsa and Guacamole

Grilled Chicken Fajitas ⇝ Easy Boiled Corn with Lime Butter

Key Lime Pie

Grilled Chicken Fajitas

You will need three 14-inch metal skewers for this recipe. This dish is fairly mild; to make it spicier, add the reserved chile seeds to the marinade in step 2. Serve with diced avocado, salsa, sour cream, shredded cheddar or Monterey Jack cheese, and lime wedges.

2	pounds red onions, sliced into ½-inch-thick rings
6	red, yellow, and/or green bell peppers, stemmed, seeded, and quartered
1	cup vegetable oil
	Salt and pepper
1	cup lime juice (8 limes)
3	jalapeño chiles, stemmed, seeds reserved, and minced
⅓	cup minced fresh cilantro
9	garlic cloves, minced
3	tablespoons Worcestershire sauce
1 ½	tablespoons brown sugar
4	pounds boneless, skinless chicken breasts, trimmed and pounded ½ inch thick
24	(6-inch) flour tortillas

1. Thread onion rounds, from side to side, onto 3 metal skewers. Brush onions and peppers with ¼ cup oil and season with salt and pepper.

2. In large bowl, whisk lime juice, jalapeños, cilantro, garlic, Worcestershire, brown sugar, 1 tablespoon salt, and 2¼ teaspoons pepper together. Whisking constantly, drizzle in remaining ¾ cup oil. Measure out and reserve ¾ cup marinade for serving. Whisk 1 tablespoon more salt into

remaining marinade and add chicken; cover and refrigerate for 15 minutes.

3A. FOR A CHARCOAL GRILL: Open bottom grill vent completely. Light large chimney starter mounded with charcoal briquettes (7 quarts). When top coals are partially covered with ash, pour evenly over grill. Set cooking grate in place, cover, and open lid vent completely. Heat grill until hot, about 5 minutes. *continued* ➤

POUNDING CHICKEN BREASTS

To ensure that boneless chicken breasts are of even thickness, and therefore will cook at the same rate, you may need to pound them. Place the breasts, smooth side down, on a large sheet of plastic wrap. Cover with a second sheet of plastic wrap and pound gently to make sure that each breast has the same thickness from end to end.

✔ **WHY THIS RECIPE WORKS**

With smoky meat and vegetables wrapped up in warm flour tortillas, fajitas are an ideal off-the-grill meal. But to avoid dry, stringy chicken and limp, flavorless vegetables that desperately need a truckload of toppings, we realized that each component needs special handling. Briefly marinating the chicken in a high-acid mixture created a bright, unadulterated tang. A mounded chimney of coals gave us the very hot fire we needed to aggressively sear the chicken and quickly cook it through. While the cooked chicken was resting, skewered red onions (preferred for their sweeter flavor) and bell peppers (a combination of red, yellow, and green was the most attractive) went on the grill. We finished the chicken and vegetables with a final burst of fresh flavor by tossing them in just a small amount of reserved marinade.

3B. FOR A GAS GRILL: Turn all burners to high, cover, and heat grill until hot, about 15 minutes. Leave all burners on high.

4. Clean and oil cooking grate. Using tongs, remove chicken from marinade and lay, smooth side down, on grill; discard used marinade. Cook (covered if using gas) until chicken is well browned on first side, 4 to 6 minutes. Flip chicken and continue to cook until it registers 160 degrees, 4 to 6 minutes longer. Transfer to cutting board, tent loosely with aluminum foil, and let rest while grilling vegetables and tortillas.

5. If using gas, turn all burners to medium. Place peppers, skin side down, and onion skewers on grill. Cook until spottily charred on both sides, 8 to 12 minutes, flipping as needed. Transfer to cutting board with chicken.

6. Working in batches, place tortillas in single layer on grill and cook until warm and lightly browned, about 20 seconds per side (do not grill too long or tortillas will become brittle). As tortillas come off grill, wrap in large sheet of foil or dish towel to keep warm and pliable.

7. Remove onions from skewer, separate into rings, and place in large bowl. Slice peppers lengthwise into ¼-inch strips and place in same bowl. Add ¼ cup reserved marinade to vegetables and toss well to combine; arrange on platter. Slice chicken into ¼-inch strips and toss with ½ cup reserved marinade; arrange on platter. Serve with warmed tortillas.

Fresh Tomato Salsa

To make this dish spicier, add the reserved chile seeds. The amount of sugar and lime juice you'll need depends on the ripeness of the tomatoes. Serve with Guacamole (page 121) and tortilla chips. Use the leftover salsa to serve with the fajitas.

✔ **WHY THIS RECIPE WORKS**
While sweet, ripe tomatoes make the best salsa, our recipe works with any tomato, even bland supermarket specimens. To get rid of excess liquid, we drained the tomatoes for 30 minutes in a colander (salting broke down the tomatoes too much). A little sugar helped bring out the sweetness of the tomatoes; because ripeness varies, we found it best to add the sugar (as well as lime juice) to taste.

1 ½ pounds tomatoes, cored and cut into ½-inch dice
1 large jalapeño chile, stemmed, seeds reserved, and minced
½ cup finely chopped red onion
1 small garlic clove, minced
¼ cup minced fresh cilantro
   Salt and pepper
2 teaspoons lime juice, plus extra as needed
   Sugar

Let tomatoes drain in colander for 30 minutes. As tomatoes drain, layer jalapeño, onion, garlic, and cilantro on top. Shake colander to drain off and discard excess tomato juice, then transfer vegetables to serving bowl. (Salsa can be refrigerated for up to 3 hours.) Before serving, stir in ½ teaspoon salt, pinch pepper, and lime juice. Season with salt, pepper, sugar, and extra lime juice to taste. (Makes 3 cups.)

Guacamole

Very ripe Hass avocados are key to this recipe. Serve with Fresh Tomato Salsa (page 120) and tortilla chips.

6	avocados, pitted and cut into ½-inch pieces
	Salt
½	cup minced fresh cilantro
¼	cup finely chopped red onion
¼	cup lime juice (2 limes)
1	large jalapeño chile, stemmed, seeded, and minced
2	garlic cloves, minced
1	teaspoon cumin

Mash 4 avocados and ½ teaspoon salt to relatively smooth puree in medium bowl with fork. Gently fold in remaining 2 diced avocados, cilantro, onion, lime juice, jalapeño, garlic, and cumin. Season with salt to taste and serve. (Guacamole can be refrigerated, with plastic wrap pressed directly onto its surface to prevent browning, for up to 1 day; bring to room temperature before serving. Makes 6 cups.)

WHY THIS RECIPE WORKS

The keys to velvety, chunky-textured guacamole are the right avocado and a minimum of mashing. We mash two-thirds of the avocados with a fork, combine with the other ingredients (onion, garlic, jalapeño, cilantro, salt, and cumin), then dice the remaining avocados and fold them in with a very light hand.

DICING AN AVOCADO

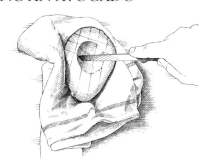 

Use a dish towel to hold the avocado steady. Make ½-inch crosshatch incisions in the flesh of each avocado half with a dinner knife, cutting down to but not through the skin. Separate the diced flesh from the skin using a spoon inserted between the skin and the flesh and gently scoop out the avocado cubes.

Easy Boiled Corn with Lime Butter

If you have a supersweet variety of corn, omit the sugar in the cooking water. Don't cook more than eight ears of corn at a time. If cooking more than eight ears, either bring another pot of water to boil or cook the corn in batches.

4	teaspoons sugar
6	tablespoons unsalted butter, melted
½	teaspoon grated lime zest plus 2 tablespoons juice
¾	teaspoon salt
¼	teaspoon pepper
8	ears corn, husks and silk removed

Bring 4 quarts water and sugar to boil in large pot over high heat. Meanwhile, combine melted butter, lime zest and juice, salt, and pepper in small bowl. Add corn to water, return to boil, and cook until tender, about 6 minutes. Using tongs, transfer corn to large serving platter, letting excess water drain back into pot. Drizzle corn with melted lime butter and serve hot.

WHY THIS RECIPE WORKS

Nothing beats the ease and flavor of freshly boiled corn on the cob. When boiling the corn, hold the salt—salted cooking water makes the corn kernels tough. We found that 4 teaspoons of granulated sugar was a welcome addition to the boiling water. The slightly sweetened water helped accentuate the natural sweetness of the corn.

Key Lime Pie

The graham cracker crust needs to be freshly baked and warm when adding the filling. The timing here is a bit different from other pies; you need to make the filling first, then bake the crust. Feel free to use Key limes if desired; note that you'll need about 20 Key limes to yield ½ cup of juice. Serve with whipped cream if desired.

- 4 large egg yolks
- 4 teaspoons grated lime zest plus ½ cup juice (4 limes)
- 1 (14-ounce) can sweetened condensed milk
- 8 whole graham crackers, broken into 1-inch pieces
- 5 tablespoons unsalted butter, melted and cooled
- 3 tablespoons granulated sugar

1. Adjust oven rack to middle position and heat oven to 325 degrees. Whisk egg yolks and zest together in medium bowl until mixture has light green tint, about 2 minutes. Whisk in condensed milk until smooth, then whisk in lime juice. Cover mixture and let sit at room temperature until thickened, about 30 minutes.

2. Meanwhile, process graham cracker pieces in food processor to fine, even crumbs, about 30 seconds. Sprinkle butter and sugar over crumbs; pulse to incorporate. Sprinkle mixture into 9-inch pie plate. Press firmly into even, compact layer over bottom and up sides of pie plate using bottom of dry measuring cup.

3. Bake until crust is fragrant and beginning to brown, 13 to 18 minutes. Pour thickened filling into warm crust and continue to bake pie until center is firm but jiggles slightly when shaken, 15 to 20 minutes. Let pie cool slightly for 1 hour, then cover loosely with plastic wrap and refrigerate until filling is chilled and set, at least 3 hours and up to 24 hours.

WHY THIS RECIPE WORKS

Classic Key lime pies are not baked; instead, the combination of egg yolks, lime juice, and sweetened condensed milk firms up when chilled because the juice's acidity causes the proteins in the eggs and milk to bind. We found that this custardy filling actually developed a much silkier consistency if briefly baked: an extra step, but well worth it. While many recipes we have tried insist on only using tiny, tart Key limes, we found that everyday limes worked just fine. A head-to-head tasting of the two proved that the flavor difference was slim, although you should feel free to use Key limes if you can find them.

Margaritas

For the best flavor, we recommend steeping the zest and juice for the full 24 hours, although the margaritas will still be great if the mixture is steeped only for 4 hours. If you're in a rush and need to serve margaritas immediately, omit the zest and skip the steeping process altogether. If you cannot find superfine sugar, process regular granulated sugar in a food processor for 30 to 40 seconds.

- 2 cups 100 percent agave tequila, preferably reposado
- 2 cups triple sec
- 8 teaspoons grated lime zest plus 1 cup juice (8 limes)
- 8 teaspoons grated lemon zest plus 1 cup juice (6 lemons)
- ½ cup superfine sugar
- ⅛ teaspoon salt
- 2 cups crushed ice, plus extra for serving

1. Combine tequila, triple sec, lime zest and juice, lemon zest and juice, sugar, and salt in 8-cup liquid measuring cup. Cover and refrigerate until flavors meld, at least 4 hours and up to 24 hours.

2. Strain margarita mixture into large pitcher. Add ice and stir until thoroughly combined and chilled, about 30 seconds. Pour into individual glasses, adding extra ice as desired. (Makes 2 quarts.)

WHY THIS RECIPE WORKS

The typical margarita tends to be a slushy, headache-inducing concoction made with little more than ice, tequila, and artificially flavored corn syrup. To achieve a balanced blend of fresh citrus flavors and tequila, we had to find the best proportions (equal parts juice, orange liqueur, and tequila) and the right alcohol (triple sec and a reposado tequila) for a mellow flavor.

Middle Eastern
Shish Kebab
Dinner

THE GAME PLAN
⬥

ONE DAY AHEAD...

MARINATE SHISH KEBAB MEAT: 30 minutes
(plus 2 hours for marinating)

MAKE ICE CREAM SANDWICHES: 1 hour
(plus 8½ hours for baking and freezing)

MAKE RICE SALAD: 40 minutes
(plus 30 minutes for cooling)

ON THE DAY OF...

MAKE WHIPPED FETA: 10 minutes

MAKE YOGURT SAUCE: 10 minutes
(plus 30 minutes for chilling)

MAKE CARROT SALAD: 40 minutes

ASSEMBLE AND GRILL SHISH KEBABS: 40 minutes
(plus 30 minutes for heating grill)

MIDDLE EASTERN
SHISH KEBAB DINNER

↗ Serves 8 ↖

Spicy Whipped Feta ↝ Lamb Shish Kebabs with Garlicky Yogurt Sauce
Persian Rice Salad with Dates and Pistachios ↝ Moroccan Carrot Salad
Pistachio-Lemon Ice Cream Sandwiches

Lamb Shish Kebabs with Garlicky Yogurt Sauce

You will need twelve 14-inch metal skewers for this recipe. To cut the onions into tidy pieces for kebabs, trim the root and stem ends, then peel and cut them in half lengthwise. Discard the onion core (or save for another use), then continue to cut the remaining onion down into 1-inch square pieces (without separating the layers). Serve with Garlicky Yogurt Sauce (page 126).

MARINADE

- 14 large fresh mint leaves
- 4 teaspoons chopped fresh rosemary
- 1 teaspoon grated lemon zest plus ¼ cup juice (2 lemons)
- 4 garlic cloves, peeled
- ¾ cup olive oil
- 1½ teaspoons salt
- ¼ teaspoon pepper

KEBABS

- 3 pounds boneless leg of lamb, trimmed and cut into 1-inch pieces
- 3 red bell peppers, stemmed, seeded, and cut into 1-inch pieces
- 2 red onions, cut into 1-inch squares
- 2 zucchini, halved lengthwise and sliced ½ inch thick

1. FOR THE MARINADE: Process all ingredients in food processor until smooth, about 1 minute, scraping down bowl as needed.

2. FOR THE KEBABS: Toss lamb with marinade in large bowl, cover, and refrigerate for at least 2 hours and up to 24 hours.

Thread marinated meat, peppers, onions, and zucchini onto 12 metal skewers in an alternating pattern. Brush skewers with leftover marinade. (Kebabs can be refrigerated for up to 4 hours before grilling.)

3A. FOR A CHARCOAL GRILL: Open bottom grill vent completely. Light large chimney starter three-quarters full with charcoal briquettes (4½ quarts). When top coals are partially covered with ash, pour evenly over grill. Set cooking grate in place, cover, and open lid vent completely. Heat grill until hot, about 5 minutes.

3B. FOR A GAS GRILL: Turn all burners to high, cover, and heat grill until hot, about 15 minutes. Turn all burners to medium-high.

4. Clean and oil cooking grate. Place kebabs on grill and cook (covered if using gas), turning as needed, until lamb and vegetables are lightly charred on all sides and meat registers 120 to 125 degrees (for medium-rare), about 8 minutes.

5. Transfer kebabs to platter, tent loosely with aluminum foil, and let rest for 5 to 10 minutes. Serve with Garlicky Yogurt Sauce.

✔ **WHY THIS RECIPE WORKS**
These colorful and fragrant skewers of lamb and vegetables benefit greatly from marinating, which added a layer of moisture that kept the kebabs from drying out on the grill while the flavors (we liked a combination of rosemary, garlic, mint, and lemon) penetrated the meat. Two hours in the marinade was sufficient time to achieve some flavor, but it took a good eight hours for these flavors to really sink in. Marinating for 12 hours, or overnight, was even better. To get the most out of the marinade and to ensure the vegetables and meat were thoroughly seasoned, we brushed some of the marinade on the skewers before grilling.

Garlicky Yogurt Sauce

WHY THIS RECIPE WORKS For a tangy, bracing sauce that cuts through the richness of lamb, but consists of minimal ingredients, we combined Greek yogurt with minced garlic, fresh cilantro, and mint.

Be sure to use Greek yogurt here, instead of regular plain yogurt, because its thicker consistency helps prevent the sauce from being watery and thin.

2 cups whole-milk Greek yogurt
3 garlic cloves, minced
¼ cup minced fresh cilantro
¼ cup minced fresh mint
½ teaspoon salt
¼ teaspoon pepper

Stir all ingredients together in medium bowl. Let sit until flavors meld, about 30 minutes. (Sauce can be refrigerated for up to 2 days.)

Spicy Whipped Feta

WHY THIS RECIPE WORKS The return on investment is huge with this Greek *meze* classic. We found rinsing the feta was the key to preventing an overly salty dip. A hefty dose of ground cayenne pepper gives this dip a subtle background heat that doesn't compete with the feta while olive oil imparts fruity notes and some richness, and lemon juice balances the saltiness of the cheese.

While a pound of feta may seem like a lot, its volume will condense dramatically when processed. This dip is fairly spicy; to make it less spicy, reduce the amount of cayenne pepper to ¼ teaspoon. Our preferred brand of feta cheese is Mt. Vikos Traditional. Serve with pita chips or warm pita bread.

1 pound feta cheese, crumbled (4 cups)
⅓ cup extra-virgin olive oil, plus
1 tablespoon for serving
1 tablespoon lemon juice
½ teaspoon cayenne pepper
½ teaspoon pepper

Rinse feta under cold water and pat dry with paper towels. Process feta, ⅓ cup oil, lemon juice, cayenne, and pepper in food processor until smooth, about 20 seconds. Transfer mixture to serving bowl, drizzle with remaining 1 tablespoon oil, and serve. (Feta can be refrigerated for up to 2 days; bring to room temperature before serving. Makes 2 cups.)

Persian Rice Salad with Dates and Pistachios

WHY THIS RECIPE WORKS This colorful and unusual rice salad is a great complement to the lamb kebabs. To rid the rice of excess starch, which would make for a sticky salad, we cooked long-grain rice as we would pasta, boiling it in a large volume of water.

Taste the rice as it nears the end of its cooking time; it should be cooked through and firm, but not crunchy. We recommend regular long-grain rice, but basmati rice will work as well.

2½ cups long-grain white rice
Salt and pepper
1 bunch scallions, chopped
1 cup pistachios, toasted (see page 29) and chopped
½ cup chopped dates
½ cup minced fresh parsley
¼ cup lemon juice (2 lemons)
⅛ teaspoon ground cinnamon
⅔ cup extra-virgin olive oil

1. Bring 4 quarts water to boil in large pot. Add rice and 1 tablespoon salt. Return to boil and cook uncovered, stirring occasionally, until rice is tender but not soft, 10 to 12 minutes. Drain rice well, spread over rimmed baking sheet, and cool to room temperature.

2. Toss cooled rice, scallions, pistachios, dates, and parsley together in large bowl. Whisk lemon juice and cinnamon together in small bowl. Whisking constantly, drizzle in oil. Pour dressing over salad and toss to combine. Season with salt and pepper to taste and serve. (Rice salad can be refrigerated for up to 2 days; bring to room temperature before serving.)

Moroccan Carrot Salad

The fastest way to shred carrots for this salad is to use the shredding disk in a food processor. Of course you could use the large holes of a box grater, but your arm may get quite tired.

4	oranges
1½	pounds carrots, peeled and grated
4	radishes, trimmed and sliced thin
¼	cup minced fresh cilantro
¼	cup orange juice
4	teaspoons lemon juice
1½	teaspoons honey
1	teaspoon ground cumin
	Salt and pepper
¼	teaspoon cayenne pepper
⅓	cup extra-virgin olive oil

1. Cut away peel and pith from oranges. Quarter oranges, then slice crosswise into ½-inch-thick pieces. Combine orange pieces, carrots, radishes, and cilantro in large bowl. Whisk orange juice, lemon juice, honey, cumin, ¾ teaspoon salt, and cayenne together in small bowl. Drizzle dressing over salad and toss gently to coat.

2. Let salad sit until liquid begins to pool in bottom of bowl, about 5 minutes. Drain salad gently through fine-mesh strainer, about 2 minutes. (Salad can be refrigerated for up to 2 days; drain again before continuing with step 3.)

3. Transfer salad to serving bowl, drizzle with oil, and toss gently to coat. Season with salt and pepper to taste and serve.

WHY THIS RECIPE WORKS

This is not your mother's mayonnaise-based carrot and raisin salad—rather it is a more exotic Moroccan-style salad featuring grated carrots tossed with orange pieces and crunchy radishes, flavored with cumin, cilantro, lemon juice, and a hit of cayenne. To get rid of the unwanted pool of liquid exuded by the dressed carrots, we tried salting the carrots, but this process required at least half an hour. We also tried squeezing the carrots in a dish towel after we grated them, but this resulted in a loss of flavor. We finally settled on increasing the amount of spices in the vinaigrette; the carrots thus received an initial overdose of spices that would stand up to the inevitable excess of liquid. By straining some of the liquid from the salad, we reached a proper level of seasoning and our salad was complete.

CUTTING CITRUS FOR SALAD

Slice the top and bottom off the orange, then cut away the rind and pith using a paring knife. Quarter the peeled orange, cutting away any seeds or chewy pith in the center, then slice each quarter crosswise into ½-inch-thick pieces.

Pistachio-Lemon Ice Cream Sandwiches

✔ **WHY THIS RECIPE WORKS**

For this sophisticated version of a childhood favorite, we paired bright, homemade slice-and-bake lemon cookies with store-bought pistachio ice cream. We knew the cookies' lemon flavor needed to be bracing enough to stand out even when served from the freezer (since cold dulls flavor). After some experimentation we found that a combination of lemon zest and juice in the cookie dough gave them the bright, tart flavor we were after. Slicing the cookies into relatively thin ¼-inch rounds and filling each sandwich with ⅓ cup slightly softened ice cream made the best cookie-to-ice cream ratio. Chopped pistachios, pressed into the sides of the sandwich, offered additional crunch and great visual appeal. Six hours in the freezer was enough to harden the ice cream and soften the cookies just enough to mesh with the ice cream and feel sandwichlike.

This recipe is best prepared the day ahead, to allow enough time for the sandwiches to freeze.

¾ cup (5¼ ounces) sugar
2 tablespoons grated lemon zest plus 2 tablespoons juice (2 lemons)
1¾ cup (8¾ ounces) all-purpose flour
¼ teaspoon baking powder
¼ teaspoon salt
12 tablespoons unsalted butter, cut into ½-inch pieces and chilled
1 large egg yolk
½ teaspoon vanilla extract
2 pints pistachio ice cream
¾ cup pistachios, toasted (see page 29) and chopped

1. Process sugar and lemon zest in food processor until sugar is pale yellow, about 30 seconds. Add flour, baking powder, and salt and pulse to combine, about 10 pulses. Add butter pieces and pulse until mixture resembles fine corneal, about 15 pulses.

2. In small bowl, whisk lemon juice, egg yolk, and vanilla to combine. With processor running, add lemon juice mixture in slow, steady stream, about 10 seconds. Continue processing until dough begins to form ball, 10 to 15 seconds.

3. Transfer dough to clean counter and roll into 7-inch log, about 3 inches in diameter. Wrap dough tightly in plastic wrap and refrigerate until cold and firm, at least 2 hours and up to 3 days.

4. Adjust oven racks to upper-middle and lower-middle positions and heat oven to 375 degrees. Line 2 rimmed baking sheets with parchment paper.

5. Slice dough into ¼-inch-thick cookies (you should have about 20). Lay cookies on prepared baking sheets, spaced about 1 inch apart. Bake until edges begin to brown, 14 to 16 minutes, switching and rotating baking sheets halfway through baking. Let cookies cool on baking sheets for 3 minutes, then transfer to wire rack to cool completely.

6. To assemble sandwiches, let ice cream soften at room temperature, 5 to 10 minutes. Place ⅓ cup ice cream between two cookies and squeeze cookies gently until ice cream is evenly distributed. Press pistachios into sides of ice cream sandwiches and lay on large platter. Wrap tightly in plastic wrap and freeze until firm, at least 6 hours and up to 2 days. Let sandwiches sit at room temperature for 10 minutes before serving.

EVEN EASIER ➤ Don't have time to make ice cream sandwiches? Portion 4 quarts (½ gallon) pistachio ice cream into individual serving bowls, then drizzle with limoncello (an Italian lemon liquor) and top with whipped cream. Serve with pizzelle cookies.

Grilled Shrimp Dinner

THE GAME PLAN

❧

ONE DAY AHEAD...

MAKE COUSCOUS: 45 minutes

MAKE LEMON POUND CAKE: 25 minutes
(plus 3 hours for baking and cooling)

ON THE DAY OF...

MAKE TOMATO TART: 30 minutes (plus 1¼ hours for baking and cooling)

MAKE MARINATED ZUCCHINI: 20 minutes

GLAZE POUND CAKE, PREP STRAWBERRIES, AND MAKE WHIPPED CREAM: 1 hour

MAKE GRILLED SHRIMP SKEWERS: 45 minutes
(plus 30 minutes for heating grill)

GRILLED SHRIMP DINNER

⇐ Serves 8 ⇐

Tomato and Mozzarella Tart ⇐ Grilled Shrimp Skewers with Lemon-Garlic Sauce
Couscous with Carrots and Chickpeas ⇐ Zucchini Ribbons with Shaved Parmesan
Glazed Lemon Pound Cake with Strawberries and Whipped Cream

Grilled Shrimp Skewers with Lemon-Garlic Sauce

You will need eight 14-inch metal skewers for this recipe. Using a warmed bowl in step 5 to toss the cooked shrimp with the butter sauce will help keep the shrimp warm for serving.

4	pounds extra-large shrimp (21 to 25 per pound), peeled and deveined (see page 304)
¼	cup olive oil
	Salt and pepper
¾	teaspoon sugar
12	tablespoons unsalted butter, cut into 12 pieces
⅓	cup lemon juice (2 lemons)
5	garlic cloves, minced
¼	teaspoon red pepper flakes
⅓	cup minced fresh parsley
	Lemon wedges

1. Pat shrimp dry with paper towels. Thread shrimp tightly onto 8 metal skewers, alternating direction of heads and tails. Brush shrimp with oil and season with salt and pepper. Sprinkle one side of each skewer with sugar.

2. Cook butter, lemon juice, garlic, pepper flakes, and ¼ teaspoon salt together in small saucepan over medium heat, stirring often, until butter melts, about 2 minutes. Remove from heat and cover to keep warm.

3A. FOR A CHARCOAL GRILL: Open bottom grill vent completely. Light large chimney starter mounded with charcoal briquettes (7 quarts). When top coals are partially covered with ash, pour evenly over grill. Set cooking grate in place, cover, and open lid vent completely. Heat grill

until hot, about 5 minutes.

3B. FOR A GAS GRILL: Turn all burners to high, cover, and heat grill until hot, about 15 minutes. Leave all burners on high.

4. Clean and oil cooking grate. Place shrimp skewers, sugared side down, on grill. Use tongs to push shrimp together on skewer if they have separated. Grill (covered if using gas) until shrimp are lightly charred, 4 to 5 minutes. Flip shrimp skewers and continue to grill (covered if using gas) until second side is pink, about 2 minutes longer.

5. Remove skewers from grill and gently slide shrimp off skewers into large, warmed bowl. Toss shrimp with warm butter sauce and parsley. Serve immediately with lemon wedges.

CROWDING SHRIMP ONTO A SKEWER

Pass the skewer through the center of each shrimp. As you add shrimp to the skewer, alternate the directions of the heads and tails for a compact arrangement of about 12 shrimp. The shrimp should be crowded and touching each other.

✔ **WHY THIS RECIPE WORKS**
Grilling shrimp in their shells protects the delicate flesh, but seasonings are peeled away at the table. To deliver tender, juicy, boldly flavored shrimp without the shells, we crammed peeled shrimp onto a skewer, which prevented overcooking. We set the skewers over a screaming hot fire, taking them off before they were completely cooked (but after they had picked up attractive grill marks). We finished cooking the shrimp in a heated bowl with warmed butter sauce boldly flavored with lemon and garlic; this last dunk gave them tons of flavor.

Tomato and Mozzarella Tart

✓ **WHY THIS RECIPE WORKS**

This beautiful tart boasts an easy-to-make savory ricotta, Parmesan, and mozzarella filling topped with sliced fresh tomatoes—the perfect opener for a summer meal. To make the tart quick, we used store-bought puff pastry. Folding over the outer edge of the pastry and "waterproofing" with egg wash forms a raised crust that looks attractive and keeps the toppings from sliding off. To get a crust that is flaky yet rigid enough to hold the toppings, we used a two-step baking method: a high temperature for initial lift and browning, then a lower temperature to dry out the shell for maximum sturdiness. We layered this tart with two kinds of cheese: grated Parmesan, for sharp nutty flavor, and ricotta, which gave the filling body and moisture (part-skim ricotta helped balance the rich puff pastry and kept the tart from being unpalatably heavy).

To thaw frozen puff pastry, allow it to sit either in the refrigerator for 24 hours or on the counter for 30 to 60 minutes.

- 2 (9½ by 9-inch) sheets frozen puff pastry, thawed
- I large egg, beaten
- 4 ounces Parmesan cheese, grated (2 cups)
- 4 plum tomatoes, cored and sliced crosswise ¼ inch thick
  Salt and pepper
- 3 tablespoons extra-virgin olive oil
- 2 garlic cloves, minced
- 8 ounces part-skim ricotta cheese (I cup)
- 2 ounces mozzarella cheese, shredded (½ cup)
- 2 tablespoons chopped fresh basil

1. Adjust oven rack to lower-middle position and heat oven to 425 degrees. Overlap sheets of pastry by 1 inch in middle of large piece of parchment. Smooth out seam with rolling pin. Brush edges of pastry with egg, then fold over short edges by 1 inch. Fold long edges of pastry over by 1 inch and press lightly to secure. Brush folded edges with egg.

2. Carefully transfer parchment with pastry onto rimmed baking sheet. Sprinkle 1 cup Parmesan evenly over center of pastry. Using fork, poke holes in center of shell. Bake for 13 to 15 minutes, then reduce oven temperature to 350 degrees and continue to bake until golden brown and crisp, 13 to 15 minutes longer. Transfer to wire rack and let cool to room temperature, about 20 minutes. (Pastry crust can be held at room temperature for up to 2 days.) Increase oven temperature to 425 degrees.

3. Meanwhile, spread tomato slices out over several layers of paper towels, and sprinkle with ½ teaspoon salt. Let sit for 30 minutes, then blot dry with paper towels. Combine 2 tablespoons oil, garlic, pinch salt, and pinch pepper in small bowl. In separate bowl, mix remaining 1 cup Parmesan, remaining 1 tablespoon oil, ricotta, and mozzarella and season with salt and pepper to taste.

4. Spread ricotta mixture evenly into baked crust. Shingle tomato slices widthwise on top of cheese, then brush with garlic oil. Bake tart until shell is deep golden brown and cheese is melted, 15 to 17 minutes. Let cool on wire rack for 5 minutes, then sprinkle with basil. Slide tart onto cutting board, cut into pieces, and serve.

EVEN EASIER ➤ Don't have time to make a tomato tart? Thinly slice 6 large tomatoes and 1½ pounds fresh mozzarella, then shingle them, alternating, on large platter. Season with salt and pepper, drizzle lightly with extra-virgin olive oil, and sprinkle with 2 tablespoons chopped fresh basil. Serve with sliced bread or Garlic Toasts (page 62).

SHAPING THE TART CRUST

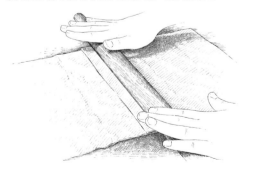 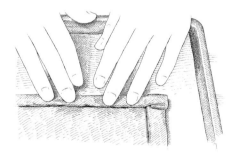

Brush egg along one edge of one sheet of puff pastry, then overlap with a second sheet of dough by 1 inch and press to seal the pieces together. Using a rolling pin, smooth out the seam to form one large sheet. Brush the edges of the pastry with egg and fold in each side to form a 1-inch raised crust. Gently slide the prepared crust onto a rimmed baking sheet.

Couscous with Carrots and Chickpeas

Do not use Israeli couscous in this recipe; its larger size requires a different cooking method. For an accurate measurement of boiling water, bring a full kettle of water to a boil, then measure out the desired amount.

2	cups plain couscous
6	tablespoons olive oil
3	carrots, peeled and grated
1	onion, chopped fine
5	garlic cloves, minced
1	teaspoon ground coriander
3	cups boiling water
1	(15-ounce) can chickpeas, rinsed
	Salt and pepper
2	tablespoons lemon juice
½	cup minced fresh cilantro or parsley

1. Toast couscous with 2 tablespoons olive oil in 12-inch skillet over medium heat, stirring occasionally, until lightly browned, 3 to 5 minutes; transfer to large bowl.

2. Heat 1 tablespoon oil in now-empty skillet over medium-high heat until shimmering. Add carrots and onion and cook until softened, 5 to 7 minutes. Stir in garlic and coriander and cook until fragrant, about 30 seconds. Transfer mixture to bowl with couscous. Stir boiling water, chickpeas, and 1 teaspoon salt into couscous. Cover tightly with plastic wrap and let sit until couscous is tender, about 12 minutes.

3. Fluff couscous with fork, breaking up any clumps. Combine remaining 3 tablespoons oil and lemon juice in small bowl, then drizzle over couscous and gently toss to incorporate. Season with salt and pepper to taste. (Couscous can be refrigerated for up to 1 day; bring to room temperature or microwave, covered, until hot, 3 to 5 minutes before serving.) Fold in cilantro and serve warm or at room temperature.

Zucchini Ribbons with Shaved Parmesan

Using in-season zucchini, good olive oil, and high-quality Parmesan is crucial in this simple side dish. Our preferred brand of regular (not extra-virgin) olive oil is DaVinci. Be ready to serve this dish shortly after it is assembled.

1½	pounds zucchini
	Salt and pepper
½	cup olive oil
¼	cup lemon juice (2 lemons)
2	tablespoons minced fresh mint
6	ounces Parmesan cheese, shaved (see page 32)

Using vegetable peeler or mandoline, slice zucchini lengthwise into very thin ribbons. (Zucchini ribbons can be refrigerated for up to 2 hours before continuing.) Gently toss zucchini ribbons with salt and pepper, then arrange attractively on shallow platter. Drizzle with olive oil and lemon juice, sprinkle with mint and Parmesan, and serve.

Glazed Lemon Pound Cake with Strawberries and Whipped Cream

This cake batter will be very fluid and look almost like a thick pancake batter. Sliced ripe peaches, nectarines, or plums can be substituted for the strawberries; just make sure you have roughly 2 pounds of prepped fruit in total. Do not substitute raspberries, blueberries, or blackberries here; they will not work well.

POUND CAKE

1½	cups (6 ounces) cake flour
1	teaspoon baking powder
½	teaspoon salt
1¼	cups (8¾ ounces) granulated sugar
4	large eggs, room temperature
2	tablespoons grated lemon zest plus 2 teaspoons juice (2 lemons)
1½	teaspoons vanilla extract
16	tablespoons unsalted butter, melted and hot

GLAZE

1¾	cups (7 ounces) confectioners' sugar
1	teaspoon grated lemon zest plus ¼ cup juice (2 lemons)
	Pinch salt

BERRIES AND WHIPPED CREAM

30	ounces strawberries, hulled and quartered (6 cups)
¼	cup (1¾ ounces) plus 1 tablespoon granulated sugar
1	cup heavy cream, chilled
1	teaspoon vanilla extract

1. FOR THE POUND CAKE: Adjust oven rack to middle position and heat oven to 350 degrees. Grease and flour 8½ by 4½-inch loaf pan. Whisk flour, baking powder, and salt together in bowl.

2. Process sugar, eggs, lemon zest and juice, and vanilla in food processor until combined, about 10 seconds. With processor running, add hot melted butter in steady stream until combined, about 30 seconds. Pour mixture into large bowl.

3. Sift one-third of flour mixture over egg mixture and whisk to combine until few streaks of flour remain. Repeat twice more with remaining flour mixture, then continue to whisk batter gently until most lumps are gone (do not overmix). Scrape batter into prepared pan and smooth top. Wipe any drops of batter off sides of pan and gently tap pan on counter to settle batter. Bake cake until toothpick inserted in center comes out clean, 50 to 60 minutes, rotating pan halfway through baking.

4. Let cake cool in pan for 10 minutes. Run small knife around edge of cake to loosen, then turn it out onto wire rack. Let cake cool completely, about 2 hours, before glazing. (Cooled cake can be stored at room temperature for up to 1 day.)

5. FOR THE GLAZE: Whisk all ingredients together in bowl until smooth and let sit until thickened, about 25 minutes. Pour glaze over top of cooled cake, letting it drip down sides. Let glaze set, at least 30 minutes and up to 4 hours.

6. FOR THE BERRIES AND WHIPPED CREAM: Combine strawberries and ¼ cup sugar in bowl and toss to coat. Let berry mixture sit at room temperature until sugar has dissolved and berries are juicy, at least 30 minutes and up to 2 hours.

7. Using stand mixer fitted with whisk, whip cream, remaining 1 tablespoon sugar, and vanilla on medium-low speed until foamy, about 1 minute. Increase speed to high and whip until soft peaks form, 1 to 3 minutes. (Whipped cream can be refrigerated for up to 8 hours; rewhisk briefly before serving.) Slice pound cake and serve with whipped cream and strawberries.

🗸 **WHY THIS RECIPE WORKS**
Served with whipped cream and strawberries, this cake makes an impressive finish to this summery menu. Although made from only a handful of ingredients, pound cake can be a finicky, disappointing dessert prone to disaster. Most classic pound cake recipes we researched use a fussy mixing method in which all the ingredients need to be at the same temperature. After trying everything we could think of to construct a foolproof recipe, we finally found the answers to our fussy batter problems: hot, melted (rather than softened) butter and the food processor. The fast-moving blade of the processor plus the hot melted butter emulsifies the liquid ingredients quickly before they have a chance to curdle. We mixed lemon zest into the cake batter and glazed the finished cake with lemon sugar syrup for a final blast of bright lemon flavor.

Little Italy Pasta Supper, page 145

Japanese Salmon Dinner, page 187

New York–Style Pizza Party, page 151

Autumn Harvest Pork Dinner, page 171

FALL

Rustic Tuscan Supper

THE GAME PLAN

ONE DAY AHEAD...

MARINATE MOZZARELLA AND OLIVES: 20 minutes
(plus 4 hours for marinating)

SOAK BEANS FOR STEW: 5 minutes
(plus 8 hours for soaking)

MAKE BREAD DOUGH: 10 minutes
(plus 8 hours for rising)

ON THE DAY OF...

MAKE BREAD: 10 minutes (plus 5 hours for rising, baking, and cooling)

MAKE BEAN STEW: 3¼ hours

MAKE APPLES WITH CARAMEL SAUCE: 1 hour

MAKE SALAD: 20 minutes

RUSTIC TUSCAN SUPPER

❦ Serves 8 ❧

Marinated Baby Mozzarella and Olives ❧ Hearty Tuscan Bean Stew
Almost No-Knead Bread ❧ Arugula and Fennel Salad with Shaved Parmesan
Skillet-Roasted Apples with Caramel Sauce

Hearty Tuscan Bean Stew

Bacon can be substituted for the pancetta. You will need at least a 6-quart Dutch oven for this recipe. We prefer the creamier texture of beans soaked for at least 8 hours as directed in step 1; however, if you're short on time you can quick-soak them. To quick-soak beans, bring 2 quarts of water and 3 tablespoons of salt to a boil in a large pot. Combine the hot salt water and beans in a large bowl and let sit for 1 hour; drain and rinse the beans well before continuing with step 2.

Salt and pepper
1½ pounds dried cannellini beans (about 3 cups), picked over and rinsed
2 tablespoons extra-virgin olive oil, plus extra for serving
8 ounces pancetta, cut into ¼-inch pieces
2 onions, chopped fine
3 celery ribs, cut into ½-inch pieces
1 pound carrots, peeled and cut into ½-inch pieces
10 garlic cloves, peeled and crushed
6 cups low-sodium chicken broth
5 cups water
2 bay leaves
1 pound kale or collard greens, stemmed and leaves cut into 1-inch pieces
1 (14.5-ounce) can diced tomatoes, drained and rinsed
1 sprig fresh rosemary

1. Dissolve 3 tablespoons salt in 4 quarts cold water in large bowl or container. Add beans and soak at room temperature for 8 to 24 hours. Drain and rinse beans well.

2. Adjust oven rack to lower-middle position and heat oven to 250 degrees. Cook oil and pancetta in Dutch oven over medium heat until pancetta is lightly browned and fat has rendered, 8 to 10 minutes. Stir in onions, celery, and carrots and cook until vegetables are softened and lightly browned, 12 to 18 minutes.

3. Stir in garlic and cook until fragrant, about 1 minute. Stir in broth, water, bay leaves, and soaked beans and bring to boil. Cover, transfer pot to oven, and cook until beans are almost tender, 45 to 60 minutes.

4. Stir in kale and tomatoes and continue to cook, covered, until beans and greens are fully tender, 30 to 40 minutes. Remove pot from oven. (Alternatively, cook stew for only 15 minutes after adding kale and tomatoes, then remove from oven and let sit at room temperature, uncovered, for up to 2 hours. Reheat gently over medium-low heat before continuing.)

5. Submerge rosemary sprig in stew, cover, and let steep off heat for 15 minutes. Remove and discard bay leaves and rosemary sprig. Season with salt and pepper to taste. Use back of spoon to mash some beans against side of pot to thicken stew. Serve, drizzling individual portions with olive oil.

✔ **WHY THIS RECIPE WORKS**
In Tuscany, creamy, flavorful beans transform rustic stews into something special. We borrowed some of this culinary wizardry by combining chunks of vegetables and greens with buttery beans for a hearty, deeply flavored stew perfect for ushering in the cool weather. Since beans are the centerpiece of this dish, we concentrated on cooking them perfectly. Determined to avoid tough, exploded beans, we soaked the beans overnight in salted water to soften the skins. Cooking the stew in a gentle 250-degree oven produced beans that were tender but intact. The final trick was to add tomatoes toward the end of cooking, since their acid interfered with the softening process. We looked to other traditional Tuscan ingredients to round out the stew, including pancetta, kale, lots of garlic, a sprig of rosemary, and, of course, a drizzle of fruity extra-virgin olive oil just before serving.

Marinated Baby Mozzarella and Olives

✔ **WHY THIS RECIPE WORKS**
Aromatic herbs and bright citrus notes enliven the flavor of fresh mozzarella, while briny, pungent olives offset its mildness. We liked a mix of green and black olives, which we rinsed to remove excess salt and patted dry so the olive oil and herb marinade would not be diluted.

Make sure to bring the mixture to room temperature before serving or the oil will look cloudy and congealed. Serve with toothpicks and a thinly sliced baguette or crackers.

¾ cup pitted green olives, halved
¾ cup pitted black olives, halved
12 ounces fresh baby mozzarella cheese balls (bocconcini)
1 cup extra-virgin olive oil
3 shallots, sliced thin
1 garlic clove, minced
1 teaspoon grated lemon zest
1 teaspoon minced fresh thyme
1 teaspoon minced fresh oregano
¾ teaspoon salt
¼ teaspoon red pepper flakes

Gently rinse olives and mozzarella in colander under cold running water. Drain well and gently pat dry with paper towels. Whisk oil, shallots, garlic, lemon zest, thyme, oregano, salt, and pepper flakes together in medium bowl. Add olives and cheese and toss gently to coat. Cover and refrigerate for at least 4 hours and up to 2 days. Bring to room temperature before serving.

Arugula and Fennel Salad with Shaved Parmesan

✔ **WHY THIS RECIPE WORKS**
Inspired by the classic Italian combination of white beans and bitter greens, this salad features assertive arugula—a natural pairing with our Hearty Tuscan Bean Stew. Thinly sliced fennel gives the salad appealing crunch. To flatter the bright, clean flavor of the arugula, we made a vinaigrette using tart lemon juice, shallot, a little chopped thyme, and a touch of Dijon to help emulsify everything.

If desired, reserve and chop some fennel fronds for garnish.

3 tablespoons lemon juice
1 shallot, minced
2 teaspoons Dijon mustard
1½ teaspoons minced fresh thyme
1 garlic clove, minced
¼ teaspoon salt
⅛ teaspoon pepper
¾ cup extra-virgin olive oil
12 ounces baby arugula (12 cups)
2 fennel bulbs, stalks discarded, halved, cored, and sliced thin (see page 22)
2 ounces Parmesan cheese, shaved (see page 32)

Whisk lemon juice, shallot, mustard, thyme, garlic, salt, and pepper together in medium bowl. Whisking constantly, drizzle in oil. In large bowl, gently toss arugula with fennel. Just before serving, whisk dressing to re-emulsify, then drizzle over salad and toss gently to coat. Garnish individual portions with Parmesan.

Almost No-Knead Bread

This bread bakes best in a heavy enameled cast-iron Dutch oven with a tight-fitting lid, but it will work in any Dutch oven. If your Dutch oven is not very heavy, the crust of the bread will turn out thinner and lighter. For the best flavor, use a mild-flavored beer, like Budweiser, Stella Artois, or Heineken; a mild nonalcoholic beer also works well.

3	cups (15 ounces) all-purpose flour
1½	teaspoons salt
¼	teaspoon instant or rapid-rise yeast
¾	cup water, room temperature
½	cup mild-flavored beer, room temperature
1	tablespoon white vinegar
	Vegetable oil spray

1. Whisk flour, salt, and yeast together in large bowl. Fold in water, beer, and vinegar with rubber spatula until dough comes together and looks shaggy. Cover bowl with plastic wrap and let sit at room temperature for at least 8 hours and up to 18 hours.

2. Lay 18 by 12-inch sheet of parchment paper inside 10-inch skillet and spray with vegetable oil spray. Turn dough out onto lightly floured counter and knead by hand to form smooth, round ball, 10 to 15 times. Shape dough into ball by pulling edges into middle with floured hands. Transfer dough, seam side down, to prepared skillet.

3. Mist dough with vegetable oil spray and cover loosely with plastic wrap. Let rise at room temperature until doubled in size and dough barely springs back when poked with knuckle, about 2 hours.

4. About 30 minutes before baking, adjust oven rack to lowest position, place covered Dutch oven on rack, and heat oven to 500 degrees.

5. Lightly flour top of dough and, using razor blade or sharp knife, make one 6-inch-long, ½-inch-deep slit along top of dough. Carefully remove pot from oven and remove lid. Pick up parchment and dough and carefully lower them into hot pot, letting any excess parchment hang over edge. Cover pot.

6. Place pot in oven, reduce oven temperature to 425 degrees, and bake covered for 30 minutes. Remove lid and continue to bake until loaf registers 210 degrees and crust is deep golden brown, 20 to 30 minutes. Carefully remove bread from pot, transfer to wire rack, and let cool to room temperature, about 2 hours, before serving.

✔ **WHY THIS RECIPE WORKS**
This easy-to-make bread is designed to require very little kneading. The trick is to make the dough quite wet and to let it rest for a long period of time on the counter before shaping and baking. The long resting time is what gives the loaf its structure (it actually develops the gluten), whereas in other breads, this structure is developed through the act of kneading. To boost the flavor of this simple bread, we found that a little beer and a dash of white vinegar lent a valuable but subtle "bready" tang.

MAKING ALMOST NO-KNEAD BREAD

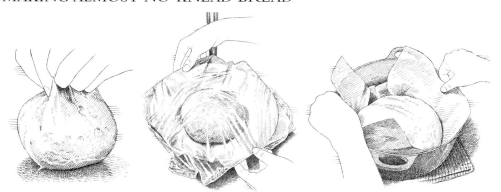

After kneading the loaf, shape the dough into a ball by pulling the edges up and into the middle. Lay an 18 by 12-inch sheet of parchment paper inside a 10-inch skillet and spray with vegetable oil spray. Transfer the dough, seam side down, to the prepared skillet. Mist the dough with vegetable oil spray and cover loosely with plastic wrap. After the dough has doubled in size, use the parchment paper to carefully transfer the dough to the preheated Dutch oven to bake.

Skillet-Roasted Apples with Caramel Sauce

WHY THIS RECIPE WORKS
Apple desserts tend to be homey, so we added a little drama by caramelizing cored apple halves—stem intact—for a burnished, enhanced silhouette. Requiring only a skillet, a handful of ingredients, and 30 minutes, our recipe is also a lot quicker and easier than an apple pie or tart. We browned the apple halves in a little sugar and butter to promote caramelization, removing them once browned and slightly softened so they wouldn't overcook as we finished the caramel sauce. Apple brandy (such as Calvados) enhanced the apple flavor and added complexity and sophistication to the sauce. Heavy cream lent a velvety, smooth consistency and a touch of salt balanced the sweetness and allowed the caramel flavor to really pop.

This dish is quite rich, so plan on serving just half an apple per person. If you can't find Pink Lady or Honeycrisp, Braeburn apples can be substituted. If the sauce bubbles up at any point after adding the cream in step 4, remove it from the heat momentarily until the bubbling subsides.

2 tablespoons unsalted butter
1 cup (7 ounces) sugar
4 Pink Lady or Honeycrisp apples, peeled, halved, and cored leaving stem intact
½ cup water
½ cup Calvados or apple-flavored brandy
1 cup heavy cream, room temperature
⅛ teaspoon salt
4 pints (½ gallon) vanilla ice cream
½ cup sliced almonds, toasted (see page 29)

1. Set wire rack in rimmed baking sheet lined with aluminum foil. Melt butter in 12-inch nonstick skillet over medium heat. Sprinkle ¼ cup sugar into skillet, then lay apples, cut side down, over sugar.

2. Cook, gently shaking pan occasionally, until apples are golden brown on cut side and sugar begins to brown, 6 to 8 minutes. Flip apples over and continue to cook until apples are almost tender (fork inserted in center of apple meets slight resistance), 3 to 5 minutes, reducing heat as needed to prevent sugar from getting too dark. Transfer apples, cut side up, to prepared wire rack. (Apples can be held at room temperature for up to 4 hours; if desired, reheat in 500-degree oven for 5 minutes before serving.)

3. Add remaining ¾ cup sugar and water to now-empty skillet. Bring to boil, scraping up browned bits. Reduce to simmer and cook until mixture thickens and is amber-colored, about 5 minutes.

4. Off heat, carefully stir in Calvados. Return to simmer and cook until alcohol has evaporated and mixture thickens again, about 5 minutes. Stir in cream and salt and continue to simmer sauce, stirring gently, until smooth and reduced to 1¼ cups, 5 to 7 minutes. (Sauce can be held in bowl at room temperature for up to 4 hours; cover and microwave until warm, about 1 minute, before serving.)

5. Portion ice cream into individual bowls and top with caramelized apple half, cut side facing up. Drizzle with caramel sauce, sprinkle with almonds, and serve.

Little Italy Pasta Supper

THE GAME PLAN

◄-◄

ONE DAY AHEAD...

MAKE SPINACH DIP: 15 minutes (plus 1 hour for chilling)

MAKE MEATBALLS AND SAUCE: 2½ hours

MAKE PUDDING CAKES: 30 minutes

ON THE DAY OF...

REHEAT MEATBALLS AND COOK SPAGHETTI: 30 minutes

MAKE GARLIC BREAD: 20 minutes

MAKE SALAD: 20 minutes

BAKE PUDDING CAKES: 40 minutes

➤ Serves 8 ➤

Herbed Spinach Dip ➤ Spaghetti and Meatballs
Classic Garlic Bread ➤ Italian-Style Salad with Fennel and Artichokes
Individual Hot Fudge Pudding Cakes

Spaghetti and Meatballs

You will need at least a 6-quart Dutch oven for this recipe. You can substitute 1 cup plain yogurt mixed with ½ cup milk for the buttermilk. Grate the onion on the large holes of a box grater; you will need 1 to 2 onions to yield 1½ cups grated onion. Panko can be found at most supermarkets, either next to the other bread crumbs or in the international foods aisle with other Asian ingredients. Plan on serving 3 to 5 meatballs per person.

MEATBALLS
2¼	cups panko bread crumbs
1½	cups buttermilk
3	tablespoons water
1½	teaspoons unflavored gelatin
6	ounces thinly sliced prosciutto, chopped fine
3	ounces Parmesan cheese, grated (1½ cups)
3	large eggs, lightly beaten
6	tablespoons minced fresh parsley
3	garlic cloves, minced
1½	teaspoons salt
½	teaspoon pepper
2	pounds 85 percent lean ground beef
1	pound ground pork

SAUCE
3	tablespoons extra-virgin olive oil
1½	cups grated onion
6	garlic cloves, minced
1	teaspoon dried oregano
½	teaspoon red pepper flakes
6	cups bottled tomato juice
3	(28-ounce) cans crushed tomatoes
6	tablespoons dry white wine
	Salt and pepper

½	cup minced fresh basil
3	tablespoons minced fresh parsley
	Sugar
1½	pounds spaghetti
2	ounces Parmesan cheese, grated (1 cup)

1. FOR THE MEATBALLS: Adjust oven racks to upper-middle and lower-middle positions and heat oven to 450 degrees. Generously spray 2 wire racks with vegetable oil spray and set in 2 rimmed baking sheets lined with aluminum foil. Combine panko and buttermilk in large bowl and let sit, mashing occasionally, until smooth paste forms, about 10 minutes. Place water in small bowl, sprinkle gelatin over top, and let sit for 5 minutes.

2. Stir gelatin mixture, prosciutto, Parmesan, eggs, parsley, garlic, salt, and pepper into panko-buttermilk mixture. Add beef and pork and gently mix until thoroughly combined using hands. Lightly shape mixture into 2-inch round meatballs (about ¼ cup each; about 40 meatballs total).

3. Spread meatballs out over prepared wire racks. Roast until browned, *continued* ➤

✔ WHY THIS RECIPE WORKS

This recipe delivers tender meatballs in flavorful, full-bodied tomato gravy in 90 minutes—without leaving a disaster in the kitchen just as the doorbell rings. Instead of the typical prepackaged "meatloaf mix" that most recipes call for, we opted for a simpler approach: a mixture of 85 percent lean ground chuck (anything less fatty would produce a dry, bland meatball) and ground pork. Then, employing a test kitchen trick, we added a little gelatin to plump the meatballs and lend them a soft richness. A panade of panko (super-crunchy Japanese bread crumbs) soaked in buttermilk kept our meatballs moist. To avoid the messy step of frying, we turned to roasting, which worked perfectly. For a flavorful sauce without drippings, we braised the meatballs in the sauce for an hour so they could beef up the sauce as they finished cooking and became tender.

about 30 minutes, switching and rotating baking sheets halfway through cooking. Remove meatballs from oven and lower oven temperature to 300 degrees.

4. FOR THE SAUCE: While meatballs cook, heat oil in Dutch oven over medium heat until shimmering. Add onion and cook until softened and lightly browned, 6 to 8 minutes. Stir in garlic, oregano, and pepper flakes and cook until fragrant, about 30 seconds. Stir in tomato juice, crushed tomatoes, wine, and 1½ teaspoons salt and bring to simmer. Reduce heat to medium-low and simmer until slightly thickened, about 15 minutes.

5. Gently add roasted meatballs to sauce, cover pot, and place in oven. Cook until meatballs are firm and sauce has thickened, about 1 hour. (Sauce can be cooled and refrigerated for up to 1 day. Gently reheat over medium-low heat, stirring occasionally, about 30 minutes.) Stir in basil and parsley. Season with sugar, salt, and pepper to taste.

6. Bring 6 quarts water to boil in large pot. Add pasta and 1½ tablespoons salt and cook, stirring often, until al dente. Drain pasta and return it to pot. Toss pasta with 1½ cups sauce. Divide pasta among individual bowls, then top with more sauce and meatballs. Serve, passing grated Parmesan separately.

Herbed Spinach Dip

✓ **WHY THIS RECIPE WORKS** Our herbed spinach dip updates this normally humdrum party dip with a rich, creamy texture and big, bold spinach taste. A combination of mayonnaise and sour cream created a smooth base that was both rich and creamy. A good dose of fresh herbs, plus garlic, red bell pepper, and hot sauce give this dip lively flavor.

Be sure to squeeze the spinach thoroughly of excess liquid or the dip will taste watery. It's important to mince or press the garlic before adding it to the food processor with the other ingredients to prevent large chunks of garlic in the dip. Serve with fresh vegetable crudités, a thinly sliced baguette, and/or crackers.

10   ounces frozen spinach, thawed and squeezed dry
½   red bell pepper, stemmed, seeded, and chopped fine
½   cup sour cream
½   cup mayonnaise
½   cup fresh parsley leaves
1   tablespoon fresh dill or 1 teaspoon dried
3   scallions, sliced thin
1   garlic clove, minced
¼   teaspoon hot sauce, plus extra as needed
    Salt and pepper

Process all ingredients with ½ teaspoon salt and ¼ teaspoon pepper in food processor until well combined, about 1 minute. Transfer to serving bowl, cover, and refrigerate until flavors have blended, about 1 hour and up to 24 hours. Season with salt, pepper, and additional hot sauce to taste before serving. (Makes 2 cups.)

Classic Garlic Bread

Look for the highest quality football-shaped loaf of Italian bread you can find. We found that long, narrow French bread produces smaller, less satisfying slices.

9 garlic cloves, unpeeled
6 tablespoons unsalted butter, softened
2 tablespoons grated Parmesan cheese
½ teaspoon salt
¼ teaspoon pepper
1 (1-pound) loaf high-quality Italian bread, halved horizontally

1. Adjust oven rack to middle position and heat oven to 500 degrees. Toast garlic cloves in small skillet over medium heat, shaking pan occasionally, until fragrant and color of cloves deepens slightly, about 8 minutes. When cool enough to handle, peel and mince garlic (you should have about 3 tablespoons). Mash garlic, butter, Parmesan, salt, and pepper together in bowl.

2. Spread garlic-butter mixture evenly on cut sides of loaf. Place bread buttered side up on rimmed baking sheet. Bake until surface of bread is golden brown and toasted, 5 to 10 minutes, rotating baking sheet halfway through baking. Cut each half into 2-inch slices and serve.

✔ WHY THIS RECIPE WORKS

For crisp garlic bread with a sweet garlic flavor, we toasted a generous amount of whole garlic cloves to mellow their harshness. We then mashed the roasted garlic with enough butter to give the bread richness without making it soggy and greasy. A sprinkle of grated Parmesan cheese added depth and complexity without interfering with the garlic flavor.

Italian-Style Salad with Fennel and Artichokes

White wine vinegar can be substituted for the white balsamic vinegar. We do not recommend using regular balsamic vinegar because it will give the salad a muddy appearance.

3 tablespoons white balsamic vinegar
1 garlic clove, minced
¼ teaspoon salt
⅛ teaspoon pepper
6 tablespoons extra-virgin olive oil
1 head romaine lettuce (12 ounces), cut into 1-inch pieces
4 ounces baby arugula (4 cups)
1 fennel bulb, stalks discarded, bulb halved, cored, and sliced thin (see page 22)
½ cup fresh parsley leaves
½ cup pitted kalamata olives, chopped coarse
1 (14-ounce) can artichoke hearts, rinsed, patted dry, and quartered
2 ounces Asiago cheese, shaved (see page 32)

Whisk vinegar, garlic, salt, and pepper together in medium bowl. Whisking constantly, drizzle in oil. In large bowl, gently toss romaine with arugula, fennel, parsley, and olives. Just before serving, whisk dressing to re-emulsify, then drizzle all but 1 tablespoon over salad and toss gently to coat. Toss artichoke hearts with remaining 1 tablespoon dressing. Garnish individual portions with dressed artichoke hearts and Asiago.

✔ WHY THIS RECIPE WORKS

For a salad that would be refreshing but robust enough to pair with spaghetti and meatballs, we started with a base of mild romaine and spicy arugula, plus a good dose of parsley leaves, which served both as salad green and herb. Thinly sliced fennel added an appealing anise crunch. To incorporate some antipasto elements, we added olives, artichoke hearts, and shaved Asiago.

Individual Hot Fudge Pudding Cakes

This recipe requires 1½ cups weak coffee; use either 1 cup coffee diluted with ½ cup water or 1½ cups water mixed with 2 teaspoons instant espresso or instant coffee.

⅔   cup (2 ounces) Dutch-processed cocoa

6   tablespoons unsalted butter, cut into 6 pieces

2   ounces bittersweet or semisweet chocolate, chopped

¾   cup (3¾ ounces) all-purpose flour

2   teaspoons baking powder

1   cup (7 ounces) granulated sugar

⅓   cup whole milk

1   tablespoon vanilla extract

1   large egg yolk

¼   teaspoon salt

⅓   cup packed (2⅓ ounces) brown sugar

1½   cups weak coffee

2   pints vanilla or coffee ice cream

1. Adjust oven rack to lower-middle position and heat oven to 400 degrees. Grease eight 6-ounce ramekins and arrange on rimmed baking sheet.

2. Microwave ⅓ cup cocoa, butter, and chocolate in medium bowl, stirring often, until smooth, 1 to 3 minutes; let cool slightly. In small bowl, whisk flour and baking powder together.

3. In large bowl, whisk ⅔ cup granulated sugar, milk, vanilla, egg yolk, and salt together until combined. Whisk in cooled chocolate mixture, followed by flour mixture until just combined. Divide batter evenly among prepared ramekins (about ¼ cup per ramekin) and smooth tops. (Ramekins can be covered and refrigerated for up to 1 day.)

4. Combine remaining ⅓ cup cocoa, remaining ⅓ cup granulated sugar, and brown sugar in bowl, breaking up clumps with fingers. Sprinkle 2 tablespoons of mixture into each ramekin, followed by 3 tablespoons coffee. Bake until cakes are puffed and bubbling, 17 to 20 minutes. (Do not overbake.) Let cakes cool for 15 minutes (cakes will fall slightly). Just before serving, place small scoops of ice cream on top of cakes. Serve in ramekins.

EVEN EASIER ⤜ Don't have time to make individual chocolate cakes? Consider serving amaretto brownie sundaes instead. Place brownies (store-bought or made from a box) in individual serving bowls and top with 4 pints (½ gallon) vanilla ice cream. Drizzle with amaretto (or any other nut-flavored liqueur) then sprinkle with ½ cup toasted sliced almonds. Top with whipped cream if desired.

✔ **WHY THIS RECIPE WORKS**

Hot fudge pudding cake is the ultimate in homey alchemy: cake batter sprinkled with a mixture of sugar and cocoa and topped with brewed coffee transforms in the oven to a moist, brownielike chocolate cake with a hidden reservoir of fudgy, gooey sauce built right underneath. A combination of Dutch-processed cocoa (less acidic than natural cocoa powder) and bittersweet chocolate gives the cake layer an intense chocolate flavor, and the coffee cuts sweetness. While it's important not to overcook the cake, a 15-minute rest before serving allows the sauce to thicken into a silky, puddinglike texture, and gives the cake a chewy crust. We baked the cakes in individual ramekins and topped them with vanilla ice cream for an irresistible finish to our hearty meal.

New York–Style Pizza Party

THE GAME PLAN
↩

ONE DAY AHEAD...

MAKE MARINATED ARTICHOKE HEARTS: 15 minutes
(plus 3 hours for marinating)

MAKE PIZZA DOUGH: 20 minutes (plus 24 hours
for rising)

MAKE CANNOLI FILLING: 15 minutes
(plus 1 hour for draining ricotta)

ON THE DAY OF...

MAKE STUFFED PEPPERS: 20 minutes

MAKE PIZZAS: 2¼ hours (plus 1 hour to heat pizza stone)

MAKE SALAD: 30 minutes

ASSEMBLE CANNOLI: 15 minutes

NEW YORK–STYLE PIZZA PARTY

⤙ Serves 8 ⤚

Marinated Artichoke Hearts and Stuffed Pickled Sweet Peppers
Thin-Crust Cheese and Basil Pizza ⤝⤞ Mushroom and Fennel Pizza
Olive, Caper, and Spicy Garlic Pizza ⤝⤞ Prosciutto and Arugula Pizza
Citrus Salad with Bitter Greens ⤝⤞ Homemade Pistachio Cannoli

Thin-Crust Pizzas

This recipe will produce four distinctly different pizzas; one pizza is simply topped with cheese and basil, while the other three pizzas have additional toppings. Timing the pizzas for a crowd can be tricky; we suggest having the sauce, cheese, and all of the toppings ready to go before you start baking. If you don't have a pizza peel, use a large rimless baking sheet to transfer the pizza to the baking stone. Make sure the peel is well floured so that it will slide easily into the oven; semolina flour is ideal for dusting the peel if you have it.

DOUGH

- 6 cups (33 ounces) bread flour
- 4 teaspoons sugar
- 1 teaspoon instant or rapid-rise yeast
- 2⅔ cups ice water
- 2 tablespoons vegetable oil
- 1 tablespoon salt

SAUCE

- 1 (28-ounce) can whole peeled tomatoes, drained with juice reserved
- 1 tablespoon extra-virgin olive oil
- 1 teaspoon red wine vinegar
- 2 garlic cloves, minced
- 1 teaspoon dried oregano
- ½ teaspoon salt
- ¼ teaspoon pepper

PIZZAS

- 2 ounces Parmesan cheese, grated (1 cup)
- 1 pound whole-milk mozzarella cheese, shredded (4 cups)
- 1 tablespoon chopped fresh basil

- 1 recipe Mushroom and Fennel Pizza Topping (page 151)
- 1 recipe Olive, Caper, and Spicy Garlic Pizza Topping (page 151)
- 1 recipe Prosciutto and Arugula Pizza Topping (page 151)

1. FOR THE DOUGH: Process flour, sugar, and yeast together in food processor until combined, about 5 seconds. With processor running, slowly add water. Continue to process until dough is just combined and no dry flour remains, about 15 seconds. Let dough sit for 10 minutes.

2. Add oil and salt and continue to process until dough forms satiny, sticky ball that clears sides of bowl, about 1 minute. Transfer dough to lightly oiled counter and knead briefly until smooth, about 1 minute. Shape dough into ball, place in large greased bowl, and cover tightly with greased plastic wrap. Refrigerate for at least 24 hours and up to 3 days. *continued* ➤

☑ **WHY THIS RECIPE WORKS**
Trendy pizza parlors, watch out: With our easy-to-make recipe, any home cook can achieve the perfect crust at home—thin, crisp, and spottily charred on the exterior; tender yet chewy within—without a roaring hot brick oven or expert pizza-tossing skills. Our foolproof recipe starts with a relatively wet—but not too wet—dough, which stretches without tearing and stays tender once baked. High-protein bread flour aids in chewy texture, and extra sugar and oil help crisp the crust. But the real breakthroughs here turned out to be a cold proof and a revised oven rack setup. Slowing down the dough's fermentation in the refrigerator limits the size of bubbles that form, leading to less rise and a thinner, more flavorful crust.

3. FOR THE SAUCE: Process drained tomatoes with oil, vinegar, garlic, oregano, salt, and pepper in food processor until smooth, about 30 seconds. Transfer mixture to liquid measuring cup and add reserved tomato juice until sauce measures 2 cups. (Sauce can be refrigerated for up to 1 week.)

4. FOR THE PIZZAS: Position oven rack 4½ inches from top of oven, set pizza stone on rack, and heat oven to 500 degrees. Let stone heat up for 1 hour. Meanwhile, remove dough from refrigerator and divide into 4 equal pieces. Shape each piece into smooth ball and place on lightly oiled baking sheet, spaced 3 inches apart. Cover loosely with greased plastic wrap and let sit at room temperature for 1 hour.

5. Working with 1 piece of dough at a time, coat dough generously with flour and place on well-floured counter. Using fingertips, gently flatten dough into 8-inch disk, leaving 1 inch of outer edge slightly thicker than center. Using hands, gently stretch dough into 12-inch round, working along edges and giving dough quarter turns as you stretch. (Rounds can be stacked between pieces of parchment on baking sheet, covered with greased plastic

wrap, and refrigerated for up to 45 minutes before continuing with step 6.)

6. Transfer 1 dough round to well-floured pizza peel and stretch into 13-inch round. Spread ½ cup tomato sauce over dough, leaving ¼-inch border around edge. Sprinkle with ¼ cup Parmesan, followed by 1 cup mozzarella.

7. Carefully slide pizza onto hot baking stone and bake until crust is well browned and cheese is bubbly, 10 to 12 minutes, rotating pizza halfway through baking. Transfer pizza to wire rack and let cool for 5 minutes. Sprinkle with basil and serve.

8. For Mushroom and Fennel Pizza, repeat step 6 then sprinkle with topping and bake as directed; drizzle with truffle oil (if using) before serving. For Olive, Caper, and Spicy Garlic Pizza, repeat step 6 then sprinkle with topping and bake as directed; sprinkle with parsley before serving. For Prosciutto and Arugula Pizza, repeat step 6 and bake as directed; sprinkle with proscuitto-arugula topping before serving. (Baked pizzas can be held at room temperature for up to 4 hours. Re-crisp on hot baking stone in 500-degree oven, about 3 minutes; sprinkle with fresh herbs or proscuitto-arugula topping before serving.)

MAKING PIZZA

On a well-floured surface and using your fingertips, gently flatten the dough into an 8-inch disk, leaving the outer edge slightly thicker than the center to create a fatter "handle." With your hands, stretch the dough into a 12-inch round, working along the edges and giving the dough quarter turns. Transfer to a well-floured pizza peel and stretch to a 13-inch round. Top the dough with sauce, cheese, and toppings (if appropriate), then slide the pizza onto a preheated baking stone located just 4½ inches from the top of the oven (or broiler element, if applicable).

Mushroom and Fennel Pizza Topping

If desired, mince the fennel fronds and sprinkle them over the pizza with the basil before serving.

4 ounces cremini mushrooms, trimmed and sliced thin

½ fennel bulb, stalks discarded, cored, and sliced thin (see page 22)

1 tablespoon extra-virgin olive oil
Salt and pepper

2 teaspoons minced thyme
White truffle oil for drizzling (optional)

Toss mushrooms, fennel, and olive oil together in bowl and season with salt and pepper. Microwave, uncovered, until vegetables are softened and release liquid, 2 to 3 minutes. Drain vegetables, then toss with thyme. Sprinkle evenly over pizza before baking. Drizzle truffle oil, if using, lightly over pizza before serving. (Makes enough topping for 1 pizza.)

Olive, Caper, and Spicy Garlic Pizza Topping

Be sure to rinse the capers and anchovies, if using, or the pizza will be very salty.

⅓ cup pitted kalamata olives, halved

2 tablespoons capers, rinsed and patted dry

2 anchovy fillets, rinsed, patted dry, and chopped coarse (optional)

1 small garlic clove, minced

1 teaspoon extra-virgin olive oil

⅛ teaspoon red pepper flakes

¼ cup fresh parsley leaves

Combine olives, capers, anchovies, if using, garlic, oil, and pepper flakes in bowl. Sprinkle evenly over pizza before baking. Sprinkle parsley over pizza before serving. (Makes enough topping for 1 pizza.)

Prosciutto and Arugula Pizza Topping

This topping is added to the fully baked pizza before serving. Don't dress the arugula too far in advance or it will turn soggy.

1 cup baby arugula

2 teaspoons extra-virgin olive oil
Salt and pepper

2 ounces thinly sliced prosciutto, cut into 1-inch strips

Toss arugula with oil in bowl and season with salt and pepper to taste. Sprinkle prosciutto and dressed arugula over pizza before serving. (Makes enough topping for 1 pizza.)

Marinated Artichoke Hearts and Stuffed Pickled Sweet Peppers

WHY THIS RECIPE WORKS The key to this quick but flavorful antipasto appetizer is to start with two ingredients that are virtually prep-free: frozen artichoke hearts and pickled cherry peppers. We tossed the thawed artichokes in a lively mixture of olive oil, fresh herbs, and lemon zest and juice. While the artichokes chilled and absorbed the bold dressing, we stuffed store-bought pickled sweet cherry peppers with prosciutto and bite-size chunks of creamy fontina cheese.

Make sure to dry the artichokes thoroughly before tossing with marinade or they will be watery. Sweet cherry peppers are sold in jars and at the deli counter alongside the olives. To help the stuffed peppers stand upright on the platter, use a paring knife to trim the bottom of the peppers level. Serve with thin breadsticks.

¼ cup minced fresh parsley or basil
1 shallot, minced
¾ teaspoon grated lemon zest plus 2 tablespoons juice
1 garlic clove, minced
Salt and pepper
¾ cup extra-virgin olive oil
18 ounces frozen artichoke hearts, thawed, patted dry, and quartered if whole
16 ounces pickled sweet cherry peppers (25 peppers)
6 ounces fontina cheese, cut into ½-inch cubes
7 ounces thinly sliced prosciutto, sliced in half lengthwise

1. Whisk parsley, shallot, lemon zest and juice, garlic, ¼ teaspoon salt, and ⅛ teaspoon pepper together in small bowl. Whisking constantly, drizzle in olive oil. Measure out and reserve 2 tablespoons dressing for stuffed peppers. Gently fold artichoke hearts into remaining dressing, cover, and refrigerate until flavors meld, at least 3 hours and up to 1 day.

2. Meanwhile, remove stem and core of peppers with paring knife. Rinse peppers well and pat dry with paper towels. Roll each piece of cheese inside 1 piece prosciutto and stuff inside cored peppers.

3. To serve, transfer artichoke hearts to serving bowl and season with salt and pepper to taste. Arrange stuffed peppers on serving platter, whisk reserved dressing to re-emulsify, then drizzle over peppers.

Citrus Salad with Bitter Greens

WHY THIS RECIPE WORKS This light and refreshing fall salad sets pieces of fresh orange and grapefruit against a backdrop of bitter endive and spicy watercress. It's crucial to drain the fruit to remove excess juice; otherwise, the salad becomes a watery mess in moments. Incorporating a little drained citrus juice into the dressing reinforces the fresh, bold flavor, and some honey enhances the fruits' sweetness.

For more information on how to cut the grapefruits and oranges, see page 127.

2 grapefruits
2 large oranges
¼ cup red wine vinegar
1 shallot, minced
1 tablespoon honey
¼ teaspoon salt
⅛ teaspoon pepper
⅔ cup extra-virgin olive oil
12 ounces watercress, trimmed (12 cups)
3 heads Belgian endive (4 ounces each), leaves separated and cut into 2-inch pieces
¼ cup fresh parsley leaves
2 ounces Parmesan cheese, shaved (see page 32)

1. Cut away peel and pith from grapefruits and oranges. Quarter grapefruits and oranges, then slice crosswise into ¼-inch-thick pieces. Transfer fruit to colander, set over bowl to catch drained liquid, until serving time.

2. Whisk 1 tablespoon drained citrus juice, vinegar, shallot, honey, salt, and pepper together in medium bowl. Whisking constantly, drizzle in olive oil.

3. In large bowl, gently combine watercress, endive, and parsley. Just before serving, add drained fruit, discarding remaining drained juice. Whisk dressing to re-emulsify, then drizzle over salad and toss gently to coat. Garnish individual portions with Parmesan.

Homemade Pistachio Cannoli

You can find cannoli shells at most markets in either the international foods aisle, the gourmet cheese section, or the bakery. Make sure to use a high-quality whole-milk ricotta, such as Calabro. Use a vegetable peeler or the large holes of a box grater to shave or grate chocolate for a garnish.

12   ounces ricotta cheese (1½ cups)
12   ounces mascarpone cheese (1½ cups)
¾   cup (3 ounces) confectioners' sugar
½   cup shelled pistachios, chopped coarse
1½   teaspoons vanilla extract
      Pinch salt
10   cannoli shells
¼   cup shaved or grated bittersweet
      chocolate

1. Line colander with triple layer of cheesecloth and place in sink. Place ricotta in prepared colander, pull edges of cheesecloth together to form pouch, and twist to squeeze out as much liquid as possible. Place taut, twisted cheese pouch in pie plate and set heavy plate on top. Weight plate with 2 large heavy cans and refrigerate for 1 hour.

2. Discard drained ricotta liquid and transfer dry ricotta to medium bowl. Stir in mascarpone, sugar, pistachios, vanilla, and salt. Cover and refrigerate until needed, or up to 1 day.

3. Transfer chilled cheese mixture into pastry bag or large zipper-lock bag. (If using zipper-lock bag, cut ¾ inch off one bottom corner.) Pipe filling evenly into cannoli shells from both ends, working outward from center. Sprinkle 1 end of each cannoli with grated chocolate and serve. (Makes 10 cannoli.)

❤ WHY THIS RECIPE WORKS

To bring a taste of Italy home, we filled store-bought cannoli shells with a traditional filling of ricotta cheese enriched with creamy, rich mascarpone, sugar, and chopped pistachios. Instead of draining the ricotta overnight, we weighted the ricotta with heavy cans to remove maximum moisture in minimal time, resulting in a desirably dense filling in only an hour. To pipe the filling into the shells, a zipper-lock bag makes a convenient stand-in for a pastry bag. We garnished one end of each cannoli with shaved chocolate as a flavorful and elegant alternative to mini chocolate chips.

MAKING CANNOLI

To drain the ricotta of excess liquid, squeeze it in a triple-layer cheesecloth pouch, twisting the cheesecloth ends taut. Place the taut pouch in a pie plate, top with a plate, and weight down with several large heavy cans; refrigerate and let drain for 1 hour. To fill the cannoli, pipe the filling evenly into cannoli shells from both ends, working from the center of the shell outward.

Provençal Bistro Dinner

THE GAME PLAN

ONE DAY AHEAD...

MAKE PÂTÉ: 30 minutes (plus 6 hours for chilling)

MAKE ROUILLE: 30 minutes

MAKE POTS DE CRÈME: 35 minutes
(plus 4½ hours for chilling)

ON THE DAY OF...

MAKE BOUILLABAISSE: 3 hours

MAKE GARLIC TOASTS: 10 minutes

MAKE SALAD: 25 minutes

WHIP CREAM FOR POTS DE CRÈME: 5 minutes

PROVENÇAL BISTRO DINNER

➤ *Serves 8* ➤

Chicken Liver Pâté ✎ Chicken Bouillabaisse with Saffron Rouille
Romaine Salad with Pears and Fennel
Chocolate Pots de Crème

Chicken Bouillabaisse

You will need at least a 6-quart Dutch oven for this recipe. Be careful not to fully submerge the chicken into the liquid during cooking, or the skin will turn soggy.

9	(6-ounce) bone-in chicken thighs, trimmed
5	(12-ounce) bone-in split chicken breasts, trimmed (see page 113) and cut in half
	Salt and pepper
¼	cup olive oil
1½	pounds leeks, white and light green parts only, halved lengthwise, sliced thin, and washed thoroughly (see page 37)
2	fennel bulbs, stalks discarded, bulbs halved, cored, and sliced thin (see page 22)
2	tablespoons all-purpose flour
6	garlic cloves, minced
2	tablespoons tomato paste
½	teaspoon saffron threads
¼	teaspoon cayenne pepper
6	cups low-sodium chicken broth, plus extra as needed
3	(14.5-ounce) cans diced tomatoes, drained
2	pounds Yukon Gold potatoes, cut into ¾-inch cubes
1	cup dry white wine
⅓	cup pastis or Pernod
3	(2-inch) strips orange zest (see page 28)
2	tablespoons minced fresh tarragon or parsley
1	recipe Saffron Rouille (page 158)
1	recipe Garlic Toasts (page 62)

1. Adjust oven rack to middle position and heat oven to 375 degrees. Pat chicken dry with paper towels and season with salt and pepper. Heat 2 tablespoons oil in Dutch oven over medium-high heat until just smoking. Brown one-third of chicken on both sides, 8 to 10 minutes, flipping as needed; transfer to bowl. Repeat with remaining 2 tablespoons oil and remaining chicken in 2 batches.

2. Add leeks and fennel to now-empty Dutch oven and cook, stirring often, until softened, 5 to 7 minutes. Stir in flour, garlic, tomato paste, saffron, and cayenne and cook until fragrant, about 30 seconds. Stir in broth, tomatoes, potatoes, wine, pastis, and orange zest and bring to simmer. Reduce heat to medium-low and simmer until vegetables are tender and flavors have combined, 10 to 12 minutes. Transfer mixture to 16 by 13-inch roasting pan.

3. Nestle chicken thighs into roasting pan with skin sitting above surface of liquid. Transfer roasting pan to oven and cook for 10 minutes. Carefully nestle chicken breasts into pan, making *continued* ➤

✔ **WHY THIS RECIPE WORKS**
Swapping readily available bone-in chicken breasts and thighs for the numerous and expensive varieties of fish in traditional bouillabaisse makes this update of the classic Provençal recipe an equally delicious but far more practical dish. Resting the chicken on the potatoes as the bouillabaisse cooks in the oven enables the skin to stay out of the liquid and become crisp. A quick blast of broiler heat before serving further enhances crispness. Traditional flavors of garlic, fennel, and tarragon lend earthy aromatics to the saffron-scented stew, and pastis or Pernod provides an extra splash of anise flavor. The stew is topped with garlicky *rouille*, a mayonnaise flavored with saffron and thickened with bread crumbs, and crunchy crostini.

sure all chicken skin stays above surface of liquid. Continue to cook in oven until breasts register 160 degrees and thighs register 175 degrees, 20 to 30 minutes. (Bouillabaisse can be refrigerated in roasting pan for up to 1 day. Reheat, covered, in 375-degree oven until sauce is simmering and chicken is heated through, 1½ to 2 hours; add additional broth as needed to adjust sauce consistency.)

4. Remove bouillabaisse from oven. Adjust oven rack 6 inches from broiler element and heat broiler. Broil bouillabaisse until chicken skin is crisp, 5 to 10 minutes.

5. Transfer chicken to large platter. Let broth settle for 5 minutes, then skim fat from surface with wide spoon. Stir in tarragon and season with salt and pepper to taste. Ladle broth and potatoes into individual shallow serving bowls, top with 2 pieces of chicken, and dollop with Saffron Rouille. Spread about 1 teaspoon rouille onto each Garlic Toast, then nestle into bowls. Serve, passing remaining rouille separately.

Saffron Rouille

Leftover rouille can be used in sandwiches or as a sauce for vegetables and fish.

WHY THIS RECIPE WORKS As if our Chicken Bouillabaisse weren't already a gloriously flavored dish, the addition of a creamy, garlicky rouille takes it up a notch. Saffron, Dijon, and cayenne give this garlicky mayonnaise its punch while bread thickens and binds it all together. We like to dollop it right into the bouillabaisse and serve it on garlic toasts that soften in the stew.

¼ cup water
½ teaspoon saffron threads
2 slices hearty white sandwich bread, crusts removed, bread torn into 1-inch pieces
5 teaspoons lemon juice
2 large egg yolks
1 tablespoon Dijon mustard
3 garlic cloves, minced
¼ teaspoon cayenne pepper
¾ cup vegetable oil
¾ cup extra-virgin olive oil
Salt and pepper

1. Microwave water and saffron in medium bowl until hot and steaming, 10 to 20 seconds; let steep for 5 minutes. Stir bread and lemon juice into saffron-water, let soak 5 minutes, then mash into paste using whisk.

2. Whisk in egg yolks, mustard, garlic, and cayenne until smooth, about 15 seconds. Whisking constantly, slowly drizzle in vegetable oil in steady stream until smooth mayonnaise-like consistency is reached, scraping down bowl as needed. Slowly whisk in olive oil in steady stream until smooth. Season with salt and pepper to taste. (Rouille can be refrigerated for up to 2 days. Makes 2 cups.)

Chicken Liver Pâté

Pressing plastic wrap against the surface of the pâté helps minimize any discoloration due to oxidation. Serve with a thinly sliced baguette, toast points, or crackers.

8   tablespoons unsalted butter
3   large shallots, sliced thin
1   tablespoon minced fresh thyme
    Salt and pepper
1   pound chicken livers, rinsed and patted dry, fat and connective tissue removed
¾   cup dry vermouth
2   teaspoons brandy

1. Melt butter in 12-inch skillet over medium-high heat. Add shallots, thyme, and ¼ teaspoon salt and cook until shallots are lightly browned, 3 to 5 minutes. Add chicken livers and cook, stirring constantly, about 1 minute. Add vermouth and simmer until livers are cooked but still have rosy interior, 4 to 6 minutes.

2. Using slotted spoon, transfer livers to food processor. Continue to simmer vermouth mixture until slightly syrupy, about 2 minutes longer.

3. Add vermouth mixture and brandy to processor and process until mixture is very smooth, about 2 minutes, scraping down bowl as needed. Season with salt and pepper to taste. Transfer to small serving bowl and smooth top. Press plastic wrap flush to surface of pâté and refrigerate until firm, at least 6 hours and up to 3 days.

4. Before serving, bring to room temperature to soften and scrape off any discolored pâté on top.

Romaine Salad with Pears and Fennel

To ripen rock-hard pears, store them in a paper bag with bananas.

2   tablespoons chopped fresh mint
1½   teaspoons grated lemon zest plus 2 tablespoons juice
      Salt and pepper
¼   cup extra-virgin olive oil
2   heads Belgian endive (4 ounces each), leaves separated and cut into 1-inch pieces
1   large head romaine lettuce (14 ounces), cut into 1-inch pieces
1   fennel bulb, stalks discarded, halved, cored, and sliced thin (see page 22)
3   very ripe Bartlett or Bosc pears

1. Whisk mint, lemon zest and juice, ¼ teaspoon salt, and ⅛ teaspoon pepper together in small bowl. Whisking constantly, drizzle in oil. In large bowl, toss endive with romaine and fennel.

2. Just before serving, peel, halve, and core pears, then slice lengthwise into ¼-inch-thick slices. Whisk dressing to re-emulsify, then drizzle over salad and toss gently to coat. Garnish individual portions with sliced pears.

Chocolate Pots de Crème

We prefer pots de crème made with 60 percent cocoa bittersweet chocolate (our favorite brands are Ghirardelli and Callebaut), but 70 percent bittersweet chocolate can also be used. If using a 70 percent bittersweet chocolate (we like Lindt, El Rey, and Valrhona), reduce the amount of chocolate to 8 ounces. A tablespoon of strong brewed coffee may be substituted for the instant espresso and water.

POTS DE CRÈME
- 10 ounces bittersweet chocolate, chopped fine
- 5 large egg yolks
- 5 tablespoons (2¼ ounces) sugar
- ¼ teaspoon salt
- 1½ cups heavy cream
- ¾ cup half-and-half
- 1 tablespoon vanilla extract
- ½ teaspoon instant espresso dissolved in 1 tablespoon hot water

GARNISH
- ½ cup heavy cream, chilled
- 2 teaspoons sugar
- ½ teaspoon vanilla extract
   Cocoa powder (optional)

1. FOR THE POTS DE CRÈME: Place chocolate in heatproof bowl; set fine-mesh strainer over bowl and set aside.

2. Whisk yolks, sugar, and salt together in bowl until combined, then whisk in heavy cream and half-and-half. Transfer mixture to medium saucepan and cook over medium-low heat, stirring constantly and scraping bottom of pot, until thickened and registers 175 to 180 degrees, 8 to 12 minutes. (Do not overcook or simmer custard.)

3. Immediately pour hot custard through strainer over chocolate. Let mixture sit to melt chocolate, about 5 minutes. Whisk gently until smooth, then whisk in vanilla and espresso. Divide mixture evenly among eight 5- or 6-ounce ramekins. Gently tap ramekins against counter to remove any air bubbles.

4. Cool pots de crème to room temperature, then cover with plastic wrap and refrigerate until chilled, at least 4 hours and up to 3 days.

5. FOR THE GARNISH: Using stand mixer fitted with whisk, whip cream, sugar, and vanilla on medium-low speed until foamy, about 1 minute. Increase speed to high and whip until soft peaks form, 1 to 3 minutes. (Whipped cream can be refrigerated for up to 8 hours; rewhisk briefly before serving.)

6. To serve, let pots de crème sit at room temperature for 20 to 30 minutes. Dollop pots de crème with whipped cream and dust with cocoa powder (if using).

Farmhouse Chicken Dinner

THE GAME PLAN
❧

ONE DAY AHEAD...

PREP CHICKEN: 45 minutes (plus 30 minutes for brining)

MAKE BARLEY PILAF: 1¼ hours

MAKE SPICED WALNUTS FOR APPETIZER: 1 hour

THE DAY OF...

MAKE PEAR CRUMBLE: 2 hours

BAKE CHICKEN AND BRUSSELS SPROUTS: 1¼ hours

ASSEMBLE GOAT CHEESE APPETIZER: 5 minutes

REHEAT BARLEY PILAF: 5 minutes

FARMHOUSE CHICKEN DINNER

➤ Serves 8 ◄

Honeyed Goat Cheese with Spiced Walnuts and Figs
Rustic Breaded Chicken with Brussels Sprouts
Herbed Barley Pilaf ✦ Autumn Pear Crumble

Rustic Breaded Chicken with Brussels Sprouts

If using kosher chicken, do not brine in step 1, and season the chicken with salt before dredging in flour in step 3. Do not use maple-flavored bacon here; it will add an unwelcome flavor to the dish.

½ cup sugar
   Salt and pepper
8 (12-ounce) bone-in split chicken breasts, skin removed, trimmed (see page 113)
1 (12-inch) baguette, torn into 1-inch pieces (5 cups)
4 tablespoons unsalted butter, melted
¼ cup minced fresh parsley
2 garlic cloves, minced
½ cup all-purpose flour
2 large eggs
4 slices bacon, cut into ½-inch pieces
3 pounds Brussels sprouts, trimmed and halved
6 shallots, peeled and quartered
3 tablespoons olive oil
   Lemon wedges

1. Dissolve sugar and ½ cup salt in 2 quarts cold water in large container. Submerge chicken in brine, cover, and refrigerate for 30 to 60 minutes.

2. Adjust oven racks to upper-middle and lower-middle positions and heat oven to 450 degrees. Process bread in food processor until coarsely chopped with pieces no larger than ¼ inch, 1½ to 2 minutes. Add melted butter, ¼ teaspoon salt, and ⅛ teaspoon pepper and pulse to incorporate, about 5 pulses. Spread crumbs over rimmed baking sheet and bake on lower rack until golden, about 6 minutes. Let crumbs cool slightly, then stir in parsley and garlic.

3. Set wire rack in rimmed baking sheet. Place flour in shallow dish. In second shallow dish, lightly beat eggs. Spread toasted crumbs into third shallow dish. Remove chicken from brine and pat dry with paper towels. Working with 1 breast at a time, dredge skinned side of chicken in flour, then dip into eggs, and finally, coat with crumbs, pressing on them to adhere. Lay chicken breaded side up on prepared wire rack. Pack remaining crumbs onto top of chicken. (Breaded chicken can be refrigerated for up to 24 hours before continuing with step 5.)

4. Meanwhile, line another rimmed baking sheet with aluminum foil. Microwave bacon in bowl until fat is rendered but bacon is still soft, 1 to 3 minutes. Toss bacon and rendered fat with Brussels sprouts, shallots, oil, ½ teaspoon salt, and ¼ teaspoon pepper. Spread vegetables onto prepared baking sheet. (Prepped vegetables can be held at room temperature for up to 4 hours before continuing.) *continued* ➤

✔ **WHY THIS RECIPE WORKS**
When it comes to comfort food, roast chicken is about as good as it gets. Bone-in chicken breasts are the answer to keeping this dish streamlined for company, and a 30-minute brining ensures juicy, tender chicken. A rustic coating of fresh bread crumbs, parsley, and garlic gives each forkful a satisfying crunch and knockout flavor and protects the breast meat from drying out. To maximize efficiency, we used the high heat and lower rack of the oven to roast a side dish of Brussels sprouts, bacon, and shallots while the chicken climbed to 160 degrees. First, we cooked bacon pieces in the microwave to render fat, which was tossed with the vegetables to provide an extra punch of flavor.

5. Place chicken on upper-middle rack and vegetables on lower-middle rack. Roast, stirring sprouts occasionally, until chicken registers 160 degrees and crumbs are well browned, 30 to 40 minutes.

6. Remove chicken from oven and let rest for 5 to 10 minutes. Continue to roast vegetables until completely tender and lightly caramelized, about 5 minutes longer. Season vegetables with salt and pepper to taste. Serve chicken and vegetables with lemon wedges.

Honeyed Goat Cheese with Spiced Walnuts and Figs

✓ WHY THIS RECIPE WORKS While simple to pull together, this appetizer is anything but ordinary. Tossing the walnuts in egg whites gives them a sticky coating for the spices to cling to as they toast. The combination of cumin and cayenne provides a savory kick to balance the sweetness of honey and creamy tang of goat cheese. What's more, the walnuts can be made up to a week ahead, making assembly a snap.

If you can't find superfine sugar, process granulated sugar in a food processor for 1 minute. If fresh figs are unavailable, substitute apple slices or seedless grapes. Serve with crackers or a thinly sliced baguette.

1	large egg white
1	teaspoon water
¼	teaspoon salt
1	cup walnuts, chopped coarse
3	tablespoons superfine sugar
½	teaspoon ground cumin
¼	teaspoon cayenne pepper
¼	teaspoon paprika
1	(10-ounce) log goat cheese
	Coarse sea salt
2	tablespoons honey
16	fresh figs, halved lengthwise

1. Adjust oven rack to middle position and heat oven to 275 degrees. Line rimmed baking sheet with parchment paper.

Whisk egg white, water, and salt together in medium bowl. Add nuts and toss to coat. Drain nuts through fine mesh strainer, about 5 minutes.

2. Mix sugar, cumin, cayenne, and paprika in large bowl. Add drained nuts and toss to coat. Spread nuts evenly over prepared baking sheet. Bake nuts, stirring occasionally, until dry and crisp, about 50 minutes. Let nuts cool completely, about 30 minutes, then break apart with hands. (Nuts can be stored at room temperature for up to 1 week.)

3. Place goat cheese on serving platter. Season with sea salt, drizzle with honey, and sprinkle with spiced nuts. Serve with figs.

Herbed Barley Pilaf

✓ WHY THIS RECIPE WORKS Firmer in texture and less likely to overcook than rice, barley provides the hearty side dish this rustic menu requires. Best of all, the barley's sturdy texture and low starch give it staying power; it can be cooked up to a day ahead and reheated before serving.

Don't substitute hulled barley for the pearl barley; hulled barley requires soaking and a longer cooking time.

4	tablespoons unsalted butter
1	onion, chopped fine
	Salt and pepper
2½	cups pearl barley, rinsed and drained
3	garlic cloves, minced
2	teaspoons minced fresh thyme
3¾	cups water
⅓	cup minced fresh parsley
3	tablespoons minced fresh chives
2	teaspoons lemon juice

1. Melt butter in large saucepan over medium heat. Add onion and ¼ teaspoon salt and cook, stirring occasionally, until onion is softened, 5 to 7 minutes.

2. Stir in barley, garlic, and thyme and cook, stirring often, until barley is lightly toasted and fragrant, about 3 minutes. Stir in water and bring to simmer. Reduce heat to low, cover, and continue to simmer until barley is tender and water is absorbed,

20 to 30 minutes.

3. Off heat, lay clean folded dish towel underneath lid and let sit for 10 minutes. Fluff barley with fork. Fold in parsley, chives, and lemon juice and season with salt and pepper to taste. Serve. (Pilaf can be refrigerated for up to 1 day; reheat in microwave until hot, 2 to 4 minutes, before serving.)

~~~~~~

Autumn Pear Crumble

Be careful not to overbake the topping in step 4, or it may get too dark when baked again with the filling in step 5. Serve with vanilla ice cream or whipped cream.

FRUIT FILLING

4	pounds Bosc or Bartlett pears, peeled, cored, and cut into ½-inch pieces
5	tablespoons (2¼ ounces) granulated sugar
1	tablespoon brandy
1	tablespoon lemon juice
1	teaspoon cornstarch
½	teaspoon cinnamon
⅛	teaspoon salt
1	cup dried cranberries

CRUMBLE

1	cup (5 ounces) all-purpose flour
¼	cup packed (1¾ ounces) brown sugar
¼	cup (1¾ ounces) plus 1 tablespoon granulated sugar
2	teaspoons vanilla extract
⅛	teaspoon salt
6	tablespoons unsalted butter, cut into 6 pieces and softened
½	cup sliced almonds

1. FOR THE FRUIT FILLING: Combine pears, sugar, brandy, lemon juice, cornstarch, cinnamon, and salt in Dutch oven. Cover and cook over medium heat, stirring often, until pears are tender when poked with fork but still hold their shape, 15 to 20 minutes. Off heat, gently stir in cranberries. Divide mixture among eight 6-ounce ramekins and set on rimmed baking sheet. (Fruit filling can be refrigerated for up to 2 days.)

2. FOR THE CRUMBLE: Adjust oven rack to middle position and heat oven to 350 degrees. Line rimmed baking sheet with parchment paper.

3. Pulse flour, brown sugar, ¼ cup granulated sugar, vanilla, and salt in food processor until combined, about 5 pulses. Sprinkle butter and ¼ cup almonds over top and process until mixture clumps together into large crumbly balls, about 30 seconds. Sprinkle remaining ¼ cup almonds over top and pulse to incorporate, about 2 pulses.

4. Spread mixture out onto prepared baking sheet, breaking it into ¼-inch pieces (with some smaller loose bits). Bake until lightly browned, 10 to 15 minutes. (Topping can be stored at room temperature for up to 3 days.)

5. Sprinkle topping evenly over filling in ramekins, breaking up any large pieces. Sprinkle with remaining 1 tablespoon granulated sugar. Bake crumble until topping is well browned and fruit is bubbling around edges, 23 to 27 minutes, rotating baking sheet halfway through baking. Let cool for 10 minutes before serving.

☑ WHY THIS RECIPE WORKS
Cooking the fruit and crumble separately is the key to this dessert's success. Precooking the pears in a Dutch oven gets them to the perfect texture—tender but not mushy—and gives them time to release their juices before adding the topping. Dried cranberries give a tart splash of flavor to balance the pears' sweetness. To keep the topping from getting soggy in the moist fruit, the crumble mixture (more cookie than streusel, in fact) is first baked on a sheet pan until lightly golden. The buttery, crisp, nutty-tasting crumble is then broken into pieces and sprinkled onto the individual bowls of cooked fruit. A final pass in the oven browns the topping and helps it cling to the bubbling filling.

EVEN EASIER ➤ Don't have time to make a pear crumble? Homemade caramel apples are a great ending to this fall dinner and are festive—especially if kids are included. Line a baking sheet with greased parchment paper. Insert popsicle sticks into 8 Granny Smith apples with stems removed. Melt two 14-ounce bags chewy caramel candies with ¼ cup water in a large heatproof bowl set over a saucepan filled with 1 inch of barely simmering water, about 10 minutes. Dip the apples into the melted caramel and turn to coat. Let the excess caramel drip off the apples, then transfer to the prepared baking sheet and let cool for 15 minutes. If desired, press chopped roasted peanuts into the caramel while warm, or drizzle with melted chocolate.

Vegetarian
Indian Night

THE GAME PLAN

⫷⫸

ONE DAY AHEAD...

MAKE RED LENTIL DAL DIP: 1 hour
(plus 30 minutes for cooling)

MAKE CILANTRO-MINT CHUTNEY: 10 minutes

MAKE CARDAMOM COOKIES: 1¼ hours
(plus 2 hours for chilling)

ON THE DAY OF...

MAKE CURRY: 1½ hours

MAKE RICE PILAF: 1 hour

ASSEMBLE DESSERT: 5 minutes

VEGETARIAN INDIAN NIGHT

❦ *Serves 8* ❦

Red Lentil Dal Dip
Indian-Style Vegetable Curry with Cilantro-Mint Chutney
Basmati Rice Pilaf ❧ Mango Sorbet with Rose Water and Cardamom Cookies

Indian-Style Vegetable Curry

You will need at least a 6-quart Dutch oven for this recipe. To make this dish spicier, add the reserved chile seeds. Serve with Cilantro-Mint Chutney (page 168) and warm naan.

2	(14.5-ounce) cans diced tomatoes
¼	cup mild curry powder
2	teaspoons garam masala
6	tablespoons vegetable oil
2	pounds onions, chopped fine
1½	pounds red potatoes, cut into ½-inch pieces
6	garlic cloves, minced
2	tablespoons grated fresh ginger
2	serrano chiles, stemmed, seeds reserved, and minced
2	tablespoons tomato paste
1	large head cauliflower (3 pounds), cored and cut into 1-inch florets
2½	cups water, plus extra as needed
2	(15-ounce) cans chickpeas, rinsed
	Salt
3	cups frozen peas
½	cup heavy cream or coconut milk

1. Pulse tomatoes in food processor until nearly smooth with ¼-inch pieces visible, about 5 pulses; set aside. Toast curry powder and garam masala in 8-inch skillet over medium-high heat, stirring constantly, until spices darken slightly and become fragrant, about 1 minute. Transfer spices to small bowl.

2. Heat ¼ cup oil in Dutch oven over medium-high heat until shimmering. Add onions and potatoes and cook, stirring occasionally, until onions are softened and lightly browned and potatoes are golden around edges, 10 to 12 minutes.

3. Reduce heat to medium. Clear center of pan, add remaining 2 tablespoons oil, garlic, ginger, chiles, and tomato paste and cook until fragrant, about 30 seconds. Add toasted spices and cook, stirring constantly, about 1 minute longer. Add cauliflower and cook until spices coat florets, about 2 minutes.

4. Stir in processed tomatoes, water, chickpeas, and 1 teaspoon salt. Increase heat to medium-high and bring to boil, scraping up browned bits. Cover, reduce heat to medium, and simmer briskly, stirring occasionally, until vegetables are tender, 10 to 15 minutes. (Curry can be held at room temperature for up to 1 hour. Reheat gently over low heat, adjusting sauce consistency with additional water as needed, before continuing.)

5. Stir in peas and cream and continue to cook until heated through, about 2 minutes. Season with salt to taste and serve.

✔ WHY THIS RECIPE WORKS
Vegetable curries can be complicated affairs, with lengthy ingredient lists and fussy techniques meant to compensate for the lack of meat. We wanted a curry we could make for company that was low on fuss but big on flavor. Toasting the curry powder in a skillet turned it into a flavor powerhouse. Further experimentation proved that adding a few pinches of garam masala added even more spice flavor. To build the rest of our flavor base, we started with a generous amount of sautéed onion, vegetable oil, garlic, ginger, fresh chile, and tomato paste for sweetness. When we chose our vegetables (chickpeas and potatoes for heartiness and cauliflower and peas for texture and color), we found that sautéing the spices and main ingredients together enhanced and melded the flavors.

Cilantro-Mint Chutney

WHY THIS RECIPE WORKS
This chutney of fresh mint and grassy cilantro mixed with yogurt and spices provides a cool contrast to the robust curry. While traditional fruit chutneys usually require cooking, this fresh green chutney can be assembled in less than a minute in the food processor.

We prefer whole-milk yogurt here, though low-fat or nonfat yogurt can be substituted.

2   cups fresh cilantro leaves
1   cup fresh mint leaves
½   cup plain yogurt
¼   cup finely chopped onion
1   tablespoon lime juice
1½   teaspoons sugar
½   teaspoon ground cumin
¼   teaspoon salt

Process all ingredients in food processor until smooth, 30 to 40 seconds, scraping down bowl as needed. (Chutney can be refrigerated for up to 24 hours. Makes 1 cup.)

Red Lentil Dal Dip

WHY THIS RECIPE WORKS
Traditional Indian dal is often served as a stew, but reducing the amount of liquid provides a thicker, more intense consistency perfect for serving with pita chips or spreading on naan. The red lentils cook quickly and break down into a smooth puree within about 20 minutes (no soaking required), making them an ideal choice for a quick dip. To intensify the flavor of the spices, we "bloomed" them in hot oil and then added onion, garlic, and ginger before adding the lentils and liquid. Coconut milk gave the dal a luxurious texture, while cilantro added color and freshness and lime juice provided a tangy finish.

You cannot substitute brown lentils for the red lentils here; the red lentils have a very different texture. The addition of coconut milk provides a lush, creamy texture and rich flavor; do not substitute light coconut milk. Serve with pita chips.

½   teaspoon ground coriander
½   teaspoon ground cumin
½   teaspoon ground cinnamon
½   teaspoon ground turmeric
⅛   teaspoon ground cardamom
⅛   teaspoon red pepper flakes
3   tablespoons olive oil
1   onion, chopped fine
3   garlic cloves, minced
1   tablespoon tomato paste
1½   teaspoons grated fresh ginger
2   cups water
1   cup coconut milk
7   ounces red lentils (1 cup), picked over and rinsed
⅓   cup minced fresh cilantro
4   teaspoons lime juice
     Salt and pepper

1. Combine coriander, cumin, cinnamon, turmeric, cardamom, and pepper flakes in small bowl. Heat 1 tablespoon oil in large saucepan over medium-high heat until shimmering. Add spices and cook until fragrant, about 10 seconds. Stir in onion and cook until softened, 5 to 7 minutes. Stir in garlic, tomato paste, and ginger and cook until fragrant, about 30 seconds.

2. Stir in water, coconut milk, and lentils and bring to boil. Reduce to simmer and cook, uncovered, until lentils are tender and resemble coarse puree, 20 to 25 minutes. Transfer to serving bowl and let cool to room temperature. (Dip can be refrigerated for up to 1 day; return to room temperature before continuing.)

3. Stir in remaining 2 tablespoons oil, cilantro, and lime juice. Season with salt and pepper to taste and serve. (Makes 2½ cups.)

EVEN EASIER ➤ Don't have time to make a red lentil dip? Make a quick canned white bean dip using similar flavors. Microwave ¼ cup olive oil, 1 minced shallot, 2 cloves minced garlic, ¾ teaspoon salt, ½ teaspoon turmeric, ½ teaspoon coriander, ½ teaspoon cumin, ¼ teaspoon cardamom, and a pinch red pepper flakes together in a medium bowl until fragrant, about 1 minute. Puree two 15-ounce cans white beans, rinsed, oil-spice mixture, and ½ cup coconut milk in a food processor until smooth, scraping down the bowl as needed. Transfer to a serving bowl and stir in ½ cup minced fresh cilantro and 1 tablespoon lime juice. Cover and refrigerate until chilled, about 30 minutes, before serving.

Basmati Rice Pilaf

Long-grain white, jasmine, or Texmati rice can be substituted for the basmati. A nonstick saucepan works best here, although a traditional saucepan will also work.

3 tablespoons olive oil
1 onion, chopped fine
  Salt and pepper
2½ cups basmati rice, rinsed and drained
3¾ cups water

1. Heat oil in large saucepan over medium heat until shimmering. Add onion and 1 teaspoon salt and cook, stirring occasionally, until onion is softened, 5 to 7 minutes. Stir in rice and cook, stirring often, until fragrant and edges of grains begin to turn translucent, about 2 minutes.

2. Stir in water and bring to simmer. Cover, reduce heat to low, and continue to simmer until water is absorbed and rice is tender, 16 to 20 minutes. Off heat, lay clean folded dish towel underneath lid and let sit for 10 minutes. Fluff rice with fork, season with salt and pepper to taste, and serve.

✔ WHY THIS RECIPE WORKS
Using the pilaf method of rice cooking, we were able to maximize flavor by first sautéing the onion and then the rice in oil. The tender, separate grains of this pilaf make it the perfect vehicle for our Indian-Style Vegetable Curry.

Mango Sorbet with Rose Water and Cardamom Cookies

Rose water is potent, so be sure to drizzle it lightly over the mango sorbet.

1 cup plus 2 tablespoons (5⅔ ounces) all-purpose flour
¾ teaspoon ground cardamom
¼ teaspoon baking powder
¼ teaspoon salt
8 tablespoons unsalted butter, softened
½ cup packed (3½ ounces) light brown sugar
1 large egg yolk
½ teaspoon vanilla extract
½ cup shelled pistachios, chopped coarse
4 pints (½ gallon) mango sorbet
  Rose water

1. Whisk flour, cardamom, baking powder, and salt together in bowl. Using stand mixer fitted with paddle, beat butter and sugar until pale and fluffy, about 3 minutes. Add egg yolk and vanilla and beat until incorporated, about 30 seconds, scraping down bowl as needed. Reduce speed to low and slowly add flour mixture until combined, about 30 seconds. Add pistachios and mix until incorporated. Cover and refrigerate until dough is no longer sticky, 10 to 15 minutes.

2. Transfer dough to clean counter and roll into 15-inch-long log, about 2 inches in diameter. Flatten top and sides of log into rectangular shape, measuring about 2½ inches wide by 1 inch thick. Wrap dough tightly in plastic wrap and refrigerate until firm, at least 2 hours and up to 3 days.

3. Adjust oven racks to upper-middle and lower-middle positions and heat oven to 350 degrees. Line 2 baking sheets with parchment paper.

4. Slice dough into ¼-inch-thick rounds. Lay cookies on prepared baking sheets, spaced about 1 inch apart. Bake until edges are lightly browned, 12 to 16 minutes, switching and rotating baking sheets halfway through baking. Let cookies cool on baking sheets for 3 minutes, then transfer to wire rack to cool completely. (Makes 3 dozen cookies.)

5. To serve, portion sorbet into individual bowls, drizzle lightly with rose water, and serve with cookies.

✔ WHY THIS RECIPE WORKS
A hint of cardamom and crunchy pistachios give an Indian spin to our rich butter cookies. Paired with tangy mango sorbet drizzled with rose water, the cookies provide an easy-to-assemble yet elegant finish to the meal.

Autumn Harvest Pork Dinner

THE GAME PLAN

ONE DAY AHEAD...

ASSEMBLE PALMIERS: 15 minutes (plus 1 hour for chilling)

ON THE DAY OF...

BAKE PALMIERS: 30 minutes

MAKE TART: 1 hour (plus 2½ hours for baking and cooling)

MAKE CILANTRO SAUCE: 15 minutes

MAKE PORK LOIN AND SWEET POTATOES:
2½ hours (plus 1½ hours for brining)

MAKE SALAD: 20 minutes

AUTUMN HARVEST PORK DINNER

⤙ *Serves 8* ⤚

Ham and Cheese Palmiers
Roast Pork Loin with Sweet Potatoes and Cilantro Sauce
Spinach Salad with Blood Oranges and Radishes
Raspberry Streusel Tart

Roast Pork Loin with Sweet Potatoes and Cilantro Sauce

A ¼-inch layer of fat on top of the roast is ideal; if the roast has a thicker fat cap, trim it back accordingly. If the pork is enhanced (injected with a salt solution), do not brine in step 1, and season with salt in step 2.

PORK AND POTATOES

½	cup sugar
	Salt and pepper
1	(4-pound) boneless pork loin roast, trimmed and tied at 1½-inch intervals (see page 175)
1	tablespoon ground coriander
1	tablespoon ground cumin
1	tablespoon plus ⅓ cup vegetable oil
5	pounds sweet potatoes, peeled, quartered, and cut into 1-inch chunks
1	pound shallots, peeled and quartered
¼	teaspoon cayenne pepper

CILANTRO SAUCE

3¾	cups fresh cilantro leaves and stems, trimmed (3 bunches)
¾	cup extra-virgin olive oil
2	tablespoons lime juice
3	garlic cloves, minced
½	teaspoon sugar
	Salt and pepper

1. FOR THE PORK AND POTATOES: Dissolve sugar and ¼ cup salt in 2 quarts cold water in large container. Submerge pork in brine, cover, and refrigerate for 1½ to 2 hours.

2. Adjust oven rack to lower-middle position and heat oven to 375 degrees. Remove pork from brine, pat dry with paper towels, and season with coriander, cumin, and ½ teaspoon pepper.

3. Heat 1 tablespoon oil in 12-inch skillet over medium-high heat until just smoking. Brown pork lightly on all sides, 6 to 8 minutes; transfer to large plate.

4. Toss sweet potatoes and shallots with remaining ⅓ cup oil and cayenne, season with salt and pepper, and spread into large roasting pan. Set V-rack over vegetables and lay pork loin on rack. Roast pork and potatoes until pork registers 140 to 145 degrees, 1 to 1¼ hours.

5. FOR THE CILANTRO SAUCE: Meanwhile, pulse all ingredients in food processor until cilantro is finely chopped, 10 to 15 pulses, scraping down bowl as needed. Season with salt and pepper to taste. (Sauce can be refrigerated for up to 1 day.)

6. Transfer pork to carving board, tent loosely with aluminum foil, and let rest for 15 minutes. Meanwhile, increase oven temperature to 500 degrees and continue to roast potatoes and shallots until nicely browned, about 10 minutes. Slice pork ¼ inch thick and serve with potatoes and cilantro sauce.

✔ **WHY THIS RECIPE WORKS**
Pairing mild pork with a bright cilantro sauce and sweet potatoes, we eased into fall with a little of summer's brightness. To ensure the lean boneless roast emerged from the oven juicy and well seasoned, we brined the pork and cooked it at a moderate 375 degrees. A mixture of ground coriander, cumin, salt, and pepper gave the pork's exterior color and flavor, and also complemented the lively cilantro sauce. For the side, we tossed sweet potato chunks and quartered shallots with some oil and a pinch of cayenne pepper and roasted them along with the pork. By the time the pork was done, the vegetables were tender but a little pale so we set aside the pork to rest, then turned up the heat and returned the roasting pan to the oven to give the vegetables some nice caramelization.

Ham and Cheese Palmiers

To thaw frozen puff pastry, allow it to sit either in the refrigerator for 24 hours or on the counter for 30 to 60 minutes. If the dough becomes too warm and sticky to work with, cover it with plastic wrap and chill in the refrigerator until firm. To round out this appetizer, consider serving it with farmhouse cheddar and sliced apples.

1 (9½ by 9-inch) sheet frozen puff pastry, thawed
2 tablespoons Dijon mustard
2 teaspoons minced fresh thyme
4 ounces thinly sliced deli ham
2 ounces Parmesan cheese, grated (1 cup)

1. Roll pastry into 12-inch square on lightly floured counter. Brush evenly with mustard, sprinkle with thyme, lay ham evenly over top (right to edge), and sprinkle with Parmesan. Roll up both sides of dough until they meet in the middle.

2. Wrap log of dough in plastic wrap and refrigerate until firm, at least 1 hour and up to 2 days.

3. Adjust oven rack to middle position and heat oven to 400 degrees. Line rimmed baking sheet with parchment paper. Trim ends of log, then slice into ⅓-inch-thick pieces with sharp serrated knife. Lay on prepared baking sheet, spaced about 1 inch apart.

4. Bake until golden brown and crisp, about 25 minutes, rotating baking sheet halfway through baking. Transfer palmiers to wire rack and let cool completely before serving. (Palmiers can be held at room temperature for up to 6 hours. Makes 32 palmiers.)

MAKING PALMIERS

Brush dough evenly with Dijon and sprinkle with thyme. Lay the ham evenly over the dough and sprinkle with grated Parmesan. Roll 2 parallel sides of dough towards the center so they meet in the middle. Wrap log of dough in plastic wrap and refrigerate until firm, at least 1 hour and up to 2 days. Trim the ends of the log, then slice the chilled log crosswise into ⅓-inch-thick pieces with a sharp serrated knife.

Spinach Salad with Blood Oranges and Radishes

Regular oranges can be substituted for the blood oranges if necessary. For information on how to cut the oranges, see page 127.

For information on how to cut the oranges, see page 127.

2 tablespoons lemon juice
1 shallot, minced
¼ teaspoon grated orange zest
¼ teaspoon sugar
Salt and pepper
⅓ cup extra-virgin olive oil
6 medium radishes, grated (½ cup)
2 blood oranges
12 ounces baby spinach (about 12 cups)

Whisk lemon juice, shallot, orange zest, sugar, ½ teaspoon salt, and ¼ teaspoon pepper together in small bowl. Whisking constantly, drizzle in oil. Cut away peel and pith from oranges. Quarter oranges, then slice crosswise into ½-inch-thick pieces. Combine orange pieces and radishes in large bowl and place spinach on top. Just before serving, whisk dressing to re-emulsify, then drizzle over salad and toss gently to coat.

✔ WHY THIS RECIPE WORKS
To make the most of sweet, tender (as well as convenient) baby spinach, we paired it with spicy radishes and juicy blood oranges for visual appeal. Shredding the radishes on a box grater ensured that crunchy bites were incorporated throughout the salad, and cutting slices from quartered oranges was easier than segmenting them.

Raspberry Streusel Tart

If raspberries taste very tart, add an extra tablespoon or two of granulated sugar to the filling to compensate.

1½ cups (7½ ounces) all-purpose flour
½ cup (3½ ounces) granulated sugar
¼ teaspoon salt
12 tablespoons unsalted butter, cut into 12 pieces and softened
½ cup (1½ ounces) old-fashioned rolled oats
½ cup sliced almonds, toasted (see page 29)
3 tablespoons light brown sugar
¾ cup raspberry jam
7½ ounces raspberries (1½ cups)
1 tablespoon lemon juice

1. Adjust oven rack to middle position and heat oven to 375 degrees. Grease 9-inch springform pan.

2. Using stand mixer fitted with paddle, mix flour, granulated sugar, and salt on low speed until combined. Add 10 tablespoons butter, 1 piece at a time, and mix until mixture resembles wet sand, 1 to 2 minutes. Reserve ½ cup mixture for topping and set aside.

3. Sprinkle remaining mixture into prepared pan and press firmly into even, compact layer with bottom of dry measuring cup. Use back of spoon to press and smooth edges. Bake until fragrant and beginning to brown, about 15 minutes. Let tart shell cool slightly while making topping and filling.

4. Mix reserved flour mixture with oats, almonds, and brown sugar in medium bowl. Add remaining 2 tablespoons butter and pinch mixture between fingers into hazelnut-size clumps.

5. In small bowl, mash jam, ½ cup raspberries, and lemon juice with fork to coarse puree. Spread berry mixture evenly over warm crust, then top with remaining 1 cup raspberries. Sprinkle streusel topping over raspberries.

6. Bake until filling is bubbling and topping is deep golden brown, 22 to 25 minutes, rotating pan halfway through baking. Let tart cool completely in pan, about 2 hours. (Tart can be held at room temperature for up to 8 hours.) To serve, remove outer metal ring of springform pan, slide thin metal spatula between tart and springform pan bottom, and carefully slide tart onto serving platter.

✔ WHY THIS RECIPE WORKS
Our raspberry streusel tart is both rustic and elegant, striking a perfect balance between the bright, tangy fruit filling and rich, buttery shortbread crust. We realized this tart would need a bottom crust that was sturdy and a topping that was light and dry so it would adhere to the filling. The key to achieving these two textures with one mixture was butter: A butter-rich shortbread made a supportive bottom crust. We then rubbed even more butter into the same dough to produce a great streusel topping. For a fresh-tasting fruity filling, we combined fresh raspberries with raspberry jam. Adding a dash of lemon juice to the jam brightened the filling further.

Classic Roast Beef Supper

THE GAME PLAN

⬥

ONE DAY AHEAD...

MAKE BLUE CHEESE SPREAD: 10 minutes

ON THE DAY OF...

MAKE STUFFED DATES: 10 minutes

MAKE ROAST BEEF WITH VEGETABLES: 3 hours

MAKE APPLE CRISP: 1¼ hours (plus 35 minutes for baking and cooling)

MAKE BRAISED KALE: 1¼ hours

CLASSIC ROAST BEEF SUPPER

⤝ *Serves 8* ⤝

Parmesan and Walnut–Stuffed Dates ⤝ Blue Cheese and Walnut Spread
Roast Beef with Caramelized Carrots, Potatoes, and Brussels Sprouts
Garlicky Braised Kale ⤝ Apple Crisp

Roast Beef with Caramelized Carrots, Potatoes, and Brussels Sprouts

Top sirloin is our favorite beef roast for this recipe, but any boneless roast from the sirloin will work well.

GARLIC-HERB BUTTER

8	tablespoons unsalted butter, softened
2	tablespoons minced fresh parsley
1	tablespoon minced fresh thyme
2	garlic cloves, minced
¼	teaspoon salt
⅛	teaspoon pepper

BEEF AND VEGETABLES

2	pounds red potatoes, cut into 1½-inch pieces
1	pound carrots, peeled, halved lengthwise, and cut into 1½-inch pieces
⅓	cup water
1	pound Brussels sprouts, trimmed and halved
1	(4-pound) boneless top sirloin roast, fat trimmed to ⅛ inch thick, tied at 1½-inch intervals
	Salt and pepper
¼	cup vegetable oil
1	tablespoon minced fresh thyme

1. FOR THE BUTTER: Beat butter in bowl with fork until light and fluffy, then mix in remaining ingredients. Place butter in center of piece of plastic wrap and shape into log. Wrap butter tightly in plastic, twisting ends of plastic to *continued* ➤

continued ➤

WHY THIS RECIPE WORKS

Our foolproof roast beef recipe starts with an inexpensive cut and roasts a medley of fall vegetables alongside the beef for a side dish. For the beef, we settled on sirloin roast, which has big beefy flavor, enough fat to stay juicy, and a tender texture. As with other large roasts, cooking slow and low was best to allow sufficient time for the even conduction of heat to the center of the roast. To get a browned crust, we used a two-pronged approach of searing the roast on the stovetop before cooking, as well as raising the temperature during the last 10 minutes of cooking for a final blast of heat to further develop the crust. To ensure the vegetables were ready at the same time as the beef, we gave them a head start in the microwave. Returning them to the hot oven while the roast rested gave them a fully caramelized, sweet exterior.

HOW TO TIE A ROAST

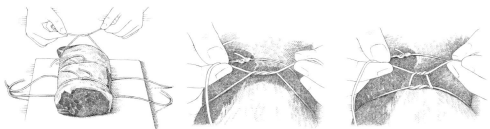

Tying a roast not only yields more attractive slices but also ensures that the roast will have the same thickness from end to end so that it cooks evenly. Cut pieces of heavy-duty kitchen twine that are at least 8 inches longer than the girth of the roast. Slide the pieces of twine underneath the roast at even 1½-inch intervals. Tightly tie each piece of twine around the roast, starting with a piece in the very center, followed by pieces at both ends, then finally the remaining pieces in between.

help tighten and shape log. Refrigerate until firm, at least 1 hour and up to 2 days.

2. FOR THE BEEF AND VEGETABLES: Adjust oven rack to lower-middle position and heat oven to 250 degrees. Combine potatoes, carrots, and water in large bowl. Cover and microwave for about 10 minutes. Stir in Brussels sprouts and continue to microwave, stirring occasionally, until all vegetables are mostly tender, 5 to 10 minutes longer.

3. Meanwhile, pat beef dry with paper towels and season with salt and pepper. Heat 1 tablespoon oil in 12-inch skillet over medium-high heat until just smoking. Brown beef well on all sides, 7 to 10 minutes; transfer to large roasting pan.

4. Drain vegetables well, then toss with remaining 3 tablespoons oil, thyme, and season with salt and pepper. Spread vegetables into roasting pan around beef. (Prepped beef roast and vegetables can be held at room temperature for up to 1 hour before roasting.) Roast beef and vegetables until meat registers 110 degrees, about 1 hour.

5. Increase oven temperature to 500 degrees and continue to roast beef and vegetables until meat registers 120 to 125 degrees (for medium-rare), 10 to 15 minutes longer.

6. Transfer beef to carving board, tent loosely with aluminum foil, and let rest for 15 to 20 minutes. Meanwhile, continue to roast vegetables, stirring occasionally, until nicely browned, 15 to 20 minutes. Remove twine from beef and slice ¼ inch thick. Unwrap butter and slice into 8 pieces. Place butter on top of beef to melt and serve with vegetables.

Parmesan and Walnut–Stuffed Dates

Use high-quality dates, such as Medjools, and authentic Parmesan cheese for this simple appetizer.

✔ WHY THIS RECIPE WORKS
This appetizer is simple to prepare ahead of time, but with only three ingredients, the devil is in the details. While the variety of dates available to you may vary, we most like Medjools, which are particularly sweet and dense textured, for our stuffed dates recipe. As for the cheese, good-quality, fresh Parmesan is a must. Look for whole walnut halves, not pieces, which have a tendency to fall out of the dates.

24   large pitted dates
1   (4-ounce) chunk Parmesan cheese
24   walnut halves, toasted (see page 29)

Using paring knife, cut dates open on 1 side. Cut Parmesan into 24 thin shards roughly same length as dates. Stuff Parmesan shard and walnut half into each date, and serve. (Dates can be held at room temperature for up to 4 hours.)

CUTTING PARMESAN INTO SHARDS

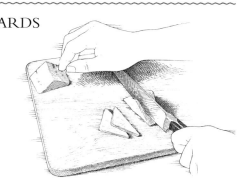

Use a chef's knife to remove the rind from a square block of Parmesan cheese. Cut the trimmed block in half on the diagonal. Place each half cut side down on a cutting board and slice the cheese into thin triangles, about ¹/₁₆ inch wide. These thin shards should be about the size of a date.

Blue Cheese and Walnut Spread

Serve with crackers or a thinly sliced baguette.

8 ounces cream cheese

2 tablespoons milk

1 cup walnuts, toasted (see page 29) and chopped coarse

4 ounces blue cheese, crumbled (1 cup)

Microwave cream cheese in medium bowl until very soft, about 20 seconds. Stir in remaining ingredients and transfer to small serving bowl. Refrigerate until set, at least 1 hour or up to 3 days. (Makes 1½ cups.)

WHY THIS RECIPE WORKS

Cream cheese is the base for this boldly flavored spread. To get the best consistency, we softened the cream cheese in the microwave before adding the other ingredients.

Garlicky Braised Kale

You will need at least a 6-quart Dutch oven for this recipe. This will look like a mountain of raw kale before it's cooked, but it wilts down substantially and will eventually all fit into the pot.

6 tablespoons olive oil

1 large onion, chopped fine

10 garlic cloves, minced

¼ teaspoon red pepper flakes

2 cups low-sodium chicken broth

1 cup water
  Salt and pepper

4 pounds kale, stemmed and leaves chopped into 3-inch pieces

1 tablespoon lemon juice, plus extra as needed

1. Heat 3 tablespoons oil in Dutch oven over medium heat until shimmering. Add onion and cook until softened and lightly browned, 5 to 7 minutes. Stir in garlic and pepper flakes and cook until fragrant, about 1 minute. Stir in broth, water, and ½ teaspoon salt and bring to simmer.

2. Stir in one-third of kale, cover, and cook, stirring occasionally, until wilted, 2 to 4 minutes. Repeat with remaining kale in 2 batches. Continue to cook, covered, until kale is tender, 13 to 15 minutes longer.

3. Remove lid and increase heat to medium-high. Cook, stirring occasionally, until most liquid has evaporated and greens begin to sizzle, 10 to 12 minutes. Off heat, stir in remaining 3 tablespoons oil and lemon juice. Season with salt, pepper, and extra lemon juice to taste. Serve.

WHY THIS RECIPE WORKS

Winter greens like kale can be problematic: Southern-style braises cook the life out of the greens, and the blanching-then-sautéing route is a complicated process that requires multiple pots. We wanted a one-pot kale recipe that would serve eight with no parcooking. To achieve this, we first briefly cooked the kale with a little bit of liquid, adding the greens in three batches to wilt so they fit in the pot. When the kale had nearly reached the tender-firm texture we wanted, we removed the lid and raised the heat to allow the liquid to cook off.

PREPPING KALE AND CHARD

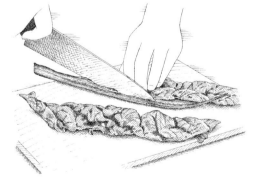 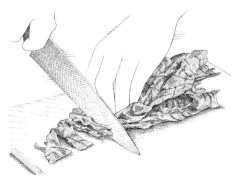

Cut away the leafy green portion from either side of the stalk or stem using a chef's knife. Stack several leaves on top of one another and chop into pieces. Wash and dry the leaves after they are cut using a salad spinner.

Apple Crisp

We like Golden Delicious apples for this recipe, but any sweet, crisp apple such as Honeycrisp or Braeburn can be substituted. Do not use Granny Smith apples in this recipe. While rolled oats are preferable in the topping, quick oats can be substituted. Serve with vanilla ice cream or whipped cream.

TOPPING

- ¾ cup (3¾ ounces) unbleached all-purpose flour
- ¾ cup pecans, chopped fine
- ¾ cup old-fashioned rolled oats
- ½ cup (3½ ounces) packed light brown sugar
- ¼ cup (1¾ ounces) granulated sugar
- ½ teaspoon ground cinnamon
- ½ teaspoon salt
- 8 tablespoons unsalted butter, melted and cooled

FILLING

- 1½ cup apple cider
- 1 tablespoon lemon juice
- 4 pounds Golden Delicious apples, peeled, cored, halved, and cut into ½-inch-thick wedges
- ⅓ cup (2⅓ ounces) granulated sugar
- ¼ teaspoon ground cinnamon
- 2 tablespoons unsalted butter

1. FOR THE TOPPING: Adjust oven rack to middle position and heat oven to 450 degrees. Combine flour, pecans, oats, brown sugar, granulated sugar, cinnamon, and salt in medium bowl. Stir in butter until thoroughly moistened and crumbly.

2. FOR THE FILLING: Bring cider to simmer in 12-inch skillet over medium heat and cook until reduced to ¾ cup, about 7 minutes. Transfer to liquid measuring cup and stir in lemon juice.

3. Toss apples with sugar and cinnamon in bowl. Melt butter in now-empty skillet over medium heat. Add apples and cook, stirring often, until they begin to soften and become translucent, 10 to 15 minutes. (Do not fully cook apples.) Off heat, gently stir in cider mixture.

4. Transfer apple mixture to 13 by 9-inch casserole dish. Sprinkle evenly with topping, breaking up any large chunks. Bake until fruit is tender and topping is deep golden brown, about 20 minutes.

5. Let crisp cool slightly on wire rack, about 15 minutes. Serve warm or at room temperature. (Crisp can be held at room temperature for up to 2 hours; if desired, reheat in 425-degree oven until slightly warm, about 5 minutes, before serving.)

✔ WHY THIS RECIPE WORKS

To complete our classic roast beef supper, we opted for a classic apple dessert. Less fussy than pie but just as delicious, apple crisp delivers big apple flavor with a crunchy, nutty topping. Starting our apple crisp recipe on the stovetop allowed us to stir the apples periodically so they would cook evenly. Plus, the stovetop's heat drove away extra moisture and allowed the fruit and butter to caramelize and lend a sweet richness to the filling. Sugar, lemon juice, and apple cider give our skillet apple crisp recipe depth and full-fledged apple flavor. To top things off, a combination of white and brown sugars, cinnamon, salt, chopped pecans, and— for extra texture—chewy rolled oats bring depth and crunch to our apple crisp.

Refined Short Ribs Dinner

THE GAME PLAN

ONE DAY AHEAD...

MAKE SHORT RIBS: 1½ hours (plus 3 hours for braising)

MAKE CAKE: 1 hour (plus 16 hours for cooling and chilling)

ON THE DAY OF...

MAKE STUFFED MUSHROOMS: 1 hour

MAKE POLENTA: 1¼ hours

MAKE SALAD: 35 minutes

REHEAT SHORT RIBS: 30 minutes

BRING CAKE TO ROOM TEMPERATURE: 30 minutes

REFINED SHORT RIBS DINNER

⤝ *Serves 8* ⤜

Stuffed Mushrooms with Boursin and Prosciutto ⤞ Braised Beef Short Ribs

Arugula Salad with Grapes, Fennel, Gorgonzola, and Pecans

Creamy Parmesan Polenta ⤞ Flourless Chocolate Cake

Braised Beef Short Ribs

You will need at least a 6-quart Dutch oven for this recipe. Make sure that the ribs are at least 4 inches long and 1 inch thick. If boneless ribs are unavailable, substitute 12 pounds of bone-in beef short ribs at least 4 inches long with 1 inch of meat above the bone (see page 182 for information on boning short ribs). To remove portobello gills, use a dinner spoon and gently scrape the gills off the underside of each mushroom cap. Season the ribs lightly with salt in step 1, or the resulting sauce will taste overly salty.

6	pounds boneless beef short ribs, trimmed
	Salt and pepper
¼	cup vegetable oil
2	large onions, halved and sliced thin
1	tablespoon tomato paste
8	garlic cloves, minced
3	cups red wine
2	cups beef broth
1	pound portobello mushroom caps, gills removed, halved, and sliced crosswise ¼ inch thick
1	pound cremini mushrooms, trimmed and sliced into ¼-inch pieces
1	teaspoon minced fresh thyme
½	cup water
1	teaspoon unflavored gelatin
¼	cup minced fresh parsley

1. Adjust oven rack to lower-middle position and heat oven to 300 degrees. Pat beef dry with paper towels and lightly season with salt and pepper. Heat 2 tablespoons oil in Dutch oven over medium-high heat until smoking. Brown one-third of beef on all sides, about 5 minutes; transfer to large bowl. Repeat with remaining 2 tablespoons oil and remaining beef in 2 batches.

2. Add onions to now-empty pot and cook over medium heat until softened and beginning to brown, 12 to 15 minutes (if onions begin to darken too quickly, add 2 tablespoons water to pan). Stir in tomato paste and cook until sides and bottom of pot begin to brown, about 2 minutes. Stir in garlic and cook until fragrant, about 30 seconds.

3. Slowly whisk in wine, scraping up browned bits. Increase heat to medium-high and simmer until reduced by half, 8 to 10 minutes. Stir in broth, mushrooms, and thyme. Nestle browned ribs with any accumulated juices into pot and return to simmer. Cover, place pot in oven, and cook until ribs are tender and fork slips easily in and out of meat, 2½ to 3 hours, turning ribs over twice during cooking.

4. Transfer meat to large plate and tent with aluminum foil. Strain *continued* ➤

cooking liquid through fine-mesh strainer into fat separator. Reserve strained vegetables. Let liquid settle for 5 minutes, then pour defatted liquid back into pot, discarding fat. Place water in small bowl, sprinkle gelatin over top, and let sit until needed.

5. Simmer strained liquid over medium heat until reduced to 3 cups, 10 to 15 minutes. Off heat, stir in gelatin mixture and strained vegetables and season with salt and pepper to taste. (Ribs can be returned to Dutch oven with sauce and refrigerated for up to 2 days. Before serving, discard hardened fat from surface and gently reheat over medium-low heat, about 30 minutes, adding hot water as needed to adjust consistency of sauce.)

6. To serve, portion ribs into individual shallow bowls, spoon mushrooms and sauce over top, sprinkle with parsley, and serve.

BONING SHORT RIBS

With the chef's knife as close as possible to the bone, carefully remove the meat. Trim the excess hard fat and silver skin from both sides of the meat.

Stuffed Mushrooms with Boursin and Prosciutto

✔ **WHY THIS RECIPE WORKS** Embracing the philosophy of "less is more," we modeled these mushrooms after the tapas-style stuffed mushrooms that feature just a few well-chosen ingredients nestled inside each mushroom cap. We started by parcooking white mushrooms to rid them of excess moisture. Forgoing fussy bread-based stuffings that usually end up soggy, we filled the caps with buttery and creamy Boursin cheese. Next we sprinkled thinly sliced prosciutto on top—the saltiness enhanced the creamy cheese and the strips crisped nicely in the oven.

Be sure to buy mushrooms with caps that measure between 1½ and 2 inches in diameter; they will shrink substantially as they roast.

24 (1½- to 2-inch-wide) white mushroom caps, stems removed completely
2   tablespoons olive oil
¼   teaspoon salt
⅛   teaspoon pepper
1   (5.2-ounce) package Boursin Garlic and Fine Herbs cheese, softened
1   ounce thinly sliced prosciutto, sliced crosswise ¼ inch thick
2   tablespoons minced fresh parsley or chives

1. Adjust oven rack to lower-middle position and heat oven to 450 degrees. Line baking sheet with aluminum foil. Toss mushroom caps with oil, salt, and pepper and lay gill side down on prepared baking sheet. Roast mushrooms until they release their moisture and shrink, about 25 minutes.

2. Remove caps from oven, let cool slightly, then flip caps over. Using 2 spoons, spoon Boursin into mushroom caps. Top with prosciutto. (Stuffed mushrooms can be covered and refrigerated up to 1 day before baking.)

3. Bake mushrooms until cheese is hot and prosciutto begins to crisp, 10 to 12 minutes. Transfer to serving platter, sprinkle with parsley, and serve.

EVEN EASIER ⤳ Don't have time to make stuffed mushrooms? Spread 6 ounces store-bought mushroom pâté (or other vegetable pâté), followed by one 5.2-ounce package Boursin cheese, over thin slices of baguette or Garlic Toasts (page 62). Garnish with ¼ cup minced fresh parsley, chives, or basil, if desired.

Arugula Salad with Grapes, Fennel, Gorgonzola, and Pecans

The fennel fronds are the small, dill-like leaves found on the fennel stems; using the fronds in this salad boosts the fennel flavor but is optional. Letting the fennel marinate in the vinaigrette for a few minutes before adding the arugula intensifies the flavor greatly. Be sure to add the arugula and grapes just before serving, however, or the salad will turn soggy.

¼ cup white wine vinegar
2 tablespoons apricot jam
1 shallot, minced
Salt and pepper
¼ cup extra-virgin olive oil
1 small fennel bulb, fronds minced (optional), stalks discarded, bulb halved, cored, and sliced thin (see page 22)
10 ounces baby arugula (10 cups)
10 ounces red seedless grapes, halved (1½ cups)
4 ounces Gorgonzola cheese, crumbled (1 cup)

¾ cup pecans, toasted (see page 29) and chopped coarse

1. Whisk vinegar, jam, shallot, ¼ teaspoon salt, and ¼ teaspoon pepper in large bowl. Whisking constantly, drizzle in oil.

2. Just before serving, whisk dressing to re-emulsify, then stir in fennel and let it absorb dressing, about 15 minutes. Add arugula, grapes, and fennel fronds, if using, and toss gently to coat. Garnish individual portions with Gorgonzola and pecans.

☑ **WHY THIS RECIPE WORKS**
We partnered spicy arugula with Gorgonzola cheese for a salad that would be refreshing but flavorful enough to stand up to rich short ribs. For the vinaigrette, we added a spoonful of jam which helped emulsify the dressing and complemented this strongly flavored salad. Thinly sliced fennel had welcome crispness, but its relatively mild flavor was somewhat lost; a brief marinade in the dressing boosted the fennel's flavor.

Creamy Parmesan Polenta

Do not use instant or quick-cooking polenta here. Coarse-ground degerminated cornmeal such as yellow grits (with uniform grains the size of couscous) will work, but do not use whole grain, stone-ground, or regular cornmeal. Do not omit the baking soda—it reduces the cooking time and makes for a creamier polenta. Using a high-quality Parmesan is crucial in this simple side dish.

9½ cups water
Salt and pepper
Pinch baking soda
2 cups polenta
5 ounces Parmesan cheese, grated (2½ cups), plus extra for serving
3 tablespoons unsalted butter

1. Bring water to boil in large saucepan over medium-high heat. Stir in 2 teaspoons salt and baking soda. Slowly add polenta while whisking constantly in circular motion to prevent clumping. Bring to simmer,

stirring constantly, about 1 minute. Reduce heat to lowest possible setting and cover.

2. Cook for 5 minutes, then whisk polenta to smooth out lumps, about 15 seconds. Cover and continue to cook, without stirring, until grains of polenta are tender but slightly al dente, about 30 minutes longer. (Polenta should be loose and barely hold its shape but will continue to thicken as it cools.)

3. Off heat, stir in Parmesan and butter and season with salt and pepper to taste. Let polenta sit, covered, for 5 minutes. Serve, passing additional Parmesan separately.

☑ **WHY THIS RECIPE WORKS**
For quick polenta with a creamy texture and deep corn flavor, we searched for the right type of cornmeal and a technique to hasten its cooking. Coarse-ground degerminated cornmeal gave us the soft but hearty texture and nutty flavor we were looking for. A pinch of baking soda cut cooking time in half and eliminated the need for stirring, giving us the best quick polenta recipe. Parmesan cheese and butter stirred in at the last minute finished our polenta.

Flourless Chocolate Cake

✔ WHY THIS RECIPE WORKS
Flourless chocolate cake should serve as an ultimate expression of pure chocolate flavor, with a rich, dense texture that still retains some delicacy. In producing an ideal recipe with only four ingredients, we found two key techniques that delivered a perfectly smooth and creamy cake. The first is to bake it in a water bath, which creates a gentle, moist-heat environment in which the cake can slowly bake. The second trick is to remove the cake from the oven while it is still a little underdone. The cake will continue to cook and firm up as it cools.

Good-quality chocolate is very important to the flavor and texture of this cake; our preferred brands of bittersweet chocolate are Callebaut and Ghirardelli. You can substitute ¼ cup warm water mixed with 1 teaspoon instant espresso or instant coffee for the strong coffee. If substituting an 8-inch springform pan, increase the baking time to 22 to 25 minutes. This cake is very rich, so small slices are best. For neat, professional-looking pieces of cake, clean the knife thoroughly between slices. Note that this cake will serve 12 to 14 people; leftovers can be covered and refrigerated for up to 4 days.

1	pound bittersweet chocolate, chopped
16	tablespoons unsalted butter, cut into chunks
¼	cup strong coffee
8	large eggs, room temperature Confectioners' sugar, for dusting
10	ounces raspberries (2 cups)

1. Adjust oven rack to lower-middle position and heat oven to 325 degrees. Grease 9-inch springform pan, then line bottom with parchment paper. Wrap outside of pan with two 18-inch square pieces heavy-duty foil and set inside roasting pan. Bring kettle of water to boil.

2. Melt chocolate, butter, and coffee together in microwave in large bowl, stirring often, 1 to 3 minutes. Let mixture cool slightly.

3. Using stand mixer fitted with whisk, whip eggs on medium-low speed until frothy, about 1 minute. Increase speed to high and whip until eggs are very thick and pale yellow, 5 to 10 minutes. Gently fold one-third of whipped eggs into chocolate mixture with rubber spatula until only a few streaks remain. Repeat twice more with remaining whipped eggs and continue to fold batter until no streaks remain.

4. Scrape batter into prepared pan and smooth top. Set roasting pan on oven rack and pour boiling water into roasting pan until it reaches about halfway up sides of springform pan. Bake cake until edges are just beginning to set, a thin crust has formed over top, and an instant-read thermometer inserted about 1 inch from edge reads 140 degrees, 18 to 20 minutes. (Do not overbake.)

5. Let cake cool in roasting pan for 45 minutes, then transfer to wire rack and let cool until barely warm, 2½ to 3 hours, running knife around edge of cake every hour or so. Wrap pan tightly in plastic wrap and refrigerate until set, at least 12 hours and up to 2 days.

6. About 30 minutes before serving, run knife around edge of cake and remove sides of pan. Carefully slide cake, still on parchment, onto serving platter. Just before serving, dust cake with confectioners' sugar and cut into wedges. Garnish slices with raspberries.

Japanese Salmon Dinner

THE GAME PLAN

ONE DAY AHEAD...

MAKE WASABI DIP: 15 minutes

MAKE SAKE-STEWED CHERRIES: 1 hour

MAKE LACE COOKIES: 1¼ hours

MARINATE SALMON: 15 minutes
(plus 5 hours for marinating)

ON THE DAY OF...

BOIL EDAMAME: 25 minutes

MAKE SUSHI RICE: 45 minutes

MAKE SALAD: 35 minutes

MAKE MISO SALMON: 15 minutes

REHEAT CHERRIES AND ASSEMBLE DESSERT:
5 minutes

JAPANESE SALMON DINNER

> ➤ *Serves 8* ◂

Edamame with Sea Salt ↭ Wasabi Dip ↭ Miso-Glazed Salmon
Sesame Sushi Rice ↭ Cucumber, Radish, and Watercress Salad
Vanilla Ice Cream with Sake-Stewed Cherries and Lace Cookies

Miso-Glazed Salmon

Be sure to buy white miso, but do not buy light or low-sodium white miso. Light or low-sodium miso will not work in this recipe; note that you'll have to read the label carefully to know if the miso is light or low-sodium. When removing the salmon from the marinade, do not wipe away any excess marinade clinging to the fish; the excess marinade will turn to a sweet-salty crust during cooking. For information on how to cut the salmon in step 1, see page 21.

1 ½	cups white miso
¾	cup sugar
¾	cup sake
1	tablespoon grated fresh ginger
2	(2-pound) skin-on salmon fillets, about 1 ½ inches thick

1. Whisk miso, sugar, sake, and ginger together in medium bowl to dissolve sugar and miso. Use sharp knife to remove any whitish fat from belly of salmon and cut each fillet into 4 equal pieces. Divide fillets between two 1-gallon zipper-lock bags and pour marinade evenly into bags. Seal bags, pressing out as much air as possible, and refrigerate at least 5 hours and up to 24 hours, flipping bags occasionally to ensure fish marinates evenly.

2. Adjust oven rack 6 inches from broiler element and heat broiler. Line broiler pan bottom with aluminum foil and top with slotted broiler pan top. Remove fish from marinade and lay on broiler pan top, skin side down. Spoon 1 tablespoon marinade over each fillet; discard extra marinade.

3. Broil salmon until center is still translucent when checked with tip of paring knife and registers 125 degrees (for medium-rare), about 7 to 10 minutes. Transfer salmon to platter or individual plates and serve.

✔ WHY THIS RECIPE WORKS

Our miso-glazed salmon is marinated in an enticing salty-sweet mixture with savory, nutty notes from the miso that, once cooked, morphs into a deeply caramelized, almost candylike crust. With only a handful of ingredients and just a few minutes of hands-on prep time, the cornerstone of our Asian menu is as simple as it is impressive. We worked out a ratio of white miso, sugar, and sake that was balanced and had a thick, clingy texture. We also tried adding fresh grated ginger; though not traditional, a small amount brightened the dish considerably. Broiling was the best way to achieve the deeply caramelized coating that we were after.

Edamame with Sea Salt

Be sure to buy edamame still in the pods, not shelled edamame.

WHY THIS RECIPE WORKS
The sweet, slightly nutty flavor of edamame in their shells, sprinkled with coarse grains of salt, is a crowd-pleasing, fun-to-eat appetizer.

1   pound frozen edamame in pods
     Coarse sea salt

Bring 4 quarts water to boil in large pot. Add edamame and 1 tablespoon salt and cook until just tender, 3 to 5 minutes. Drain well and toss with 2 teaspoons salt. Serve warm, with extra bowl for discarded pods.

Wasabi Dip

This dip is slightly spicy; add more or less wasabi paste to make it more or less spicy. Serve with rice crackers.

WHY THIS RECIPE WORKS
For a playful note in our Japanese salmon dinner, we punched up a base of tangy cream cheese with savory soy sauce and the cool heat of wasabi paste. We like the clean flavor of crisp rice crackers with this dip.

1   pound cream cheese, softened
¼   cup milk
2   tablespoons soy sauce
2   tablespoons lemon juice
5   teaspoons wasabi paste
4   scallions, minced
¼   cup minced fresh cilantro

Whisk cream cheese, milk, soy sauce, lemon juice, wasabi paste, and scallions together until well combined. Transfer dip to serving bowl. (Dip can be refrigerated for up to 3 days; let sit at room temperature for 30 minutes before continuing.) Sprinkle cilantro over top and serve. (Makes 2 cups.)

EVEN EASIER   Don't have time to cook edamame or make wasabi dip? Consider buying sushi from a restaurant or supermarket and arranging it on a platter with soy sauce for dipping, wasabi, pickled ginger, chopsticks, and little plates. You'll need 35 to 40 pieces of sushi for eight people. If you're not familiar with sushi, stick to the basics: two rolls with cooked fish (such as California or dragon), two rolls with raw fish (such as spicy tuna and hirame), one vegetarian roll (such as avocado or cucumber), and six pieces of shrimp sushi (called ebi).

Cucumber, Radish, and Watercress Salad

Salting the cucumbers will help rid them of excess moisture and prevent the salad from tasting watery.

3   cucumbers, peeled, halved lengthwise, seeded (see page 89), and cut on bias into ¼-inch pieces (about 3 cups)
    Salt
¼   cup rice vinegar
I   tablespoon honey
I   teaspoon grated ginger
½   teaspoon grated orange zest plus I tablespoon juice
½   teaspoon grated lime zest plus I tablespoon juice
¼   cup vegetable oil
I   pound watercress (16 cups)
8   ounces radishes, trimmed and sliced thin

1. Toss cucumbers with ½ teaspoon salt and let drain in colander for 15 minutes. In small bowl, whisk vinegar, honey, ginger, orange zest and juice, and lime zest and juice together. Whisking constantly, drizzle in oil.

2. Combine drained cucumbers, watercress, and radishes in large bowl. Just before serving, whisk dressing to re-emulsify, then drizzle over salad and toss gently to coat.

✔ WHY THIS RECIPE WORKS
We paired mild cucumber with spicy radishes and watercress for a bold and refreshing salad that cuts the richness of the salmon and complements the salty-sweet miso glaze. For cucumbers with good crunch, we seeded, salted, and drained them for 15 minutes to draw out excess moisture (this also prevented watery dressing).

Sesame Sushi Rice

Short-grain rice contains a higher percentage of starch than other varieties, which is what gives sushi rice its trademark stickiness. Handle the cooked rice very gently and do not stir it too much when adding the flavorings in step 2, or the rice will turn gluey.

4   cups water
3½ cups short-grain rice, rinsed and drained
¼   cup seasoned rice vinegar
¼   cup mirin
I   teaspoon salt
4   scallions, sliced thin
3   tablespoons toasted sesame oil
I   tablespoon sesame seeds, toasted (see page 29)

1. Bring water and rice to boil in large saucepan over medium-high heat. Cover, reduce heat to low, and cook for 6 minutes. Remove rice from heat and let sit until tender, about 15 minutes.

2. Meanwhile, microwave vinegar, mirin, and salt together in bowl until hot, about 1 minute. Gently fold hot vinegar mixture, scallions, sesame oil, and sesame seeds into rice, and serve. (Rice can be covered and held for up to 30 minutes before serving.)

✔ WHY THIS RECIPE WORKS
The pleasantly sticky and tangy flavor of sushi rice makes it an ideal partner for the salty-sweet glazed salmon. To achieve the right amount of stickiness and chew without gumminess, the best technique was to simmer water and rice together for several minutes before removing it from the heat, still covered, to finish cooking gently and evenly.

Vanilla Ice Cream with Sake-Stewed Cherries and Lace Cookies

✔ **WHY THIS RECIPE WORKS**
Traditional tuile-shaped lace cookies spiced with Chinese five-spice powder and crunchy sesame seeds make a stunning presentation atop a bowl of creamy ice cream and sweet-tart sake-stewed cherry sauce—essentially an Asian riff on cherries jubilee. These gossamer-thin wafers look difficult but are actually very simple to make. The reason they are so rarely made is their tendency to stick to the baking sheet, bunching and tearing when you attempt to remove them. We eliminated the sticking problem with a three-part solution: removing eggs from the batter (they have a tendency to make cookie dough sticky), using parchment paper, and letting the cookies firm up for a minute or two before shaping.

If frozen cherries are not available, you can substitute canned morello cherries. The lace cookies emerge from the oven soft and malleable and turn crisp as they cool. If you're tight on time, delicate gingersnaps (such as Anna's Ginger Thins) are a nice substitution.

CHERRY SAUCE
- 1½ pounds frozen sweet cherries
- 2 cups sake
- ½ cup (3½ ounces) granulated sugar
- ¼ cup light corn syrup
- 2 tablespoons lemon juice
- 2 teaspoons grated fresh ginger
- 2 star anise pods
  Pinch salt
- 4 teaspoons cornstarch

LACE COOKIES
- 6 tablespoons packed (2⅔ ounces) dark brown sugar
- 4 tablespoons unsalted butter
- ¼ cup light corn syrup
- 3 tablespoons all-purpose flour
- 2 tablespoons sesame seeds, toasted (see page 29)
- 1½ teaspoons heavy cream
- ¾ teaspoon five-spice powder
- ½ teaspoon vanilla extract
- ⅛ teaspoon salt
  Pinch cinnamon

- 4 pints (½ gallon) vanilla ice cream

1. FOR THE CHERRY SAUCE: Bring cherries, 1½ cups sake, sugar, corn syrup, lemon juice, ginger, star anise, and salt to boil in medium saucepan over medium-high heat. Simmer until cherries just begin to break down, about 10 minutes.

2. Combine cornstarch and remaining ½ cup sake in small bowl, then gently whisk into cherry mixture. Continue to simmer until sauce thickens slightly and coats back of spoon, about 1 minute. Remove from heat and let cool slightly, 15 to 30 minutes. (Sauce can be refrigerated for up to 3 days; reheat in microwave, about 2 minutes.)

3. FOR THE LACE COOKIES: Adjust oven rack to upper-middle position and heat oven to 350 degrees. Line baking sheet with parchment paper.

4. Bring sugar, butter, and corn syrup to boil in medium saucepan over medium heat, stirring often. Off heat, whisk in flour, sesame seeds, cream, five-spice powder, vanilla, salt, and cinnamon until smooth. Let cool slightly, 5 to 10 minutes. (Mixture can be refrigerated for up to 3 days; let dough soften at room temperature before continuing.)

5. Drop six 1-teaspoon portions of batter onto prepared baking sheet, spaced 4 inches apart. Bake cookies until they spread thin, are no longer bubbling, and are deep golden brown, 5 to 7 minutes, rotating baking sheet halfway through baking.

6. Let cookies cool slightly on baking sheet for 1 minute, then transfer to wire rack using thin metal spatula and let cool completely, about 15 minutes. (Alternatively, drape warm cookies over rolling pin to curl, then transfer to wire rack to cool.) Repeat with remaining dough in 2 batches, using freshly lined baking sheet. (Cookies can be stored at room temperature for up to 1 week. Makes 18 cookies.)

7. To serve, portion ice cream into individual bowls, spoon warm cherry sauce over top, and serve with cookies.

SHAPING LACE COOKIES

Drape cookies over a rolling pin (or wine bottle) while still warm so that the cookies form a gentle curve. Hold the cookie in place until it is set, about 10 seconds, then let cool on a wire rack.

Easy and Elegant Cornish Game Hen Dinner, page 211

New England Cod and Potato Dinner, page 201

Family-Style Italian Sunday Supper, page 207

Hearty French Lamb Shank Dinner, page 227

⇀ WINTER ↼

Mushroom Pasta Supper   195

Crispy Polenta Squares with Olive Tapenade
Pasta with Sautéed Wild Mushrooms
Apple and Celery Salad with Roquefort
Cappuccino Semifreddo with Hazelnuts

New England Cod
and Potato Dinner   201

Cheddar and Apple Panini Bites
Lemon-Herb Cod Fillets with Garlic Potatoes
Roasted Fennel and Mushroom Salad
Cranberry Upside-Down Cake

Family-Style Italian Sunday Supper   207

Homemade Ricotta Cheese
One-Pot Bolognese
Arugula Salad with Figs and Prosciutto
Chocolate-Dipped Pistachio Biscotti with Vin Santo

Easy and Elegant Cornish
Game Hen Dinner   211

Caramelized Onion, Blue Cheese, and Prosciutto Tart
Balsamic-Glazed Cornish Game Hens
Farro with Fennel and Parmesan
Garlicky Broccoli Rabe
Pear and Ginger Turnovers

A Taste of India   217

Goat Cheese with Homemade Mango Chutney
Chicken Tikka Masala
Basmati Rice Pilaf
Mango and Jícama Salad with Mint Vinaigrette
Cardamom and Pistachio Ice Milk

Snowed-In Slow-Roasted
Pork Supper   221

Easy Mushroom Pâté
Slow-Roasted Pork with Cherry Sauce
Sweet Potato Puree
Broccolini with Garlic and Browned Butter
Apple Strudel

Hearty French Lamb Shank Dinner   227

Skillet-Caramelized Pears with Blue Cheese
Braised Lamb Shanks
White Bean Gratin
Garlicky Swiss Chard
Crème Brûlée

Steakhouse Prime Rib Dinner   233

Shrimp Cocktail
Prime Rib au Jus
Winter Root Vegetable Gratin
Haricots Verts with Garlic and Herbs
Dark Chocolate–Orange Mousse

Belgian Stew Supper   239

Easy Baked Brie with Jam
Carbonnade
Buttered Egg Noodles
Roasted Winter Squash Salad
Glazed Ginger Bundt Cake with Vanilla Ice Cream

Paella Night   245

Serrano Ham and Manchego Cheese Crostini
Paella
Green Salad with Marcona Almonds
Almond Cake with Clementines and Whipped Cream

Mushroom Pasta Supper

THE GAME PLAN
◄►

ONE DAY AHEAD...

MAKE SEMIFREDDO: 1 hour (plus 8 hours for freezing)

MAKE POLENTA FOR APPETIZER: 30 minutes (plus 2½ hours for cooling)

MAKE TAPENADE FOR APPETIZER: 10 minutes

ON THE DAY OF...

MAKE PASTA: 1 hour

FINISH POLENTA APPETIZER: 25 minutes

MAKE SALAD: 30 minutes

MUSHROOM PASTA SUPPER

⤙ *Serves 8* ⤚

Crispy Polenta Squares with Olive Tapenade
Pasta with Sautéed Wild Mushrooms ⤙ Apple and Celery Salad with Roquefort
Cappuccino Semifreddo with Hazelnuts

Pasta with Sautéed Wild Mushrooms

To make this dish vegetarian, substitute vegetable broth for the chicken broth.

4	tablespoons unsalted butter
2	tablespoons extra-virgin olive oil
I	red onion, chopped fine
I	pound shiitake mushrooms, stemmed and sliced ¼ inch thick
I	pound cremini mushrooms, trimmed and sliced ¼ inch thick
	Salt and pepper
5	garlic cloves, minced
4½	teaspoons minced fresh thyme
2	cups low-sodium chicken broth
¾	cup heavy cream
4½	teaspoons lemon juice
I½	pounds farfalle
3	ounces Parmesan cheese, grated (1½ cups)
¼	cup minced fresh parsley

1. Heat butter and oil in 12-inch skillet over medium heat until butter is melted. Add onion and cook until softened, about 5 minutes. Stir in shiitakes, cremini, and ½ teaspoon salt, cover, and cook until mushrooms have released their liquid, about 8 minutes. Uncover and continue to cook until mushrooms are dry and browned, about 8 minutes longer. Stir in garlic and thyme and cook until fragrant, about 30 seconds; transfer to bowl and cover to keep warm.

2. Add broth and cream to now-empty skillet and bring to simmer, scraping up browned bits. Off heat, stir in lemon juice and season with salt and pepper to taste. (Sauce can be covered and held at room temperature for up to 2 hours. Add mushrooms, cover, and return to brief simmer over medium-low heat before adding to pasta in step 4.)

3. Meanwhile, bring 6 quarts water to boil in large pot. Add pasta and 1½ tablespoons salt and cook, stirring often, until al dente. Reserve 1 cup cooking water, then drain pasta and return it to pot.

4. Add mushrooms, sauce, Parmesan, and parsley to pasta and toss to combine. Before serving, add reserved cooking water as needed to adjust consistency.

✔ **WHY THIS RECIPE WORKS**
This recipe combines the intense flavor of sautéed mushrooms with a light cream sauce for a woodsy, full-flavored pasta dish. To eke out deep flavor from supermarket mushrooms we used a combination of cremini for their rich and meaty nature and shiitake mushrooms for their hearty flavor and pleasant texture. To jump-start the cooking and minimize shrinking, we overloaded the skillet, cooking the mushrooms covered until they had released their juices before removing the lid to drive off moisture and maximize browning. Garlic, red onion, and thyme round out the flavors in a simple sauce of chicken broth, heavy cream, and lemon juice.

Crispy Polenta Squares with Olive Tapenade

Be sure to buy instant polenta, which has a much shorter cooking time than regular polenta. Don't be tempted to process the green and kalamata olives together or their colors will bleed, making the tapenade look muddy.

TAPENADE

- ¾ cup pitted green olives
- ¾ cup pitted kalamata olives
- ¼ cup chopped fresh basil
- 3 tablespoons extra-virgin olive oil
- 1 tablespoon capers, rinsed and minced
- 4 anchovy fillets, rinsed, patted dry, and minced

POLENTA

- 3 tablespoons olive oil
- 6 garlic cloves, minced
- 1 teaspoon minced fresh rosemary
- 4 cups water
  Salt and pepper
- 1 cup instant polenta
- ¼ cup vegetable oil

1. FOR THE TAPENADE: Pulse green olives in food processor until finely chopped, about 10 pulses; transfer to serving bowl. Pulse remaining ingredients together until finely chopped, about 8 pulses, then stir into green olives until well combined. (Tapenade can be refrigerated for up to 3 days.)

2. FOR THE POLENTA: Line bottom of 8½ by 4½-inch loaf pan with parchment paper and coat lightly with vegetable oil spray. Cook olive oil and garlic in 8-inch nonstick skillet over low heat, stirring often, until garlic is golden and fragrant, about 10 minutes. Off heat, stir in rosemary; let cool.

3. Meanwhile, bring water to boil, covered, in large saucepan over high heat. Reduce heat to low and stir in ¾ teaspoon salt. Slowly add polenta while whisking constantly in circular motion to prevent clumping. Continue to cook uncovered, stirring often, until polenta is soft and smooth, 3 to 5 minutes. Off heat, stir in garlic-rosemary mixture and season with pepper to taste.

4. Pour polenta into prepared loaf pan, smooth top, and let cool to room temperature, about 30 minutes. Wrap tightly in

CUTTING POLENTA SQUARES

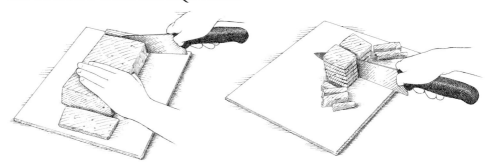

Run a small knife around the edge of the polenta, then flip it out onto a cutting board and remove the parchment. Trim ¼ inch off both ends of the polenta loaf and discard. Slice the polenta crosswise into ¼-inch-thick slabs. Stack about 6 slabs on top of one another, trim the edges, then cut in half to make 1½-inch squares.

plastic wrap and refrigerate until polenta is very firm, at least 2 hours and up to 1 day.

5. Run small knife around edge of polenta, then flip out onto cutting board and remove parchment. Trim ¼ inch off both ends of loaf and discard. Slice polenta crosswise into ¼-inch-thick slabs. Stack about 6 slabs on top of one another, trim edges, then cut in half to make 1½-inch squares. (You should have 50 squares total. Sliced polenta can be refrigerated for up to 1 day.)

6. Adjust oven rack 3 inches from broiler element, place rimmed baking sheet on rack, and heat broiler for 10 minutes. Carefully remove baking sheet from oven. Working quickly, drizzle vegetable oil evenly on hot baking sheet and arrange polenta squares in single layer. Broil polenta until spotty-brown and crisp, 8 to 10 minutes. Transfer polenta squares to platter and serve alongside tapenade with spoon or spreader.

Apple and Celery Salad with Roquefort

We like the rich, creamy flavor of Roquefort in this salad, but other varieties of blue cheese can be substituted. You can slice the apples or celery by hand or use a mandoline or V-slicer if you prefer. Blanched slivered almonds can be substituted for the hazelnuts.

3	tablespoons cider vinegar
1	tablespoon honey
¼	teaspoon salt
⅛	teaspoon pepper
3	tablespoons extra-virgin olive oil
2	celery ribs, sliced thin on bias
1	Braeburn or Fuji apple, cored, halved, and sliced thin
1	head red leaf lettuce (12 ounces), cut into 1-inch pieces
¼	cup fresh parsley leaves
6	ounces Roquefort cheese, crumbled (1½ cups)
½	cup hazelnuts, toasted (see page 29), skinned (see page 24), and chopped coarse

Whisk vinegar, honey, salt, and pepper in large bowl. Whisking constantly, drizzle in oil. Just before serving, whisk dressing to re-emulsify. Stir in celery and apple and let them absorb dressing, about 5 minutes. Add lettuce and parsley and toss gently to coat. Garnish individual portions with Roquefort and hazelnuts.

✔ WHY THIS RECIPE WORKS Strong blue cheese really shines when paired with thinly sliced sweet apple and crisp celery. A good shot of cider vinegar gives necessary tartness to the dressing, and a spoonful of honey tempers the acidity of the vinegar and highlights the saltiness of the cheese. As for the greens, we liked a combination of mild red leaf lettuce with bold and aromatic parsley, while a sprinkling of toasted hazelnuts gave additional crunch.

Cappuccino Semifreddo with Hazelnuts

For a milder flavor, instant coffee can be substituted for the instant espresso. To make chocolate shavings, use a vegetable peeler to shave them off a large block of chocolate (see page 10).

✔ **WHY THIS RECIPE WORKS**
A cross between a custard and ice cream, this semifreddo recipe features a light mousse flavored with coffee and speckled with nuts. We started with an Italian meringue, in which hot sugar syrup is poured into egg whites as they are beaten. The syrup cooks the whites, making for a stable meringue that can hold up to the additional ingredients. Because it can be made far ahead of time (even up to two weeks) and is frozen in individual ramekins, this semifreddo is both refined and simple to serve.

1   cup heavy cream, chilled
½   cup (3½ ounces) plus 2 tablespoons sugar
¼   cup water
3   large egg whites, room temperature
    Pinch cream of tartar
2   tablespoons instant espresso, dissolved in 1 tablespoon warm water
1   teaspoon vanilla extract
¼   cup hazelnuts, toasted (see page 29), skinned (see page 24), and chopped coarse
    Chocolate shavings (optional)

1. Using stand mixer fitted with whisk, whip cream on medium-low speed until frothy, about 1 minute. Increase speed to high and whip until soft peaks form, 1 to 3 minutes. Transfer whipped cream to bowl, cover, and refrigerate until needed.

2. Bring ½ cup sugar and water to boil in small saucepan over medium-high heat and cook until mixture is slightly thickened and syrupy and registers 235 degrees, 3 to 4 minutes. Remove syrup from heat and cover to keep warm.

3. Using dry, clean bowl and whisk attachment, whip egg whites and cream of tartar on medium-low speed until foamy, about 1 minute. Increase speed to medium-high and whip whites to soft, billowy mounds, about 1 minute. Gradually add remaining 2 tablespoons sugar and whip until glossy, soft peaks form, 1 to 2 minutes.

4. Reduce speed to medium and slowly add hot syrup, avoiding whisk and sides of bowl. Increase speed to medium-high and continue to whip until meringue has cooled slightly (just warm) and is very thick and shiny, 2 to 5 minutes. Add dissolved espresso and vanilla and continue to whip until incorporated, 30 to 60 seconds.

5. Gently stir one-third of whipped cream into meringue with rubber spatula. Fold in remaining whipped cream and 2 tablespoons hazelnuts until just incorporated.

6. Divide mixture evenly among eight 4-ounce ramekins and gently tap ramekins on counter to settle batter. Cover each ramekin tightly with plastic wrap, pressing it flush to surface of batter, and freeze until firm, at least 8 hours and up to 2 weeks.

7. Before serving, let ramekins sit at room temperature until slightly softened, 5 to 10 minutes. Sprinkle with remaining 2 tablespoons hazelnuts and chocolate shavings, if using.

New England Cod and Potato Dinner

THE GAME PLAN

ON THE DAY OF...

MAKE CRANBERRY CAKE: 1 ¼ hours
(plus 50 minutes for baking and cooling)

MAKE SALAD: 30 minutes (plus 1 ¼ hours
for roasting and cooling vegetables)

MAKE COD WITH POTATOES: 1 ½ hours

MAKE PANINI BITES: 35 minutes

Lemon-Herb Cod Fillets with Garlic Potatoes

Slicing the potatoes 3/16 inch thick (the thickness of three stacked pennies) is crucial for the success of this dish; use a mandoline, a V-slicer, or a food processor fitted with a slicing blade. Make sure to toss the potatoes with oil right after slicing to prevent browning; do not store the sliced potatoes in water or they'll turn soggy when cooked. Halibut or haddock can be substituted for the cod.

6	tablespoons unsalted butter, softened
1	tablespoon minced fresh thyme
1	tablespoon minced fresh parsley
2	teaspoons grated lemon zest plus 2 lemons, sliced thin
	Salt and pepper
6	tablespoons olive oil
3	pounds russet potatoes, sliced 3/16 inch thick
6	garlic cloves, minced
8	(6- to 8-ounce) skinless cod fillets, 1 to 1½ inches thick

1. Adjust oven rack to lower-middle position and heat oven to 425 degrees. Mash butter, thyme, parsley, lemon zest, ¼ teaspoon salt, and ⅛ teaspoon pepper together in bowl. (Butter can be refrigerated for up to 1 week.)

2. Brush rimmed baking sheet with 2 tablespoons oil. In large bowl, toss potatoes with remaining ¼ cup oil and garlic. Shingle potatoes tightly into even rows, lengthwise, on baking sheet. (Assembled potatoes can be wrapped *continued* ➤

continued ➤

WHY THIS RECIPE WORKS
A play on the classic cod and potato duo, this dish features flaky, moist fish atop a bed of crisp, creamy potatoes. Cooking fish and potatoes together on one pan (the kitchen workhorse, the rimmed baking sheet) has the benefit of flavoring both with mingled juices and aromatics, as well as limiting pans that need to be watched and washed. After slicing the potatoes thin and shingling them attractively on the sheet pan, we gave them a head start in the oven before adding the fish so that both would finish cooking at the same time. An easy compound butter made with garlic, thyme, parsley, and lemon zest, plus a shingling of lemon slices, flavored the fish and kept it moist.

SHINGLING POTATOES FOR LEMON-HERB COD

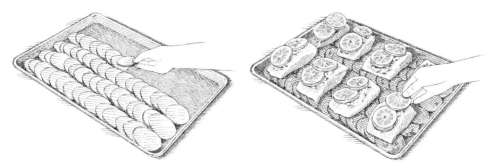

Shingle the sliced potatoes tightly into even rows lengthwise on the baking sheet; you should have about 5 rows of potatoes and no gaps. Once the potatoes are parcooked, carefully arrange the fish buttered side up on top of the potatoes and top each piece of fish with lemon slices.

tightly and refrigerated for up to 2 hours.) Season potatoes with salt and pepper and roast until spotty brown and just tender, 35 to 40 minutes, rotating baking sheet halfway through roasting.

3. Pat cod dry with paper towels, season with salt and pepper, and rub herb butter evenly over top of each fillet. Carefully arrange fish on top of potatoes and top each

fillet with lemon slices.

4. Roast fish and potatoes until fish flakes apart when gently prodded with paring knife and registers 140 degrees, about 15 minutes. Gently score potatoes around each piece of fish into individual portions with edge of spatula. Slide spatula underneath potatoes and fish, carefully transfer to individual plates, and serve.

Roasted Fennel and Mushroom Salad

Fennel fronds (the delicate greenery attached to the fennel stalks) add a good amount of flavor to this salad; if they are unavailable, substitute 3 tablespoons chopped fresh tarragon.

✔ **WHY THIS RECIPE WORKS**
We wanted a roasted vegetable salad with vegetables that had compatible colors, flavors, and textures and would roast well together. Earthy cremini mushrooms and slightly sweet fennel fit the bill—we halved the mushrooms and cut the fennel into ½-inch pieces, tossing both with oil, salt, and pepper, plus a little sugar (to enhance browning), before roasting them together. Cut this way, the vegetables kept their structure and cooked to a firm yet tender consistency, while achieving significant, flavorful browning.

¼   cup lemon juice (2 lemons)
2   teaspoons Dijon mustard
     Salt and pepper
6   tablespoons extra-virgin olive oil
4   fennel bulbs, fronds minced, stalks discarded, bulbs quartered, cored, and cut crosswise into ½-inch-thick slices (see page 22)
2   pounds cremini mushrooms, trimmed and halved if small or quartered if large
½   teaspoon sugar
4   ounces baby arugula (4 cups)

1. Adjust oven racks to upper-middle and lower-middle positions and heat oven to 500 degrees. Whisk lemon juice, mustard, ¼ teaspoon salt, and ⅛ teaspoon pepper

together in large bowl. Whisking constantly, drizzle in 2 tablespoons oil.

2. In separate bowl, toss sliced fennel and mushrooms with remaining ¼ cup oil, sugar, ½ teaspoon salt, and ¼ teaspoon pepper. Spread evenly over 2 rimmed baking sheets. Roast until vegetables are well browned and tender, 35 to 45 minutes, switching and rotating baking sheets halfway through baking.

3. Whisk dressing to re-emulsify, then add roasted vegetables and toss to combine. Let cool to room temperature, about 30 minutes. (Cooled vegetables can be covered and held at room temperature for up to 1½ hours.) Just before serving, add fennel fronds and arugula and toss gently to coat.

Cheddar and Apple Panini Bites

You can substitute any fruit chutney for the apple chutney. We like to use rustic, artisanal bread for this recipe; don't use a baguette, but rather look for a wide loaf that will yield big slices. Nut breads also work well here. We like the attractive grill marks that a grill pan gives the panini, but you can substitute a 12-inch nonstick skillet if necessary.

½ cup apple chutney
2 teaspoons minced fresh thyme or sage (optional)
8 (½-inch-thick) slices crusty bread
8 ounces thinly sliced sharp cheddar cheese
4 slices bacon, cooked and crumbled
1 Granny Smith apple, cored, halved, and sliced thin
2 tablespoons olive oil

1. Spread chutney evenly over 1 side of each piece of bread and sprinkle with thyme, if using. Build 4 sandwiches, using prepared bread (with chutney inside sandwich), cheddar, bacon, and apple. (Assembled sandwiches can be held for up to 4 hours.)

2. Brush outside of sandwiches lightly with oil. Heat 12-inch nonstick grill pan over medium heat for 1 minute. Place 2 sandwiches in pan and weight with Dutch oven. Cook until bread is golden brown and crisp on both sides and cheese is melted, about 8 minutes, removing pot and flipping sandwiches over halfway through cooking.

3. Transfer to wire rack and repeat with remaining 2 sandwiches. Slice sandwiches crosswise into ¾-inch-thick strips and serve.

COOKING PANINI

To make panini without using a panini press, heat up a 12-inch nonstick grill pan over medium heat for 1 minute. Place 2 sandwiches in the pan and place a Dutch oven on top to weigh down the sandwiches. Cook until bread is golden brown and crisp on both sides and cheese has melted, about 8 minutes, removing the pot and flipping the sandwiches over halfway through the cooking time.

Cranberry Upside-Down Cake

To prevent this cake from sticking, do not let it cool in the pan for more than 10 minutes.

TOPPING

6	tablespoons unsalted butter
12	ounces fresh or thawed frozen cranberries (3 cups)
¾	cup (5¼ ounces) sugar
2	tablespoons seedless raspberry jam
½	teaspoon vanilla extract

CAKE

1	cup (5 ounces) all-purpose flour
¼	cup blanched slivered almonds
1	teaspoon baking powder
¼	teaspoon salt
½	cup milk
½	teaspoon vanilla extract
½	teaspoon almond extract
6	tablespoons unsalted butter, softened
¾	cup (5¼ ounces) sugar
3	large eggs, separated
	Pinch cream of tartar

WHIPPED CREAM

1	cup heavy cream, chilled
1	tablespoon sugar
¼	teaspoon vanilla extract
	Pinch salt

1. FOR THE TOPPING: Adjust oven rack to middle position and heat oven to 350 degrees. Grease 9-inch round cake pan, line with parchment paper, grease parchment, then flour pan. Melt butter in 12-inch nonstick skillet over medium heat. Add cranberries, sugar, and jam and cook until cranberries are just softened, about 4 minutes. Strain cranberry mixture over bowl, reserving juices.

2. Return strained juices to skillet and simmer over medium heat until syrupy and reduced to 1 cup, about 4 minutes. Off heat, stir in vanilla. Arrange strained berries in single layer in prepared pan. Pour juice mixture over berries and refrigerate for 30 minutes.

3. FOR THE CAKE: Meanwhile, process ¼ cup flour and almonds in food processor until finely ground, about 45 seconds. Add remaining ¾ cup flour, baking powder, and salt, and pulse to combine; set aside. Whisk milk and extracts together in liquid measuring cup.

4. Using stand mixer fitted with paddle, beat butter and sugar until pale and fluffy, about 3 minutes. Add egg yolks, 1 at a time, and beat until combined. Add flour mixture in 3 additions, alternating with 2 additions of milk mixture, scraping down bowl as needed. Give batter final stir by hand, then transfer batter to large bowl.

5. Using dry, clean bowl and whisk attachment, whip egg whites and cream of tartar on medium-low speed until foamy, about 1 minute. Increase speed to medium-high and whip until soft peaks form, 2 to 3 minutes. Whisk one-third of whipped whites into batter, then fold in remaining whites.

6. Pour batter over chilled cranberry mixture and bake until toothpick inserted in center comes out clean, 35 to 40 minutes. Let cake cool on wire rack 10 minutes, then run paring knife around edge of cake and invert onto serving plate. (Cake can be held at room temperature for up to 8 hours before serving.)

7. FOR THE WHIPPED CREAM: Using stand mixer fitted with whisk, whip cream, sugar, vanilla, and salt on medium-low speed until foamy, about 1 minute. Increase speed to high and whip until soft peaks form, 1 to 3 minutes. (Whipped cream can be refrigerated for up to 8 hours; rewhisk briefly before serving.) Slice cake into pieces and serve with whipped cream.

EVEN EASIER ➜ Don't have time to make a cranberry cake? Serve sliced pound cake with a homemade cranberry sauce and whipped cream. For the sauce, bring 1¼ cups sugar, ¾ cup water, 1 tablespoon grated orange zest, and ¼ teaspoon salt to a boil in a medium saucepan over high heat. Stir in one 12-ounce bag cranberries and simmer until thickened and most of the berries have popped open, about 5 minutes. Transfer to a bowl and stir in 2 tablespoons triple sec or Grand Marnier. Cover and refrigerate until chilled, about 30 minutes, before serving.

✔ WHY THIS RECIPE WORKS

This ruby-crowned cake boasts a sweet-tart cranberry topping and a tender, buttery cake. But as with all upside-down cakes, its preparation (the berries are baked on the bottom of the cake, then the cake is flipped over to allow the berries to appear on top) can easily lead to collapsed, soggy cakes. We found that folding fluffy beaten egg whites into the batter produced a light cake that was still sturdy enough to support the fruit topping. Ground almonds lent a moist richness and hearty texture to the crumb. Precooking the cranberries and sugar on the stovetop to evaporate some of the fruit's moisture kept the topping from being runny.

Family-Style Italian Sunday Supper

THE GAME PLAN

◄▸

ONE DAY AHEAD...

MAKE RICOTTA CHEESE: I hour
(plus 2 hours for chilling)

MAKE BISCOTTI: I hour (plus 3 hours
for baking and cooling)

ON THE DAY OF...

MAKE BOLOGNESE: 2¼ hours

MAKE SALAD: 45 minutes

SEASON RICOTTA AND MAKE GARLIC TOASTS:
I5 minutes

FAMILY-STYLE ITALIAN
SUNDAY SUPPER

⤙ *Serves 8* ⤙

Homemade Ricotta Cheese
One-Pot Bolognese ⤛ Arugula Salad with Figs and Prosciutto
Chocolate-Dipped Pistachio Biscotti with Vin Santo

One-Pot Bolognese

You will need at least a 6-quart Dutch oven for this recipe. If you can't find meatloaf mix, substitute 12 ounces each of 85 percent lean ground beef and ground pork. Be careful not to break up the meat too much when cooking it with the milk in step 3; the meat will continue to break down while the pasta cooks in step 5.

3	carrots, peeled and cut into 1-inch pieces
1	onion, cut into 1-inch pieces
4	ounces thinly sliced pancetta, cut into 1-inch pieces
¾	ounce dried porcini mushrooms, rinsed
2	anchovy fillets, rinsed
3	(14.5-ounce) cans diced tomatoes
3	tablespoons unsalted butter
	Salt and pepper
3	tablespoons tomato paste
1	tablespoon sugar
2	garlic cloves, minced
1½	pounds meatloaf mix
2	cups whole milk
¾	cup dry white wine
5	cups water
1½	pounds ziti (7½ cups)
2	ounces Parmesan cheese, grated (1 cup)

1. Pulse carrots and onion in food processor until finely chopped, 15 to 20 pulses; transfer to bowl. Process pancetta, porcini mushrooms, and anchovies until finely chopped, 30 to 35 seconds; transfer to separate bowl. Pulse tomatoes with their juice until mostly smooth, about 10 pulses; transfer to separate bowl.

2. Melt butter in Dutch oven over medium heat. Add processed pancetta mixture and cook until browned, 3 to 5 minutes. Stir in processed carrot mixture and 1½ teaspoons salt and cook until vegetables are softened, 8 to 10 minutes.

3. Stir in tomato paste and sugar and cook for 1 minute. Stir in garlic and cook until fragrant, about 30 seconds. Add meatloaf mix, breaking meat into 1-inch pieces with wooden spoon, and cook for 1 minute. Stir in milk, scraping up any browned bits, and simmer until nearly evaporated, 25 to 28 minutes.

4. Stir in wine and simmer until nearly evaporated, 13 to 15 minutes. Stir in processed tomatoes and bring to simmer. (Sauce can be covered and held at room temperature for up to 3 hours. Return to simmer, covered, over medium-high heat, about 6 minutes, before continuing.)

5. Stir in water and ziti and bring to rapid simmer. Cover and simmer vigorously, stirring often and scraping bottom of pot, until pasta is tender and sauce is thickened, 18 to 20 minutes. Off heat, season with salt and pepper to taste and serve with Parmesan.

✔ **WHY THIS RECIPE WORKS**
Rich and meaty, Bolognese sauce is everything you could ask for in a meat sauce except quick. For a quick one-pot pasta Bolognese that tasted as if it had simmered all day, we started by using the food processor to chop most of the ingredients. Dried porcini and pancetta boosted the meaty depth of the sauce, while white wine added sweetness and complexity. Cooking the meatloaf mix in milk helped break it down and soften it to give it that long-cooked flavor and texture. Adding extra water to the sauce allowed us to cook the pasta right in the sauce—giving the pasta extra flavor and, as an added bonus, eliminating extra dishes.

Homemade Ricotta Cheese

WHY THIS RECIPE WORKS Kicking off the meal with an appetizer of homemade cheese will impress your guests, and this cheese is actually quite simple to make. Traditional ricotta (which means "re-cooked" in Italian) is made from the whey left over from cheese making, but our version starts with fresh whole milk, which is heated and then lemon juice is added; the combination of lemon juice and heated milk denatures the milk proteins until they separate into liquid whey and soft, billowy curds. We found lemon juice produced a better flavor than other acids such as vinegar, and gentle handling was crucial to prevent grainy cheese.

Make sure to use fresh homogenized and pasteurized milk here; do not use ultra-pasteurized (UHT or long-life) milk in this recipe, as it will not curdle properly. Try to handle the ricotta as little as possible after draining in step 3; excessive handling will give the ricotta a gummy texture. A sliced baguette or crackers can be substituted for the Garlic Toasts.

1   gallon whole milk
     Salt and pepper
¼   teaspoon grated lemon zest plus
     ⅔ cup juice (3 lemons)
¼   cup minced fresh basil
2   tablespoons extra-virgin olive oil,
     plus extra for drizzling
1   garlic clove, minced
1   recipe Garlic Toasts (page 62)

1. Heat milk and 1 teaspoon salt in Dutch oven over medium-high heat, stirring frequently with rubber spatula to prevent scorching, until milk registers 185 degrees, about 15 minutes.

2. Remove pot from heat. Slowly stir in lemon juice until fully incorporated and milk curdles, about 15 seconds. Let mixture sit undisturbed until it separates into solid curds and translucent liquid whey, about 5 minutes. Once separated, let curds rest for 20 minutes longer.

3. Line large colander with double layer of cheesecloth and place in sink. Very gently pour mixture into prepared strainer. Let drain, undisturbed, until whey no longer runs freely from colander and cheese looks moist, about 10 minutes. Transfer cheese to bowl and refrigerate until cold, at least 2 hours and up to 3 days.

4. Before serving, gently fold in lemon zest, basil, oil, garlic, ¾ teaspoon salt, and ½ teaspoon pepper. Transfer to serving bowl, cover, and refrigerate until flavors meld, at least 1 hour and up to 6 hours. Drizzle additional oil over ricotta and serve with Garlic Toasts. (Makes 3 cups.)

EVEN EASIER   Don't have time to make homemade ricotta? Buy the best ricotta you can find, and stir in the seasonings. Depending on the flavor and texture of the ricotta you find, you may need to add extra salt, lemon juice, basil, and olive oil for flavor, along with a few tablespoons of heavy cream to help loosen up the texture.

Arugula Salad with Figs and Prosciutto

WHY THIS RECIPE WORKS Here strips of salty, meaty prosciutto tame sharp peppery arugula while dried figs provide a sweet, fruity counterpoint. Frying the prosciutto gives it a crisp texture, and we plumped the figs by microwaving them in a mixture of balsamic vinegar and raspberry jam. We added walnuts for crunch and finished with slivers of briny, tangy Parmesan.

Honey can be substituted for the jam, if desired.

5   tablespoons extra-virgin olive oil
3   ounces thinly sliced prosciutto, cut into
     ¼-inch-wide ribbons
¼   cup balsamic vinegar
4   teaspoons raspberry jam
¾   cup dried figs, stemmed and chopped
     into ¼-inch pieces
1   shallot, minced
¼   teaspoon salt
⅛   teaspoon pepper
10   ounces baby arugula (10 cups)
¾   cup walnuts, toasted (see page 29)
     and chopped coarse
3   ounces Parmesan cheese, shaved
     (see page 32)

1. Heat 1 tablespoon oil in 10-inch nonstick skillet over medium heat until shimmering. Add prosciutto and cook until crisp, about 7 minutes. Using slotted spoon, transfer to paper towel–lined plate.

2. Whisk vinegar and jam together in medium bowl, then stir in figs. Cover and microwave until figs are plump, about 1 minute. Stir in remaining ¼ cup oil, shallot, salt, and pepper. Let cool to room temperature.

3. In large bowl, gently toss arugula with walnuts. Just before serving, stir fig mixture to recombine, then drizzle over salad and toss gently to coat. Garnish individual portions with crisp prosciutto and Parmesan.

Chocolate-Dipped Pistachio Biscotti with Vin Santo

Biscotti are Italian cookies that are baked twice—the first baking actually cooks the dough, while the second baking makes the cookies crisp and dry. Slicing the loaves while warm is important; if allowed to cool, the loaves will be tough and difficult to slice. Make sure you melt the chocolate in a bowl wide enough to fit the biscotti when dipping in step 6. Vin Santo is an Italian dessert wine classically served with biscotti; feel free to substitute another dessert wine if desired.

2 cups (10 ounces) all-purpose flour
1 teaspoon baking powder
¼ teaspoon salt
4 tablespoons unsalted butter, softened
1 cup (7 ounces) sugar
2 large eggs
½ teaspoon vanilla extract
¾ cup unsalted pistachios, toasted (see page 29) and chopped coarse
8 ounces bittersweet chocolate, chopped fine
   Vin Santo

1. Adjust oven rack to middle position and heat oven to 350 degrees. Line baking sheet with parchment paper. Whisk flour, baking powder, and salt together in medium bowl.

2. Using stand mixer fitted with paddle, beat butter and sugar on medium-high speed until pale and fluffy, about 3 minutes. Add eggs, 1 at a time, then vanilla extract, and beat until combined, about 30 seconds.

3. Reduce speed to low and slowly mix in flour mixture until combined, about 30 seconds, scraping down bowl as needed. Give batter final stir by hand, then mix in pistachios until just incorporated.

4. Press dough into two 13 by 2-inch loaves on prepared baking sheet, spaced about 3 inches apart. Bake loaves until golden and just beginning to crack on top, about 35 minutes, rotating baking sheet halfway through baking. Let loaves cool on baking sheet for 10 minutes. Lower oven temperature to 325 degrees.

5. Transfer warm loaves to cutting board and slice each on diagonal into ½-inch-thick slices with serrated knife. Lay slices about ½ inch apart on baking sheet and bake until crisp and golden brown on both sides, about 15 minutes, flipping slices over halfway through baking. Transfer biscotti to wire rack and let cool completely, about 1 hour.

6. Microwave chocolate in small, wide bowl on 50 percent power, stirring occasionally, until melted, 2 to 4 minutes. Dip bottom half of each biscotti into melted chocolate and transfer, chocolate side down, to parchment-lined baking sheet; let chocolate set, about 1 hour. (Biscotti can be held at room temperature for up to 3 days. Makes 3 dozen cookies.) Serve with small glasses of Vin Santo.

✓ **WHY THIS RECIPE WORKS**
Coated with bittersweet chocolate and served with Vin Santo, these biscotti make a fine ending to this family-style Italian dinner. Lean doughs made with just egg whites and no butter make very dry cookies—the type you need to dunk in coffee before eating. Doughs made with a little butter and whole eggs, such as this one, turn out softer cookies that don't require dunking (although they still taste good that way).

MAKING BISCOTTI

Using floured hands, shape each piece of dough into a smooth 13 by 2-inch loaf on a parchment-lined baking sheet, spacing the loaves about 3 inches apart. Bake the loaves until golden and cracked on top, about 35 minutes. Let the loaves cool for 10 minutes, then slice on the diagonal into ½-inch-thick slices. Lay the slices about ½ inch apart on the baking sheet and bake until crisp, about 15 minutes, flipping them over halfway through baking.

Easy and Elegant Cornish Game Hen Dinner

THE GAME PLAN
◆◆

ONE DAY AHEAD...

MAKE TART DOUGH: 15 minutes
(plus 1½ hours for rising)

CARAMELIZE ONIONS FOR TART: 25 minutes

MAKE AND FREEZE TURNOVERS: 45 minutes

ON THE DAY OF...

BAKE TURNOVERS: 30 minutes

ASSEMBLE AND BAKE TART: 30 minutes

MAKE GAME HENS: 45 minutes (plus 1 hour for roasting)

MAKE FARRO: 1¾ hours

MAKE BROCCOLI RABE: 30 minutes

EASY AND ELEGANT
CORNISH GAME HEN DINNER

➤ *Serves 8* ◄

Caramelized Onion, Blue Cheese, and Prosciutto Tart

Balsamic-Glazed Cornish Game Hens ✎ Farro with Fennel and Parmesan

Garlicky Broccoli Rabe ✎ Pear and Ginger Turnovers

Balsamic-Glazed Cornish Game Hens

Try to buy hens that are the same size so that they will cook at the same rate; if the hens vary widely in size, be ready to remove them individually from the oven as they finish cooking.

1⅓ cups packed dark brown sugar
1 cup balsamic vinegar
   Salt and pepper
8 (1¼- to 1½-pound) Cornish game hens, giblets removed

1. Adjust oven rack to middle position and heat oven to 450 degrees. Set wire rack in rimmed baking sheet lined with aluminum foil. Whisk sugar, vinegar, and 1 teaspoon salt together in 4-cup liquid measuring cup and microwave until thickened and reduced to about 1⅓ cups, 8 to 10 minutes. Measure out and reserve ⅓ cup glaze for serving. Cover remaining glaze to keep warm. (Glaze will thicken as it cools between bastings; rewarm as needed to loosen).

2. Tuck wings and tie legs of each hen together with kitchen twine. Pat hens dry with paper towels and season with salt and pepper. Arrange hens breast side down, with wings facing out, on prepared wire rack. Roast for 15 minutes.

3. Remove hens from oven and brush with ⅓ cup glaze. Flip hens breast side up with legs facing out, and brush with ⅓ cup glaze. Continue to roast for 20 minutes.

4. Brush hens with remaining ⅓ cup glaze and continue to roast until hens are spotty brown and breasts register 160 degrees and thighs register 175 degrees, 15 to 20 minutes. Transfer hens to carving board and brush with glaze reserved for serving. Let rest for 10 minutes before serving.

PROTECTING THE WINGS

Tucking the wings of a game hen, chicken, or turkey, behind the back will keep them out of the way and prevent the wingtips from burning. Simply twist each wing back behind the back and close the joints of the wings tightly. The tension of the closed, tucked wing will help to keep it in place.

TRUSSING CORNISH HENS

Tie the legs of each hen together with kitchen twine.

Caramelized Onion, Blue Cheese, and Prosciutto Tart

✔ **WHY THIS RECIPE WORKS** This pizzalike tart features the concentrated flavors of salty prosciutto and bold blue cheese against a backdrop of sweet caramelized onions and figs. Bread flour gives the crust the crackerlike exterior and chewy crumb we wanted. (Although this dough comes together quickly in the food processor, you can also use store-bought pizza dough to save time.) Fig jam, a winter-friendly pantry ingredient, provides a stable and tasty base for the other toppings.

You can substitute 8 ounces of store-bought pizza dough or pizza dough from your favorite local pizzeria here. All-purpose flour can be substituted for the bread flour in the pizza dough, but the resulting crust will be a little less crisp and chewy. If desired, you can slow down the dough's rising time by letting it rise in the refrigerator for 8 to 16 hours in step 2; let the refrigerated dough soften at room temperature for 30 minutes before using. If fig jam is not available, you can substitute apricot jam.

PIZZA DOUGH

1–1¼	cups (5½ to 6¾ ounces) bread flour
¾	teaspoon instant or rapid-rise yeast
½	teaspoon salt
2	teaspoons olive oil
7	tablespoons warm water

TART

5	teaspoons olive oil
1	onion, halved and sliced ¼ inch thick
¼	teaspoon brown sugar
¼	cup fig jam, loosened with 1 teaspoon water
⅛	teaspoon pepper
2	ounces blue cheese, crumbled (½ cup)
2	ounces thinly sliced prosciutto, cut into 1-inch strips
¼	teaspoon chopped fresh thyme

1. FOR THE PIZZA DOUGH: Pulse 1 cup flour, yeast, and salt together in food processor (fitted with dough blade if possible) to combine. With processor running, pour in oil, then water, and process until rough ball forms, 20 to 30 seconds. Let dough rest for 2 minutes and then process for 30 seconds longer.

2. Turn dough onto lightly floured counter and knead by hand to form smooth, round ball, about 5 minutes, adding remaining ¼ cup flour, 1 tablespoon at a time, to prevent dough from sticking to counter. Place dough in lightly greased bowl, cover tightly with greased plastic wrap, and let rise in warm place until doubled in size, 1 to 1½ hours. (Risen dough can be frozen for up to 1 month; let thaw on counter for several hours before using.)

3. FOR THE TART: Heat 2 teaspoons oil in 10-inch nonstick skillet over medium-low heat until shimmering. Add onion and brown sugar, cover, and cook, stirring occasionally, until onion has softened and released its liquid, about 5 minutes. Uncover, increase heat to medium-high, and continue to cook, stirring often, until onions are deeply browned, 10 minutes; set aside. (Onion can be refrigerated for up to 2 days.)

4. Adjust oven rack to lowest position and heat oven to 500 degrees. Brush rimmed baking sheet with remaining 1 tablespoon oil. Turn dough out onto lightly floured counter. Press and roll dough into 14 by 8-inch oval. Transfer dough to prepared sheet, reshape as needed, and gently dimple with fingertips.

5. Brush fig jam evenly over dough, leaving ½-inch border around edge, and season with pepper. Scatter caramelized onions, blue cheese, prosciutto, and thyme evenly over top. (Assembled tart can be held at room temperature for up to 4 hours before baking.)

6. Bake until tart is deep golden brown, 8 to 12 minutes, rotating baking sheet halfway through baking. Cut into 16 equal pieces and serve warm.

EVEN EASIER ➴ Don't have time to make a caramelized onion tart? Buy thin, crisp bread sticks (called grissini), and wrap thinly sliced prosciutto around the middle of each stick. (You'll need about 24 bread sticks and 8 ounces of prosciutto.) Serve with a wedge of sweet blue cheese, fig or onion jam, and plain crackers.

Farro with Fennel and Parmesan

For a creamy texture, be sure to stir the farro often in step 3. Farro can be found at the market alongside the other grains (such as barley) or next to the dried pasta.

¼ cup olive oil
1 onion, chopped fine
1 fennel bulb, stalks discarded, bulb halved, cored, and chopped fine (see page 22)
  Salt and pepper
6 garlic cloves, minced
2 teaspoons minced fresh thyme
3½ cups farro
4 cups low-sodium chicken broth
3 cups water, plus extra as needed
2 ounces Parmesan cheese, grated (1 cup)
½ cup minced fresh parsley
4 teaspoons balsamic vinegar

1. Heat oil in Dutch oven over medium heat until shimmering. Add onion, fennel, and ½ teaspoon salt and cook until softened, about 10 minutes. Stir in garlic and thyme and cook until fragrant, about 30 seconds. Stir in farro and cook until lightly toasted, about 3 minutes.

2. Stir in broth and water and bring to boil. Cover, reduce heat to low, and simmer until farro is nearly tender yet still firm in center, 45 to 50 minutes.

3. Uncover, increase heat to medium, and simmer, stirring often, until farro is tender and most of liquid has evaporated, about 10 minutes. If pot looks dry before farro is tender, add additional water as needed. (Farro can be covered and held at room temperature for up to 4 hours; reheat gently over medium-low heat, adding extra water as needed, before continuing.)

4. Off heat, stir in Parmesan, parsley, and vinegar. Season with salt and pepper to taste and serve.

WHY THIS RECIPE WORKS
This wonderfully nutty, slightly sweet grain is traditionally cooked by Italians in the same manner as Arborio rice to create a creamy dish called *farrotto*. We found it best to modify the traditional risotto technique and employed a more hands-off hybrid approach. We sautéed the farro with aromatics to enhance its flavor, then simmered it covered with plenty of liquid until nearly tender. We then removed the lid and stirred it frequently during the last minutes of cooking, releasing starches in the farro to create a rich and creamy consistency.

Garlicky Broccoli Rabe

Be careful not to overtrim the broccoli rabe; just trim the very ends of the stems and remove any wilted leaves. Shocking the blanched broccoli rabe in ice water is important to prevent overcooking, and it allows you to get most of the work and mess out of the way ahead of time.

3 pounds broccoli rabe, trimmed
  Salt and pepper
6 tablespoons extra-virgin olive oil
6 garlic cloves, minced
½ teaspoon red pepper flakes
  Lemon wedges

1. Bring 6 quarts water to boil in large pot over high heat. Fill large bowl with ice water. Add broccoli rabe and 1½ tablespoons salt to boiling water and cook until wilted and just tender, about 3 minutes.

2. Drain broccoli rabe, then plunge immediately into ice water to chill, about 2 minutes. Drain broccoli rabe well, discarding any ice, and dry thoroughly with paper towels. (Broccoli rabe can be refrigerated for up to 1 day.)

3. Heat ¼ cup oil, garlic, pepper flakes, and ½ teaspoon salt in 12-inch nonstick skillet over medium heat until garlic begins to sizzle, about 1 minute. Increase heat to medium high, add blanched broccoli rabe, and cook until heated through, 3 to 5 minutes. Drizzle with remaining 2 tablespoons oil and serve with lemon wedges.

WHY THIS RECIPE WORKS
For broccoli rabe that would be intensely flavored but not intensely bitter, we blanched it in plenty of salted water to tame its edge. For a dramatic, attractive look, we left the stalks of rabe whole and followed the blanching with an ice water bath, which halted cooking and locked in the vegetable's vibrant green color. We finished with a quick sauté with bold and simple ingredients that complemented the broccoli rabe's strong flavor.

Pear and Ginger Turnovers

The pears should be ripe but firm, which means the base of the stem should give slightly when gently pressed with a finger. To thaw frozen puff pastry, allow it to sit either in the refrigerator for 24 hours or on the counter for 30 to 60 minutes.

¾ cup (5¼ ounces) sugar

1 pound Bartlett or Bosc pears, peeled, cored, and chopped

1 tablespoon lemon juice

½ teaspoon ground ginger

⅛ teaspoon salt

2 (9½ by 9-inch) sheets frozen puff pastry, thawed

½ cup applesauce

1 teaspoon ground cinnamon

2 pints vanilla ice cream

1. Adjust oven rack to middle position and heat oven to 400 degrees. Line rimmed baking sheet with parchment paper.

2. Pulse ½ cup sugar, pears, lemon juice, ginger, and salt together in food processor until largest pieces of pear are no larger than ½ inch, about 6 pulses. Let mixture sit for 5 minutes, then transfer to fine-mesh strainer set over bowl and let drain, reserving juice, until needed.

3. Roll each sheet of dough into 10-inch square between 2 lightly floured sheets of parchment paper. Remove top sheets of parchment paper and cut dough into four 5-inch squares (you will have 8 squares total).

4. Combine drained pears and applesauce in bowl. Place 2 tablespoons pear mixture in center of each piece of dough. Brush edges of dough with some reserved pear juice. Fold dough over filling into triangle, crimp edges with fork to seal, and transfer to prepared baking sheet. Freeze turnovers until firm, about 15 minutes. (Turnovers can be frozen for 1 hour, then transferred to zipper-lock bag and frozen for up to 1 month. Let sit at room temperature for 20 minutes before baking.)

5. Brush turnovers with more reserved pear juice. Combine remaining ¼ cup sugar and cinnamon, then sprinkle over turnovers. Bake turnovers until well browned, 20 to 26 minutes, rotating baking sheet halfway through baking. Immediately transfer turnovers to wire rack and let cool slightly. Serve with vanilla ice cream. (Baked turnovers can be held at room temperature for up to 4 hours; if desired, reheat in 400-degree oven for 5 minutes before serving. Makes 8 turnovers.)

SEALING TURNOVERS

After placing the pear mixture into the center of each pastry square and brushing the edges of the squares with the reserved pear juice, bring 1 corner over the pastry to meet the opposite corner to form a triangle. Use a fork to crimp the edges and seal the turnovers.

✔ WHY THIS RECIPE WORKS
These crisp, juicy turnovers capture all the flavor of pears encased in flaky pastry without a difficult-to-make pastry and a cooked filling. The secret? Store-bought frozen puff pastry and applesauce. For a quick filling, we processed the pears in the food processor, then drained them to remove the excess liquid that would make the turnovers soggy. Cooked fruit—in the form of applesauce—added complexity to the raw pears, while lemon juice brightened the flavor, and ginger and cinnamon rounded out the filling. The sticky, sugary juice shed by the pears worked perfectly as a glue to hold the seams of the turnovers together and we also brushed it on top to ensure a shiny, crackly top.

A Taste of India

THE GAME PLAN
⌐

ONE DAY AHEAD...

MAKE ICE MILK: 15 minutes (plus 10 hours for freezing)

MAKE MANGO CHUTNEY: 45 minutes
(plus 2 hours for chilling)

ON THE DAY OF...

MAKE CHICKEN TIKKA MASALA: 1¼ hours
(plus 30 minutes for marinating)

MAKE RICE PILAF: 1 hour

MAKE SALAD: 25 minutes

ASSEMBLE GOAT CHEESE APPETIZER: 5 minutes

A TASTE OF INDIA

⤝ Serves 8 ⤜

Goat Cheese with Homemade Mango Chutney ⤝ Chicken Tikka Masala
Basmati Rice Pilaf ⤝ Mango and Jícama Salad with Mint Vinaigrette
Cardamom and Pistachio Ice Milk

Chicken Tikka Masala

You will need at least a 6-quart Dutch oven for this recipe. This dish is best when prepared with whole-milk yogurt, but low-fat yogurt can be substituted. To make this dish spicier, add the reserved chile seeds. Serve with Basmati Rice Pilaf (page 218) and warm naan bread.

CHICKEN

2	teaspoons salt
1	teaspoon ground cumin
1	teaspoon ground coriander
¼	teaspoon cayenne pepper
8	(6- to 8-ounce) boneless, skinless chicken breasts, trimmed
2	cups plain whole-milk yogurt
¼	cup vegetable oil
2	tablespoons grated fresh ginger
4	garlic cloves, minced

MASALA SAUCE

¼	cup vegetable oil
1	onion, chopped fine
	Salt
4	garlic cloves, minced
4	teaspoons grated fresh ginger
1	serrano chile, stemmed, seeds reserved, and minced
2	tablespoons garam masala
2	tablespoons tomato paste
2	(28-ounce) cans crushed tomatoes
1	tablespoon sugar
1⅓	cups heavy cream
½	cup minced fresh cilantro

1. FOR THE CHICKEN: Combine salt, cumin, coriander, and cayenne in small bowl. Pat chicken dry with paper towels, sprinkle with spice mixture, and press gently to help spices adhere. Transfer chicken to large platter, cover with plastic wrap, and refrigerate for 30 to 60 minutes. Whisk yogurt, oil, ginger, and garlic together in large bowl; set aside until needed.

2. FOR THE MASALA SAUCE: Heat oil in Dutch oven over medium heat until shimmering. Add onion and ¼ teaspoon salt and cook until softened and lightly browned, 5 to 7 minutes. Stir in garlic, ginger, chile, garam masala, and tomato paste and cook until fragrant, about 30 seconds.

3. Add crushed tomatoes and sugar and bring to boil. Reduce heat to medium–low, cover, and simmer, stirring occasionally, for 15 minutes. Stir in cream and return to simmer. Remove pan from heat and cover to keep warm. (Sauce can be refrigerated for up to 1 day. Reheat gently over low heat before continuing.)

4. While sauce cooks, adjust oven rack to upper-middle position and heat broiler. Set wire rack in rimmed baking sheet lined with aluminum foil. Using tongs, dip chicken into yogurt mixture (chicken should be coated with thick layer of yogurt) and lay on prepared baking sheet. Discard excess yogurt mixture. *continued* ➤

✔ **WHY THIS RECIPE WORKS**
Although tikka masala is not an authentic Indian dish (it was invented in a London curry house in the 1970s), diners worldwide have fallen in love with the tender, moist pieces of chicken napped with a lightly spiced tomato cream sauce. We wanted a chicken masala that was exotic-tasting but simple to make with readily available ingredients. To get there, we rubbed the chicken with a mixture of salt, coriander, cumin, and cayenne and then dipped it in yogurt mixed with oil, garlic, and ginger. For a winter-friendly recipe, we chose the broiler rather than the grill, and we cooked the chicken in large pieces to prevent it from drying out.

5. Broil chicken until exterior is lightly charred in spots and chicken registers 160 degrees, 10 to 18 minutes, flipping chicken halfway through cooking. Let chicken rest for 5 minutes, then cut into 1-inch chunks and stir into warm sauce (do not simmer). Stir in cilantro, season with salt to taste, and serve.

Goat Cheese with Homemade Mango Chutney

✔ **WHY THIS RECIPE WORKS**
In India, no meal would be complete without some sort of chutney, whether served as a condiment, sauce, or dip. We paired the spicy-sweet flavor of mango chutney with creamy, mild goat cheese for a perfect opener to our tikka masala meal. Since the fruit is cooked, frozen mangos proved to be just as good as fresh, but more convenient. Ditto for dried ginger (as opposed to fresh). Raisins and brown sugar played up the sweetness of the fruit, and dry mustard and garlic provided a savory, tangy background.

Depending on how sweet your mangos are, you may need to add more sugar to taste. Serve with crackers, a thinly sliced baguette, or pita chips.

- 1   pound frozen chopped mangos (2½ cups), thawed
- 1   tablespoon unsalted butter
- 1   red onion, chopped fine
-     Salt and pepper
- ½   teaspoon dry mustard
- ¼   teaspoon ground ginger
- ⅛   teaspoon ground cinnamon
-     Pinch ground cloves
- 2   garlic cloves, minced
- 6   tablespoons light brown sugar, plus extra as needed
- 1   cup water
- ¼   cup raisins
- 2   tablespoons white vinegar
- 1   (10-ounce) log goat cheese

1. Pulse mangos in food processor to ¼-inch chunks, about 6 pulses. Melt butter in medium saucepan over medium heat. Add onion, ½ teaspoon salt, mustard, ginger, cinnamon, and cloves and cook until onion is softened, about 5 minutes.

2. Stir in garlic and cook until fragrant, about 30 seconds. Stir in mangos and sugar and cook until mangos release their liquid and mixture thickens, 6 to 8 minutes. Stir in water, raisins, and vinegar and simmer, stirring occasionally, until thickened, about 12 minutes.

3. Off heat, season with salt, pepper, and additional sugar if needed. Transfer to a serving bowl and refrigerate until cold, at least 2 hours and up to 4 days. (Makes 2 cups.) Serve chutney, with spoon or spreader, alongside goat cheese.

Basmati Rice Pilaf

✔ **WHY THIS RECIPE WORKS**
For light, fluffy, aromatic basmati rice, we cooked it pilaf style, toasting the rice in oil to build flavor before adding the water. We found it important to first rinse the rice to remove excess starch—this produced grains that were more tender.

Long-grain white, jasmine, or Texmati rice can be substituted for the basmati. A nonstick saucepan works best here, although a traditional saucepan will also work.

- 3   tablespoons olive oil
- 1   onion, chopped fine
-     Salt and pepper
- 2½   cups basmati rice, rinsed and drained
- 3¾   cups water

1. Heat oil in large saucepan over medium heat until shimmering. Add onion and 1 teaspoon salt and cook, stirring occasionally, until onion is softened, 5 to 7 minutes. Stir in rice and cook, stirring often, until fragrant and edges of grains begin to turn translucent, about 2 minutes.

2. Stir in water and bring to simmer. Cover, reduce heat to low, and continue to simmer until water is absorbed and rice is tender, 16 to 20 minutes. Off heat, lay clean folded dish towel underneath lid and let rice sit for 10 minutes. Fluff rice with fork, season with salt and pepper to taste, and serve.

Mango and Jícama Salad with Mint Vinaigrette

Jícama is a sweet, crisp root vegetable that looks a little like a turnip; its unique flavor and crunch suits it well for this refreshing salad.

1	tablespoon minced fresh mint
2	teaspoons honey
1	teaspoon mayonnaise
1	teaspoon Dijon mustard
½	teaspoon ground cumin
¼	teaspoon lemon zest plus 2 tablespoons juice
¼	teaspoon salt
⅛	teaspoon pepper
⅓	cup extra-virgin olive oil
12	ounces jícama, peeled and sliced into ¼-inch-thick strips
2	mangos, peeled, pitted, and cut into ¼-inch-thick strips
½	cup roasted cashews, coarsely chopped
10	ounces baby spinach (10 cups)

1. Whisk mint, honey, mayonnaise, mustard, cumin, lemon zest and juice, salt, and pepper together in small bowl. Whisking constantly, drizzle in oil.

2. Combine jícama, mangos, and cashews in large bowl and place spinach on top. Just before serving, whisk dressing to re-emulsify, then drizzle over salad and toss gently to coat.

✔ WHY THIS RECIPE WORKS
For a cooling salad to go with our spicy chicken, we combined mild baby spinach with crisp jícama and sweet, tender mango. Honey and Dijon mustard lent both flavor and thickness to the bright dressing, and a little mayonnaise added further stability, while mint enhanced the clean, soothing flavor. While frozen mangos worked well in our chutney, we found fresh mangos were key here since their creamy texture and sweet flavor are the focus of this salad.

Cardamom and Pistachio Ice Milk

Ice milk has a distinctive milky flavor and slightly icy texture when compared to ice cream. This recipe tastes best when made with whole milk; we don't recommend substituting low-fat or nonfat milk. Do not omit the vodka; it plays an important role in the frozen texture of the ice milk. When portioning the ice milk into the ramekins, you may have some left over, which can be packed into an airtight container and frozen for up to 1 week. Serve with delicate gingersnaps.

5	cups whole milk
2	(14-ounce) cans sweetened condensed milk
¼	cup vodka
½	teaspoon ground cardamom
¼	teaspoon salt
½	cup pistachios, 5 tablespoons chopped and 3 tablespoons chopped fine

1. Blend milk, condensed milk, vodka, cardamom, and salt together in blender until thoroughly combined and emulsified, about 10 seconds. Pour mixture into bowl or container, press plastic wrap flush to surface of mixture, and freeze until mostly frozen but stirrable, 4 to 5 hours.

2. Stir in 5 tablespoons chopped pistachios and ladle mixture evenly into eight 6-ounce ramekins. Cover ramekins tightly with plastic and continue to freeze until solid, at least 5 hours and up to 1 week.

3. Before serving, let ice milk soften slightly at room temperature, about 10 minutes, and sprinkle 3 tablespoons finely chopped pistachios evenly over top.

✔ WHY THIS RECIPE WORKS
Often described as "traditional Indian ice cream," this frozen milk-based dessert known as *kulfi* offers a cooling, sweet finish to heavily spiced meals. It is easier to make then regular ice cream, and doesn't require an ice cream maker. Many recipes for kulfi require reducing fresh milk on the stovetop, but we saved time by starting with a base of sweetened condensed milk, which we supplemented with some regular milk for fresh flavor.

Snowed-In Slow-Roasted Pork Supper

THE GAME PLAN

ONE DAY AHEAD...

PREP PORK ROAST: 10 minutes
(plus 12 hours for salting)

MAKE MUSHROOM PÂTÉ: 50 minutes
(plus 2 hours for chilling)

MAKE SWEET POTATO PUREE: 1½ hours

ON THE DAY OF...

ROAST PORK: 7¼ hours

MAKE APPLE STRUDEL: 1¾ hours

MAKE CHERRY SAUCE FOR PORK: 1 hour

MAKE BROCCOLINI: 40 minutes

REHEAT SWEET POTATO PUREE: 5 minutes

SNOWED-IN SLOW-ROASTED PORK SUPPER

⤳ Serves 8 ⬿

Easy Mushroom Pâté ⤳ Slow-Roasted Pork with Cherry Sauce

Sweet Potato Puree ⤳ Broccolini with Garlic and Browned Butter

Apple Strudel

Slow-Roasted Pork with Cherry Sauce

We prefer natural to enhanced pork (pork that has been injected with a salt solution) though either will work in this recipe. We also prefer to use kosher salt in step 1, but 2½ tablespoons of table salt can be substituted if necessary. Add more water to the roasting pan as necessary during the last hours of cooking to prevent the drippings from burning.

1	(6- to 8-pound) bone-in pork butt roast, fat cap intact
	Kosher salt and pepper
⅓	cup packed light brown sugar
10	ounces fresh or frozen pitted cherries
2	cups dry red wine
¾	cup granulated sugar
5	tablespoons red wine vinegar
¼	cup ruby port

1. Using sharp knife, cut slits 1 inch apart in crosshatch pattern in fat cap of roast, being careful not to cut into meat. Combine ⅓ cup salt and brown sugar in bowl. Rub salt mixture over entire pork shoulder and into slits. Wrap meat tightly with plastic wrap, place in large bowl, and refrigerate for at least 12 hours and up to 24 hours.

2. Adjust oven rack to lowest position and heat oven to 325 degrees. Lightly coat V-rack with vegetable oil spray and set in large roasting pan. Unwrap roast, brush excess salt mixture from surface, and season with pepper. Lay roast in prepared V-rack and add 1 quart water to roasting pan.

3. Roast pork until meat is extremely tender and registers 190 degrees, 5 to 6 hours, basting twice during cooking. Transfer pork to carving board, tent loosely with aluminum foil, and let rest for 1 hour. Pour drippings from roasting pan into fat separator. Let liquid settle for 5 minutes, then pour off and reserve ¼ cup defatted liquid; discard fat and remaining liquid.

4. Bring ¼ cup defatted liquid, cherries, wine, granulated sugar, ¼ cup vinegar, and port to simmer in small saucepan over medium heat. Cook, stirring occasionally, until reduced to 1½ cups, about 45 minutes. Off heat, stir in remaining 1 tablespoon vinegar and cover to keep warm.

5. Using paring knife, cut around inverted T-shaped bone until it can be pulled from roast (use clean dish towel to grasp bone). Using serrated knife, slice pork thin and serve with cherry sauce.

✔ WHY THIS RECIPE WORKS
This fork-tender roast with its flavorful, crisp crust (dubbed "meat-candy" in the test kitchen) recalls the glory days of old-fashioned, better-tasting pork and is the perfect centerpiece for a cold-weather dinner. We started our recipe by rubbing the roast's exterior with a combination of brown sugar and salt, and then left it to rest overnight. The sugar pulled the water from the outer layers of the meat, drying out the exterior, and boosted browning. A 325-degree oven proved best; a five-hour stint broke down the meat's collagen and rendered the interior meltingly tender yet sliceable. Finally, a fruity sauce with sweet and sour elements cuts the richness of the slow-roasted pork shoulder.

Easy Mushroom Pâté

Serve with crackers, a thinly sliced baguette, or Garlic Toasts (page 62).

1   ounce dried porcini mushrooms, rinsed
1   pound white mushrooms, trimmed and halved
3   tablespoons unsalted butter
2   large shallots, minced
    Salt and pepper
3   garlic cloves, minced
1½ teaspoons minced fresh thyme
2   ounces cream cheese
2   tablespoons heavy cream
1   tablespoon minced fresh parsley
1½ teaspoons lemon juice

1. Microwave 1 cup water and porcini in covered bowl until steaming, about 1 minute. Let sit until softened, about 5 minutes. Drain porcini through fine-mesh strainer lined with coffee filter set over bowl. Reserve ⅓ cup liquid.

2. Pulse porcini and white mushrooms in food processor until finely chopped and all pieces are pea-size or smaller, about 10 pulses, scraping down bowl as needed.

3. Melt butter in 12-inch skillet over medium heat. Add shallots and ¾ teaspoon salt and cook until softened, 3 to 5 minutes. Add garlic and thyme and cook until fragrant, 30 seconds. Add mushrooms and cook, stirring occasionally, until liquid released from mushrooms evaporates and they begin to brown, 10 to 12 minutes.

4. Add reserved porcini liquid and cook until liquid has nearly evaporated, about 1 minute. Off heat, stir in cream cheese, cream, parsley, and lemon juice and season with salt and pepper to taste. Transfer to serving bowl and smooth top. Press plastic wrap flush to surface of pâté and refrigerate until firm, at least 2 hours and up to 3 days. Before serving, bring pâté to room temperature to soften. (Makes 2 cups.)

Sweet Potato Puree

Slicing the sweet potatoes evenly is important so they cook at the same rate.

5   pounds sweet potatoes, peeled and sliced ¼ inch thick
1   cup water
½   cup low-sodium chicken broth
2   teaspoons minced fresh thyme
2   teaspoons sugar
    Salt and pepper
½   cup half-and-half, warmed, plus extra as needed
2   tablespoons unsalted butter, melted

1. Combine sweet potatoes, water, broth, thyme, sugar, and 1 teaspoon salt in Dutch oven. Bring to simmer over medium-high heat. Cover, reduce heat to medium-low, and cook, stirring occasionally, until potatoes fall apart easily when poked with fork and liquid has been absorbed, 50 to 60 minutes.

2. Process potatoes, half-and-half, and butter in food processor until mixture is completely smooth, 2 to 3 minutes, scraping down bowl as needed. Season with salt and pepper to taste and serve. (Potatoes can be transferred to bowl, covered, and refrigerated for up to 1 day. Microwave, covered, until hot, 3 to 5 minutes before serving; add extra half-and-half as needed to adjust consistency.)

Broccolini with Garlic and Browned Butter

You will need at least a 6-quart Dutch oven for this recipe. Make sure to watch the butter closely as it browns in step 3; it can go from nutty brown to black and burnt in a matter of seconds.

2 tablespoons olive oil
3 pounds broccolini, trimmed
   Salt and pepper
¾ cup water
6 tablespoons unsalted butter
4 garlic cloves, minced
1 teaspoon minced fresh thyme
¼ teaspoon red pepper flakes

1. Heat oil in Dutch oven over medium-high heat until just smoking. Add broccolini and ½ teaspoon salt and cook, stirring occasionally, until they begin to brown, about 5 minutes.

2. Reduce heat to medium, add water, and cover. Cook broccolini, tossing often, until bright green but still crisp, 6 to 8 minutes. Uncover and continue to cook, tossing often, until water has evaporated, and broccolini is tender, 5 to 7 minutes longer. Transfer to large bowl.

3. Add butter to now-empty pot and melt over medium-high heat, swirling occasionally, until butter is browned and has nutty aroma, 2 to 3 minutes. Off heat, stir in garlic, thyme, pepper flakes, ½ teaspoon salt, and ¼ teaspoon pepper until fragrant, about 30 seconds. Add broccolini, toss to coat evenly with browned butter, and serve.

Apple Strudel

To thaw the phyllo dough, allow it to sit either in the refrigerator for 24 hours or on the counter for 4 to 5 hours. If the phyllo sheets have small cuts or tears in the same location, flip the alternating sheets of phyllo when assembling the strudel in step 4, so that the cuts will not line up and cause a weak spot in the crust. To make fresh bread crumbs, pulse white sandwich bread (with crust) in a food processor to fine crumbs, about 6 pulses; one slice of bread will make about 1 cup of fresh crumbs. Serve with vanilla ice cream or whipped cream.

¾ cup golden raisins
¼ cup Calvados, applejack, or apple cider
⅓ cup fresh white bread crumbs
9 tablespoons unsalted butter, melted and cooled
3 Golden Delicious apples, peeled, cored, cut into 8 wedges, and sliced crosswise ¼ inch thick
1 McIntosh apple, peeled, cored, cut into 8 wedges, and sliced crosswise ¼ inch thick
⅓ cup walnuts, toasted (see page 29) and chopped fine
½ cup (3½ ounces) sugar

1½ teaspoons lemon juice
½ teaspoon ground cinnamon
⅛ teaspoon salt
20 (14 by 9-inch) sheets phyllo dough, thawed
   Confectioners' sugar, for dusting

1. Adjust oven rack to middle position and heat oven to 425 degrees. Line rimmed baking sheet with parchment paper. Bring raisins and Calvados to simmer in small saucepan over medium heat; remove from heat and let sit, covered, until needed. *continued* ➤

2. Toast bread crumbs with 1 tablespoon melted butter in 8-inch skillet over medium heat, stirring frequently, until golden brown, about 2 minutes; transfer to large bowl.

3. Drain raisins, discarding liquid. Add raisins, apples, walnuts, ¼ cup sugar, lemon juice, cinnamon, and salt to bowl with bread crumbs and toss to combine.

4. Lay one phyllo sheet, with long side facing you, on clean, dry surface. Brush sheet with melted butter and sprinkle with ½ teaspoon sugar. Layer 9 more sheets phyllo on top, brushing each layer with more butter and sprinkling with ½ teaspoon sugar.

5. Mound half apple filling into narrow log along bottom edge of phyllo, leaving 2-inch border at bottom and ½-inch border on sides. Carefully fold bottom edge of dough over filling, then, holding apples in place, continue to roll dough around filling into tight log, leaving ends open. Gently transfer strudel, seam side down, to prepared baking sheet. Repeat with remaining 10 sheets phyllo, more butter, 5 teaspoons sugar, and remaining filling.

6. Brush strudels with butter and sprinkle with remaining 2 teaspoons sugar. (Strudels can be covered tightly with plastic wrap and refrigerated for up to 4 hours.)

7. Bake strudels until golden brown, 20 to 25 minutes, rotating baking sheet halfway through baking. Let cool on baking sheet until warm, at least 15 minutes and up to 4 hours. Just before serving, dust with confectioners' sugar. Using serrated knife, slice each strudel into 8 pieces (2 per person).

MAKING APPLE STRUDEL

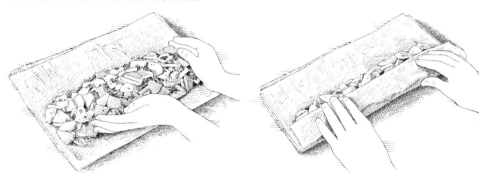

Mound half of the apple mixture into a narrow log along the bottom edge of the buttered and sugared stack of phyllo, leaving a 2-inch border at the bottom and a ½-inch border on the sides. Carefully fold the bottom edge of the dough over the filling, then, holding the apples in place, continue to roll the dough around the filling into a tight log, leaving the ends open. Gently transfer the strudel, seam side down, to the prepared baking sheet. Repeat with the remaining filling and phyllo. Brush the strudels with melted butter and sprinkle with 2 teaspoons sugar.

Hearty French Lamb Shank Dinner

THE GAME PLAN
❧

ONE DAY AHEAD...

MAKE LAMB SHANKS: 1 hour
(plus 3½ hours for braising)

MAKE CRÈME BRÛLÉE: 50 minutes
(plus 4½ hours for baking and cooling)

ON THE DAY OF...

REHEAT LAMB SHANKS: 1½ hours

MAKE WHITE BEAN GRATIN: 1½ hours

MAKE PEAR APPETIZER: 50 minutes

MAKE SWISS CHARD: 45 minutes

FINISH CRÈME BRÛLÉE: 10 minutes

HEARTY FRENCH LAMB SHANK DINNER

Serves 8

Skillet-Caramelized Pears with Blue Cheese
Braised Lamb Shanks ❧ White Bean Gratin
Garlicky Swiss Chard ❧ Crème Brûlée

Braised Lamb Shanks

Make sure the shanks are well trimmed and all large pockets of fat have been removed.

8	(12- to 16-ounce) lamb shanks, trimmed
	Salt and pepper
3	tablespoons olive oil
2	onions, chopped fine
2	celery ribs, minced
1	carrot, peeled and cut into 2-inch pieces
5	garlic cloves, minced
2	teaspoons minced fresh thyme
2	teaspoons minced fresh rosemary
½	cup all-purpose flour
2	tablespoons tomato paste
2½	cups dry red wine
3½	cups low-sodium chicken broth, plus extra as needed

1. Adjust oven rack to lower-middle position and heat oven to 325 degrees. Pat lamb shanks dry with paper towels and season with salt and pepper.

2. Heat oil in Dutch oven over medium heat until shimmering. Add onions, celery, carrot, and ¼ teaspoon salt and cook, stirring often, until softened and lightly browned, 8 to 10 minutes. Stir in garlic, thyme, and rosemary and cook until fragrant, about 30 seconds. Stir in flour and tomato paste and cook, stirring constantly, for 1 minute. Slowly whisk in wine, scraping up any browned bits. Whisk in broth until smooth and bring to simmer. Carefully transfer liquid to large roasting pan.

3. Nestle shanks into pan, cover pan with aluminum foil, and transfer to oven. Cook until shanks are very tender and fork slips easily in and out of meat, but meat is not falling off bone, 3 to 3½ hours, turning shanks over once during cooking.

4. Transfer shanks to platter and tent with foil. Strain cooking liquid through fine-mesh strainer into fat separator, pressing on solids to extract as much liquid as possible; discard solids. Let liquid settle for 5 minutes, then pour defatted liquid into liquid measuring cup; discard fat. Season sauce with salt and pepper to taste. (Shanks and sauce can be returned to roasting pan and refrigerated for up to 1 day; reheat, covered, in 375-degree oven until sauce is simmering and lamb is heated through, about 1½ hours, turning shanks over once. Add additional broth as needed to adjust sauce consistency.)

5. To serve, portion shanks into individual shallow bowls and spoon sauce over top.

✔ WHY THIS RECIPE WORKS Rich and hearty, these braised lamb shanks are the perfect centerpiece for a winter meal. The key was to build a flavorful braising sauce that would ultimately be strained and served with the meltingly tender shanks. We started by sautéing a traditional mirepoix (onion, celery, and carrot), adding garlic and herbs, and then adding flour and tomato paste (for meaty depth of flavor). After deglazing the pan with wine and broth, we had a flavorful sauce to add to the roasting pan. We found we could skip the step of browning the lamb shanks because it made them tough and they became browned enough from the heat of the oven. Best of all, the flavors of the lamb and sauce were even better upon reheating, making this a great make-ahead entrée.

Skillet-Caramelized Pears with Blue Cheese

WHY THIS RECIPE WORKS
Set out a platter with
Stilton cheese and these
caramelized pears drizzled
with caramel sauce and just
wait for the praise, as this
is no ordinary appetizer.
The pungent flavor of blue
cheese is the perfect foil for
the sweetness of the pears,
and the caramel sauce leans
more savory than sweet
with the addition of salt
and crushed peppercorns.
The pears are cooked in
the skillet with the caramel
sauce, instead of separately,
saving time and keeping
things easy. We added cream
to the pan to transform
the sticky sugar syrup
into a smooth sauce that
clings lightly to the pears.

Select ripe but firm pears for this recipe. If the sauce bubbles up at any point after adding the cream in step 3, remove it from the heat momentarily until the bubbling subsides. You can serve this appetizer either on a large platter (which is more casual) or arrange the cheese and pears on individual plates.

½	cup water
¾	cup sugar
4	Bosc or Bartlett pears, halved and cored
¾	cup heavy cream
½	teaspoon black peppercorns, crushed coarse
⅛	teaspoon salt
8	ounces Stilton or other strong blue cheese

1. Set wire rack in rimmed baking sheet lined with aluminum foil. Pour water into 12-inch nonstick skillet, then pour sugar into center of pan (being careful not to let it hit sides of pan). Bring to boil over high heat, stirring occasionally, until sugar is fully dissolved and liquid is bubbling, about 1 minute.

2. Add pears to skillet, cut side down. Cover, reduce heat to medium, and cook until pears are almost tender, and fork inserted into center of pears meets slight resistance, 13 to 16 minutes.

3. Uncover, increase heat to medium-high, and cook until sauce is deep amber-colored and cut sides of pears are golden brown, about 5 minutes. Pour heavy cream around pears and let bubbling subside. Cook, shaking pan until sauce is smooth and just combined, about 1 minute longer.

4. Off heat, transfer pears, cut side up, to prepared wire rack and let cool slightly. (Pears can be held at room temperature for up to 4 hours). Stir pepper and salt into sauce and transfer to small bowl. (Sauce can be covered and held at room temperature for up to 4 hours; reheat in microwave until warm, stirring frequently, 1 to 2 minutes.)

5. Carefully slice each pear half lengthwise into 3 wedges and arrange on serving platter or individual plates. Drizzle pears with caramel sauce and serve with Stilton.

White Bean Gratin

WHY THIS RECIPE WORKS
This Tuscan-inspired
gratin is a fitting side for
our rustic lamb shanks.
Canned cannellini beans
cut down the prep time
for this flavorful gratin. We
found that a brief simmer
in chicken broth with
rosemary infused the beans
with long-cooked flavor.

Make sure to cook the onions until they are well caramelized and darkly colored in step 1. Our favorite brand of white beans is Westbrae Organic Great Northern Beans. If you have made the lamb shanks ahead and are reheating them, place the shanks on the lower-middle rack of the oven and this gratin on the upper-middle rack of the oven.

3	tablespoons extra-virgin olive oil		1	cup low-sodium chicken broth
3	onions, halved and sliced thin		1	teaspoon minced fresh rosemary or ¼ teaspoon dried
½	teaspoon brown sugar		2	ounces Parmesan cheese, grated (1 cup)
6	garlic cloves, minced			Salt and pepper
⅛	teaspoon red pepper flakes		4	ounces Gruyère cheese, shredded (1 cup)
½	cup dry white wine		2	tablespoons minced fresh parsley
4	(15-ounce) cans cannellini beans, rinsed			

1. Adjust oven rack to middle position and heat oven to 375 degrees. Heat 2 tablespoons oil in Dutch oven over medium-high heat until shimmering. Add onions and brown sugar and cook, stirring often, until softened, about 5 minutes. Reduce heat to medium-low and continue to cook, stirring often, until onions are dark golden and caramelized, 20 to 25 minutes.

2. Stir in garlic and pepper flakes and cook until fragrant, about 30 seconds. Stir in wine and cook until nearly evaporated, about 1 minute. Transfer onions to 13 by 9-inch baking dish and spread into even layer.

3. Add beans, broth, and rosemary to now-empty pot and bring to brief simmer, about 1 minute. Off heat, gently stir in remaining 1 tablespoon oil and Parmesan. Season with salt and pepper to taste and spread evenly over onions. Sprinkle Gruyère evenly over top. (Gratin can be covered and held at room temperature for up to 2 hours.)

4. Bake, uncovered, until cheese is lightly golden and edges are bubbling, 15 to 20 minutes. Sprinkle with parsley and serve.

Garlicky Swiss Chard

You will need at least a 6-quart Dutch oven for this recipe. Don't dry the chard greens completely after washing; a little extra water clinging to the leaves will help them wilt when cooking in step 2. Make sure to only use 3 cups of sliced chard stems; depending on the size of your stems, there may be extra which can be discarded or saved for another use.

- 3 tablespoons extra-virgin olive oil
- 3 pounds Swiss chard, leaves sliced 1 inch thick, and 3 cups stems sliced ¼ inch thick on bias (see page 177)
- 2 shallots, minced
  Salt and pepper
- 4 garlic cloves, minced
- 1 tablespoon minced fresh thyme
- 1 tablespoon lemon juice

1. Heat 2 tablespoons oil in Dutch oven over medium-high heat until shimmering. Stir in chard stems, shallots, and ¼ teaspoon salt and cook, stirring often, until softened, 8 to 10 minutes.

2. Stir in garlic and thyme and cook until fragrant, about 30 seconds. Add chard leaves to pot, cover, and cook until leaves begin to wilt, about 2 minutes. Uncover and continue to cook, stirring constantly with tongs, until leaves are wilted and tender, 3 to 6 minutes.

3. Off heat, stir in lemon juice and season with salt and pepper to taste. Using slotted spoon, transfer chard to serving dish. Drizzle with remaining 1 tablespoon oil and serve.

✔ WHY THIS RECIPE WORKS
This garlicky chard is surprisingly flavorful and very easy to make at the last minute if the chard is prepped in advance. Chard stems are delicious when cooked, so we included some of them here, too; since they take longer to cook than the leaves, we sautéed them first. Shallots and garlic added sweetness and heat to balance the chard's earthy, mineral flavor, and a final splash of lemon juice minimized bitterness.

Crème Brûlée

For the caramelized sugar crust, we recommend turbinado sugar (sometimes sold as Sugar in the Raw). Regular granulated sugar will work in a pinch, but use only 1 teaspoon per custard. If using shallow ramekins, which normally hold 4 to 5 ounces, you may find that you have enough custard base for 1 or 2 extra custards.

- 4 cups heavy cream
- ⅔ cup (4⅔ ounces) granulated sugar
- I vanilla bean, halved lengthwise, seeds removed and reserved (see page 35)
  Pinch salt
- 10 large egg yolks
- ¼ cup turbinado sugar

1. Adjust oven rack to lower-middle position and heat oven to 300 degrees. Cover bottom of roasting pan with dish towel and arrange eight 6-ounce ramekins in pan, making sure they don't touch. Bring kettle of water to boil.

2. Combine 2 cups cream, granulated sugar, vanilla bean and seeds, and salt in medium saucepan. Bring mixture to boil over medium heat, stirring occasionally to dissolve sugar. Off heat, cover and let steep for 15 minutes.

3. Stir in remaining 2 cups cream. Place egg yolks in large bowl and slowly whisk in 1 cup of cream mixture until smooth. Whisk in remaining cream mixture until thoroughly combined. Strain through fine-mesh strainer into large liquid measuring cup or pitcher. Pour custard evenly into ramekins.

4. Transfer pan to oven and carefully pour enough boiling water into pan to reach two-thirds of way up sides of ramekins. Bake until centers of custards are just barely set, 30 to 35 minutes (25 to 30 minutes for shallow fluted dishes).

5. Transfer ramekins to wire rack and let cool to room temperature, about 2 hours. Set ramekins on rimmed baking sheet, cover tightly with plastic wrap, and refrigerate until cold, at least 2 hours and up to 4 days.

6. Before serving, uncover ramekins and gently blot tops dry with paper towel. Sprinkle 1½ teaspoons turbinado sugar onto each ramekin and gently shake ramekin to spread sugar out evenly. Pour out any excess sugar and wipe inside rim of ramekin clean. Ignite torch and caramelize sugar. Serve.

CARAMELIZING CRÈME BRÛLÉE

After sprinkling the sugar over the surface of the custard, tilt and tap the ramekin to distribute the sugar into a thin, even layer; dump out any excess sugar. Ignite the torch, and holding the flame about 2 inches above the sugar, slowly sweep the flame over the sugar until it bubbles and turns a deep golden brown.

> **WHY THIS RECIPE WORKS**
> Crème brûlée is all about the contrast between the crisp sugar crust and the silky custard underneath. All too often, the custard is too lean and runny and the topping is so thick that it practically requires a hammer to crack. For the smoothest, richest custard, we learned that a lot of egg yolks (rather than whole eggs) were necessary, as was heavy cream. Sugar, a vanilla bean, and a pinch of salt were the only other additions. A propane or butane torch (not the broiler) along with an even sprinkling of turbinado sugar are the keys to a perfect caramelized sugar crust.

EVEN EASIER ➤ Don't have time to make Crème Brûlée? Make a burnt sugar caramel sauce and serve over 4 pints (½ gallon) vanilla ice cream. To make a burnt sugar caramel sauce, carefully combine ¾ cup water and 1½ cups sugar in a medium saucepan. Gently stir the sugar with a clean spatula to wet it thoroughly. Bring to a boil over medium-high heat and cook, without stirring, until the sugar has dissolved completely and the liquid has a faint golden color, about 12 minutes. Reduce the heat to medium-low and continue to cook, stirring occasionally, until the caramel is very dark, just begins to smoke, and smells slightly burnt, about 375 degrees on a candy thermometer, 5 to 7 minutes. Off heat, slowly whisk in 1½ cups heavy cream (mixture will bubble vigorously). Stir in ¾ teaspoon vanilla extract, ¾ teaspoon lemon juice, and ¼ teaspoon salt.

Steakhouse Prime Rib Dinner

THE GAME PLAN

ONE DAY AHEAD...

MAKE ROOT VEGETABLE GRATIN: 40 minutes
(plus 2 hours for baking and cooling)

MAKE CHOCOLATE MOUSSE: 1 hour
(plus 4 hours for chilling)

PREP PRIME RIB ROAST: 5 minutes
(plus 6 hours for salting)

ON THE DAY OF...

MAKE SHRIMP COCKTAIL: 1 hour (plus 1 hour
for chilling)

MAKE PRIME RIB: 1 hour (plus 4 hours for roasting
and resting)

MAKE HARICOTS VERTS: 45 minutes

FINISH GRATIN: 1½ hours

MAKE WHIPPED CREAM FOR MOUSSE: 5 minutes

STEAKHOUSE PRIME RIB DINNER

~ Serves 8 ~

Shrimp Cocktail ~ Prime Rib au Jus

Winter Root Vegetable Gratin ~ Haricots Verts with Garlic and Herbs

Dark Chocolate–Orange Mousse

Prime Rib au Jus

A 7-pound roast should contain three or four rib bones. Ask your butcher for the first cut of a rib roast (the loin end), with ribs 9 or 10 through 12; it's much less fatty than the second cut (the chuck end). We prefer to use kosher salt in step 1, but 1 tablespoon of table salt can be substituted if necessary.

1	(7-pound) standing rib roast, trimmed and tied
	Kosher salt and pepper
2	tablespoons vegetable oil
1	onion, chopped coarse
1	carrot, peeled and chopped coarse
1	celery rib, chopped coarse
1	cup dry red wine
½	ounce dried porcini mushrooms, rinsed and minced
2	sprigs fresh thyme
1	bay leaf
2	cups low-sodium chicken broth
2	cups beef broth

1. Pat roast dry with paper towels and season with 2 tablespoons kosher salt and 2 teaspoons pepper. Wrap meat tightly in plastic wrap, place in large bowl, and refrigerate for at least 6 hours and up to 24 hours.

2. Adjust oven rack to lowest position and heat oven to 250 degrees. Spray large roasting pan with vegetable oil spray. Heat 1 tablespoon oil in 12-inch skillet over medium-high heat until just smoking. Brown roast on all sides, 12 to 14 minutes, reducing heat if pan begins to scorch; transfer to large plate.

3. Heat remaining 1 tablespoon oil in now-empty skillet over medium heat until shimmering. Add onion, carrot, and celery and cook until softened and beginning to brown, 5 to 7 minutes. Stir in wine, porcini mushrooms, thyme, and bay leaf, scraping up any browned bits, and cook until liquid has nearly evaporated, about 3 minutes. Transfer mixture to prepared roasting pan.

4. Spray V-rack with vegetable oil and set inside roasting pan. Place browned roast in V-rack and roast for *continued* ➤

TYING PRIME RIB

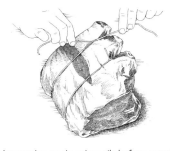

It is imperative to tie prime rib before roasting or the outer layer of meat will pull away from the rib-eye muscle and overcook. To prevent this problem, tie the roast at both ends, running the string parallel to the bone.

✔ WHY THIS RECIPE WORKS

Most of us cook prime rib only once a year, if that, so the stakes are high to get the juicy, tender, rosy meat that prime rib should have. Surprisingly, we found that a roast cooked at a temperature of only 250 degrees was rosy from the center all the way out. Additionally, it retained more juice than a roast cooked at a higher temperature, and the internal temperature rose less during resting, so we had more control over the final degree of doneness. Searing before roasting gave us a crusty brown exterior. For seasoning, prime rib needs nothing more than salt and pepper. Dry-aging the seasoned prime rib for up to 24 hours enhanced the flavor even further. Finally, because we sautéed the aromatics first and then roasted them under the prime rib in the oven, the jus developed extra flavor with less mess and little fuss.

1½ hours. Carefully add chicken broth and beef broth to roasting pan and continue to roast until meat registers 125 degrees (for medium-rare), 1½ to 2 hours longer.

5. Transfer roast to carving board, tent loosely with aluminum foil, and let rest for 30 minutes. Strain drippings from pan through fine-mesh strainer into fat separator, pressing on solids to extract as much liquid as possible; discard solids. Let liquid settle for 5 minutes, then pour defatted jus into sauce boat, discarding fat. Season jus with salt and pepper to taste. (Jus can be reheated in microwave until hot, 1 to 3 minutes, before serving.) Remove twine from roast, carve, and serve with jus.

HOW TO CARVE PRIME RIB

Carving a bone-in roast as large (and expensive) as a prime rib can be a bit intimidating. Here's the best way to remove the bone and carve this centerpiece roast into perfect slices: Holding the roast in place with a carving fork, remove the meat from the bone by cutting parallel to the rib bones. Place the now-boneless roast cut side down and cut the meat across the grain into ½-inch-thick slices.

Shrimp Cocktail

We prefer to use extra-large shrimp for this recipe; if your shrimp are smaller or larger, they will have slightly different cooking times.

✔ WHY THIS RECIPE WORKS For perfectly cooked shrimp infused with great flavor, we love this poaching method where the shrimp cooks off the heat in a flavorful liquid that is a far cry from a traditional court-bouillon. The secret is a hefty dose of Old Bay seasoning in addition to lemon juice and bay leaves. Once you try this method, you'll never be tempted to buy already cooked shrimp again. And forget the jarred cocktail sauce. This one is bursting with fresh flavor and a spicy kick— plus it's a snap to make.

SHRIMP

4 teaspoons lemon juice
4 bay leaves
2 teaspoons salt
2 teaspoons black peppercorns
2 teaspoons Old Bay Seasoning
2 pounds extra-large shrimp (21 to 25 per pound), peeled and deveined (see page 304)

COCKTAIL SAUCE

2 cups ketchup
¼ cup lemon juice (2 lemons)
¼ cup prepared horseradish, plus extra as needed
4 teaspoons hot sauce, plus extra as needed
1 teaspoon salt
½ teaspoon pepper

1. FOR THE SHRIMP: Fill large bowl with ice water. Bring lemon juice, bay leaves, salt, peppercorns, Old Bay, and 8 cups water to boil in large pot for 2 minutes. Remove pot from heat and add shrimp. Cover and steep off heat until shrimp are firm and pink, about 7 minutes. Drain shrimp and plunge immediately into ice water. Drain and refrigerate shrimp until thoroughly chilled, at least 1 hour and up to 1 day.

2. FOR THE COCKTAIL SAUCE: Stir all ingredients together in small bowl. Season with additional horseradish and hot sauce to taste. (Sauce can be refrigerated for up to 1 day. Makes 2½ cups.) To serve, arrange shrimp on serving platter with cocktail sauce.

Winter Root Vegetable Gratin

Use a mandoline, V-slicer, or food processor fitted with a ⅛-inch slicing blade, or slice the vegetables carefully by hand using a very sharp knife. This gratin needs to be cooked in advance, then reheated quickly before serving while the prime rib rests.

2	pounds russet potatoes, peeled and sliced ⅛ inch thick
1	pound carrots, peeled and sliced ⅛ inch thick
1	pound parsnips, peeled and sliced ⅛ inch thick
4	tablespoons unsalted butter
6	tablespoons all-purpose flour
2	cups heavy cream
1½	cups low-sodium chicken broth
4	ounces sharp cheddar cheese, shredded (1 cup)
2	teaspoons salt
1	teaspoon minced fresh thyme
½	teaspoon pepper
1	tablespoon minced fresh parsley

1. Adjust oven rack to middle position and heat oven to 350 degrees. Grease shallow 3-quart casserole dish. Place potatoes, carrots, and parsnips in very large bowl.

2. Melt butter in medium saucepan over medium heat. Stir in flour and cook for 1 minute. Whisk in cream and broth, bring to simmer, and cook until slightly thickened, about 2 minutes. Off heat, whisk in cheddar, salt, thyme, and pepper.

3. Pour sauce over vegetables and toss to coat. Transfer mixture to prepared dish and gently pack into even layer, removing any air pockets. Cover dish with aluminum foil and bake until vegetables are tender and fork inserted in center meets little resistance, about 1 hour 20 minutes, rotating dish halfway through baking.

4. Transfer gratin to wire rack, remove foil, and let cool until just warm, about 45 minutes. Wrap dish tightly with plastic wrap and refrigerate for to up 1 day.

5. Let gratin sit at room temperature for 1 hour. As soon as tenderloin is removed from oven, adjust oven rack to middle position and increase oven temperature to 450 degrees. Bake gratin, uncovered, until top just begins to brown and sauce bubbles gently around edges, about 20 minutes. Let cool for 10 minutes, then sprinkle with parsley and serve.

WHY THIS RECIPE WORKS
A classic dinner of prime rib wouldn't be complete without potatoes, so we developed a potato gratin worthy of this rich and elegant roast. Adding carrots and parsnips to the russet potatoes gives the gratin bright color and complex flavor, and the sharp tang of cheddar cheese in the sauce contrasts the sweetness of the root vegetables. Since the gratin and prime rib use different baking temperatures, we found it best to cook the gratin fully ahead of time, then simply heat it through and brown the top while the roasted prime rib rests.

Haricots Verts with Garlic and Herbs

To preserve the bright green color of the beans, be sure to add the lemon juice just before serving, as the acidity will cause the beans to discolor.

2	tablespoons unsalted butter, softened
4	garlic cloves, minced
1½	teaspoons minced fresh thyme
	Salt and pepper
2	pounds haricots verts, trimmed
2	teaspoons lemon juice
1	tablespoon minced fresh parsley

1. Mash butter, garlic, thyme, ½ teaspoon salt, and ¼ teaspoon pepper together in bowl. (Butter can be refrigerated for up to 1 week.)

2. Bring 6 quarts water to boil in large pot over high heat. Stir in haricots verts and 1½ tablespoons salt and cook until crisp-tender, 4 to 8 minutes. Drain beans and return to pot. Add butter, cover, and let sit off heat until butter has melted, about 2 minutes. Add lemon juice and parsley, toss gently to coat, and serve.

WHY THIS RECIPE WORKS
The freshness of slender, crisp-tender haricots verts offsets the richness of the prime rib and root vegetable gratin. Boiling the beans in salted water sets their color and deepens their flavor. Combining the garlic and thyme in a compound butter makes it easy to evenly distribute the flavors without needing to sauté the beans.

Dark Chocolate–Orange Mousse

We prefer to use either Ghirardelli Bittersweet Chocolate or Callebaut Intense Dark Chocolate, which each contain about 60 percent cacao.

MOUSSE

- 1 cup plus 2 tablespoons heavy cream, plus extra as needed
- 8 (2-inch) strips orange zest (2 oranges) (see page 28)
- 8 ounces bittersweet chocolate, chopped fine
- ¼ cup water
- 2 tablespoons Dutch-processed cocoa
- 1 teaspoon instant espresso
- 2 tablespoons Grand Marnier
- 2 large eggs, separated
- 1 tablespoon sugar
- ⅛ teaspoon salt

GARNISH

- ½ cup heavy cream, chilled
- 2 teaspoons sugar
- ½ teaspoon vanilla extract
  Chocolate shavings (optional)

1. FOR THE MOUSSE: Bring heavy cream and orange zest to brief simmer in medium saucepan over medium heat. Remove from heat, cover, and let steep for 10 minutes. Transfer to liquid measuring cup and refrigerate until chilled, about 2 hours. Remove and discard zest; add additional cream as needed until liquid measures 1 cup plus 2 tablespoons.

2. Microwave chocolate, water, cocoa, and espresso in bowl on 50 percent power, stirring occasionally, until melted, 2 to 4 minutes. Stir in Grand Marnier.

3. Whisk egg yolks, 1½ teaspoons sugar, and salt together in large bowl until mixture lightens in color and thickens slightly,

about 30 seconds. Whisk in melted chocolate mixture until combined. Let cool until just slightly warm, 3 to 5 minutes.

4. Using stand mixer fitted with whisk, whip egg whites on medium-low speed until foamy, about 1 minute. Increase speed to medium-high and whip whites to soft, billowy mounds, about 1 minute. Gradually add remaining 1½ teaspoons sugar and whip until glossy, soft peaks form, 1 to 2 minutes. Using whisk, stir about one-quarter of whipped egg whites into chocolate mixture to lighten it; gently fold in remaining egg whites with rubber spatula until few white streaks remain.

5. Using stand mixer fitted with whisk, whip orange-scented cream on medium-low speed until foamy, about 1 minute. Increase speed to high and whip until soft peaks form, 1 to 3 minutes. Using rubber spatula, fold whipped cream into chocolate mixture until no white streaks remain. Divide mousse evenly among 8 ramekins, wine glasses, or goblets. Cover with plastic wrap and refrigerate until set and chilled, at least 2 hours and up to 24 hours.

6. FOR THE GARNISH: Using stand mixer fitted with whisk, whip cream, sugar, and vanilla on medium-low speed until foamy, about 1 minute. Increase speed to high and whip until soft peaks form, 1 to 3 minutes. (Whipped cream can be refrigerated for up to 8 hours; rewhisk briefly before serving.) To serve, let mousse sit at room temperature for 10 minutes, then dollop with whipped cream and sprinkle with chocolate shavings, if using.

✔ **WHY THIS RECIPE WORKS**
This chocolate mousse is a surefire hit, combining a light, meltingly smooth texture with substantial chocolate flavor with undertones of orange. Since the downfall of many mousse recipes is their heaviness, we used fewer egg whites and yolks than other recipes we tested, as well as eliminating butter from the recipe. To make up for the lost volume of the eggs, we whipped the cream to soft peaks before adding it to the chocolate. A combination of bittersweet chocolate and cocoa powder maximizes the chocolate presence in the mousse. And to further deepen the chocolate flavor, we found that a small amount of instant espresso powder, salt, and Grand Marnier worked wonders.

Belgian Stew Supper

THE GAME PLAN

ONE DAY AHEAD...

ASSEMBLE BAKED BRIE: 20 minutes

MAKE BUNDT CAKE: 50 minutes
(plus 3 hours for baking and cooling)

MAKE CARBONNADE: 1½ hours
(plus 2½ hours for braising)

ON THE DAY OF...

MAKE SALAD: 50 minutes (plus 1¼ hours
for roasting and cooling)

BAKE BRIE: 30 minutes (plus 50 minutes
for freezing and cooling)

REHEAT CARBONNADE: 35 minutes

MAKE BUTTERED EGG NOODLES: 30 minutes

Easy Baked Brie with Jam ✦ Carbonnade
Buttered Egg Noodles ✦ Roasted Winter Squash Salad
Glazed Ginger Bundt Cake with Vanilla Ice Cream

Carbonnade

Cooking this stew the day before will be crucial if you only have one oven; the stew can then be reheated on the stovetop while you bake the brie and roast the squash for the salad. You will need at least a 6-quart Dutch oven for this recipe. When it comes to beer for carbonnade, we prefer a traditional copper-colored Belgian ale with fruity, spicy aromas and a pleasant hoppy bitterness—our favorite is Chimay Pères Trappistes Ale Première. Pilsners and other sweet, light-bodied beers lack the necessary bitterness, while very bitter beers (like India pale ales) lack the necessary sweetness.

1	(6-pound) boneless beef chuck-eye roast, pulled apart at seems, trimmed, and cut into 1½-inch pieces
	Salt and pepper
3	tablespoons vegetable oil
6	slices bacon, cut into 1-inch pieces
3	pounds onions, halved and sliced ¼ inch thick
3	garlic cloves, minced
1½	tablespoons minced fresh thyme or 1 teaspoon dried
⅛	teaspoon ground nutmeg
¼	cup all-purpose flour
1½	tablespoons tomato paste
1	cup low-sodium chicken broth
1	cup beef broth
3	cups beer
3	bay leaves
1½	tablespoons cider vinegar
2	tablespoons minced fresh parsley

1. Adjust oven rack to lower-middle position and heat oven to 325 degrees. Pat beef dry with paper towels and season with salt and pepper. Heat 2 tablespoons oil in Dutch oven over medium-high heat until just smoking. Brown one third of beef on all sides, about 8 minutes; transfer to medium bowl. Using fat left in the pot, repeat with remaining beef in 2 batches. *continued* ➤

WHY THIS RECIPE WORKS

In a good carbonnade recipe, the heartiness of the beef should meld with the soft sweetness of sliced onions in a lightly thickened broth laced with the malty flavor of beer. We found that the chuck-eye roast was our best (and most economical) beef option, given its generous fat marbling, which provides flavor and a tender, buttery texture. Lots of thinly sliced yellow onions, a spoonful of tomato paste, and a few minced garlic cloves boost the flavor. The key element of this Belgian stew, however, is a good dose of beer as part of the braising liquid for flavor that is rich, deep, and satisfying.

CUTTING BEEF STEW MEAT

 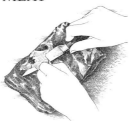 

Pull apart the roast at its major seams (delineated by lines of fat and silverskin); use a knife as necessary. With a sharp, thin-tipped knife, trim off the excess fat and silverskin. Cut the meat into pieces as directed in specific recipes.

2. Add bacon to now-empty pot and cook over medium heat until beginning to brown and fat is rendered, about 5 minutes. Stir in remaining 1 tablespoon oil, onions, and ½ teaspoon salt and cook, stirring often, until softened, 5 to 7 minutes. Stir in garlic, thyme, and nutmeg and cook until fragrant, about 30 seconds. Stir in flour and tomato paste and cook, stirring constantly, for 1 minute.

3. Slowly whisk in chicken broth and beef broth, scraping up any browned bits. Gradually whisk in beer until smooth and bring to simmer. Stir in browned meat with any accumulated juices, bay leaves, and vinegar, and return to simmer. Cover pot partially (lid should be just off center to leave about 1 inch open), transfer to oven, and cook until meat is tender and sauce is thickened and glossy, 2 to 2½ hours, stirring well after 1 hour.

4. Remove stew from oven and remove and discard bay leaves. (Stew can be cooled and refrigerated for up to 2 days. Discard hardened fat from surface and gently reheat over medium-low heat, about 30 minutes.)

5. Gently stir in parsley, season with salt and pepper to taste, and serve.

Easy Baked Brie with Jam

To thaw frozen puff pastry, allow it to sit either in the refrigerator for 24 hours or on the counter for 30 to 60 minutes. It is best to use a firm, fairly unripe Brie for this recipe. Serve with crackers.

1	(9½ by 9-inch) sheet frozen puff pastry, thawed
1	large egg, lightly beaten
1	(8-ounce) wheel firm Brie cheese
¼	cup fig, apricot, or cranberry jam

1. Roll puff pastry into 12-inch square on lightly floured counter. Using 9-inch round plate (or pie plate) as guide, trim pastry into 9-inch circle with paring knife. Brush edges lightly with egg. Place Brie in center of pastry circle and wrap in pastry, lifting pastry up over cheese, pleating it at even intervals, and leaving opening in center where Brie is exposed. Press pleated edge of pastry up to form rim. Brush exterior of pastry with beaten egg. (Brie can be wrapped tightly in plastic wrap and refrigerated for up to 24 hours.)

2. Line rimmed baking sheet with parchment paper. Transfer Brie to prepared baking sheet and freeze for 20 minutes. Adjust oven rack to middle position and heat oven to 425 degrees. Bake cheese until exterior is deep golden brown, 20 to 25 minutes.

3. Transfer cheese to wire rack. Spoon jam into exposed center of Brie, and let cool for about 30 minutes before serving.

WRAPPING BRIE IN PUFF PASTRY

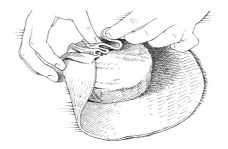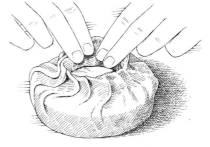

Lift the pastry up over the cheese, pleating it at even intervals and leaving an opening in the center where the Brie is exposed. Press the pleated edge of the pastry up to form a rim, which will be filled with the jam or preserves after baking.

Buttered Egg Noodles

Egg noodles are available in a wide variety of sizes; be sure to use wide noodles here because their larger size is better suited to accompany the stew.

1	pound wide egg noodles
	Salt and pepper
4	tablespoons unsalted butter

Bring 4 quarts water to boil in large pot. Add noodles and 1 tablespoon salt and cook until tender, 6 to 8 minutes. Drain noodles and return to pot. Stir in butter, season with salt and pepper to taste, and serve.

Roasted Winter Squash Salad

Apple juice can be substituted for the cider; simply omit the honey. The onions should not marinate longer than 15 minutes; prolonged soaking in the vinaigrette will cause them to lose their crisp texture. The squash can be served warm or at room temperature.

1	cup apple cider
5	teaspoons cider vinegar
1½	teaspoons honey
2	teaspoons minced shallot
¼	teaspoon minced fresh sage
	Salt and pepper
5	tablespoons extra-virgin olive oil
3	pounds butternut squash, peeled, seeded, and cut into 1-inch cubes (8½ cups)
1	small red onion, halved and sliced thin
10	ounces baby arugula (10 cups)
4	ounces feta cheese, crumbled (1 cup)
½	cup walnuts, toasted (see page 29) and chopped coarse

1. Simmer cider in small saucepan over medium-high heat until reduced to ⅓ cup, about 8 minutes. Transfer to large bowl, let cool, then whisk in vinegar, honey, shallot, sage, ¼ teaspoon salt, and ¼ teaspoon pepper. Whisking constantly, drizzle in 3 tablespoons oil.

2. Meanwhile, adjust oven rack to upper-middle position and heat oven to 475 degrees. Line rimmed baking sheet with parchment paper. Toss squash with remaining 2 tablespoons oil, ½ teaspoon salt, and ¼ teaspoon pepper and spread out over prepared baking sheet. Roast squash until tender and golden brown, 30 to 40 minutes.

3. Transfer squash to medium bowl, drizzle with 3 tablespoons dressing, and toss gently to coat; let cool to room temperature, about 30 minutes. (Squash can be held at room temperature for up to 1½ hours.)

4. Just before serving, whisk dressing to re-emulsify, then stir in onion and let it absorb dressing, 10 to 15 minutes. Add arugula, feta, and walnuts and toss gently to coat. Garnish individual portions with roasted squash.

Glazed Ginger Bundt Cake with Vanilla Ice Cream

Guinness is the test kitchen's favorite brand of stout. Be sure to use finely ground black pepper here. Do not use blackstrap molasses in this recipe. An equal amount of orange or lemon juice can be substituted for the ginger ale in the glaze. Our favorite brand of vanilla ice cream is Ben & Jerry's.

CAKE
2½   cups (12½ ounces) all-purpose flour
2   teaspoons baking powder
¾   teaspoon baking soda
¾   teaspoon salt
16   tablespoons unsalted butter
2   tablespoons ground ginger
2   teaspoons ground cinnamon
1   teaspoon ground allspice
¼   teaspoon pepper
4   large eggs, room temperature
1½   cups (10½ ounces) sugar
4   teaspoons grated fresh ginger
¾   cup robust or dark molasses
¾   cup stout beer

GLAZE
1¾   cups (7 ounces) confectioners' sugar
3   tablespoons ginger ale
1   teaspoon ground ginger

2   pints vanilla ice cream

1. FOR THE CAKE: Adjust oven rack to middle position and heat oven to 375 degrees. Grease and flour 12-cup nonstick Bundt pan. Whisk flour, baking powder, baking soda, and salt together in large bowl.

2. Melt butter in medium saucepan over medium heat. Stir in ground ginger, cinnamon, allspice, and pepper and cook until fragrant, about 30 seconds. Remove from heat and let cool slightly.

3. Whisk eggs, sugar, and fresh ginger together in large bowl until light and frothy. Stir in melted butter mixture, molasses, and beer until incorporated. Whisk flour mixture into egg mixture until no lumps remain.

4. Pour batter into prepared pan and smooth top. Wipe any drops of batter off sides of pan and gently tap pan on work surface to release air bubbles. Bake cake until skewer inserted in center comes out clean, about 45 minutes. Let cake cool in pan on wire rack for 20 minutes. Remove cake from pan and let cool completely, about 2 hours.

5. FOR THE GLAZE: Whisk all ingredients together in bowl until smooth. Pour glaze over top of cooled cake and let drip down sides. Let glaze set, about 15 minutes, before serving. (Cake can be stored at room temperature for up to 2 days.) Serve with vanilla ice cream.

WHY THIS RECIPE WORKS
This recipe takes gingerbread from snack cake to elegant dessert, first by moving the cake into a Bundt pan, and second, by intensifying the ginger flavor. A hefty 2 tablespoons of ground ginger plus 4 teaspoons grated fresh ginger give this cake an appealing and unmistakable punch while robust molasses (rather than mild) and stout beer give the cake a deep, malty tang. While it may seem out of place in a cake, pepper plays a pivotal role in bringing out the ginger's burn.

Paella Night

THE GAME PLAN
❧

ONE DAY AHEAD...

MAKE ALMOND CAKE: 30 minutes
(plus 3 hours for baking and cooling)

ON THE DAY OF...

MAKE PAELLA: 2¼ hours

MAKE SALAD: 15 minutes

MAKE CROSTINI: 15 minutes

FINISH ALMOND CAKE: 15 minutes

Paella

You will need at least a 6-quart Dutch oven for this recipe, or a 15- to 16-inch paella pan. If using a paella pan, be sure to follow the specific paella pan instructions on page 246. Spanish chorizo is the sausage of choice for paella, but Mexican chorizo or linguiça are acceptable substitutes. Soccarat, a layer of crusty browned rice that forms on the bottom of the pan, is a traditional part of paella, but we've made it optional; if desired, see instructions for how to make a soccarat at the end of step 6.

1½	pounds extra-large shrimp (21 to 25 per pound), peeled and deveined (see page 304), tails removed
3	tablespoons olive oil, plus extra as needed
12	garlic cloves, minced
	Salt and pepper
1	pound boneless, skinless chicken thighs, trimmed and halved crosswise
1	red bell pepper, stemmed, seeded, and cut into ½-inch-wide strips
12	ounces Spanish chorizo, sliced ½ inch thick on the bias
1	onion, chopped fine
1	(14.5-ounce) can diced tomatoes, drained, minced, and drained again
3¼	cups low-sodium chicken broth
2½	cups Valencia or Arborio rice
½	cup dry white wine
½	teaspoon saffron threads, crumbled
2	bay leaves
½	cup frozen peas, thawed
1½	pounds mussels, scrubbed and debearded (see page 246)
3	tablespoons minced fresh parsley
	Lemon wedges

1. Adjust oven rack to lower-middle position and heat oven to 350 degrees. Toss shrimp with 2 tablespoons oil, 2 teaspoons garlic, ¼ teaspoon salt, and ¼ teaspoon pepper in medium bowl; cover and refrigerate until needed. Pat chicken thighs dry with paper towels and season with salt and pepper.

2. Heat 2 teaspoons oil in Dutch oven over medium-high heat until shimmering. Add bell pepper and cook until skin begins to blister and turn spotty black, about 3 minutes; transfer to plate.

3. Add 1 teaspoon oil to now-empty pot and place over medium-high heat until shimmering. Brown chicken on both sides, 6 to 8 minutes; transfer to bowl. Reduce heat to medium, add chorizo, and cook, stirring frequently, until deeply browned and some of fat is rendered, about 6 minutes; transfer to bowl with chicken.

4. Add enough oil to fat left in pot to equal 2 tablespoons. Add onion and cook over medium heat until softened, 5 to 7 minutes. Stir in remaining garlic and cook until fragrant, about *continued* ➤

✔ WHY THIS RECIPE WORKS

With its bright array of colors and flavors, nothing beats the drama of paella. But while paella is a big hit at restaurants, it can be an unwieldy production at home. To keep things simpler, we pared down our ingredients, dismissing lobster (too much work), diced pork (sausage would be enough), fish (flakes too easily), and rabbit and snails (too unconventional). For our recipe we stuck with chorizo, chicken (boneless, skinless thighs), shrimp, and mussels (favored over scallops, clams, and calamari). When we focused on the rice, we found we preferred medium-grain varieties. Valencia was our favorite, with Italian Arborio a close second.

30 seconds. Stir in tomatoes and cook until pan is nearly dry, about 3 minutes.

5. Stir in chicken broth, rice, wine, saffron, bay leaves, and ½ teaspoon salt. Return chicken and chorizo to pot, increase heat to medium-high, and bring to boil. Cover pot, transfer to oven, and cook until rice absorbs almost all of liquid, about 15 minutes.

6. Remove pot from oven. Working quickly, evenly scatter shrimp and bell pepper over rice. Sprinkle with peas, then scatter mussels on top of peas. Cover, return to oven, and cook until shrimp are opaque and mussels have opened, 15 to 20 minutes. (If soccarat is desired, remove pot from oven, uncover, and cook over medium-high heat for 3 to 6 minutes, rotating pot as needed for even browning.)

7. Let paella sit, covered, for 5 minutes. Remove and discard bay leaves. Transfer mussels to large bowl, discarding any that have not opened, and cover to keep warm. Sprinkle parsley over paella and gently stir to incorporate shrimp into rice. Portion paella into individual serving bowls, top with mussels, and serve with lemon wedges.

DEBEARDING MUSSELS

Mussels often contain a weedy beard protruding from the crack between the two shells. It's fairly small and can be difficult to tug out of place. We have found the flat surface of a knife gives some leverage to help remove the pesky beard. Trap the beard between the side of a small paring knife and your thumb and pull to remove it.

MAKING PAELLA USING A PAELLA PAN

A paella pan makes an attractive and impressive presentation. Use one that is at least 15 inches in diameter. Follow recipe for Paella, using aluminum foil to tightly cover pan when directed. When placing mussels in pan, nestle them hinged side down into rice. To serve, do not remove mussels from pan or stir rice to incorporate shrimp directed in step 7; rather, sprinkle with parsley and bring paella pan to the table for serving.

Serrano Ham and Manchego Cheese Crostini

If you can't find Serrano ham, substitute thinly sliced prosciutto.

1	recipe Garlic Toasts (page 62)
¼	cup honey
8	ounces thinly sliced Serrano ham
6	ounces Manchego cheese, shaved (see page 32)

Drizzle honey over one side of garlic toasts, then top with Serrano ham and Manchego. (Makes 20 crostini.)

Green Salad with Marcona Almonds

We prefer the flavor of sherry vinegar in this salad; however, red wine vinegar can be substituted. If you can't find Marcona almonds, substitute regular blanched almonds, toasted (see page 29).

5	teaspoons sherry vinegar
1	shallot, minced
1	teaspoon Dijon mustard
¼	teaspoon salt
¼	teaspoon pepper
¼	cup extra-virgin olive oil
12	ounces mesclun greens (12 cups)
¾	cup Marcona almonds, chopped coarse
2	ounces Manchego or Parmesan cheese, shaved (see page 32)

Whisk vinegar, shallot, mustard, salt, and pepper together in small bowl. Whisking constantly, drizzle in oil. In large bowl, gently toss mesclun with almonds. Just before serving, whisk dressing to re-emulsify, then drizzle over salad and toss gently to coat. Garnish individual portions with Manchego.

Almond Cake with Clementines and Whipped Cream

This cake has a dense, pound cake–like texture. Do not substitute low-fat or nonfat milk for the whole milk. Be careful not to overtoast the almonds or the cake will have a dry, crumbly texture. An equal amount of blanched whole almonds can be substituted for the slivered, but you will need to increase their processing time to 30 seconds in step 2. When serving, be sure to use a serrated knife to cut the cake and take your time when slicing through the decorative clementines on top.

CAKE

2¼	cups (10 ounces) slivered almonds, toasted (see page 29)
1	cup (7 ounces) sugar
	Pinch salt
½	cup (2 ounces) cake flour
½	teaspoon baking powder
6	tablespoons unsalted butter, cut into 6 pieces and softened
2	large eggs, room temperature
⅓	cup whole milk

TOPPING

¾	cup heavy cream, chilled
1½	teaspoons sugar
¼	teaspoon vanilla extract
4	clementines, peeled and sliced crosswise into ⅛-inch-thick rings

1. Adjust oven rack to middle position and heat oven to 350 degrees. Grease 9-inch round cake pan and line bottom of pan with parchment paper. *continued* ➤

Process almonds, ¼ cup sugar, and salt in food processor until very finely ground, about 15 seconds. Add flour and baking powder and pulse to incorporate, about 5 pulses.

2. Using stand mixer fitted with paddle, beat butter and remaining ¾ cup sugar on medium speed until pale and fluffy, about 3 minutes. Add eggs, 1 at a time, and beat until combined. Add ground almond mixture and beat until just incorporated, about 30 seconds. Add milk and beat until just incorporated, about 30 seconds more. Give batter final stir by hand.

3. Scrape batter into prepared pan and smooth top. Gently tap pan on counter to release air bubbles. Bake until cake is puffed and golden on top and toothpick inserted in center comes out clean, 30 to 40 minutes, rotating pan halfway through baking.

4. Let cake cool in pan for 10 minutes. Run small knife around edge of cake, then flip out onto wire rack. Peel off parchment, flip cake right side up, and let cool, about 2 hours. (Cake can be wrapped and stored at room temperature for up to 5 days.)

5. FOR THE TOPPING: Using stand mixer fitted with whisk, whip cream, sugar, and vanilla on medium-low speed until foamy, about 1 minute. Increase speed to high and whip until soft peaks form, 1 to 3 minutes. (Whipped cream can be refrigerated for up to 8 hours; rewhisk briefly before using.)

6. Place cake on cake platter and spread whipped cream over top of cake, leaving ¼-inch border around edge. Shingle sliced clementines attractively over top. (Assembled cake can be held at room temperature for up to 1 hour.) Use serrated knife to gently slice through clementines and cake and serve.

EVEN EASIER ↬ Don't have time to make an almond-clementine cake? Drizzle 10 peeled and thinly sliced clementines with a spiced, red wine reduction and serve with lightly sweetened whipped cream and almond biscotti. To make a spiced red wine reduction, simmer 1½ cups dry red wine, ⅓ cup sugar, 1 whole clove, 1 (3-inch) strip orange zest (see page 28), ½ teaspoon vanilla extract, and pinch salt together in a small saucepan until syrupy and reduced to ½ cup, about 20 minutes; discard clove and zest before serving.

TOPPING THE ALMOND CAKE

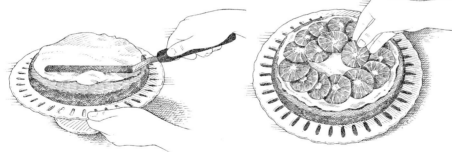

Spread the whipped cream evenly over the top of the cake, leaving a ¼-inch border at the edge. Shingle the sliced clementines attractively over the top of the cake. When serving the cake, be sure to use a sharp, serrated knife to carefully cut through the clementines.

Sunday Brunch Celebration, page 289

Spring Leg of Lamb, page 295

Lasagna Dinner for a Crowd, page 253

Upscale Picnic Spread, page 283

Lasagna Dinner for a Crowd

THE GAME PLAN

⫸

ONE DAY AHEAD...

MAKE CHEESE TERRINE: 30 minutes
(plus 4 hours for chilling)

MAKE TIRAMISÙ: 45 minutes (plus 6 hours for chilling)

PREP SAUCES AND VEGETABLES FOR LASAGNA:
1½ hours

ON THE DAY OF...

ASSEMBLE AND BAKE LASAGNA: 15 minutes
(plus 1¾ hours for baking and cooling)

BRING TERRINE TO ROOM TEMPERATURE: 1 hour

MAKE TOMATO SKEWERS: 45 minutes

MAKE CAESAR SALAD: 1 hour

LASAGNA DINNER FOR A CROWD

⊱ Serves 12 ⊰

Pesto and Sun-Dried Tomato Cheese Terrine

Tomato, Olive, and Basil Skewers ⤫ Hearty Vegetable Lasagna

Caesar Salad ⤫ Tiramisù

Hearty Vegetable Lasagna

You will need a 15 by 10-inch casserole dish, or shallow 4-quart casserole dish, for this recipe. We prefer kosher salt for salting the eggplant in step 3; if using table salt, reduce all salt amounts in the recipe by half. Part-skim mozzarella can substituted for the whole-milk mozzarella if desired; do not buy preshredded cheese as it does not melt well. Food-safe, undyed paper towels can be substituted for the coffee filters in step 3. Note that you will need two boxes of no-boil lasagna noodles for this recipe.

TOMATO SAUCE

1½	(28-ounce) cans crushed tomatoes (4½ cups)
⅓	cup minced fresh basil
3	tablespoons extra-virgin olive oil
3	garlic cloves, minced
1	teaspoon kosher salt
¼	teaspoon red pepper flakes

CHEESE FILLING

12	ounces whole-milk cottage cheese (1½ cups)
1½	cups heavy cream
6	ounces Parmesan cheese, grated (3 cups)
3	garlic cloves, minced
1½	teaspoons cornstarch
½	teaspoon kosher salt
¾	teaspoon pepper

VEGETABLE FILLING

2	pounds eggplant, peeled and cut into ½-inch pieces
	Kosher salt and pepper
1½	pounds zucchini, cut into ½-inch pieces
1½	pounds yellow squash, cut into ½-inch pieces

6	tablespoons plus 1 teaspoon extra-virgin olive oil
6	garlic cloves, minced
4½	teaspoons minced fresh thyme
1	pound baby spinach (16 cups)

18	no-boil lasagna noodles
¾	cup pitted kalamata olives, minced
1	pound whole-milk mozzarella cheese, shredded (4 cups)
3	tablespoons chopped fresh basil

1. FOR THE TOMATO SAUCE: Whisk all ingredients together in bowl. (Sauce can be refrigerated for up to 1 day.)

2. FOR THE CHEESE FILLING: Whisk all ingredients together in bowl. (Filling can be refrigerated for up to 1 day.)

3. FOR THE VEGETABLE FILLING: Adjust oven rack to middle position and heat oven to 450 degrees. Line large plate with double layer of coffee filters and coat lightly with vegetable oil spray. Toss eggplant with 1 teaspoon salt, then spread evenly over coffee filter–lined plate. Microwave, uncovered, until eggplant is dry to touch and slightly shriveled, about 15 minutes, *continued* ➤

✓ WHY THIS RECIPE WORKS

For a complex vegetable lasagna with bold flavor, we started with a summery mix of zucchini, yellow squash, and eggplant, salting and microwaving the eggplant and sautéing the vegetables to cut down on excess moisture and deepen their flavor. Spinach and olives added textural contrast and flavor without much work. We dialed up the usual cheese filling by switching mild-mannered ricotta for tangy cottage cheese mixed with heavy cream for richness and Parmesan and garlic for added flavor. Our quick no-cook tomato sauce brought enough moisture to our lasagna to ensure that the no-boil noodles softened properly while baking.

tossing halfway through cooking. Let cool slightly.

4. Combine cooled eggplant, zucchini, yellow squash, ½ teaspoon salt, and ½ teaspoon pepper in bowl. In small bowl, combine 2 tablespoons oil, garlic, and thyme. Heat 2 tablespoons oil in 12-inch nonstick skillet over medium-high heat until shimmering. Add half of vegetables and cook until spotty brown, about 10 minutes. Clear center of skillet, add half of garlic mixture, and cook, mashing mixture into pan, until fragrant, about 30 seconds. Stir garlic mixture into vegetables; transfer to bowl. Repeat with 2 tablespoons oil, remaining eggplant mixture, and remaining garlic mixture.

5. Heat remaining 1 teaspoon oil in now-empty skillet over medium-high heat until shimmering. Add spinach, handful at a time, and cook, stirring frequently, until wilted, about 3 minutes. Transfer spinach to paper towel–lined plate, let drain for 2 minutes, then stir into cooked vegetables.

(Cooked vegetables can be refrigerated for up to 1 day.)

6. Grease 15 by 10-inch baking dish. Spread 1½ cups tomato sauce evenly over bottom of dish. Arrange 6 noodles into dish (noodles will overlap). Spread half of vegetable mixture over noodles, followed by half of olives. Spoon half of cheese filling over top and sprinkle with 1 cup mozzarella. Repeat layering with 6 noodles, 1½ cups tomato sauce, remaining vegetables, remaining olives, remaining cheese filling, and 1 cup mozzarella. For final layer, arrange remaining 6 noodles on top, cover completely with remaining tomato sauce, and sprinkle with remaining 2 cups mozzarella.

7. Cover dish tightly with aluminum foil that has been sprayed with vegetable oil spray and set on foil-lined baking sheet. Bake until edges are bubbling, about 1 hour and 15 minutes, rotating dish halfway through baking. Let cool for 30 minutes. Sprinkle with basil before serving.

Tomato, Olive, and Basil Skewers

You will need about 40 sturdy wooden toothpicks for this recipe; avoid using very thin, flimsy toothpicks here. Placing a halved grape tomato, with its flat side facing down, on the bottom of the toothpick makes it easy to stand the skewers upright on a serving platter.

½   teaspoon grated orange zest plus 2 tablespoons juice
½   teaspoon grated lemon zest plus I tablespoon juice
I   garlic clove, minced
½   teaspoon Dijon mustard
½   teaspoon honey
¼   teaspoon fennel seeds, chopped
¼   teaspoon salt
⅛   teaspoon pepper
⅓   cup extra-virgin olive oil
I   pound grape tomatoes, halved
I   cup pitted kalamata olives
I   cup fresh basil leaves

1. Whisk orange zest and juice, lemon zest and juice, garlic, mustard, honey, fennel seeds, salt, and pepper together in large bowl. Whisking constantly, drizzle in oil. Gently stir in tomatoes and olives. Skewer tomatoes, olives, and basil leaves in following order from top to bottom: tomato half, olive, basil leaf (folded if large), and tomato half with flat side facing down.

2. Stand skewers upright on serving platter. Reserve remaining dressing leftover in bowl. (Skewers can be held at room temperature for up to 4 hours.) Just before serving, whisk reserved dressing to re-emulsify, then drizzle over skewers, and serve. (Makes 40 skewers.)

Pesto and Sun-Dried Tomato Cheese Terrine

Parmesan can be substituted for the Pecorino Romano if desired. Serve with a thinly sliced baguette or Garlic Toasts (see page 62).

1   cup fresh basil leaves plus 1 tablespoon shredded basil
1   ounce baby spinach (1 cup)
1   ounce Pecorino Romano cheese, grated (½ cup)
2   garlic cloves, minced
2   tablespoons olive oil
1   pound cream cheese, softened
8   ounces goat cheese, softened
½   cup walnuts, toasted (see page 29) and chopped
½   cup oil-packed sun-dried tomatoes, rinsed, patted dry, and chopped fine

1. Line 1-quart bowl with plastic wrap, leaving 4-inch overhang. Process 1 cup basil, spinach, Pecorino, garlic, and oil in food processor until smooth, about 1 minute. In medium bowl, combine cream cheese and goat cheese.

2. Spread one-third of cheese mixture into bottom of prepared bowl. Spread half of basil mixture evenly over cheese. Sprinkle with half of walnuts and half of tomatoes. Repeat with half of remaining cheese mixture, followed by remaining basil mixture, remaining walnuts, and remaining tomatoes. Top with remaining cheese mixture.

3. Fold plastic wrap over top of cheese and refrigerate until firm, at least 4 hours and up to 24 hours. Before serving, unwrap plastic on top, flip terrine out of bowl onto platter, then remove plastic completely. Let sit at room temperature for 1 hour and sprinkle with shredded basil.

✔ **WHY THIS RECIPE WORKS**
For an impressive but easy cheese terrine, we alternated layers of a creamy goat cheese–cream cheese mixture with a brightly flavored pesto, walnuts, and chopped sun-dried tomatoes. Spinach enhanced the bright color of the basil layer, while strong, tangy Pecorino Romano cheese intensified its punch.

Caesar Salad

WHY THIS RECIPE WORKS
We wanted to strip away the superfluous trappings and return to the basics that made Caesar salad a culinary sensation: crisp-tender romaine lettuce napped with a creamy, garlicky dressing boasting a pleasing salty undertone, with crunchy, savory croutons strewn throughout. A combination of extra-virgin olive oil and canola oil gave our dressing a neutral base. We minced garlic into a paste, then steeped it in lemon juice. To get all of our recipe's ingredients to emulsify, we beat the egg yolks, anchovies, and Worcestershire sauce into the lemon juice and garlic, then slowly whisked in the oil and some of the cheese. For the all-important croutons, we used ciabatta bread. Sprinkling the bread cubes with a little water and salt preserved their moistness and ensured they were perfectly tender at the center and browned around the edges after we toasted them.

If you can't find ciabatta bread, substitute any kind of crusty, rustic bread. You may substitute ½ cup of Egg Beaters for the egg yolks. Measuring out the amount of garlic paste in the salad dressing is very important. We prefer to use finely grated Parmesan in the dressing so that it incorporates more easily.

CROUTONS

⅓   cup olive oil
¼   cup grated Parmesan cheese
2   garlic cloves, minced
¼   teaspoon salt
10   ounces ciabatta bread, cut into ¾-inch cubes (8 cups)
⅓   cup water

SALAD

1½   teaspoons garlic, minced to paste (about 3 cloves)
¼   cup lemon juice (2 lemons)
4   large egg yolks
8   anchovy fillets, rinsed, patted dry, and minced to paste
1   teaspoon Worcestershire sauce
¼   teaspoon pepper
½   cup canola oil
3   tablespoons extra-virgin olive oil
2   ounces Parmesan cheese, grated fine (1 cup), plus 3 ounces shaved (see page 32)
6   romaine lettuce hearts (2 pounds), cut crosswise ¾-inch-thick

1. FOR THE CROUTONS: Adjust oven rack to middle position and heat oven to 450 degrees. Whisk oil, Parmesan, garlic, and salt together in small bowl. Place bread cubes in large bowl, sprinkle with water, and squeeze bread gently to absorb water. Toss bread with oil mixture and spread onto rimmed baking sheet. Bake bread, shaking pan occasionally, until golden brown, about 15 minutes. Let cool to room temperature. (Croutons can be stored in airtight container at room temperature for up to 6 hours.)

2. FOR THE SALAD: Whisk garlic paste and lemon juice together in large bowl, then let sit for 10 minutes. Whisk in egg yolks, anchovies, Worcestershire, and pepper. Whisking constantly, drizzle in canola oil and olive oil. Just before serving, whisk dressing to re-emulsify, then whisk in grated Parmesan. Add romaine, toss gently to coat, then add croutons and toss to incorporate. Garnish individual portions with shaved Parmesan.

MINCING GARLIC TO A PASTE

To make a garlic paste, start by mincing the garlic fine. Sprinkle the minced garlic with salt, then drag the side of the knife repeatedly over the mixture to form a fine puree. If possible, use kosher or coarse salt for this job; the larger crystals do a better job than fine table salt of breaking down the garlic.

Tiramisù

The test kitchen prefers a tiramisù with a pronounced rum flavor; for a less potent rum flavor, reduce amount of rum added to the coffee mixture in step 3 as desired. Brandy or whiskey can be substituted for the dark rum. Do not allow the mascarpone to warm to room temperature before using it or it may curdle.

6	large egg yolks
⅔	cup sugar
¼	teaspoon salt
9	tablespoons dark rum
1½	pounds mascarpone cheese (3 cups)
¾	cup heavy cream, chilled
2½	cups strong brewed coffee, room temperature
1½	tablespoons instant espresso powder
14	ounces dried ladyfingers (42 to 60 cookies, depending on size)
3½	tablespoons Dutch-processed cocoa
¼	cup grated semisweet or bittersweet chocolate (optional)

1. Using stand mixer fitted with whisk, whip egg yolks on low speed until just combined. Add sugar and salt, increase speed to medium-high, and beat until pale yellow, 1½ to 2 minutes, scraping down bowl as needed. Reduce speed to medium, add ¼ cup rum, and beat until just combined, 20 to 30 seconds. Add mascarpone and beat until no lumps remain, 30 to 45 seconds. Transfer mixture to large bowl.

2. In now-empty mixer bowl, beat cream at medium speed until frothy, 1 to 1½ minutes. Increase speed to high and continue to beat until cream holds stiff peaks, 1 to 1½ minutes longer. Using rubber spatula, fold one-third of whipped cream into mascarpone mixture to lighten, then gently fold in remaining whipped cream until no white streaks remain; set aside.

3. Stir coffee, espresso, and remaining 5 tablespoons rum together in bowl to dissolve espresso. Working with 1 ladyfinger at a time, drop cookie into coffee mixture, quickly flip it over, then remove it from liquid. (Do not submerge ladyfingers in liquid; soaking process should take only 2 to 3 seconds per cookie.) Lay soaked cookie in 13 by 9-inch baking dish. Repeat until soaked ladyfingers cover bottom of dish in single layer, breaking ladyfingers as needed to fit neatly into dish.

4. Spread half of mascarpone mixture evenly over ladyfingers, right to edge of dish. Place 2 tablespoons cocoa in fine-mesh strainer, then dust evenly over top. Repeat dipping and arrangement of ladyfingers to make second layer. Spread remaining mascarpone mixture over top and dust with remaining 1½ tablespoons cocoa. Wipe edges of dish clean, cover with plastic wrap, and refrigerate for at least 6 hours and up to 24 hours. Before serving, sprinkle with grated chocolate, if using.

✓ **WHY THIS RECIPE WORKS**

The luxurious combination of delicate ladyfingers soaked in a spiked coffee mixture layered with a sweet, creamy filling can be irresistible, but not if it is one of the soggy versions often served at Italian-American restaurants. We wanted to return to the roots of this classic recipe, but with a modern, streamlined approach. Instead of hauling out a double boiler to make the fussy custard-based filling (called zabaglione), we instead simply whipped egg yolks, sugar, salt, rum (our preferred spirit), and mascarpone together. We then folded in a little whipped cream to lighten the filling. For the coffee soaking mixture, we combined strong brewed coffee and instant espresso powder (along with more rum). We also perfected our dipping technique so that the ladyfingers were properly moistened but not saturated with the mixture.

ASSEMBLING TIRAMISÙ

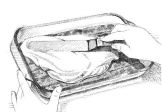

Working with 1 ladyfinger at a time, quickly soak both sides of each cookie in the coffee mixture (2 to 3 seconds total), then transfer to a 13 by 9-inch baking dish. Line the bottom of the dish completely with the soaked ladyfingers, breaking them as needed in order to fit snugly. Spread half of the mascarpone mixture evenly over the ladyfingers, right to the edge of the dish. Place 2 tablespoons cocoa in a fine-mesh strainer, then dust cocoa over top. Repeat layering with soaked ladyfingers, remaining mascarpone mixture, and cocoa.

French Country Stew Supper

THE GAME PLAN

◆

ONE DAY AHEAD...

MAKE STEW: 1¼ hours (plus 3¾ hours for braising)

MAKE TART DOUGH: 15 minutes (plus 2 hours for chilling)

ON THE DAY OF...

MAKE CHOCOLATE TART: 1¾ hours
(plus 5¼ hours for baking and chilling)

REHEAT STEW: 1 hour

MAKE SALMON CANAPÉS: 40 minutes

MAKE EGG NOODLES: 30 minutes

MAKE SALAD: 20 minutes

FRENCH COUNTRY STEW SUPPER

➤ Serves 12 ◄

Smoked Salmon Canapés ✦ Beef Stew Provençal

Endive Salad with Blue Cheese and Walnut Vinaigrette

Buttered Egg Noodles ✦ Chocolate Caramel Walnut Tart

Beef Stew Provençal

You will need a large roasting pan that measures roughly 18 by 13 inches with 4-inch sides for this recipe. If you can't find salt pork, you can substitute bacon; tie the bacon into a tidy bundle that can be easily removed. If niçoise olives are not available, kalamata olives can be substituted.

7	pounds boneless beef chuck-eye roast, pulled apart at seams, trimmed, and cut into 1½- to 2-inch pieces
	Salt and pepper
2	pounds carrots, peeled and cut into 1-inch pieces
6	ounces salt pork, rind removed, tied tightly with kitchen twine
7	(3-inch-long) strips orange zest (see page 28), cut into matchsticks (2 oranges)
1½	cups pitted niçoise olives, rinsed and chopped coarse
7	garlic cloves, sliced thin
5	anchovy fillets, rinsed and minced
8	sprigs fresh thyme, tied together with kitchen twine
3	bay leaves
7	tablespoons olive oil
2	pounds onions, halved and sliced thin
1	ounce dried porcini mushrooms, rinsed and minced
1	cup all-purpose flour
¼	cup tomato paste
4⅔	cups dry red wine (1½ bottles)
4	cups low-sodium chicken broth
1	(28-ounce) can whole tomatoes, drained and cut into ½-inch pieces
⅓	cup minced fresh parsley

1. Adjust oven rack to lower-middle position and heat oven to 325 degrees. Pat beef dry with paper towels and season with salt and pepper. Place carrots, salt pork, orange zest, half of olives, garlic, anchovies, thyme bundle, bay leaves, and half of beef in large roasting pan.

2. Heat 2 tablespoons oil in Dutch oven over medium-high heat until just smoking. Working in 2 batches, brown remaining beef on all sides, about 8 minutes per batch; transfer to roasting pan.

3. Heat remaining 5 tablespoons oil in now-empty pot over medium heat until shimmering. Add onions, porcini, and 1 teaspoon salt and cook until softened, 7 to 10 minutes. Stir in flour and tomato paste and cook for 1 minute. Slowly whisk in wine, scraping up browned bits. Whisk in broth until smooth and bring to simmer. Pour mixture into roasting pan and stir to combine.

4. Cover roasting pan tightly with aluminum foil, and cook until meat is just tender and sauce is thickened and glossy, 3¼ to 3¾ hours.

5. Remove and discard salt pork (identified by twine), thyme, and bay leaves. Stir in remaining olives. Season *continued* ➤

✓ **WHY THIS RECIPE WORKS**
This beef stew is country cooking at its best: bold and full-flavored. We started with earthy porcini, briny niçoise olives, bright tomatoes, floral orange peel, and the regional Provençal herbs, thyme and bay leaves. Anchovies added complexity without fishiness, and salt pork contributed rich body, while a generous bottle and a half of wine provided a bold base. Scaling this stew to serve a crowd required a little ingenuity, since a large Dutch oven is too small to hold enough stew for 12 in the oven (our preferred method for cooking beef stew). Larger pots cooked unevenly, but a turkey-size roasting pan was perfect: The broad, flat surface area allowed the large volume of stew to cook uniformly. Plus the roasting pan made it easier to maneuver a big batch of stew in and out of a hot oven.

with salt and pepper to taste. (Stew can be refrigerated for up to 2 days. Discard any hardened fat from top, gently transfer to Dutch oven, and bring to simmer over medium-low heat, gently stirring occasionally, about 45 minutes.) Stir in tomatoes, cover, and let sit for 10 minutes. Garnish individual portions with parsley before serving.

Smoked Salmon Canapés

✔ **WHY THIS RECIPE WORKS** Rich and a little tangy, a kicked-up crème fraîche makes a perfect partner for smoked salmon in this easy-to-make and elegant appetizer. For the toast, we liked pumpernickel cocktail bread, but its texture needed some work; a generous coat of olive oil spray and a stint in the oven gave it just the right crisp crust. To make sure that each bite-size canapé was bursting with flavor, we stirred plenty of aromatics into the crème fraîche.

We also like to use dense, German-style pumpernickel bread here instead of the cocktail bread; it is sold in rectangular, bricklike packages. Do not toast the German pumpernickel, but cut it into smaller pieces and assemble the canapés as directed in step 2.

1 (1-pound) loaf pumpernickel cocktail bread
    Olive oil spray
1 cup crème fraîche
1 shallot, minced
3 tablespoons capers, rinsed, patted dry, and minced
¼ teaspoon grated lemon zest
⅛ teaspoon pepper
1 pound thinly sliced smoked salmon
2 tablespoons minced fresh chives

1. Adjust oven racks to upper-middle and lower-middle positions and heat oven to 350 degrees. Cut bread slices in half on diagonal into triangles and spread out onto 2 rimmed baking sheets. Spray both sides of bread liberally with olive oil spray. Bake bread until lightly toasted, about 15 minutes, switching and rotating baking sheets halfway through baking. Let toasts cool.

2. Mix crème fraîche, shallot, capers, lemon zest, and pepper together in bowl. Cut salmon slices in half widthwise, then roll up each piece into little cylinder. Spread half of crème fraiche over toasts and top with salmon roll. Dollop with remaining crème fraîche, sprinkle with chives, and serve. (Makes 50 to 60 canapés.)

Endive Salad with Blue Cheese and Walnut Vinaigrette

✔ **WHY THIS RECIPE WORKS** A salad featuring a bitter green such as endive is the perfect foil to a hearty stew. Mesclun greens provide a fluffy, mild base for the endive. Chopped walnuts provide crunch and echo the walnut flavor of the vinaigrette, while a garnish of soft, crumbled blue cheese adds another layer of flavor and texture.

If walnut oil is unavailable, simply substitute additional olive oil.

¼ cup lemon juice (2 lemons)
1 shallot, minced
1 teaspoon Dijon mustard
1 teaspoon honey
    Salt and pepper
½ cup olive oil
⅓ cup walnut oil
6 heads Belgian endive (1½ pounds), leaves separated and halved crosswise
12 ounces mesclun greens (12 cups)
¾ cup walnuts, toasted (see page 29) and chopped coarse
6 ounces blue cheese, crumbled (1½ cups)

Whisk lemon juice, shallot, mustard, honey, ¼ teaspoon salt, and ¼ teaspoon pepper together in small bowl. Whisking constantly, drizzle in olive oil and walnut oil. In large bowl, gently toss endive, mesclun, and walnuts together. Just before serving, whisk dressing to re-emulsify, then drizzle over salad and toss to coat. Garnish individual portions with blue cheese.

Buttered Egg Noodles

Egg noodles are available in a wide variety of sizes; be sure to use wide noodles here because their larger size is better suited to accompany the stew.

1½	pounds wide egg noodles
	Salt and pepper
6	tablespoons unsalted butter

Bring 6 quarts water to boil in large pot. Add noodles and 1 tablespoon salt and cook until tender, 6 to 8 minutes. Drain noodles and return to pot. Stir in butter, season with salt and pepper to taste, and serve.

✔ WHY THIS RECIPE WORKS
In keeping with the rustic roots of this stew, we served it with a simple side dish of boiled egg noodles tossed with butter—the perfect bed for the stew's fragrant sauce.

Chocolate Caramel Walnut Tart

The walnuts used to make the tart dough, the filling, and the garnish must all be toasted—the entire amount can be toasted together. To cut clean slices of this dense and sticky tart, dip the blade of the knife in warm water and wipe with a dish towel before making each cut.

✔ WHY THIS RECIPE WORKS
A layer of caramel packed with chopped walnuts and topped with a smooth layer of rich, dark chocolate ganache compose the filling of this tart, which is firm enough to slice neatly but is neither dense nor overpowering. For the tart shell, we started with a modified French tart dough called pâte sucrée. Adding ground walnuts to boost the flavor meant we had to reduce the amount of butter (to account for the lesser quantity of flour and the extra fat from the ground walnuts). A chilled chocolate ganache layer proved too dense and overpowered the walnuts and caramel; the solution was to lighten the ganache with eggs and bake it to set it. Caramel-coated walnuts, arranged neatly around the perimeter of the tart, provided an elegant final touch.

TART SHELL

1	large egg
¾	teaspoon vanilla extract
¾	cup walnuts, toasted (see page 29)
¾	cup (3 ounces) confectioners' sugar
1½	cups (7½ ounces) all-purpose flour
⅛	teaspoon salt
8	tablespoons unsalted butter, cut into ¼-inch pieces and chilled

CARAMEL-WALNUT FILLING

⅓	cup water
1½	cups (10½ ounces) sugar
1	cup heavy cream
4	tablespoons unsalted butter, cut into 4 pieces
¾	teaspoon vanilla extract
¾	teaspoon lemon juice
¼	teaspoon salt
24	walnut halves, toasted (see page 29)
1½	cups (6 ounces) walnuts, toasted (see page 29) and coarsely chopped

CHOCOLATE FILLING

3	large egg yolks
2	tablespoons plus ⅔ cup heavy cream
½	cup whole milk
9	ounces semisweet chocolate, chopped fine
3	tablespoons unsalted butter, cut into 3 pieces

1. FOR THE TART SHELL: Whisk egg and vanilla together in bowl. Process nuts and sugar together in food processor until finely ground, 8 to 10 seconds. Add flour and salt and pulse to combine. Scatter butter over top and pulse until mixture resembles coarse cornmeal, about 15 pulses. With processor running, add egg mixture and continue to process until dough just comes together around processor blade, about 12 seconds.

2. Turn dough onto sheet of plastic wrap and flatten into 6-inch disk. Wrap dough tightly in plastic and refrigerate for at least 2 hours and up to 2 days.

3. Let chilled dough soften slightly at room temperature, about 10 minutes. Roll dough out to 13-inch circle on lightly floured counter. Roll dough loosely around rolling pin, then unroll over 11-inch tart pan with removable bottom. Fit dough into tart pan, pressing it firmly into pan corners and fluted edge. Trim excess dough hanging over edge of pan and use trimmings to patch weak spots. Set tart pan on large plate, cover with plastic, and freeze for at least 30 minutes and up to 1 week.

4. Adjust oven rack to middle position and heat oven to 375 degrees. Set tart pan on baking sheet. Press double layer of aluminum foil into tart shell and *continued* ➤

over edges of pan, then fill with pie weights. Bake until tart shell is golden brown and set, about 30 minutes, rotating baking sheet halfway through baking. Carefully remove weights and foil and let tart shell cool slightly on sheet while making filling.

5. FOR THE CARAMEL-WALNUT FILLING: Reduce oven temperature to 300 degrees. Pour water in medium saucepan and pour sugar into center of pan (don't let sugar hit sides of pan). Gently stir sugar with clean spatula to wet it thoroughly. Bring to boil over medium-high heat and cook, without stirring, until sugar has dissolved completely and liquid has faint golden color (about 300 degrees on candy thermometer), 6 to 10 minutes.

6. Reduce heat to medium-low and continue to cook, stirring occasionally, until caramel has dark amber color (about 350 degrees on candy thermometer), 1 to 3 minutes. Off heat, slowly whisk in cream until combined (mixture will bubble and steam vigorously). Stir in butter, vanilla, lemon juice, and salt. Stir in walnut halves to coat. Let caramel mixture sit until slightly thickened, about 8 minutes.

7. Set wire rack over piece of parchment paper. Using slotted spoon, transfer caramel-coated walnuts to rack, right side up, and let cool completely. Stir chopped walnuts into caramel, and then pour caramel mixture into tart shell. Refrigerate tart, uncovered, until caramel is firm and does not run when pan is tilted, about 20 minutes.

8. FOR THE CHOCOLATE FILLING: While caramel sets, whisk egg yolks and 2 tablespoons cream together in small bowl. Bring milk and remaining ⅔ cup cream to simmer in small saucepan. Off heat, stir in chocolate and butter, cover, and let stand until chocolate is mostly melted, about 3 minutes. Gently stir mixture until smooth, then stir in egg yolk mixture.

9. Pour chocolate filling evenly over chilled caramel in tart shell, and smooth to even layer by tilting pan. Bake tart on baking sheet until tiny bubbles are visible on surface and chocolate layer is just set, about 25 minutes.

10. Arrange caramel-coated walnut halves around edge of tart. Let tart cool slightly on baking sheet for 30 minutes, then refrigerate, uncovered, until chocolate is firm, about 3 hours. (Cooled tart can be covered and refrigerated up to 1 day.) To serve, remove outer metal ring of tart pan, slide thin metal spatula between tart and tart pan bottom, and carefully slide tart onto serving platter.

EVEN EASIER ✒ Don't have time to make a chocolate-walnut tart? Make a simple chocolate torte using a boxed brownie mix instead; our favorite brownie mix is Ghirardelli Chocolate Syrup Brownie Mix. Combine 2½ cups toasted and finely ground walnuts (or pecans), 1 (17.6–22.5 ounce) box brownie mix, 6 tablespoons melted unsalted butter, ⅓ cup milk, and 1 large egg together in a large bowl until combined. Scrape the batter into a greased and parchment-lined 9-inch round cake pan. Bake in a 325-degree oven until a toothpick inserted in the center comes out clean, 30 to 40 minutes. Let cool for 10 minutes, then flip out onto a wire rack and let cool 30 minutes longer. Serve warm or at room temperature with 2 pints vanilla ice cream and store-bought caramel sauce.

MAKING A TART SHELL

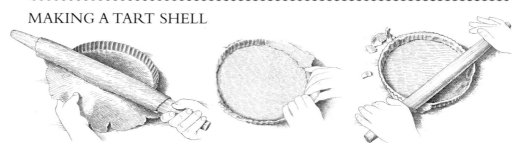

After rolling the dough out to be about 2 inches larger than the size of the tart pan, roll it loosely around the rolling pin, then gently unroll it over the tart pan. Lift the edges of the dough and ease it gently into the corners of the pan. Be gentle with the dough here to prevent it from tearing against the pan's sharp edge. Press the dough firmly into the fluted sides of the pan, forming a distinct, reinforced seam in the pan corners. Run the rolling pin over the top edge of the pan to remove excess dough. Use the excess dough as needed to reinforce any weak or thin spots in the crust.

Exotic Chicken Tagine Dinner

THE GAME PLAN

◅▸

ONE DAY AHEAD...

MAKE TAGINE: 2 hours

MAKE CARAMEL SAUCE: 30 minutes

ASSEMBLE PASTRY SWIRLS: 20 minutes
(plus 1 hour for chilling)

MAKE HUMMUS: 15 minutes

ON THE DAY OF...

MAKE CAKE: 30 minutes
(plus 2¼ hours for baking and cooling)

REHEAT TAGINE: 1¼ hours

CUT AND BAKE PASTRY SWIRLS: 35 minutes

MAKE COUSCOUS: 40 minutes

MAKE SALAD: 20 minutes

EXOTIC CHICKEN TAGINE DINNER

≻ Serves 12 ≺

Spinach and Feta Puff Pastry Swirls ≁ Roasted Red Pepper Hummus
Chicken Tagine ≁ Couscous with Pistachios and Cilantro
Bibb and Radicchio Salad with Orange Vinaigrette
Gingerbread Cake with Vanilla Ice Cream and Caramel Sauce

Chicken Tagine

You will need at least a 12-quart stockpot for this recipe. If the olives are particularly salty, give them a rinse. If you cannot find pitted olives, and don't want to pit them yourself, substitute pimento-stuffed olives, being sure to rinse them very well under cold running water.

3	pounds boneless skinless, chicken thighs, trimmed
	Salt and pepper
¼	cup all-purpose flour
6	tablespoons olive oil
3	onions, halved and sliced ¼ inch thick
7	(2-inch) strips lemon zest (see page 28) plus 1 teaspoon grated zest and ⅔ cup juice (4 lemons)
17	garlic cloves (14 cloves minced and 3 minced to paste) (see page 256)
1½	tablespoons paprika
2	teaspoons ground cumin
1	teaspoon ground ginger
1	teaspoon ground coriander
1	teaspoon ground cinnamon
½	teaspoon cayenne pepper
8	cups low-sodium chicken broth, plus extra as needed
¼	cup honey
3	pounds boneless, skinless chicken breasts, trimmed
2	pounds carrots, peeled and sliced ½ inch thick
4	cups pitted green olives, halved
2	cups dried apricots (12 ounces), chopped
½	cup minced fresh cilantro

1. Pat chicken thighs dry with paper towels, season with salt and pepper, then coat with flour, shaking to remove excess. Heat 2 tablespoons oil in 12-inch skillet over medium-high heat until just smoking. Add half of chicken thighs and cook until golden brown on both sides, 6 to 9 minutes; transfer to large bowl. Repeat with 2 tablespoons oil and remaining chicken thighs.

2. Heat remaining 2 tablespoons oil in 12-quart stockpot over medium heat until shimmering. Add onions, lemon zest strips, and 2 teaspoons salt and cook, stirring often, until onions are browned at edges, about 10 minutes. Stir in minced garlic, paprika, cumin, ginger, coriander, cinnamon, and cayenne and cook until fragrant, about 30 seconds. Slowly whisk in broth and honey, scraping up any browned bits. Add browned chicken thighs, bring to simmer, and cook for 10 minutes.

3. Pat chicken breasts dry with paper towels and season with salt and pepper. Sprinkle carrots into pot, then arrange breasts on top in single layer. Return to simmer, cover, and cook until chicken breasts *continued* ➤

♥ WHY THIS RECIPE WORKS

Our chicken tagine recipe captures all the depth and flavor of an authentic tagine—an exotically spiced, assertively flavored stew slow-cooked in an earthenware vessel of the same name—without the special pot and hard-to-find ingredients. We used boneless, skinless breasts and thighs, which are quicker to prep and cook than bone-in chicken parts. And given the intense spices in this stew, we found we didn't need to brown all the meat. Searing just the thighs provided plenty of flavorful fond (browned bits), and had the added advantage of protecting the breast meat from overcooking. To further ensure moist breast meat, we gave the thighs a head start during simmering and propped the breasts above the cooking liquid on a layer of carrots, so they could steam gently.

register 160 degrees, about 15 minutes.

4. Transfer all chicken to clean platter and tent with aluminum foil. Stir in olives and apricots, return to simmer, and cook, uncovered, until liquid has thickened slightly and carrots are tender, about 10 minutes. Meanwhile, shred chicken into bite-size pieces.

5. Remove and discard lemon zest strips, stir in shredded chicken, and season with salt and pepper to taste. (Tagine can be refrigerated for up to 2 days. Reheat gently over medium-low heat, covered, until hot, 50 to 60 minutes; add additional broth as needed to adjust sauce consistency).

6. Stir in lemon juice, grated lemon zest, and minced garlic paste and let stand for 5 to 10 minutes. Season with salt and pepper to taste. Garnish individual portions with cilantro before serving.

~~~~~~

Spinach and Feta Puff Pastry Swirls

☑ **WHY THIS RECIPE WORKS**
Store-bought puff pastry is the basis for these clever, streamlined pastry swirls, which we filled with a combination of thawed frozen spinach, feta cheese, and cream cheese to help the filling stay put. Garam masala, a combination of warm Indian spices, gave a lot of bang in one ingredient, while garlic and lemon zest and juice kept the flavor fresh. After slathering the no-cook filling on sheets of puff pastry, we rolled them up and refrigerated them so they'd be ready to go when we were.

To thaw frozen puff pastry, allow it to sit either in the refrigerator for 24 hours or on the counter for 30 to 60 minutes. Be sure to squeeze the spinach thoroughly of excess liquid or the pastries will not be crisp.

1¼   pounds frozen chopped spinach, thawed and squeezed dry
4   ounces cream cheese, softened
2   garlic cloves, minced
1   teaspoon garam masala
¼   teaspoon grated lemon zest plus 2 teaspoons juice
   Salt and pepper
2   (9½ by 9-inch) sheets frozen puff pastry, thawed
4   ounces feta cheese, crumbled (1 cup)

1. Stir spinach, cream cheese, garlic, garam masala, lemon zest and juice, ¼ teaspoon salt, and ⅛ teaspoon pepper together in bowl.

2. Lay sheets of puff pastry on lightly floured counter. Spread spinach mixture evenly over dough (right to edges) and sprinkle with feta. Roll each dough up into tight log, wrap tightly in plastic wrap, and refrigerate until firm, at least 1 hour and up to 2 days.

3. Adjust oven racks to upper-middle and lower-middle positions and heat oven to 425 degrees. Line 2 rimmed baking sheets with parchment paper. Trim ends of logs, then slice into ⅓-inch-thick pieces with sharp serrated knife. Lay on prepared baking sheets, spaced about 1 inch apart.

4. Bake until brown and crisp, 25 to 30 minutes, switching and rotating baking sheets halfway through baking. Transfer pastries to wire rack and let cool before serving. (Pastries can be held at room temperature for up to 6 hours. Makes 50 pastries.)

Roasted Red Pepper Hummus

Our favorite brand of chickpeas is Pastene.

½ cup tahini
¼ cup extra-virgin olive oil, plus extra for drizzling
2 (15-ounce) cans chickpeas, rinsed
1 cup jarred roasted red peppers, rinsed and patted dry
1 garlic clove, minced
1 teaspoon salt
Pinch cayenne
3 tablespoons lemon juice
3 tablespoons sliced almonds, toasted (see page 29)
1 tablespoon minced fresh parsley

1. Whisk tahini and oil together in small bowl or liquid measuring cup. Process chickpeas, roasted red peppers, garlic, salt, and cayenne in food processor until almost fully ground, about 15 seconds, scraping down bowl as needed. With processor running, add lemon juice and process for 1 minute. With processor running, add tahini mixture and continue to process until hummus is smooth and creamy, about 15 seconds.

2. Transfer hummus to serving bowl and let sit at room temperature until flavors meld, about 30 minutes. (Hummus can be refrigerated for up to 2 days. Makes 3 cups.) Before serving, sprinkle with almonds and parsley and drizzle with extra olive oil to taste.

✔ WHY THIS RECIPE WORKS
This light, silky hummus starts, surprisingly enough, with a can. Canned chickpeas were close in flavor to dried beans, and their convenience made them perfect for a quick appetizer (ditto for jarred roasted red peppers). We processed the chickpeas with the red peppers in the food processor before slowly adding lemon juice. To finish, we whisked the olive oil and tahini together and then drizzled this mixture into the food processor for a smooth emulsion.

Couscous with Pistachios and Cilantro

Do not use Israeli couscous in this recipe; its larger size requires a different cooking method. For an accurate measurement of boiling water, bring a full kettle of water to a boil, and then measure out the desired amount.

3½ cups couscous
½ cup olive oil
1 large onion, chopped fine
6 garlic cloves, minced
4¼ cups boiling water
Salt and pepper
¾ cup pistachios, toasted (see page 29) and chopped coarse
¼ cup lemon juice (2 lemons)
½ cup minced fresh cilantro

1. Toast couscous with 3 tablespoons oil in 12-inch skillet over medium heat, stirring occasionally, until lightly browned, 3 to 5 minutes; transfer to large bowl.

2. Heat 2 tablespoons oil in now-empty skillet over medium-high heat until shimmering. Add onion and cook until softened, about 5 minutes. Stir in garlic and cook until fragrant, about 30 seconds. Transfer to bowl with couscous.

3. Stir boiling water and 1 teaspoon salt into couscous. Cover tightly with plastic wrap and let sit until couscous is tender, about 12 minutes.

4. Fluff couscous with fork, breaking up any clumps. Add remaining 3 tablespoons oil, pistachios, and lemon juice and gently toss to incorporate. Season with salt and pepper to taste. (Couscous can be refrigerated for up to 1 day; microwave, covered, until hot, 3 to 5 minutes.) Fold in cilantro and serve.

✔ WHY THIS RECIPE WORKS
For the best couscous, we use the "pilaf method" often applied to rice, and start by sautéing the couscous in olive oil to gently brown the grains so they cook up fluffy and separate. We then transfer the couscous to a bowl and sauté onion and garlic, adding the softened aromatics to the couscous along with boiling water and setting it aside, covered, to finish cooking. When the couscous is tender, we fluff it with a fork and finish with olive oil, lemon juice, toasted pistachios, and fresh cilantro.

Bibb and Radicchio Salad with Orange Vinaigrette

✔ WHY THIS RECIPE WORKS For a salad with a balance of flavors and textures, we combined crunchy, slightly bitter radicchio with mild and soft Bibb lettuce, and dressed them with a lively vinaigrette made with orange juice. For a cohesive, clingy dressing, we needed to compensate for the additional liquid added by the juice, so we recruited a few ingredients to help emulsify: mayonnaise, Dijon mustard, and honey.

Any kind of orange juice will work in this recipe; however, freshly squeezed juice will make the flavor of the vinaigrette really sparkle.

½ cup orange juice
¼ cup white wine vinegar
1 shallot, minced
2 tablespoons minced fresh mint
2 teaspoons mayonnaise
1 teaspoon Dijon mustard
1 teaspoon honey
Salt and pepper
½ cup extra-virgin olive oil
3 heads Bibb lettuce (1½ pounds), cut into 1-inch pieces
1 head radicchio (10 ounces), cut into 1-inch pieces

½ cup sliced almonds, toasted (see page 29)
6 ounces feta, crumbled (1½ cups)

Whisk orange juice, vinegar, shallot, mint, mayonnaise, mustard, honey, ½ teaspoon salt, and ¼ teaspoon pepper together in small bowl. Whisking constantly, drizzle in olive oil. In large bowl, gently toss lettuce, radicchio, almonds, and feta. Just before serving, whisk dressing to re-emulsify, then drizzle over salad and toss gently to coat.

Gingerbread Cake with Vanilla Ice Cream and Caramel Sauce

✔ WHY THIS RECIPE WORKS For a cake that truly tasted like ginger, we used both ground and grated fresh ginger. Dark stout added a bittersweet flavor, and replacing butter with vegetable oil let the ginger flavor shine through. To give our gingerbread a sturdy texture, we beat the batter vigorously to develop gluten. Since acidity interferes with baking powder's ability to leaven, we neutralized the stout and other acidic ingredients with baking soda before incorporating them into the batter.

This cake has a potent yet well-balanced, spicy heat. If you're sensitive to spice, reduce the amount of dried ginger to 2 tablespoons. Our favorite brand of stout is Guinness.

2¼ cups (11¼ ounces) all-purpose flour
3 tablespoons ground ginger
¾ teaspoon baking powder
¾ teaspoon salt
½ teaspoon ground cinnamon
¼ teaspoon pepper
1 cup stout
¾ teaspoon baking soda
1 cup mild molasses
1¼ cups packed (8¾ ounces) light brown sugar
¼ cup (1¾ ounces) granulated sugar
3 large eggs
⅔ cup vegetable oil
1½ tablespoons grated fresh ginger

2 pints vanilla ice cream
1 recipe Caramel Sauce (page 269)

1. Adjust oven rack to middle position and heat oven to 350 degrees. Grease and flour 13 by 9-inch baking dish. Whisk flour, ground ginger, baking powder, salt, cinnamon, and pepper together in large bowl.

2. Bring stout to brief boil in medium saucepan over medium-high heat (watch closely to preventing boiling over). Off heat, stir in baking soda (mixture will foam vigorously). When foaming subsides, stir in molasses, brown sugar, and granulated sugar until dissolved and mixture has cooled.

3. Transfer stout mixture to large bowl. Whisk in eggs, oil, and grated ginger until combined. Whisk stout mixture into flour mixture in 3 additions, stirring vigorously until completely smooth after each addition.

4. Scrape batter into prepared pan and gently tap pan on counter to settle batter.

Bake until top of cake is just firm to touch and toothpick inserted in center comes out clean, about 40 minutes. Let cake cool in pan on wire rack, about 1½ hours. (Cake can be held at room temperature for up to 8 hours.) Cut cake into squares and serve with vanilla ice cream and caramel sauce.

Caramel Sauce

Be careful when stirring in the cream in step 2, because the hot mixture may splatter.

- ¾ **cup water**
- 1½ **cups (10½ ounces) sugar**
- 1½ **cups heavy cream**
- ¾ **teaspoon vanilla extract**
- ¾ **teaspoon lemon juice**
- ¼ **teaspoon salt**

1. Pour water into large saucepan and pour sugar into center of pan (don't let sugar hit sides of pan). Gently stir sugar with clean spatula to wet it thoroughly. Bring to boil over medium-high heat and cook, without stirring, until sugar has dissolved completely and liquid has faint golden color and registers 300 degrees, about 12 minutes.

2. Reduce heat to medium-low and continue to cook, stirring occasionally, until caramel has dark amber color and registers 350 degrees, 3 to 5 minutes. Off heat, slowly whisk in cream until combined (mixture will bubble and steam vigorously).

3. Stir in vanilla, lemon juice, and salt. Serve warm. (Sauce can be refrigerated for up to 2 weeks; reheat in microwave, stirring often, until warm and smooth, 1 to 2 minutes. Makes 2 cups.)

Big Game Day Party

THE GAME PLAN
◅◢

ONE DAY AHEAD...

MAKE CHILI: 50 minutes
(plus 2½ hours for simmering)

MAKE FUDGE BARS: 45 minutes
(plus 3½ hours for baking and cooling)

ON THE DAY OF...

MAKE RANCH DIP AND CRUDITÉS: 20 minutes
(plus 1 hour for chilling)

MAKE CORNBREAD: 20 minutes (plus 1 hour
for baking and cooling)

MAKE WINGS: 1¾ hours

MAKE RICE: 1¼ hours

REHEAT CHILI: 1 hour

Smoky Beef Chili with Black Beans and Corn

If the chili begins to stick to the bottom of the pot at any time during simmering, stir in ½ cup water. This chili is not very spicy; to make it spicier, stir in an additional 1 to 2 tablespoons minced chipotles with the corn in step 4. Serve with lime wedges, diced fresh tomatoes, diced avocado, sliced scallions, chopped red onion, minced cilantro, sour cream, and/or shredded Monterey Jack cheese.

¼ cup vegetable oil

4 onions, chopped fine

2 red bell peppers, stemmed, seeded, and cut into ½-inch pieces

12 garlic cloves, minced

½ cup chili powder

2 tablespoons minced canned chipotle chile in adobo sauce

2 tablespoons ground cumin

4 teaspoons ground coriander

2 teaspoons dried oregano
Salt

4 pounds 85 percent lean ground beef

2 (15-ounce) cans black beans, rinsed

2 (28-ounce) cans diced tomatoes

2 (28-ounce) cans tomato puree

4 cups frozen corn kernels, thawed

1. Heat oil in 12-quart stockpot over medium heat until shimmering. Add onions, bell peppers, garlic, chili powder, chipotle, cumin, coriander, oregano, and 1 teaspoon salt and cook, stirring often, until vegetables have softened, 15 to 17 minutes.

2. Increase heat to medium-high. Stir in beef, 1 pound at a time, and cook while breaking up chunks with wooden spoon until no longer pink, about 3 minutes per pound. Stir in beans, diced tomatoes, and tomato puree and bring to boil. Cover and simmer over low heat, stirring occasionally, for 1 hour.

3. Uncover and continue to simmer, stirring occasionally, until beef is tender and chili is dark, rich, and slightly thickened, about 1½ hours longer. (Chili can be refrigerated for up to 2 days. Reheat gently, covered, over medium-low heat, stirring often, 50 to 60 minutes; add water as needed to adjust consistency.)

4. Stir in corn and simmer until heated through, about 2 minutes. Season with salt to taste and serve.

✔ **WHY THIS RECIPE WORKS**

This easy chili recipe, made with supermarket staples, packs a smoky punch of intense flavor that will please the most discriminating of guests. To start, we added the spices to the pan with the aromatics (bell peppers, onions, and lots of garlic) to get the most flavor. For the meat, we found that 85 percent lean ground beef gave us the fullest flavor. A combination of diced tomatoes and tomato puree gave our chili a well-balanced, saucy backbone. We added quick-cooking canned black beans with the tomatoes so that they heated through and absorbed flavor. And to kick things up a notch we added canned chipotle in adobo sauce for smoky heat.

Fiery Mustard Wings

WHY THIS RECIPE WORKS
Since frying 7 pounds of chicken wings was out of the question, we needed to find a cooking method that would achieve crisp skin without the hassle and mess. Tossing the wings with baking powder before roasting helped draw moisture from the skin, enabling it to dry in the oven. A final pass under the broiler yielded crisp, golden brown wings. We made a thick and spicy sauce that clung to the wings (and our fingers) for a kick of fiery mustard flavor. Classic yellow and dry mustard provided a base for the sauce, while chili sauce and brown sugar sweetened the deal. Pickled banana peppers and lemon juice added tartness, and 3 habanero chiles brought home the heat. Not for the faint of heart (or stomach), these wings are guaranteed to attract a crowd.

These wings are very spicy; to make them milder, reduce the number of habaneros to two and remove the seeds. Be careful when handling the habaneros; wear gloves, don't touch your eyes or face, and wash your hands, knife, and cutting board thoroughly after prepping.

SAUCE
- ½   cup sliced pickled banana peppers, chopped fine, plus ¼ cup pickling liquid
- ½   cup lemon juice (3 lemons)
- ½   cup vegetable oil
- ½   cup yellow mustard
- 6   scallions, sliced thin
- ⅓   cup dry mustard
- ⅓   cup Heinz chili sauce
- ⅓   cup packed brown sugar
- 4   garlic cloves, minced
- 3   habanero chiles, minced
- 2   tablespoons water
    Salt and pepper

WINGS
- 7   pounds whole chicken wings (about 33 wings), separated at joints, wingtips discarded
- 2   tablespoons baking powder
- I   tablespoon salt

1. FOR THE SAUCE: Whisk all ingredients together in bowl and season with salt and pepper to taste. (Makes 3 cups.)

2. FOR THE WINGS: Adjust oven racks to upper-middle and lower-middle positions and heat oven to 475 degrees. Line 2 rimmed baking sheets with aluminum foil and top with wire racks. Pat chicken dry with paper towels.

3. Toss half of wings with 1 tablespoon baking powder, and 1½ teaspoons salt in large bowl to coat; spread into single layer over 1 wire rack. Repeat with remaining wings, 1 tablespoon baking powder, and 1½ teaspoons salt; spread over second wire rack.

4. Roast wings until golden on both sides, about 50 minutes, flipping wings over and switching and rotating baking sheets halfway through roasting. Remove wings from oven. (Roasted wings can be held at room temperature for up to 1 hour.)

5. Position oven rack 8 inches from broiler element and heat broiler. Working with 1 rack of wings at a time, broil wings until golden brown on both sides, 8 to 12 minutes, flipping wings over halfway through broiling; transfer wings to large bowl. Toss wings with 2 cups sauce, and transfer to platter. Serve with remaining sauce on side.

Ranch Dip and Crudités

WHY THIS RECIPE WORKS
While mayonnaise and sour cream do the heavy lifting in this thick dip, buttermilk provides an unmistakable tang and loosens the dressing to the right consistency for dipping crudités and cooling the heat of our fiery mustard wings. Fresh herbs and garlic add classic ranch flavors.

Fresh herbs are essential for the flavor of this dip; do not use dried herbs.

- I½   cups mayonnaise
- I½   cups sour cream
- 3   tablespoons buttermilk
- 3   tablespoons minced shallot or red onion
- 3   tablespoons minced fresh parsley
- 3   tablespoons minced fresh cilantro or dill
- I   tablespoon lemon juice
- 2   garlic cloves, minced
- I   teaspoon salt
- ½   teaspoon pepper
- ¼   teaspoon sugar
- 8   celery ribs, cut into thin sticks
- I   pound carrots, peeled and cut into thin sticks

Whisk all ingredients, except celery and carrot sticks, together in serving bowl until smooth. Cover and refrigerate until dip is thickened and chilled, at least 1 hour and up to 2 days. (Makes about 3½ cups.) Serve dip with celery and carrot sticks.

Easy Baked White Rice

Be sure to cover the water when bringing it to a boil in step 1. Our favorite brand of long-grain white rice is Lundberg Organic.

3½   cups long-grain white rice, rinsed
5¼   cups water
      Salt and pepper

1. Adjust oven rack to middle position and heat oven to 375 degrees. Spread rice into 13 by 9-inch baking dish. Combine water and 1 teaspoon salt in large saucepan, cover, and bring to brief boil over high heat.

2. Immediately pour boiling water over rice and cover baking dish tightly with double layer of aluminum foil. Bake rice until tender and no water remains, 40 to 50 minutes.

3. Remove dish from oven, uncover, and fluff rice with fork, scraping up any rice that has stuck to bottom. Re-cover dish with foil and let rice stand for 10 minutes. Season with salt and pepper to taste and serve.

WHY THIS RECIPE WORKS Moving the rice from the stovetop to the oven not only means hands-free cooking, but it also eliminates issues like burnt rice and scorched pans. Rinsing the rice before cooking washes away the exterior starch and minimizes clumping.

Northern Cornbread

Do not use stone-ground whole grain cornmeal here; it will yield a drier and less tender cornbread. When corn is in season, fresh cooked kernels can be substituted for the frozen corn. For more information on making a foil sling for the baking pan, see page 287.

2¼   cups (11¼ ounces) all-purpose flour
1½   cups (7½ ounces) yellow cornmeal
2½   teaspoons baking powder
¼   teaspoon baking soda
1   teaspoon salt
1½   cups buttermilk
1   cup frozen corn kernels, thawed
6   tablespoons packed (2¾ ounces) light brown sugar
3   large eggs
12   tablespoons unsalted butter, melted and cooled

1. Adjust oven rack to middle position and heat oven to 400 degrees. Line 13 by 9-inch baking pan with aluminum foil sling and grease foil.

2. Whisk flour, cornmeal, baking powder, baking soda, and salt together in medium bowl. Process buttermilk, corn, and brown sugar in food processor until combined, about 5 seconds. Add eggs and continue to process until well combined (some corn lumps will remain), about 5 seconds. Fold buttermilk mixture into flour mixture with rubber spatula. Fold in melted butter until just incorporated (do not overmix).

3. Scrape batter into prepared pan and smooth top. Bake until golden brown and toothpick inserted in center comes out clean, 25 to 35 minutes, rotating pan halfway through baking. Let cornbread cool in pan for 10 minutes, then remove from pan using sling and let cool on wire rack for 20 minutes. Serve warm or at room temperature.

WHY THIS RECIPE WORKS Northern cornbread is famous for its sweet, cakey texture, in contrast to its crumbly, more rustic Southern counterpart. In order to get serious corn flavor into our cornbread, we found we needed to add real corn kernels to the batter (for flavor) and use more flour than cornmeal (for texture). To prevent the corn kernels from tasting overly gummy and tough in the bread, we pureed them in a food processor with the buttermilk and eggs.

Oatmeal Fudge Bars

✔ **WHY THIS RECIPE WORKS**
To give our oatmeal fudge bars a truly fudgy texture, we minimized the flour and loaded up on the chocolate. To fortify the chocolate flavor we added 4 teaspoons of instant espresso (or instant coffee) powder. This small amount of coffee deepened the chocolate flavor without calling attention to itself.

Old-fashioned rolled oats may be substituted for the quick-cooking oats, although the bars will be more chewy. Be sure to let the crust cool completely before adding the filling in step 5. For more information on making a foil sling for the baking pan, see page 287.

CRUST AND TOPPING

- 1½ cups (4½ ounces) quick oats
- 1½ cups packed (10½ ounces) light brown sugar
- 1 cup (5 ounces) all-purpose flour
- ½ teaspoon baking powder
- ¼ teaspoon baking soda
- ⅛ teaspoon salt
- 12 tablespoons unsalted butter, melted and cooled

FILLING

- ½ cup (2½ ounces) all-purpose flour
- ½ cup packed (3½ ounces) light brown sugar
- 4 teaspoons instant espresso or coffee powder
- ½ teaspoon salt
- 3 cups semisweet chocolate chips (18 ounces)
- 4 tablespoons unsalted butter
- 2 large eggs

1. FOR THE CRUST AND TOPPING: Adjust oven rack to middle position and heat oven to 325 degrees. Line 13 by 9-inch baking pan with aluminum foil sling and grease foil.

2. Whisk oats, sugar, flour, baking powder, baking soda, and salt together in large bowl. Stir in melted butter until combined.

Measure out and reserve 1¼ cups of mixture separately for topping.

3. Sprinkle remaining oat mixture into prepared pan and press into even layer with bottom of measuring cup. Use back of spoon to press and smooth edges. Bake crust until light golden brown, about 8 minutes. Let crust cool completely on wire rack, about 1 hour.

4. FOR THE FILLING: Whisk flour, sugar, espresso, and salt together in medium bowl. Melt chocolate chips and butter together in microwave, stirring often, 1 to 3 minutes. Transfer chocolate mixture to large bowl and let cool slightly. Whisk in eggs until combined. Stir in flour mixture until just incorporated.

5. Adjust oven rack to middle position and heat oven to 325 degrees. Spread filling evenly over cooled crust and smooth top. Sprinkle with reserved oat topping. Bake until toothpick inserted in center comes out with a few moist crumbs attached and filling begins to pull away from sides of pan, 25 to 30 minutes, rotating pan halfway through baking.

6. Let bars cool completely in pan, about 2 hours. Remove bars from pan using sling, cut into squares, and serve. (Bars can be stored at room temperature for up to 1 day. Makes 24 squares.)

Fourth of July Block Party

THE GAME PLAN

ONE DAY AHEAD...

MAKE PIMENTO CHEESE: 15 minutes

MAKE BARBECUE SAUCE: 45 minutes

PREP PORK: 10 minutes (plus 1 hour for seasoning)

MAKE SLAW: 30 minutes (plus 2 hours for salting and chilling)

MAKE MACARONI SALAD: 45 minutes

ON THE DAY OF...

COOK AND SHRED PORK: 6½ hours

MAKE CAKE: 1¼ hours (plus 2½ hours for baking and cooling)

MAKE DEVILED EGGS: 1¼ hours

FOURTH OF JULY BLOCK PARTY

➤ Serves 12 ➤

Herbed Deviled Eggs ➤ Pimento Cheese Spread
Pulled Pork Barbecue Sandwiches ➤ Macaroni Salad with Cheddar and Chipotle
Tangy Apple-Cabbage Slaw ➤ Flag Cake

Pulled Pork Barbecue Sandwiches

Boneless pork butt (also labeled Boston butt) is often wrapped in elastic netting; be sure to remove the netting before rubbing with the spices in step 1. When using a charcoal grill, we prefer wood chunks to wood chips whenever possible; substitute 4 medium wood chunks, soaked in water for 1 hour, for the wood chip packets.

PULLED PORK

- ¼ cup paprika
- ¼ cup pepper
- ¼ cup brown sugar
- 2 tablespoons salt
- 2 (4- to 5-pound) boneless pork butts
- 4 cups wood chips, soaked in water for 15 minutes and drained

BARBECUE SAUCE

- 2 tablespoons vegetable oil
- 2 onions, chopped fine
  Salt and pepper
- 2 garlic cloves, minced
- 2 teaspoons chili powder
- ½ teaspoon cayenne pepper
- 2½ cups ketchup
- ¾ cup molasses
- 6 tablespoons cider vinegar
- ¼ cup Worcestershire sauce
- ¼ cup Dijon mustard
- 2 teaspoons hot sauce

- 12 hamburger buns
  Pickle chips, for serving

1. FOR THE PULLED PORK: Combine paprika, pepper, sugar, and salt in bowl. Pat meat dry with paper towels and rub it evenly with spice mixture. Wrap meat in plastic wrap and let sit at room temperature for at least 1 hour or refrigerate for up to 24 hours. (If refrigerated, let sit at room temperature for 1 hour before grilling.) Using 2 large pieces of heavy-duty aluminum foil, wrap soaked chips into 2 foil packets and cut several vent holes in top.

2A. FOR A CHARCOAL GRILL: Open bottom vent halfway. Light large chimney starter three-quarters full with charcoal briquettes (4½ quarts). When top coals are partially covered with ash, pour into steeply banked pile against 1 side of grill. Place wood chip packets on top of coals. Set cooking grate in place, cover, and open lid vent halfway. Heat grill until hot and wood chips begin to smoke heavily, about 5 minutes.

2B. FOR A GAS GRILL: Place wood chip packets directly on primary burner. Turn all burners to high, cover, and heat grill until hot and wood chips begin to smoke heavily, about 15 minutes. Turn primary burner to medium–high and turn off other burner(s). (Adjust primary burner as needed to maintain grill temperature around 325 degrees.)

3. Clean and oil cooking grate. Place meat on cool part of grill, away from coals and flames. Cover (positioning *continued* ➤

lid vents over meat if using charcoal) and cook until pork has dark, rosy crust, about 2 hours. During final 20 minutes of grilling, adjust oven rack to lower-middle position and heat oven to 325 degrees.

4. Transfer pork to roasting pan, cover pan tightly with foil, and roast pork until very tender and fork inserted in center meets no resistance, 2 to 3 hours. Remove pork from oven and let rest, still covered with foil, for 30 minutes.

5. FOR THE BARBECUE SAUCE: Heat oil in medium saucepan over medium heat until shimmering. Add onions and pinch salt and cook until softened, 5 to 7 minutes. Stir in garlic, chili powder, and cayenne and cook until fragrant, about 30 seconds. Whisk in ketchup, molasses, vinegar, Worcestershire, mustard, and hot sauce. Bring sauce to simmer and cook, stirring occasionally, until thickened and reduced to 4 cups, about 15 minutes. Let cool to room temperature and season with salt and pepper to taste. (Sauce can be refrigerated for up to 4 days.)

6. When pork is cool enough to handle,

unwrap and pull meat into thin shreds, discarding excess fat and gristle. Toss pork with 2 cups of sauce, adding more sauce as needed to keep meat moist. (Shredded meat can be refrigerated for up to 2 days. Reheat in microwave until hot, 5 to 10 minutes; add additional sauce as needed to moisten meat.) Serve with hamburger buns, pickle chips, and remaining sauce.

MAKING A WOOD CHIP PACKET

After soaking the wood chips in water for 15 minutes, drain and spread them in the center of a large piece of heavy-duty foil. Fold to seal the edges, then cut several slits to allow smoke to escape.

Herbed Deviled Eggs

✔ **WHY THIS RECIPE WORKS** For perfectly hard-cooked eggs (and no unattractive green ring around the yolks), we brought the eggs to a boil and then immediately removed them from the heat. The residual heat of the water cooked the eggs in exactly 10 minutes. The hard part over, we mashed the yolks and mixed in a blend of mayonnaise, sour cream, white wine vinegar, and Dijon mustard for tang, and a small amount of sugar for balance. For a fresh twist on this classic party dish we added chopped tarragon, parsley, and chives.

Be sure to use a large pot and plenty of water for cooking the eggs in step 1, or they will not cook correctly. We find it easiest to pipe the filling into the eggs using either a pastry bag or zipper-lock bag, but you can use a spoon to fill the eggs if desired.

18	large eggs
⅓	cup mayonnaise
¼	cup sour cream
2	tablespoons minced fresh tarragon
2	tablespoons minced fresh parsley
2	tablespoons minced fresh chives
1½	teaspoons white wine vinegar
1½	teaspoons Dijon mustard
¾	teaspoon sugar
½	teaspoon salt
¼	teaspoon pepper

1. Place eggs in large pot, cover with 1 inch of water, and bring to boil over high heat. Remove pan from heat, cover, and let stand 10 minutes. Fill large bowl with ice water. Pour off water from saucepan then gently shake pan back and forth to lightly crack shells. Transfer eggs to ice water, let cool for 5 minutes, then peel.

2. Halve eggs lengthwise. Transfer yolks to fine-mesh strainer set over medium bowl, and arrange whites on large serving platter. Using spatula, press yolks through strainer into bowl, then stir in remaining ingredients until smooth. Transfer yolk mixture to pastry bag fitted with star tip (or plastic bag with corner snipped off) and pipe mixture into whites. Serve. (Deviled eggs can be refrigerated for up to 6 hours. Makes 36 eggs.)

Pimento Cheese Spread

Both white and orange extra-sharp cheddar work well here. Don't substitute store-bought preshredded cheese; it doesn't blend well and will make the spread taste dry and crumbly. If you can't find jarred pimentos, substitute jarred roasted red peppers.

1	(4-ounce) jar pimento peppers, drained and patted dry (½ cup)
6	tablespoons mayonnaise
2	garlic cloves, minced
1½	teaspoons Worcestershire sauce
1	teaspoon hot sauce, plus extra to taste
1	pound extra-sharp cheddar cheese, shredded (4 cups)
	Salt and pepper

Process pimento peppers, mayonnaise, garlic, Worcestershire, and hot sauce together in food processor until smooth, about 20 seconds. Add cheddar and pulse until uniformly blended, with fine bits of cheese throughout, 20 to 25 pulses. Season with salt, pepper, and extra hot sauce to taste. Serve. (Cheese spread can be refrigerated for up to 2 weeks; let soften at room temperature before serving. Makes about 2½ cups.)

✓ **WHY THIS RECIPE WORKS**
This deconstructed cheese ball is a popular Southern spread that can be slathered on anything from crackers and sandwiches to crudités. Drained jarred pimentos give the cheesy spread its name and trademark color, but we found that adding garlic, Worcestershire sauce, and hot sauce to the base gives the mixture a pleasant kick and complexity. We used a light hand with the mayo, adding just enough to bind everything together. After a quick spin in the food processor, this spread will hold in the refrigerator for up to two weeks, making it a go-to appetizer for any get-together.

Macaroni Salad with Cheddar and Chipotle

Barilla is our favorite brand of elbow macaroni, and Hellmann's (also known as Best Foods) is our favorite brand of mayonnaise. You can substitute Hellmann's Light Mayonnaise, but we're not fans of Hellmann's Low Fat Mayonnaise or Miracle Whip here.

1½	pounds elbow macaroni (6 cups)
	Salt and pepper
8	ounces extra-sharp cheddar cheese, shredded (2 cups)
3	tablespoons minced canned chipotle chile in adobo sauce
⅓	cup minced red onion
2	celery ribs, minced
⅓	cup minced fresh parsley
3	tablespoons lemon juice
5	teaspoons Dijon mustard
¼	teaspoon garlic powder
⅛	teaspoon cayenne pepper
2¼	cups mayonnaise

1. Bring 6 quarts water to boil in large pot. Add pasta and 1½ tablespoons salt and cook until tender, 6 to 8 minutes. Drain pasta and rinse with cold water until cool. Drain again briefly and transfer to large bowl.

2. Stir in cheddar, chipotle, onion, celery, parsley, lemon juice, mustard, garlic powder, and cayenne and let sit until flavors are absorbed, about 2 minutes. Stir in mayonnaise and let sit until salad is no longer watery, 5 to 10 minutes. Season with salt and pepper and serve. (Salad can be refrigerated for up to 1 day. Before serving stir in hot water, 1 tablespoon at a time, to refresh salad and season with salt and pepper to taste.)

✓ **WHY THIS RECIPE WORKS**
Rinsing the cooked elbow macaroni in cold running water for about a minute stops its cooking; you shouldn't add mayonnaise to hot pasta. Also, the water rinses away excess starch, keeping the elbows from sticking together. Briefly draining the pasta is the key to achieving the right salad consistency; if the pasta is too dry, it will soak up the mayonnaise dressing and become gummy. Cheddar cheese and chipotle chiles make this salad the perfect match for sweet and spicy pulled pork barbecue.

Tangy Apple-Cabbage Slaw

✔ WHY THIS RECIPE WORKS
This Southern-style coleslaw
uses a mixture of oil
and vinegar, rather than
mayonnaise, as the base of
its dressing, giving the slaw
a lighter, brighter texture
and flavor. To keep the
flavor vibrant, we salted
the cabbage to draw out
moisture that can dilute the
salad. Tart Granny Smith
apples add a surprisingly
fresh twist and make this
coleslaw far from ordinary.

We prefer kosher salt for salting the cabbage in step 1; if using table salt, reduce salt amount to 1 tablespoon. To cut the apples into matchsticks, first core them, then slice into ¼-inch-thick planks, stack the planks, and cut them into thin matchsticks.

1½	heads green cabbage (3 pounds), cored and chopped fine (18 cups)
2	tablespoons kosher salt
3	Granny Smith apples, cored and cut into 2-inch-long matchsticks
3	scallions, sliced thin
¾	cup cider vinegar
⅔	cup vegetable oil
¾	cup sugar
5	teaspoons Dijon mustard
¼	teaspoon red pepper flakes

1. Toss cabbage with salt in colander set over medium bowl. Let stand until wilted, about 1 hour. Rinse cabbage under cold water, drain, dry well with paper towels. Transfer cabbage to large bowl, add apples and scallions, and toss to combine.

2. Bring vinegar, oil, sugar, mustard, and pepper flakes to boil in saucepan over medium heat. Pour over cabbage mixture and toss to coat. Cover with plastic wrap and refrigerate for at least 1 hour and up to 1 day. Serve.

Flag Cake

✔ WHY THIS RECIPE WORKS
Fresh berries in a patriotic
pattern turn a simple but
delicious yellow cake into
a showstopping holiday
dessert. Our no-fail classic
yellow sheet cake relies on
cake flour and an ample
amount of butter for its
tender crumb. To give the
berries a smooth canvas, we
ice the cake with a light and
fluffy no-cook vanilla frosting.

Be sure to use unsalted butter in the frosting. We like the look of fresh raspberries on the cake to make the red stripes, but quartered or sliced strawberries can be substituted if desired.

CAKE

2¾	cups (11 ounces) cake flour
2	teaspoons baking powder
¾	teaspoon salt
16	tablespoons unsalted butter, softened
1¾	cups (12¼ ounces) sugar
4	large eggs, room temperature
1	tablespoon vanilla extract
1½	cups whole milk, room temperature

FROSTING AND GARNISH

24	tablespoons (3 sticks) unsalted butter, cut into chunks and softened
3	tablespoons heavy cream
2½	teaspoons vanilla extract
¼	teaspoon salt
3	cups (12 ounces) confectioners' sugar
5	ounces blueberries (1 cup)
15	ounces raspberries (3 cups)

1. FOR THE CAKE: Adjust oven rack to middle position and heat oven to 350 degrees. Grease 13 by 9-inch baking pan, line with parchment paper, grease parchment, and flour pan. Whisk flour, baking powder, and salt together in medium bowl.

2. Using stand mixer fitted with paddle, beat butter and sugar on medium-high speed until pale and fluffy, about 3 minutes. Add eggs, 1 at a time, and beat until combined. Add vanilla. Reduce speed to low and add flour mixture in 3 additions, alternating with 2 additions of milk, scraping down bowl as needed. Give batter final stir by hand.

3. Scrape batter into prepared pan, smooth top, and gently tap pan on counter to settle batter. Bake cake until toothpick

inserted in center comes out with few moist crumbs attached, 25 to 30 minutes, rotating pan halfway through baking.

4. Let cake cool completely in pan, about 2 hours. Run paring knife around edge of cake and flip cake out onto wire rack. Peel off parchment, then flip cake right side up onto serving platter.

5. FOR THE FROSTING AND GARNISH: Using stand mixer fitted with paddle, beat butter, cream, vanilla, and salt together in large bowl on medium-high speed until smooth, 1 to 2 minutes.

6. Reduce mixer speed to medium-low, slowly add confectioners' sugar, and beat until incorporated and smooth, 4 to 6 minutes. Increase mixer speed to medium-high and beat until frosting is light and fluffy, 5 to 10 minutes. (Frosting can be refrigerated for up to 3 days. Before using, let soften at room temperature for 2 hours, then whip using stand mixer fitted with whisk on medium speed until smooth, 2 to 5 minutes.)

7. Spread frosting evenly over top and sides of cake. Arrange blueberries and raspberries over top of cake to make American flag design and serve. (Cake can be refrigerated for up to 6 hours; bring to room temperature before serving.)

EVEN EASIER ✦ Don't have time to make a homemade sheet cake? Consider using a boxed yellow cake mix and following the instructions for making the frosting and the flag decoration. We taste-tested eight supermarket cake mixes against one another and found Betty Crocker Super Moist Butter Recipe Yellow Cake Mix to come in pretty close to homemade.

MAKING A FLAG CAKE

 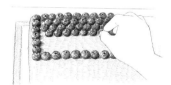 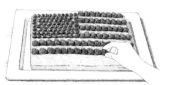

Using fresh blueberries, outline a 6 by 4½-inch rectangle in the top left corner of the frosted cake, and fill it in with rows of blueberries. Gently press on the berries so that they adhere and have an even height. For the red stripes, lay raspberries on their side and gently nestle them into one another. There should be 4 short rows of raspberry stripes across the top of the cake and 3 long rows of raspberry stripes across the bottom of the cake. Gently press on the berries to adhere.

Upscale Picnic Spread

THE GAME PLAN

ONE DAY AHEAD...

MAKE PEACH SQUARES: 45 minutes
(plus 2½ hours for baking and cooling)

PREP CHICKEN: 20 minutes (plus 6 hours for seasoning)

MAKE WHIPPED GOAT CHEESE: 10 minutes
(plus 1 hour for chilling)

ON THE DAY OF...

BAKE AND COOL CHICKEN: 1½ hours

MAKE CHERRY TOMATO SALAD: 1¼ hours

MAKE PASTA SALAD: 1 hour

ASSEMBLE MELON AND PROSCIUTTO: 10 minutes

UPSCALE PICNIC SPREAD

⮞ Serves 12 ⮜

Whipped Goat Cheese with Lemon and Scallions ⮞ Melon and Prosciutto
Spice-Rubbed Picnic Chicken ⮞ Cherry Tomato Salad with Feta and Olives
Pesto Pasta Salad ⮞ Easy Peach Squares

Spice-Rubbed Picnic Chicken

We prefer kosher salt in the spice rub; if using table salt, reduce the salt amount to 2 tablespoons. This chicken is mildly spicy; for more heat, use the increased amount of cayenne.

6	tablespoons brown sugar
¼	cup kosher salt
¼	cup chili powder
¼	cup paprika
4	teaspoons pepper
½–¾	teaspoon cayenne pepper
8	(12-ounce) bone-in split chicken breasts, trimmed, skin slashed, and cut in half
7	(6-ounce) bone-in chicken thighs, trimmed and skin slashed
7	(6-ounce) bone-in chicken drumsticks, trimmed and skin slashed

1. Line 2 rimmed baking sheets with aluminum foil and top with wire racks. Combine sugar, salt, chili powder, paprika, pepper, and cayenne in small bowl. Coat chicken pieces with spice mixture, gently lifting skin to distribute spices underneath but leaving it attached to chicken. Place chicken skin-side up on prepared wire racks, tent with foil, and refrigerate for at least 6 hours and up to 24 hours.

2. Adjust oven racks to upper-middle and lower-middle positions and heat oven to 475 degrees. Remove foil and roast chicken until brown, crisp, and breasts register 160 degrees, 30 to 40 minutes; switching and rotating baking sheets halfway through roasting. Transfer breast pieces to large platter. Continue to roast thighs and drumsticks until they register 175 degrees, 10 to 15 minutes longer; transfer to platter.

3. Let chicken cool completely, about 30 minutes, and serve. (Chicken can be refrigerated for up to 1 day; return to room temperature before serving.)

SLASHING CHICKEN SKIN

To ensure crisp skin when making Spice-Rubbed Picnic Chicken, use a paring knife to make slashes in the skin of each piece of chicken to help render the fat.

✔ **WHY THIS RECIPE WORKS**
Cold barbecued chicken may be a picnic favorite, but the flabby skin and sticky mess that go with it are less beloved. To achieve authentic barbecue flavor without all the mess, we turned to a flavorful dry rub of brown sugar, chili powder, paprika, salt, and pepper. We found that not only did applying the rub to the chicken before chilling overnight allow the flavor to penetrate the meat, but the salt in the rub helped keep the chicken moist during roasting. We partly solved the flabby skin problem by diligently trimming the chicken pieces, and then we went one step further by slitting the skin before cooking, which allowed the excess fat to render.

Whipped Goat Cheese with Lemon and Scallions

We've found that goat cheese can vary dramatically in texture and requires slightly different amounts of milk in order to achieve a nice spreadable texture.

1½	pounds goat cheese, crumbled
6	tablespoons whole milk
2	tablespoons extra-virgin olive oil
4	teaspoons grated lemon zest (2 lemons)
	Salt and pepper
4	scallions, sliced thin

Process goat cheese, ¼ cup milk, oil, lemon zest, ½ teaspoon salt, and ¼ teaspoon pepper together in food processor until smooth, about 1 minute. Mixture should have consistency of softened cream cheese; if it is too stiff, add remaining milk, 1 tablespoon at a time, and process to incorporate, about 10 seconds. Transfer mixture to bowl, stir in scallions, and season with salt and pepper to taste. Cover and refrigerate until flavors have blended, at least 1 hour and up to 2 days. (Makes 3 cups.)

Cherry Tomato Salad with Feta and Olives

If you don't have a salad spinner, after the salted tomatoes have stood for 30 minutes, wrap the bowl tightly with plastic wrap and gently shake to remove seeds and excess liquid. Strain the liquid and proceed with the recipe as directed.

4½	pounds ripe cherry tomatoes, quartered
1½	teaspoons sugar
	Salt and pepper
3	shallots, minced
6	garlic cloves, minced
3	tablespoons red wine vinegar
1½	teaspoons dried oregano
6	tablespoons extra-virgin olive oil
3	cucumbers, peeled, halved lengthwise, seeded (see page 89), and cut into ½-inch pieces
1¾	cups pitted kalamata olives, chopped
12	ounces feta cheese, crumbled (3 cups)
½	cup chopped fresh parsley

1. Toss tomatoes, sugar, and ¾ teaspoon salt in large bowl and let stand for 30 minutes. Transfer tomatoes to salad spinner and spin until seeds and excess liquid have been removed, about 1 minute, stopping to redistribute tomatoes several times during spinning. Return tomatoes to bowl. Strain tomato liquid through fine-mesh strainer into liquid measuring cup, pressing on solids to extract 1 cup of tomato liquid (discard any extra liquid).

2. Bring 1 cup tomato liquid, shallots, garlic, vinegar, and oregano to simmer in small saucepan and cook until reduced to ½ cup, 8 to 10 minutes. Transfer mixture to small bowl and refrigerate until cool, about 10 minutes. Whisking constantly, drizzle in oil until combined and season with salt and pepper to taste.

3. Add cucumbers, olives, feta, parsley, and dressing to tomatoes. Toss gently to coat and serve. (Salad can be held at room temperature for up to 4 hours.)

Melon and Prosciutto

Cantaloupe is the classic choice, but any ripe melon, including honeydew, can be used in this recipe.

12　ounces thinly sliced prosciutto
1　large cantaloupe, peeled, halved, seeded, and cut into 12 thin crescents

Wrap prosciutto around middle of each melon slice, arrange on platter, and serve. (Makes 12 pieces.)

PEELING CANTALOUPE

Trim a ¼-inch slice from the top and bottom of the melon so that it will sit flat on the cutting board. Using a chef's knife and working from top to bottom, carefully cut away the rind in long strips.

WHY THIS RECIPE WORKS

This classic pairing of sweet, juicy melon and salty, toothsome prosciutto takes little time to prepare, but such a simple dish demands the best ingredients. Make sure your melon is as sweet and ripe as can be and purchase high-quality prosciutto di Parma. It is best not to let the melon and prosciutto sit around together for too long, or the salt from the meat will draw moisture out of the melon.

Pesto Pasta Salad

We like to use farfalle in this salad, but any small pasta shape will work fine. Our favorite brand of mayonnaise is Hellmann's (also known as Best Foods). You can substitute Hellmann's Light Mayonnaise, but we're not fans of Hellmann's Low Fat Mayonnaise or Miracle Whip here.

3　garlic cloves, unpeeled
6　ounces fresh basil leaves (6 cups)
1½　ounces baby spinach (1½ cups)
1¼　cups (6¼ ounces) pine nuts, toasted (see page 29)
⅓　cup plus 2 tablespoons extra-virgin olive oil
3　tablespoons lemon juice
　　Salt and pepper
2　ounces Parmesan cheese, grated (1 cup)
½　cup mayonnaise
1½　pounds farfalle

1. Toast garlic in small skillet over medium heat, shaking pan occasionally, until fragrant and color of cloves deepens slightly, about 7 minutes. Let garlic cool, then peel and chop coarse.

2. Process garlic, basil, spinach, ½ cup pine nuts, ⅓ cup oil, lemon juice, 1¼ teaspoons salt, and ¾ teaspoon pepper in food processor until smooth, stopping to scrape down bowl as needed. Add Parmesan and mayonnaise and continue to process until thoroughly combined. Transfer pesto to small bowl, cover, and refrigerate until needed. (Mixture can be refrigerated for up to 1 day.)

3. Bring 6 quarts water to boil in large pot. Stir 1 tablespoon salt and pasta into boiling water and cook, stirring often, until pasta is just past al dente. Reserve ¼ cup of pasta cooking water and drain pasta. Toss pasta with remaining 2 tablespoons oil and spread into single layer on rimmed baking sheet. Let pasta cool to room temperature, about 30 minutes.

4. In large bowl, toss cooled pasta with pesto, adding reserved pasta water, 1 tablespoon at a time, until pesto evenly coats pasta. Fold in remaining ¾ cup nuts. (Salad can be refrigerated for up to 1 day. Before serving stir in hot water, 1 tablespoon at a time, to refresh salad and season with salt and pepper to taste.)

WHY THIS RECIPE WORKS

This pesto pasta salad is the perfect side dish for a picnic—fresh, green, garlicky, and full of herbal flavor. The textured surface of farfalle guarantees that the pesto won't slide off. To ensure that the pesto coated the pasta, we didn't rinse the pasta after cooking. Instead, we spread the pasta out to cool in a single layer on a baking sheet with a splash of oil to prevent the pasta from sticking. For the pesto, we toasted the garlic to tame its harsh bite and added mild-tasting baby spinach to keep the green color from fading. For a creamy, not greasy, pesto, we enriched it with mayonnaise. Finally, folding in extra pine nuts gave the salad an extra hit of nutty flavor and a pleasant crunchy texture.

Easy Peach Squares

Lay the thawed peaches on a dish towel to rid them of excess moisture before using.

1½ cups (7½ ounces) all-purpose flour
1¾ cups (6⅛ ounces) sliced almonds
⅓ cup (2⅓ ounces) granulated sugar
⅓ cup packed (2⅓ ounces) plus
    1 tablespoon light brown sugar
    Salt
12 tablespoons unsalted butter, cut into
    12 pieces and softened
1½ pounds frozen peaches, thawed and
    drained
½ cup peach jam
½ teaspoon grated lemon zest plus
    1 teaspoon juice

1. Adjust oven rack to middle position and heat oven to 375 degrees. Line 13 by 9-inch baking pan with aluminum foil sling and grease foil. Process flour, 1¼ cups almonds, granulated sugar, ⅓ cup brown sugar, and ½ teaspoon salt in food processor until combined, about 5 seconds. Add butter and pulse mixture until it resembles coarse meal with few pea-size pieces of butter, about 20 pulses.

2. Measure out and reserve ½ cup of mixture separately for topping. Sprinkle remaining mixture into prepared pan and press into even layer with bottom of measuring cup. Use back of spoon to press and smooth edges. Bake crust until fragrant and golden, about 15 minutes.

3. Stir remaining 1 tablespoon brown sugar into reserved mixture for topping and pinch mixture between your fingers into hazelnut-size clumps of streusel.

4. Pulse peaches and jam together in food processor until peaches are roughly ¼-inch chunks, 5 to 7 pulses. Transfer peach mixture to large nonstick skillet and cook over high heat until it is thickened and jamlike, about 10 minutes. Off heat, stir in lemon zest, lemon juice, and pinch of salt.

5. Spread cooked peach mixture evenly over hot crust, then sprinkle with streusel topping and remaining ½ cup almonds. Bake until almonds are golden, about 20 minutes, rotating pan halfway through baking.

6. Let bars cool completely in pan, about 2 hours. Remove bars from pan using sling, cut into squares, and serve. (Squares can be stored at room temperature for up to 1 day. Makes 24 squares.)

✓ WHY THIS RECIPE WORKS
Easy to pick up and eat, all-season peach squares are a handy dessert for your picnic basket. Surprisingly, we found that frozen peaches rather than fresh produced the best peach squares. Not only are frozen peaches more convenient than fresh (no peeling, pitting, or chopping), but the quality is also more consistent. Combining the peaches with peach jam helps thicken the fruity filling in our bars, and adding a dash of lemon juice to the jam brightens the filling further. For a golden brown bottom crust, we prebaked it before layering it with the filling and sprinkling on the top crust.

MAKING A SLING

Place 2 sheets of aluminum foil or parchment paper perpendicular to each other in the pan, pushing the foil into the corners. When ready to serve, use the edges of the sling to help you remove the bars from the pan in a single piece.

Sunday Brunch Celebration

THE GAME PLAN

~

ONE DAY AHEAD...

MAKE LEMON-DILL SAUCE: 5 minutes

MAKE SALMON: 25 minutes (plus 2¾ hours for cooking and chilling)

ASSEMBLE SCONES: 25 minutes

MAKE MINI CHEESECAKES: 20 minutes (plus 2 hours for baking and chilling)

ON THE DAY OF...

BAKE SCONES: 30 minutes

MAKE CUCUMBER SALAD: 30 minutes

MAKE FRUIT SALAD: 20 minutes

MAKE ASPARAGUS APPETIZER: 25 minutes

GARNISH CHEESECAKES: 15 minutes

SUNDAY BRUNCH CELEBRATION

➤ Serves 12 ➤

Prosciutto-Wrapped Asparagus ✦ Oven-Poached Salmon with Lemon-Dill Sauce
Frisée, Spinach, and Cucumber Salad ✦ Cream Scones with Scallions
Berry and Star Fruit Salad ✦ Mini Lemon Cheesecakes with Strawberries

Oven-Poached Salmon with Lemon-Dill Sauce

Be sure to follow our directions for wrapping the salmon in foil; otherwise, the fish's juices may leak onto the bottom of your oven, creating a pesky mess. To test the fish for doneness, simply poke an instant-read thermometer right through the top of the foil. If your sides of salmon are larger, they will obviously have slightly longer cooking times.

SALMON

2   (2½- to 3-pound) sides of salmon
    Salt
3   tablespoons cider or white wine vinegar
8   sprigs plus 3 tablespoons minced fresh tarragon
3   lemons, sliced thin, plus lemon wedges for serving

LEMON-DILL SAUCE

2   cups sour cream
2   shallots, minced
2   tablespoons minced fresh dill
1   tablespoon lemon juice
    Salt and pepper

1. FOR THE SALMON: Adjust oven racks to upper-middle and lower-middle positions and heat oven to 250 degrees. For each side of salmon, cut 3 sheets heavy-duty aluminum foil about 1 foot longer than fish. Overlap 2 pieces of foil lengthwise by 1 inch and fold to secure seam. Lay third sheet of foil over seam and coat well with vegetable oil spray.

2. Lay fish down center of foil, season with salt, sprinkle with vinegar, and arrange tarragon sprigs and lemon slices on top. Fold foil over top of fish and crimp edges of foil together to seal; leave a slight air pocket between top of fish and foil. *continued ➤*

✔ **WHY THIS RECIPE WORKS**
Poached side of salmon makes an impressive showing on a brunch table, but most pots can't fit a whole side of salmon, let alone two, and fish poachers are expensive. We decided to get rid of the water altogether and steam the fish in its own moisture for an easier "poached" salmon. We sprinkled two sides of salmon with vinegar, whole herbs, and sliced lemons, wrapped them in heavy-duty aluminum foil, and placed them directly on the oven racks in a relatively cool 250-degree oven.

MAKING OVEN-POACHED SALMON

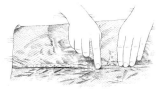  

For each side of salmon, cut 3 sheets of heavy-duty foil about a foot longer than the fish. Using 2 of the sheets, overlap their edges by 1 inch, and fold to secure the seam. Lay the third sheet of foil over the seam and coat the foil generously with vegetable oil spray. Lay the fish down the center of each piece foil, sprinkle with the vinegar, and arrange the herbs and lemon slices on top. Bring the edges of the foil up over the salmon and fold the edges tightly to secure the seam. Don't crimp the foil too close to the fish; leave a little air pocket between the fish and the foil.

3. Lay foil-wrapped fish directly on oven racks (without baking sheet) and cook until color of flesh has turned from pink to orange and fish registers 140 degrees, 1 to 1¼ hours. Remove fish from oven, open foil packets, and discard lemon slices and herbs. Let salmon cool on foil at room temperature for 30 minutes.

4. Pour off any accumulated liquid, reseal salmon in foil, and refrigerate until cold, about 1 hour. (Poached salmon can be refrigerated for up to 2 days. Let sit at room temperature for 30 minutes before serving.)

5. FOR THE LEMON-DILL SAUCE: Combine all ingredients in serving bowl and season with salt and pepper to taste. Cover and refrigerate until flavors meld, about 30 minutes and up to 1 day.

6. Unwrap salmon and brush away any gelled poaching liquid. Slide your hands under both ends of salmon and carefully transfer fish to serving platters. Sprinkle with minced tarragon and serve with lemon wedges and lemon-dill sauce.

Prosciutto-Wrapped Asparagus

✔ **WHY THIS RECIPE WORKS**
While you can't go wrong when wrapping anything in prosciutto, asparagus makes a particularly attractive subject. A few minutes of broiling is a fast and unfussy method to parcook the asparagus, rendering it tender but allowing it to remain crisp and brightly colored. A pat of spreadable Boursin cheese provides tang and makes a handy paste to hold the prosciutto around the spears.

Do not add any additional salt to this recipe because the prosciutto is already very salty. If necessary, thin asparagus can be substituted for thick; just roll 2 thin spears into each bundle. Don't overcook the asparagus in step 3 or the prosciutto will turn tough and leathery; the spears should just be warmed through before serving.

2 pounds thick asparagus, trimmed
2 teaspoons extra-virgin olive oil
1 (5.2-ounce) package Boursin Garlic and Fine Herbs cheese, softened
12 ounces thinly sliced prosciutto, cut in half crosswise

1. Adjust oven rack 3 inches from broiler element and heat broiler. (If necessary, set upside-down rimmed baking sheet on oven rack to get closer to broiler element.) Toss asparagus with oil and lay in single layer on large rimmed baking sheet. Broil until asparagus is crisp-tender, about 5 minutes, tossing halfway through broiling. Let asparagus cool slightly.

2. Spread Boursin over each piece of prosciutto. Roll prosciutto around center of each asparagus spear and transfer to rimmed baking sheet. (Wrapped asparagus can be held at room temperature for up to 4 hours.)

3. Before serving, adjust oven rack to middle position and heat oven to 450 degrees. Bake prosciutto-wrapped asparagus until just warmed through, about 5 minutes. Serve warm.

Frisée, Spinach, and Cucumber Salad

✔ **WHY THIS RECIPE WORKS**
For a refreshing salad for our brunch table, we punctuated crunchy cucumbers and soft spinach with bites of slightly peppery, bitter frisée. Salting and draining the cucumbers is the key to drawing out excess moisture.

Salting the cucumbers will help rid them of excess moisture and prevent the salad from tasting watery.

3 cucumbers, peeled, halved lengthwise, seeded (see page 89), and sliced thin
 Salt and pepper
3 tablespoons lemon juice
1 shallot, minced
2 tablespoons minced fresh mint
1 tablespoon white wine vinegar

2 teaspoons Dijon mustard
1 garlic clove, minced
½ cup extra-virgin olive oil
4 small heads frisée (1 pound), cut into 2-inch pieces
10 ounces baby spinach (10 cups)

1. Toss cucumbers with ½ teaspoon salt and let drain in colander for 15 minutes. Whisk lemon juice, shallot, mint, vinegar, mustard, garlic, ¼ teaspoon salt, and ¼ teaspoon pepper together in small bowl.

Whisking constantly, drizzle in oil.

2. Combine drained cucumbers, frisée, and spinach in large bowl. Just before serving, whisk dressing to re-emulsify, then drizzle over salad and toss gently to coat.

Cream Scones with Scallions

Make sure to cut the scones into uniform wedges in step 3 so that they bake at the same rate.

4	cups (20 ounces) all-purpose flour
2	tablespoons sugar
2	tablespoons baking powder
I	teaspoon salt
¼	teaspoon cayenne pepper
10	tablespoons unsalted butter, cut into ¼-inch pieces and chilled
8	scallions, sliced thin
2¼	cups heavy cream

1. Adjust oven racks to upper-middle and lower-middle positions and heat oven to 450 degrees. Line 2 baking sheets with parchment paper.

2. Pulse flour, sugar, baking powder, salt, and cayenne together in food processor to combine, about 5 pulses. Scatter butter evenly over top and continue to pulse until mixture resembles coarse cornmeal with few butter lumps, about 25 pulses. Transfer mixture to large bowl and stir in scallions. Stir in cream with rubber spatula until dough begins to form, about 30 seconds.

3. Turn dough and any floury bits out onto lightly floured counter and knead until it forms rough, slightly sticky ball, 5 to 10 seconds. Divide dough into 2 equal pieces. Working with 1 piece of dough at a time, press evenly into lightly floured 9-inch round cake pan. Gently remove dough from pan and cut into 12 wedges. Place wedges on prepared baking sheets. (Scones can be covered and refrigerated for up to 24 hours.)

4. Bake scones until tops are lightly golden brown, 15 to 17 minutes, switching and rotating pans halfway through baking. Transfer scones to wire rack and let cool for at least 10 minutes. Serve warm or at room temperature. (Makes 24 scones.)

❂ **WHY THIS RECIPE WORKS**
To produce fluffy scones with a delicate texture, we found it important to work the dough quickly and with a light hand. Using a food processor to cut the cold butter into the dry ingredients prevented the butter from overheating and we mixed the liquid ingredients in by hand to avoid overmixing (and tough scones). We flavored our savory scones with scallions and a little cayenne, and the addition of sugar brought out the flavors. For evenly cooked scones, they need to be the same size: a cake pan served as a handy mold to shape the dough into disks before slicing into wedges.

MAKING CREAM SCONES

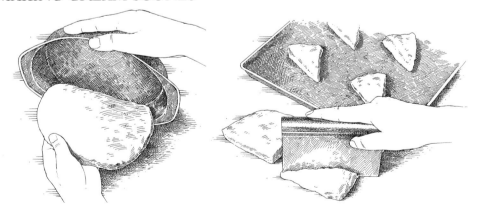

Working with 1 piece of dough at a time, press it evenly into a lightly floured 9-inch round cake pan. Gently turn the dough out of the pan onto a lightly floured counter. Use a bench scraper or knife to cut the dough into 12 wedge-shaped scones, then transfer the scones to the prepared baking sheets.

Berry and Star Fruit Salad

WHY THIS RECIPE WORKS
For a superior fruit salad, we selected our fruit carefully and made a dressing to add moisture and flavor. We combined whole berries with dramatic slices of star fruit. A simple syrup coaxed flavor from the fruit. Rather than toss everything together, we strategically layered the berries with the most fragile on top, drizzling each layer with the syrup.

We like using berries in this salad because they require no prep other than a quick rinse, but any freshly cut fruit can be substituted.

¼	cup sugar
¼	cup water
1	tablespoon grated lime zest (2 limes)
20	ounces blueberries (4 cups)
15	ounces blackberries (3 cups)
15	ounces raspberries (3 cups)
2	star fruits, sliced ¼ inch thick
3	tablespoons chopped fresh mint

1. Bring sugar and water to simmer in small saucepan over medium heat and cook until sugar dissolves and mixture measures ⅓ cup, about 2 minutes. Off heat, stir in lime zest and let cool to room temperature.

2. In large serving bowl, layer blueberries and drizzle with 1 tablespoon syrup. Layer blackberries and drizzle with 1 tablespoon syrup. Layer raspberries and 1 tablespoon syrup. Arrange star fruit on top and drizzle with remaining syrup. (Salad can be covered and refrigerated for up to 4 hours.) Sprinkle with mint before serving.

Mini Lemon Cheesecakes with Strawberries

WHY THIS RECIPE WORKS
These easy-to-make individual cheesecakes make an appealing presentation and are much simpler to prepare and serve than a full-size cheesecake. Using sweetened condensed milk allowed us to eliminate sugar, sour cream, and vanilla extract from the batter. And instead of struggling with crafting 12 individual crusts, we opted to use a single shortbread cookie for each mini cheesecake. Lining the muffin tin with cupcake liners proved to be essential for getting the cheesecakes out of the muffin tin without ruining them in the process. (It also makes cleanup easier.) Sliced strawberries macerated in a little sugar makes a simple and yet dressy topping.

We like to use Keebler Sandies when making these individual cheesecakes; they measure 2 inches wide and ½ inch thick. You can substitute any similar size, round shortbread cookie. Do not use low-fat or nonfat cream cheese or the filling will never set. If you make these cheesecakes a day ahead, note that the crust will have a much softer texture.

12	Keebler Sandies cookies
8	ounces cream cheese, softened
2	teaspoons grated lemon zest plus 1 tablespoon juice
½	cup sweetened condensed milk
2	large eggs
8	ounces strawberries, hulled and sliced thin (1½ cups)
1	tablespoon sugar

1. Adjust oven rack to middle position and heat oven to 300 degrees. Line a 12-cup muffin tin with cupcake liners. Place 1 cookie in each muffin cup.

2. Using stand mixer fitted with paddle, beat cream cheese and lemon zest on medium-high speed until light and fluffy, about 2 minutes. Gradually beat in condensed milk until incorporated, about 1 minute, scraping down bowl as needed. Add eggs, 1 at a time, and beat until smooth, 2 to 3 minutes. Add lemon juice and mix until just incorporated, about 15 seconds.

3. Divide batter evenly among muffin cups. Bake until set, about 20 minutes. Let cheesecakes cool in tin, about 30 minutes. Wrap tin with plastic wrap and refrigerate until cakes are chilled and firm, at least 1 hour and up to 1 day.

4. Before serving, toss strawberries with sugar and let sit until juicy, about 10 minutes. Remove cheesecakes from muffin tin, fan sliced strawberries attractively over top of each cake, and serve.

EVEN EASIER ⮞ Don't have time to make mini cheesecakes? Make individual strawberry parfaits instead. Hull and slice 2 pounds fresh strawberries and toss with ¼ cup sugar in a large bowl. Using a stand mixer fitted with whisk, whip 2 cups heavy cream, ½ cup sour cream, 2 tablespoons sugar, 1 teaspoon grated lemon zest, and pinch salt together until the mixture forms soft peaks. Finely crush 7 ounces Italian amaretti cookies into coarse crumbs (you should have 2 cups of crumbs). Layer half of the strawberries into 12 parfait glasses. Dollop each with 2 tablespoons whipped cream mixture and sprinkle with 1 tablespoon amaretti crumbs; repeat the layering once more. Dollop the remaining whipped cream over the top and sprinkle with the remaining crumbs.

Spring
Leg of Lamb

THE GAME PLAN
➤

ONE DAY AHEAD...

MAKE CHEESE BALL: 15 minutes (plus 3 hours for chilling)

MAKE TART DOUGH: 15 minutes (plus 1 hour for chilling)

MAKE NUTELLA TART: 2 hours (plus 2 hours for chilling)

PREP LAMB: 45 minutes

ON THE DAY OF...

COOK LAMB: 45 minutes (plus 2¼ hours for roasting and resting)

MAKE STUFFED DATES: 20 minutes

MAKE MINT RELISH: 10 minutes

MAKE RED POTATOES: 1 hour

MAKE SALAD: 45 minutes

WHIP CREAM FOR TART: 5 minutes

SPRING LEG OF LAMB

➤ *Serves 12* ◄

Port Wine–Blue Cheese Ball ❧ Dates Stuffed with Prosciutto and Nuts
Boneless Leg of Lamb with Garlic-Herb Crumb Crust
Fresh Mint Relish ❧ Roasted Red Potatoes with Sea Salt
Asparagus and Spinach Salad ❧ Nutella Tart

Boneless Leg of Lamb with Garlic-Herb Crumb Crust

In order to serve 12 people, you will need to cook two half legs of lamb. Butterflied bone-less legs of lamb (as opposed to boneless corkscrewed legs of lamb) are the easiest to work with. Make sure that each leg of lamb is in one piece before buying; if it is packaged in elastic netting, ask the butcher to cut open the netting so that you can inspect the meat before purchasing.

2	slices hearty white sandwich bread, torn into quarters
⅔	cup fresh parsley leaves
¼	cup minced fresh rosemary
6	garlic cloves, minced
6	tablespoons olive oil
2	ounces Parmesan cheese, grated (1 cup)
2	(4- to 5-pound) butterflied boneless half legs of lamb
	Salt and pepper
3	tablespoons Dijon mustard

1. Pulse bread in food processor to fine crumbs, about 16 pulses; transfer to bowl. Process parsley, rosemary, garlic, and 2 table-spoons oil together in food processor until finely minced, about 1 minute. Measure out and reserve 3 tablespoons of herb mixture separately. Toss remaining herb mixture with bread crumbs, Parmesan, and 2 table-spoons oil.

2. Lay lamb, rough side facing up, on counter and trim away any *continued* ➤

☑ WHY THIS RECIPE WORKS
These crusted boneless legs of lamb make a great centerpiece for a celebratory dinner and are easy to prep in advance and easy to slice and serve. Pounding the roasts makes it easier to roll them into a uniform shape and, more importantly, it breaks down the muscle fibers, resulting in more tender lamb. Before rolling, we coated the meat with a simple rub of aromatics to enhance and season it through and through.

PREPARING A BONELESS LEG OF LAMB

Lay lamb, rough side facing up, on counter and trim away any fat and gristle. Cover the meat with plastic wrap and pound to a uniform ¾-inch thickness. Season with salt and pepper, then spread the herb mixture evenly over the meat, leaving a 1-inch border around the edge. Roll up the meat lengthwise and tie into a tidy roast with kitchen twine at 2-inch intervals. If there are holes in the meat, patch it together as best you can before rolling and tying.

fat and gristle. Press meat flat to counter, cover meat with plastic wrap, and pound to uniform ¾-inch thickness. Remove plastic, season meat with salt and pepper, then spread reserved herb mixture evenly over each roast, leaving 1-inch border at edge. Roll and tie each piece of meat into tidy roast and tie with kitchen twine at 2-inch intervals. Pat roasts dry with paper towels and season with salt and pepper. (Lamb roasts and bread crumbs can be refrigerated for up to 1 day.)

3. Adjust oven rack to lower-middle position and heat oven to 250 degrees. Line rimmed baking sheet with aluminum foil and top with wire rack. Heat 1 tablespoon oil in 12-inch skillet over medium-high heat until just smoking. Brown 1 roast on all sides, including ends, 12 to 14 minutes. Transfer browned roast, seam side down, to prepared wire rack. Repeat with remaining 1 tablespoon oil and remaining roast; transfer to wire rack. (Browned lamb roasts can be held at room temperature for up to 1 hour before roasting.)

4. Roast lamb until it registers 100 degrees, 50 to 70 minutes. Remove lamb from oven and increase oven temperature to 425 degrees. Remove twine from lamb, coat top and sides of roasts with mustard, then press bread-crumb mixture into mustard to adhere. Continue to roast lamb until crumbs are browned and meat registers 125 degrees (for medium-rare), 25 to 30 minutes longer. (If topping becomes brown before meat is done, lightly cover meat with foil and continue to roast.)

5. Transfer roasts to carving board and let rest, uncovered, for 30 minutes. Slice roasts into ¼-inch-thick slices and serve.

Fresh Mint Relish

Consider using a food processor to help mince the parsley and mint.

☑ **WHY THIS RECIPE WORKS**
Mint jam can be stodgy and overly sweet, and we prefer this cleaner, brighter relish which pairs fresh mint with parsley, olive oil, red wine vinegar, shallot, and plenty of garlic. A little water keeps the relish from being overly thick and a touch of sugar balances the pungency.

1	cup minced fresh parsley
1	cup minced fresh mint
1	cup extra-virgin olive oil
⅓	cup red wine vinegar
¼	cup water
1	shallot, minced
4	garlic cloves, minced
1	tablespoon sugar
1	teaspoon salt

Combine all ingredients in bowl and refrigerate until needed. (Relish can be refrigerated for up to 6 hours.) Bring to room temperature before serving. (Makes 2¼ cups.)

Dates Stuffed with Prosciutto and Nuts

Look for dates that are soft and fresh; old dates will have tough outer skins and be very chewy.

6	ounces thinly sliced prosciutto
1	cup pecans or walnuts, toasted (see page 29)
¾	cup fresh parsley leaves
3	tablespoons extra-virgin olive oil
	Salt and pepper
18	dates, halved and pitted

Pulse prosciutto, pecans, and parsley in food processor until coarsely chopped, about 20 pulses. Transfer mixture to bowl, stir in olive oil, and season with salt and pepper to taste. Mound 1 generous teaspoon of filling into each date half. Serve. (Dates can be covered and held at room temperature for up to 4 hours. Makes 36 dates.)

☑ **WHY THIS RECIPE WORKS**
These addictively sweet-salty stuffed dates are impressive and boldly flavored, yet require only five ingredients, no cooking (save toasting the nuts), and no chopping (save slicing the dates). The stuffing comes together in seconds in the food processor.

Port Wine–Blue Cheese Ball

Serve with crackers, a sliced baguette, or Garlic Toasts (page 62).

8	ounces cream cheese, softened
4	ounces blue cheese, crumbled (1 cup)
4	ounces mozzarella cheese, shredded (1 cup)
2	tablespoons mayonnaise
1	tablespoon port wine
1	garlic clove, minced
½	cup pecans, toasted (see page 29) and chopped fine

Process cream cheese, blue cheese, mozzarella, mayonnaise, wine, and garlic in food processor until smooth, scraping down sides as needed, about 1 minute. Transfer mixture to center of large sheet of plastic wrap. Holding corners of wrap in 1 hand, twist cheese with other hand to shape cheese into rough ball. Refrigerate plastic-wrapped cheese until firm, at least 3 hours and up to 2 days. Before serving, reshape cheese into ball, unwrap, and roll in nuts to coat. Let soften slightly at room temperature.

EVEN EASIER ↝ Don't have time to make and chill a cheese ball? Simply transfer the processed cheese mixture to a serving bowl and sprinkle the pecans over the top. It can be served immediately or refrigerated until needed. If chilled, let soften at room temperature before serving.

☑ **WHY THIS RECIPE WORKS**
Port wine and blue cheese give an edge of sophistication to this homemade cheese ball, a playful homage to the popular but mediocre supermarket variety. We cut the strong flavor of blue cheese with the same quantity of mild mozzarella, stirring both cheeses into a cream cheese base to produce a firm, yet spreadable consistency. A couple tablespoons of mayonnaise imparted a silky texture, while a clove of assertive garlic enhanced the cheese flavor without compromising the texture. A roll in toasted and chopped pecans gave the ball an attractive and crunchy coating.

Roasted Red Potatoes with Sea Salt

✓ **WHY THIS RECIPE WORKS**
For crisp, aggressively browned roasted potatoes with moist, creamy flesh, we started with low-starch red potatoes, which hold their shape during cooking. To ensure they would cook through in the oven in the time that the lamb was resting, we gave the potatoes a head start by microwaving them with some water. Limiting the oven time also produced potatoes that were brown but not leathery.

We prefer to use extra-small red potatoes, measuring 1 inch or less in diameter, in this recipe. If your potatoes are slightly larger than 1 inch, you should quarter them. Make sure to thoroughly drain the potatoes in step 2 (there should be no water in the bottom of the colander). In terms of timing, plan on roasting these potatoes while the lamb rests.

6 pounds extra-small red potatoes, halved or quartered if large
⅓ cup olive oil
   Sea salt and pepper

1. Adjust oven racks to upper-middle and lower-middle positions and heat oven to 450 degrees. Combine potatoes with ½ cup water in large bowl. Cover and microwave, stirring occasionally, until potatoes begin to soften but still hold their shape, about 15 minutes.

2. Drain potatoes well, then toss with oil and season with salt and pepper. Arrange potatoes cut side down in single layer on 2 large rimmed baking sheets. Roast until cut sides are golden brown and potatoes are fully tender, about 30 minutes, switching and rotating baking sheets halfway through roasting. Transfer potatoes to serving bowl, sprinkle with salt to taste, and serve.

Asparagus and Spinach Salad

✓ **WHY THIS RECIPE WORKS**
For an asparagus salad with bold flavor and crisp-tender texture, sautéing proved more flavorful than blanching, and quicker than waiting for a pot of water to boil. Strips of sautéed red bell pepper bring color and sweetness to this salad, while sautéed sliced shallots add an appealing mellow flavor. The vegetables can be cooked hours ahead of time, making this an easy and impressive salad to assemble at the last minute.

We like to use thick asparagus here; however, thin asparagus will work fine too. Do not overcook the asparagus in step 1, or it will taste mushy in the salad; the cooked asparagus should still have some crunch in the center.

½ cup extra-virgin olive oil
2 red bell peppers, stemmed, seeded, and cut into ¼-inch strips
2 pounds asparagus, trimmed and cut on bias into 1-inch lengths
   Salt and pepper
2 shallots, sliced thin
3 tablespoons sherry vinegar
2 garlic cloves, minced
1 pound baby spinach (16 cups)
8 ounces goat cheese, crumbled (2 cups)

1. Heat 1 tablespoon oil in 12-inch nonstick skillet over medium-high heat until shimmering. Add bell peppers and cook until lightly browned and crisp-tender, about 5 minutes; transfer to large plate.

2. Heat 2 tablespoons oil until shimmering. Add asparagus, ½ teaspoon salt, and ⅛ teaspoon pepper, and cook until asparagus is lightly browned and almost tender, about 6 minutes. Stir in shallots and cook until asparagus is crisp-tender, about 2 minutes longer. Transfer to plate with bell peppers and let cool for at least 10 minutes and up to 2 hours.

3. Whisk vinegar, garlic, ¼ teaspoon salt, and ¼ teaspoon pepper together in small bowl. Whisking constantly, drizzle in remaining 5 tablespoons oil. Transfer vegetables to large bowl and place spinach on top. Just before serving, whisk dressing to re-emulsify, then drizzle over salad and toss gently to coat. Garnish individual portions with goat cheese.

Nutella Tart

For more information on making a tart shell, see page 262.

TART SHELL

I	large egg yolk
2	tablespoons heavy cream
¾	teaspoon vanilla extract
2	cups (10 ounces) all-purpose flour
I	cup (4 ounces) confectioners' sugar
¼	teaspoon salt
12	tablespoons unsalted butter, cut into ¼-inch pieces and chilled

FILLING

⅓	cup hazelnuts, toasted (see page 29), skinned (see page 24), and chopped coarse
I	tablespoon sugar
¾	cup heavy cream
3	ounces bittersweet chocolate, chopped fine
3	tablespoons unsalted butter, softened
1½	cups Nutella

WHIPPED CREAM

1½	cups heavy cream, chilled
I	tablespoon sugar
½	teaspoon vanilla extract
	Pinch salt

WHY THIS RECIPE WORKS
Nutella is the surprise base for the no-bake filling of this easy-to-make chocolate tart featuring the irresistible combination of rich chocolate and hazelnuts. For a dense and velvety filling, we stirred Nutella into a simple ganache (made with chocolate and cream). Butter isn't uncommon in ganache, and it gave our filling an optimally smooth texture. We poured the chocolate over a layer of hazelnuts toasted with sugar and the tart was firm enough to slice in about 2 hours.

1. FOR THE TART SHELL: Whisk egg yolk, cream, and vanilla together in bowl. Pulse flour, sugar, and salt in food processor until combined, about 5 pulses. Scatter butter pieces over top and pulse until mixture resembles coarse cornmeal, about 15 pulses. With processor running, add egg mixture and continue to process until dough just comes together around processor blade, about 12 seconds.

2. Turn dough onto sheet of plastic wrap and flatten into 6-inch disk. Wrap dough tightly in plastic and refrigerate for at least 1 hour and up to 2 days.

3. Let chilled dough soften slightly at room temperature, about 10 minutes. Roll dough out to 13-inch circle on lightly floured counter. Roll dough loosely around rolling pin, then unroll over 11-inch tart pan with removable bottom. Fit dough into tart pan, pressing it firmly into pan corners and fluted edge. Trim excess dough hanging over edge of pan and use trimmings to patch weak spots. Set tart pan on large plate, cover with plastic, and freeze for at least 30 minutes and up to 1 week.

4. Adjust oven rack to middle position and heat oven to 375 degrees. Set tart pan on baking sheet. Press double layer of aluminum foil into tart shell and over edges of pan, then fill with pie weights. Bake until tart shell is golden brown and set, about 30 minutes, rotating baking sheet halfway through baking. Carefully remove weights and foil and continue to bake until crust is fully baked and golden, 5 to 10 minutes. Let tart shell cool slightly on baking sheet while making filling.

5. FOR THE FILLING: Cook nuts and sugar together in 10-inch nonstick skillet over medium heat, stirring constantly, until nuts are golden and caramelized, about 2 minutes; transfer to bowl and let cool.

6. Bring cream to brief simmer in small saucepan over medium-high heat. Off heat, stir in chocolate and butter, cover, and let stand until chocolate is mostly melted, about 5 minutes. Gently stir mixture until smooth, then stir in Nutella.

7. Sprinkle cooled nuts over bottom of tart shell, breaking up any clumps. Pour chocolate filling evenly over nuts and refrigerate tart until filling is firm, about 2 hours. (Once firm, tart can be covered and refrigerated for up to 1 day.)

8. FOR THE WHIPPED CREAM: Using stand mixer fitted with whisk, whip all ingredients together on medium-low speed until foamy, about 1 minute. Increase speed to high and whip until soft peaks form, 1 to 3 minutes. (Whipped cream can be refrigerated for up to 8 hours; rewhisk briefly before serving.)

9. To serve, remove outer metal ring of tart pan, slide thin metal spatula between tart and tart pan bottom, and carefully slide tart onto serving platter. Serve with whipped cream.

Holiday Ham Dinner

THE GAME PLAN

◂▸

> ❧ *Serves 12* ☙

Baked Brie in Phyllo Cups ❧ Shrimp Salad on Endive

Spiral-Sliced Ham with Carrots, Fennel, and Red Potatoes

Buttermilk Biscuits ❧ Baby Greens with Strawberries

Apricot-Almond Bundt Cake

Spiral-Sliced Ham with Carrots, Fennel, and Red Potatoes

Make sure the plastic or foil covering the ham is intact and waterproof before covering the ham with warm water in step 1; if there is a hole in the covering, wrap the ham in several layers of plastic wrap. In step 3, instead of using a plastic oven bag, the ham may be placed cut side down in the roasting pan and covered tightly with aluminum foil, but you will need to add 3 to 4 minutes per pound to the heating time. If the stem ends of your carrots are very thick, slice them in half lengthwise first to ensure even cooking. We prefer to use medium-size red potatoes, measuring 2 to 3 inches in diameter, in this recipe.

HAM AND VEGETABLES

- 1 (7- to 10-pound) spiral-sliced, bone-in half ham, preferably shank end, plastic or foil covering intact
- 3 pounds carrots, peeled and cut into 2-inch lengths
- 4 garlic cloves, peeled
- 3 fennel bulbs, stalks discarded, bulbs halved, cored, and sliced lengthwise into ½-inch-thick slices (see page 22)
- 3 pounds medium red potatoes, quartered
- ½ cup olive oil
- 1 tablespoon minced fresh thyme
  Salt and pepper
- 1 large plastic oven bag
- 3 tablespoons minced fresh parsley

GLAZE

- 1½ cups maple syrup
- 1¼ cups orange marmalade
- 4 tablespoons unsalted butter, melted
- 2 tablespoons Dijon mustard
- 2 teaspoons pepper
- ½ teaspoon ground cinnamon

1. FOR THE HAM AND VEGETABLES: Place wrapped ham in stockpot or large container, cover with hot tap water, and let sit 45 minutes. Drain, cover again with hot tap water, and let sit for 45 minutes longer.

2. Meanwhile, combine carrots, garlic, and ¼ cup water in large bowl. Cover and microwave until softened, about 10 minutes; drain. Combine fennel, potatoes, and ¼ cup water in large bowl. Cover and microwave until softened, about 15 minutes; drain and combine with carrots. Toss vegetables with oil, thyme, ½ teaspoon salt, and ¼ teaspoon pepper.

3. Adjust oven rack to lowest position and heat oven to 250 degrees. Unwrap ham, discarding plastic disk covering bone. Place ham in oven bag. Gather top of bag tightly so bag fits snugly around ham, tie bag securely, and trim excess plastic. Place bagged ham, cut side down, in large roasting pan and cut 4 slits in top of bag. Arrange vegetables in roasting pan around ham. Bake until ham registers 100 degrees, 1 to *continued* ➤

WHY THIS RECIPE WORKS

Our foolproof method for a perfectly moist spiral-sliced holiday ham starts with a bone-in ham, preferably shank-end because they contain less gristle and fat and are easier to carve than butt-end hams. To minimize baking time—and reduce the risk of a dried-out ham—we soaked the ham in hot water so that it didn't go into the oven ice-cold. Using an oven bag created a moist microclimate and sped up the warming process, which allowed us to reduce the cooking time further. For the glaze, we threw out the packet that came with our ham and made a sweet, fruit-based glaze to complement the moist, tender meat. While low and slow was our preferred cooking method for the majority of the time the ham was in the oven, a short blast of higher heat at the end helped the coating caramelize without drying out the meat.

1½ hours (about 10 minutes per pound).

4. FOR THE GLAZE: Whisk all glaze ingredients together in medium bowl. Microwave until mixture thickens slightly, about 5 minutes; cover to keep warm. (Glaze will thicken as it cools between bastings; rewarm as needed to loosen.)

5. Remove ham from oven and increase oven temperature to 350 degrees. Cut open oven bag and roll back sides to expose ham. Brush ham with ½ cup glaze and continue to cook until glaze becomes sticky, about 10 minutes longer.

6. Remove roasting pan from oven and increase oven temperature to 450 degrees.

Transfer ham to carving board and reserve ¾ cup of juice accumulated in bag; discard extra juice and bag. Brush ham with ½ cup glaze, tent loosely with foil, and let rest for 20 minutes.

7. While ham rests, stir vegetables and continue to roast until fully tender, 20 to 30 minutes. Transfer vegetables to serving bowl, toss with parsley, and cover to keep warm.

8. Whisk ¾ cup reserved ham juice into remaining glaze and microwave until thickened and saucy, 3 to 5 minutes; transfer to serving bowl and cover to keep warm. Carve ham and serve, passing sauce separately.

CARVING A SPIRAL-SLICED HAM

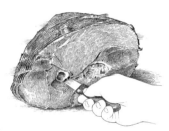  

With the tip of a paring or carving knife, cut around the bone to loosen the attached slices. Using a long carving knife, slice the meat horizontally above the bone and through the spiral-cut slices, towards the back of the ham. Pull the cut meat away from the bone and cut between the slices to fully separate them. Beginning at the tapered end, slice above the bone to remove the remaining chunk of meat. Flip the ham over and repeat the procedure for the other side.

Baked Brie in Phyllo Cups

You can either use store-bought onion jam here, or make the Caramelized Onion Jam with Port (page 50). Other flavors of jam, jelly, or preserves can be substituted for the onion jam if desired.

45	frozen mini phyllo shells (3 packages)
8	ounces Brie cheese, rind removed, cut into ½-inch pieces
⅓	cup caramelized onion jam
2	tablespoons minced fresh parsley

Adjust oven rack to middle position and heat oven to 350 degrees. Line large rimmed baking sheet with parchment paper. Place phyllo shells on prepared baking sheet. Place piece of Brie in each cup and spoon generous ¼ teaspoon jam over top. Bake until cheese has melted and phyllo cups are golden brown and crisp, 6 to 8 minutes. Sprinkle with parsley and serve warm.

Shrimp Salad on Endive

✓ **WHY THIS RECIPE WORKS**

For a shrimp salad with firm and tender shrimp and a dressing that wouldn't mask the flavor of the shrimp in a sea of mayonnaise, we added the shrimp to a cold court bouillon (a flavorful liquid of lemon juice, herbs, spices and water) and then slowly heated them together over medium heat. The gentle, slow cooking enabled the poaching liquid to add more flavor to the shrimp and also kept them moist and tender. Mayonnaise was still the best binder for the shrimp, adding moisture and fat, as long as we kept the amount modest. Shallot, fresh herbs (parsley and tarragon), and lemon juice perked up and rounded out the flavors. Chopped apple added sweet crunch and leaves of endive made an ideal vehicle: crisp and a little bitter, which contrasted nicely with the creamy dressing and sweet shrimp.

If your shrimp are smaller than 21 to 25 per pound, the cooking time will obviously be slightly shorter.

1½   pounds extra-large shrimp (21 to 25 per pound), peeled, deveined, and tails removed

6   tablespoons lemon juice (2 lemons), spent lemon halves reserved

8   sprigs fresh parsley plus 1 tablespoon minced

6   sprigs fresh tarragon plus 1 tablespoon minced

1   teaspoon whole peppercorns

1   tablespoon sugar

    Salt and pepper

⅔   cup mayonnaise

1   shallot, minced

1   Granny Smith apple, peeled, cored, and chopped fine

4   large heads Belgian endive (1½ pounds), leaves separated

1. Combine shrimp, ¼ cup lemon juice, spent lemon halves, parsley sprigs, tarragon sprigs, peppercorns, sugar, and 1 teaspoon salt with 3 cups cold water in medium saucepan. Place saucepan over medium heat and cook shrimp, stirring often, until pink, firm to touch, and centers are no longer translucent, 8 to 10 minutes. Off heat, cover and let shrimp sit for 2 minutes.

2. Meanwhile, fill medium bowl with ice water. Drain shrimp, discarding aromatics, then plunge immediately into ice water to chill, about 3 minutes. Drain shrimp well, discarding any ice, and dry thoroughly with paper towels. Chop shrimp into small pieces.

3. Whisk mayonnaise, shallot, remaining 2 tablespoons lemon juice, minced parsley, and minced tarragon together in medium bowl. Stir in shrimp and apple and season with salt and pepper to taste. (Shrimp salad can be refrigerated for up to 1 day.) Lay endive leaves on large platter, spoon 1 tablespoon shrimp salad into each leaf, and serve. (Makes about 36 leaves.)

DEVEINING SHRIMP

Hold the peeled shrimp between your thumb and forefinger and cut down the length of its back, about ⅛ to ¼ inch deep, with a sharp paring knife. If the shrimp has a vein, it will be exposed and can be pulled out easily. Once you have freed the vein with the tip of the knife, just touch the knife to a paper towel and the vein will slip off the knife and stick to the towel.

Baby Greens with Strawberries

We like the combination of baby spinach and mesclun greens in this salad, but any type of baby greens will taste nice here.

I	shallot, minced
3	tablespoons cider vinegar
2	tablespoons honey
I	tablespoon Dijon mustard
I	tablespoon poppy seeds
	Salt and pepper
¾	cup extra-virgin olive oil
13	ounces baby spinach (13 cups)
5	ounces mesclun greens (5 cups)
I	pound strawberries, hulled and quartered (3 cups)

Whisk shallot, vinegar, honey, mustard, poppy seeds, ½ teaspoon salt, and ¼ teaspoon pepper together in medium bowl. Whisking constantly, drizzle in olive oil until well combined. In large bowl, gently toss spinach, mesclun, and strawberries. Just before serving, whisk dressing to re-emulsify, drizzle over salad, and toss gently to coat. Serve.

✔ WHY THIS RECIPE WORKS
We used mesclun greens to fluff up spinach leaves and added fresh strawberries for a bright, clean flavor. For a fruity, bright dressing, we balanced a good amount of honey with cider vinegar. Dijon mustard cut through the sweetness with a nice pungency, while poppy seeds added nutty crunch.

Buttermilk Biscuits

Baking the biscuits upside down ensures a more even rise.

5	cups (25 ounces) all-purpose flour
2	tablespoons sugar
2	tablespoons baking powder
2	teaspoons salt
I½	teaspoons baking soda
16	tablespoons unsalted butter, cut into ½-inch pieces and chilled
6	tablespoons shortening, cut into ½-inch pieces and chilled
I½	cups buttermilk

1. Adjust oven rack to middle position and heat oven to 450 degrees. Line baking sheet with parchment paper.

2. Pulse flour, sugar, baking powder, salt, and baking soda in food processor until combined, about 5 pulses. Scatter butter and shortening evenly over top and continue to pulse until mixture resembles coarse meal, 12 to 15 pulses.

3. Transfer flour mixture to large bowl. Stir in buttermilk with rubber spatula until dough comes together. Turn dough out onto well-floured counter. Lightly flour hands and dough and knead dough gently until uniform, about 30 seconds. Roll dough into 12-inch round, about 1 inch thick.

4. Using floured 2½-inch biscuit cutter, stamp out 15 biscuits, gently patting dough scraps back into uniform 1-inch-thick piece as needed. Arrange biscuits upside down on prepared baking sheet, spaced about 1 inch apart. (Unbaked biscuits can be covered and refrigerated up to 24 hours; bake as directed.)

5. Bake for 5 minutes. Rotate pan, reduce oven temperature to 400 degrees, and continue to bake until golden brown, 12 to 15 minutes. Transfer to wire rack, let cool 5 to 10 minutes. Serve warm. (Biscuits can be held at room temperature up to 4 hours; rewarm in 400-degree oven for 5 minutes before serving. Makes 15 biscuits.)

✔ WHY THIS RECIPE WORKS
For perfect, fluffy buttermilk biscuits, we pulsed chilled butter and shortening with the dry ingredients in the food processor so that they would be incorporated quickly without melting. (You want the pieces of fat to melt in the oven, creating pockets of steam, which result in flaky biscuits.) Stirring the buttermilk into the mixture by hand and gently kneading the dough prevents the overworking that leads to tough biscuits. For even, not lopsided, biscuits, we baked them upside down (with the flat underside on top, they rose evenly).

Apricot-Almond Bundt Cake

✔ WHY THIS RECIPE WORKS
To really fortify the apricot flavor of our cake we used both dried apricots and apricot jam. We first chopped the dried apricots then reconstituted them in hot water to soften them. The chopped apricots gave the cake slices an appealing speckled appearance. The apricot jam further built up the apricot flavor and made the cake deliciously moist.

Prepping the Bundt pan with a butter-flour paste ensures that the cake will release from the pan easily and in one piece; be sure to use the paste even if you have a nonstick Bundt pan.

PAN PREP

1	tablespoon unsalted butter, melted
1	tablespoon all-purpose flour

CAKE

1	cup dried apricots, chopped fine
3	cups (15 ounces) all-purpose flour
1	teaspoon salt
1	teaspoon baking powder
½	teaspoon baking soda
½	cup buttermilk, room temperature
1	tablespoon vanilla extract
1	tablespoon grated lemon zest plus 1 tablespoon juice
18	tablespoons unsalted butter (2¼ sticks), cut into pieces and softened
1½	cups (10½ ounces) sugar
½	cup apricot jam
3	large eggs plus 1 large yolk, room temperature
½	cup slivered almonds, toasted (see page 29) and chopped coarse

CITRUS GLAZE

1¾	cups (7 ounces) confectioners' sugar
1	teaspoon grated orange zest plus ¼ cup juice
	Pinch salt

1. FOR THE PAN PREP: Mix butter and flour into paste. Using pastry brush, thoroughly coat interior of 12-cup Bundt pan.

2. FOR THE CAKE: Adjust oven rack to lower-middle position and heat oven to 350 degrees. In small bowl, cover apricots with boiling water and let sit until softened and plump, about 5 minutes; drain apricots and pat dry. In medium bowl, whisk flour, salt, baking powder, and baking soda together. In another medium bowl, whisk buttermilk, vanilla, lemon zest, and lemon juice together.

3. Using stand mixer fitted with paddle, beat butter and sugar together on medium speed until pale and fluffy, about 3 minutes. Add jam and beat until incorporated. Add eggs and egg yolk, 1 at a time, and beat until combined.

4. Reduce speed to low and add flour mixture in 3 additions, alternating with 2 additions of buttermilk mixture, scraping down bowl as needed. Add softened apricots and almonds and mix until incorporated.

5. Scrape batter into prepared pan and smooth top. Wipe any drops of batter off sides of pan and gently tap pan on counter to release air bubbles. Bake until skewer inserted in center comes out with few crumbs attached, 50 to 60 minutes, rotating pan halfway through baking.

6. Let cake cool in pan for 10 minutes, and then flip out onto wire rack. Let cake cool completely, about 2 hours. (Cake can be wrapped tightly and stored at room temperature for up to 1 day.)

7. FOR THE GLAZE: Whisk all ingredients together in medium bowl until smooth and let sit until thickened, about 25 minutes. Pour glaze over top of cooled cake, letting glaze drip down sides. Let glaze set before serving, about 25 minutes.

New Year's Eve Blowout

THE GAME PLAN
⤝

NEW YEAR'S EVE BLOWOUT

⇒ *Serves 12* ⇐

Oysters on the Half Shell with Ginger Mignonette Sauce
Broiled Shrimp Cocktail with Coriander and Lemon ⇒ Stuffed Beef Tenderloin
Sour Cream Smashed Potatoes ⇒ Haricots Verts with Sea Salt
Triple-Chocolate Mousse Cake

Stuffed Beef Tenderloin

When shopping, note that center-cut beef tenderloins are also referred to as Châteaubriand. We prefer to use kosher salt in the oil rub in step 3; if using table salt, reduce all salt amounts in the recipe by half. See page 310 for information on butterflying the roasts.

STUFFING

- 1 tablespoon unsalted butter
- 2 teaspoons olive oil
- 2 onions, halved and sliced ¼ inch thick
- 1 teaspoon kosher salt
- ¼ teaspoon pepper
- 1 pound cremini mushrooms, trimmed and chopped coarse
- 2 garlic cloves, minced
- 1 cup Madeira or sweet Marsala

ROASTS

- 2 (2- to 3-pound) center-cut beef tenderloin roasts, trimmed
  Kosher salt and pepper
- 1 ounce baby spinach (1 cup)
- 6 tablespoons olive oil

HERB BUTTER

- 8 tablespoons unsalted butter, softened
- 2 tablespoons whole grain mustard
- 2 tablespoons minced fresh parsley
- 2 garlic cloves, minced
- 1½ teaspoons minced fresh thyme
- ¼ teaspoon kosher salt
- ¼ teaspoon pepper

1. FOR THE STUFFING: Heat butter and oil in 12-inch nonstick skillet over medium-high heat until butter is melted. Add onions, salt, and pepper and cook until onions are softened, about 10 minutes. Stir in mushrooms and cook until all moisture has evaporated, about 10 minutes. Reduce heat to medium and continue to cook, stirring frequently, until vegetables are deeply browned and sticky, about 15 minutes. Stir in garlic and cook until fragrant, 30 seconds. Stir in Madeira and cook, scraping up any browned bits, until evaporated, about 5 minutes. Transfer stuffing to plate and let cool.

2. FOR THE ROASTS: Using chef's knife, butterfly each roast by inserting chef's knife 1 inch from bottom of roast and cutting through meat horizontally stopping just before the edge; open up meat like a book and cut diagonally into thicker portion of roast, opening up this flap and pressing meat flat. Season with salt and pepper, then spread stuffing over top, leaving ½-inch border at edge. Lay spinach on top of stuffing. Roll each piece of meat lengthwise into tidy roast and tie firmly with kitchen twine at 1½-inch intervals, staring at ends and working towards center. (Roasts can be refrigerated for up to 1 day.)

3. Combine 2 tablespoons olive oil, 1 tablespoon salt, and 1 tablespoon pepper in bowl. Rub roasts with oil mixture and let stand at room temperature for 1 hour. Adjust oven rack to middle position and heat oven to 450 degrees. *continued* ➤

✓ WHY THIS RECIPE WORKS

For a deeply charred crust, a tender, rosy-pink interior, and an intensely flavored stuffing that stayed neatly rolled in the meat, we chose the almost perfectly cylindrical Châteaubriand and used a "double-butterfly" procedure—making two cuts so the roasts opened up into three parts (like a business letter). In this way each roast accommodated 50 percent more filling than a conventionally butterflied roast. We created a suitable crust for our tenderloins in a shortened cooking time by coating the exterior of the roasts with a layer of kosher salt an hour before searing, which allowed the salt to begin to break down the protein fibers in the outermost layer of meat, so that it browned quickly. We made an intense stuffing with earthy cremini and caramelized onions, which contributed sweetness and bound the mushrooms into a thick, slightly sticky, jamlike stuffing that stayed in place during carving.

Line rimmed baking sheet with aluminum foil and top with wire rack.

4. Heat 2 tablespoons oil in 12-inch nonstick skillet over medium-high heat until just smoking. Brown 1 roast on all sides, 8 to 10 minutes. Transfer browned roast, seam side down, to prepared wire rack. Wipe skillet clean with paper towels, then repeat with remaining 2 tablespoons oil and remaining roast; transfer to wire rack. (Browned roasts can be held at room temperature for up to 1 hour before continuing.) Place roasts in oven

and cook until meat registers 125 degrees (for medium-rare), 20 to 25 minutes.

5. FOR THE HERB BUTTER: Mash ingredients together in bowl. (Butter can be refrigerated for up to 1 week; let soften before using.)

6. Transfer tenderloins to carving board. Spread half of herb butter over top of meat, loosely tent with foil, and let rest for 15 minutes. Slice roasts between pieces of twine. Remove twine and serve, topping individual portions with remaining herb butter.

STUFFING AND TYING TENDERLOIN

Insert a chef's knife about 1 inch from the bottom of the roast and cut through the meat horizontally, stopping just before the edge. Open up the meat like a book. Make another cut diagonally into the thicker portion of the roast. Open up this flap and gently press the meat flat. Spread the filling evenly over the meat, leaving ½-inch border at the edges. Lay the spinach leaves evenly on top of the filling. Using both hands, roll up the tenderloin, making it as compact as possible without squeezing out the filling. Tightly tie the roast with kitchen twine at 1½-inch intervals, starting at the ends and working your way to the middle; working inward from the ends prevents the filling from being squeezed out.

Broiled Shrimp Cocktail with Coriander and Lemon

✔ WHY THIS RECIPE WORKS
For an updated version of classic shrimp cocktail, we skipped the poaching and used the high heat of the broiler and a spice rub to give the shrimp great flavor. Our simple rub got a huge boost from a little sugar. The sugar caramelized quickly under the broiler, adding a nice sear on the outside of the shrimp and helping to bring out the fresh, sweet shrimp flavor.

It's important to dry the shrimp thoroughly before cooking. Other fresh herbs, such as dill, basil, cilantro, or mint, can be substituted for the tarragon. We prefer to use jumbo shrimp here, but extra-large shrimp (21 to 25 per pound) can be substituted; if using smaller shrimp, reduce the broiling time by about 2 minutes.

SAUCE
1 cup mayonnaise
¼ cup lemon juice (2 lemons)
3 scallions, minced
3 tablespoons minced fresh tarragon
½ teaspoon salt
¼ teaspoon pepper

SHRIMP
1 teaspoon salt
1 teaspoon ground coriander
½ teaspoon pepper
½ teaspoon sugar
⅛ teaspoon cayenne pepper
3 pounds jumbo shrimp (16 to 20 per pound), peeled and deveined (see page 304)
3 tablespoons olive oil

1. FOR THE SAUCE: Stir all ingredients together in serving bowl. Cover and refrigerate until flavors have blended, at least 30 minutes and up to 1 day. (Makes 1½ cups.)

2. FOR THE SHRIMP: Adjust oven rack 3 inches from broiler element and heat broiler. (If necessary, set upside-down rimmed baking sheet on oven rack to get closer to broiler element.) Combine salt, coriander, pepper, sugar, and cayenne in small bowl. Pat shrimp dry with paper towels, then toss with oil and spice mixture in large bowl.

3. Spread half of shrimp in single layer on rimmed baking sheet. Broil shrimp until opaque and edges begin to brown, about 6 minutes. Transfer shrimp to serving platter and cover to keep warm. Repeat with remaining shrimp; transfer to platter. Serve with sauce.

Oysters on the Half Shell with Ginger Mignonette Sauce

In addition to the mignonette sauce, consider serving the oysters with lemon wedges, prepared horseradish, and hot sauce. Serving the oysters on a bed of crushed ice helps to keep them both chilled and upright; to quickly crush a large amount of ice, place ice cubes in a double layer of zipper-lock bags and pound with a mallet or rolling pin.

⅔	cup rice vinegar
1	teaspoon grated orange zest plus
	⅓ cup juice
1	shallot, minced
2	scallions, minced
1	teaspoon grated fresh ginger
½	teaspoon sugar
½	teaspoon pepper
36	large oysters, well scrubbed

Whisk vinegar, orange zest and juice, shallot, scallions, ginger, sugar, and pepper together in serving bowl. Line large serving platter with ½ inch crushed ice. Using oyster knife and dish towel, carefully pry off and discard flat-sided shell from top of each oyster. Run knife underneath oyster in bottom shell to loosen completely, then nestle into crushed ice. Serve with sauce.

✔ **WHY THIS RECIPE WORKS**
Raw oysters served with a bracing mignonette are a simple but unbeatable first course. We traded out the red wine vinegar of traditional mignonette sauce for orange juice and rice vinegar infused with a kick of fresh ginger. We rounded out the sauce with orange zest, minced scallions, a little black pepper, and a touch of sugar for balance. It's crucial to serve oysters ice cold; nestle them in a bed of crushed ice to maintain a chilled temperature. They should also be opened as carefully as possible, in order to preserve as much of the brine (or liquor) that surrounds the oyster meat.

SHUCKING OYSTERS

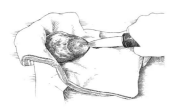 

Holding the oyster cupped side down in a dish towel, locate the hinge with the tip of an oyster knife. Push between the edges of the shells, wiggling the knife back and forth to pry the shells apart. Detach the meat from the top shell and discard the shell. Slide the knife underneath the oyster to sever the muscle that attaches it to the bottom shell. Try to keep the oyster flat as you work to keep the flavorful juices from spilling out.

Sour Cream Smashed Potatoes

✔ WHY THIS RECIPE WORKS
Our smashed potato recipe features a good contrast of textures, with chunky potatoes and skins bound by a rich, creamy puree. Low-starch, high-moisture red potatoes were the best choice here, as they hold their shape and texture through cooking. For the best chunky texture, we smashed the potatoes with a rubber spatula (you can also use the back of a wooden spoon). To prevent glueyness caused by overworking, we combined sour cream with the melted butter and other dairy before adding the mixture to the cooked potatoes. This technique required less stirring of the potatoes, and helped meld flavors.

Do not peel or cut the potatoes before cooking. We prefer to use small red potatoes, measuring 1 to 2 inches in diameter, in this recipe; if using larger potatoes, you will need to increase the simmering time in step 1.

6	pounds small red potatoes
12	tablespoons unsalted butter
12	scallions, whites minced and greens sliced thin
3	cups sour cream
1½	cups half-and-half, plus extra as needed
	Salt and pepper

1. Cover potatoes by 1 inch water in large pot and bring to boil over high heat. Reduce to simmer and cook until potatoes are tender, about 30 minutes.

2. Meanwhile, melt butter in medium saucepan over medium-low heat. Add scallion whites and cook until softened, about 5 minutes. Whisk in sour cream, half-and-half, 1 tablespoon salt, and ¾ teaspoon pepper and heat through, about 1 minute. Remove from heat and cover to keep warm.

3. Drain potatoes well, then return to pot and let sit 5 minutes. Using rubber spatula, break potatoes into large chunks. Fold in sour cream mixture until incorporated and only small chunks of potato remain. Stir in scallion greens and season with salt and pepper to taste. Stir in extra half-and-half, warmed, as needed to adjust consistency. Serve.

Haricots Verts with Sea Salt

✔ WHY THIS RECIPE WORKS
For a classic but simple dish to complement our rich stuffed tenderloin, we chose haricots verts, French green beans. A quick stint in boiling salted water was all these slender beans needed to soften them slightly without losing their color.

We prefer the flaky, coarse grains of sea salt for seasoning here, but kosher salt can be substituted. Use table salt for the cooking water.

3	pounds haricots verts, trimmed
	Salt and pepper
2	tablespoons extra-virgin olive oil
	Sea salt

Bring 6 quarts water to boil in large pot over high heat. Stir in haricots verts and 1 tablespoon salt and cook until crisp-tender, 4 to 8 minutes. Drain beans and return to pot. Toss gently with olive oil, season with sea salt and pepper to taste, and serve.

Triple-Chocolate Mousse Cake

This recipe requires a springform pan with sides at least 3 inches tall. It's important to make each layer in sequential order. Be sure to let the bottom layer cool completely before adding the middle layer. Our favorite brand of bittersweet chocolate is Ghirardelli, and our favorite brand of white chocolate chips is Guittard.

BOTTOM LAYER

- 7 ounces bittersweet chocolate, chopped fine
- 6 tablespoons unsalted butter, cut into 6 pieces
- ¾ teaspoon instant espresso powder
- 4 large eggs, separated
- 1½ teaspoons vanilla extract
  Pinch cream of tartar
  Pinch salt
- ⅓ cup packed (2⅓ ounces) light brown sugar

MIDDLE LAYER

- 7 ounces bittersweet chocolate, chopped fine
- 2 tablespoons Dutch-processed cocoa
- 5 tablespoons hot water
- 1½ cups heavy cream, chilled
- 1 tablespoon granulated sugar
- ⅛ teaspoon salt

TOP LAYER

- ¾ teaspoon unflavored gelatin
- 1 tablespoon water
- 1 cup (6 ounces) white chocolate chips
- 1½ cups heavy cream, chilled
  Shaved chocolate or cocoa powder for serving (optional)

1. FOR THE BOTTOM LAYER: Adjust oven rack to middle position and heat oven to 325 degrees. Grease 9½-inch springform pan. Melt chocolate, butter, and espresso in large heatproof bowl set over saucepan filled with 1 inch of barely simmering water, stirring occasionally, until smooth.

Remove from heat and let mixture cool slightly, about 5 minutes. Whisk in egg yolks and vanilla; set aside.

2. In stand mixer fitted with whisk, whip egg whites, cream of tartar, and salt together on medium-low speed until foamy, about 1 minute. Add half of sugar and whip until combined, about 15 seconds. Add remaining sugar, increase speed to high, and whip until soft peaks form, about 1 minute longer. Gently fold one-third of beaten egg whites into chocolate mixture to lighten. Fold in remaining egg whites until no white streaks remain. Carefully transfer batter to prepared springform pan and smooth top.

3. Bake until cake has risen, is firm around edges, and center has just set but is still soft (center will spring back when gently pressed with finger), 13 to 18 minutes. Let cake cool completely in pan, about 1 hour. (Cake will collapse as it cools.)

4. FOR THE MIDDLE LAYER: Melt chocolate in large heatproof bowl set over saucepan filled with 1 inch of barely simmering water, stirring occasionally, until smooth; let cool slightly, 2 to 5 minutes. In small bowl, combine cocoa and hot water.

5. Using stand mixer fitted with whisk, whip cream, sugar, and salt on medium-low speed until foamy, about 1 minute. Increase speed to high and whip until soft peaks form, 1 to 3 minutes.

6. Whisk cocoa mixture into melted chocolate until smooth. Gently fold one-third of whipped cream into chocolate mixture to lighten. Fold in *continued* ➤

✔ **WHY THIS RECIPE WORKS**
Triple-chocolate mousse cake is a truly decadent dessert. We aimed to create a triple-decker that was incrementally lighter in texture—and richness—from bottom to top. For simplicity's sake, we decided to build the whole dessert, layer by layer, in the same springform pan. For a base layer that had the heft to support the upper two tiers, we chose flourless chocolate cake instead of the typical mousse. Folding egg whites into the batter helped lighten the cake without affecting its structural integrity. For the middle layer, we started with a traditional chocolate mousse, but the texture seemed too heavy when combined with the cake, so we removed the eggs and cut back on the chocolate a bit—this resulted in a lighter, creamier layer. And for the crowning layer, we made an easy white chocolate mousse by folding whipped cream into melted white chocolate, and to prevent the soft mousse from oozing during slicing, we added a little gelatin to the mix.

remaining whipped cream until no white streaks remain. Spoon mixture into cake pan on top of bottom layer and smooth top. Wipe any drops of batter off sides of pan and gently tap pan on counter to release air bubbles. Refrigerate cake while preparing top layer.

7. FOR THE TOP LAYER: In small bowl, sprinkle gelatin over water and let sit for at least 5 minutes. Place white chocolate in medium heatproof bowl. Bring ½ cup cream to simmer in small saucepan over medium-high heat. Off heat, add gelatin mixture and stir until fully dissolved. Pour cream mixture over white chocolate, cover, and let sit for 5 minutes. Whisk mixture smooth and let cool to room temperature, stirring occasionally.

8. Using stand mixer fitted with whisk, whip remaining 1 cup cream on medium-low speed until foamy, about 1 minute. Increase speed to high and whip until soft peaks form, 1 to 3 minutes. Gently fold one-third of whipped cream into white chocolate mixture to lighten. Fold remaining whipped cream into white chocolate mixture until no white streaks remain. Spoon mixture into cake pan on top of middle layer and smooth top. Refrigerate cake until chilled and set, at least 2½ hours and up to 1 day.

9. To serve, let cake soften at room temperature for 30 to 45 minutes. Garnish top of cake with shaved chocolate and/or dust with cocoa, if using. Run thin knife between cake and sides of pan; remove sides of pan. Run cleaned knife along outside of cake to smooth. Using cheese wire (or dental floss), gently slice cake, wiping wire clean as needed between slices.

EVEN EASIER ⤙ Don't have time to make a mousse cake? Buy about 3 dozen chocolate truffles from a good chocolatier, and serve with Kir Imperials. To make a Kir Imperial, pour 1 tablespoon Chambord (or other raspberry liqueur) into champagne flutes, add a fresh raspberry, then fill each glass with dry champagne. You will need 2 (750-ml) bottles of champagne to make 12 Kir Imperials.

SLICING A TRIPLE-CHOCOLATE MOUSSE CAKE

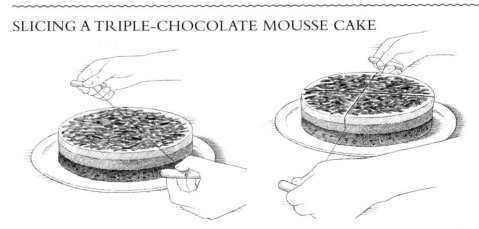

To create perfectly smooth slices of mousse cake, the best tool is not a knife. It's a cheese wire—the minimal surface area produces less drag for cleaner, neater slices. (If you don't have a cheese wire, dental floss will work almost as well.) Hold the handles and pull the wire taut. Using your thumbs to apply even pressure, slice down through the cake. Wipe the wire clean with a dry towel. Make a second cut, perpendicular to the first. Continue to make cuts around the circumference.

Classic Thanksgiving Dinner

THE GAME PLAN
‹›

FIVE DAYS AHEAD...

THAW FROZEN TURKEY:
1 day for every 4 pounds

**MAKE TURKEY BROTH
FOR GRAVY:** 15 minutes
(plus 4 hours for roasting,
simmering, and cooling)

**ASSEMBLE AND FREEZE
APPLE PIE:** 1½ hours (plus
2½ hours for chilling)

ONE DAY AHEAD...

**ASSEMBLE BREAD
STUFFING:** 1½ hours

**MAKE CRANBERRY
SAUCE:** 20 minutes
(plus 1 hour for chilling)

MAKE GRAVY: 45 minutes

MAKE PECAN PIE:
1¼ hours (plus 5 hours for
chilling, baking, and cooling)

ON THE DAY OF...

**BAKE AND COOL
FROZEN APPLE PIE:**
3 hours

**ROAST AND REST
TURKEY:** 4 hours (plus
15 minutes for carving)

**MAKE WHIPPED
POTATOES:** 1¼ hours

BAKE BREAD STUFFING:
1 hour (while roasted
turkey rests)

MAKE PEAS: 20 minutes

REHEAT GRAVY:
10 minutes

**ASSEMBLE CHEESE
BOARD:** 5 minutes

REHEAT PIES: 15 minutes

CLASSIC THANKSGIVING DINNER

➤ Serves 12 ➤

Big American Cheese Board ➤ Roast Turkey for a Crowd
Make-Ahead Turkey Gravy ➤ Whipped Potatoes ➤ Herbed Bread Stuffing
Cranberry Sauce with Pears and Ginger ➤ Buttery Peas with Shallots and Thyme
Deep-Dish Apple Pie ➤ Classic Pecan Pie

Roast Turkey for a Crowd

Be careful to dry the skin thoroughly before brushing the turkey with butter or it will have spotty brown skin. Flipping the bird during roasting helps produce evenly cooked meat, but you may opt not to rotate it; in this case, skip the step of lining the V-rack with foil, roast the bird breast side up for the entire cooking time, and be prepared to extend the cooking time by ½ hour.

1   (18- to 22-pound) frozen Butterball
    or kosher turkey
4   tablespoons unsalted butter, melted
    Salt and pepper
1   cup water, plus extra as needed

1. Place frozen turkey in large disposable aluminum roasting pan supported by baking sheet and let it thaw in refrigerator. Plan on 1 day of defrosting for every 4 pounds of turkey; 20-pound bird will take about 5 days. (To thaw frozen turkey quickly, leave wrapped in original packaging, and place in large bucket of cold water. Plan on 30 minutes of defrosting for every 1 pound of turkey; 20-pound bird will take about 10 hours. Change cold water every ½ hour to guard against bacteria growth.)

2. Adjust oven rack to lowest position, remove remaining oven racks, and heat oven to 425 degrees. Line large V-rack with heavy-duty aluminum foil, poke holes in foil, and set it inside 15 by 12-inch roasting pan.

3. Remove and discard any plastic or metal trussing device holding drumsticks. Remove and discard turkey neck and giblet packet; if timing permits, you may add them to Make-Ahead Turkey Gravy (page 319). Pat turkey dry with paper towels, then brush with 2 tablespoons melted butter and sprinkle with ½ teaspoon salt and ½ teaspoon pepper. Set turkey breast side down in V-rack. Pat back of turkey dry with paper towels, then brush with remaining 2 tablespoons butter and sprinkle with ½ teaspoon salt and ½ teaspoon pepper.

4. Pour water into roasting pan. Roast turkey for 1 hour. Remove turkey from oven and, using clean dish towels or potholders, flip turkey breast side up in V-rack. Lower oven temperature to 325 degrees and continue to roast turkey, adding more water as needed to prevent drippings in pan from burning, until breast registers 160 degrees and thighs register 175 degrees, about 2 hours longer.

5. Tip turkey to drain juices from cavity into roasting pan. Transfer turkey to carving board and let it rest until ready to carve, about 45 minutes. (If desired, scrape up drippings in roasting pan and pour into fat separator; let drippings sit until fat has separated, about 20 minutes. Add defatted drippings to gravy to taste.) Carve turkey and serve with gravy.

⚓ WHY THIS RECIPE WORKS
Unless you have access to multiple ovens, only a very large turkey will do when you've got a crowd coming to dinner. But finding a container large enough to brine a gargantuan bird can be tricky. Instead, we chose a Butterball turkey, which has already been brined for juicy flavor (a kosher bird, which has been salted, works well too). A combination of high and low heat resulted in a tender, juicy bird with deeply browned skin. After roasting, we allowed the turkey to rest for 45 minutes so the juices would redistribute, but didn't tent it with foil so the skin wouldn't become soggy; this resting time also gave us time to bake the stuffing.

How to Carve a Turkey

Carving a turkey is an art form. And since most cooks tackle this task but once a year, it's a hard task to master. Below we've assembled step-by-step instructions for the best way to carve up the big bird. The overall idea is to cut up the turkey, and arrange the pieces attractively on a large serving platter as you go. Also, have two carving boards (one for the carcass and the other for slicing the meat into serving portions) along with a couple different types of knives on hand, including a chef's knife, a boning knife, and either a slicing knife or electric knife. As you transfer the meat to the platter, keep the meat covered with aluminum foil to prevent it from cooling off and drying out.

1. Start by slicing the skin between the meat of the breast and the leg.

2. Continue to cut down to the joint, using a fork to pull the leg away from the bird while the tip of the knife severs the joint between the leg and breast.

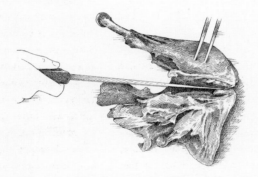

3. Lay the leg skin side down and use the blade to locate the joint between the thigh and drumstick (where the thigh and drumstick form the sharpest angle). Cut through the joint. If you have properly located it, this should be easy, as you will not be cutting through bone.

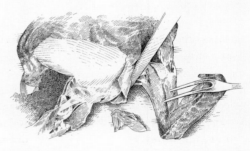

4. Use a fork to pull the wing away from the body. Cut through the joint between the wing and the breast to separate the wing from the bird.

5. Using the tip of the knife, cut along the length of the breastbone. Angle the blade of the knife and slice along the line of the rib cage to remove the entire breast half. Use a fork to pull the breast half away from the rib cage in a single piece.

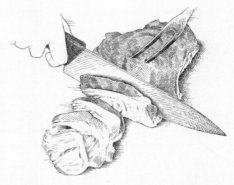

6. Cut thin slices from the breast, slicing across the grain of the meat.

Big American Cheese Board

It's fun to highlight American-made cheese and sausage on this American holiday, but obviously all types of cheese will work well here.

8 ounces sharp cheddar cheese, room temperature
8 ounces Maytag Blue cheese, room temperature
8 ounces soft goat cheese, room temperature
8 ounces sliced cured sausage or hard salami

3 cups cranberry-nut trail mix
1½ cups fig jam or fruit chutney
1 large bunch seedless red grapes
   Crackers and/or thinly sliced baguette

Arrange all ingredients attractively on large serving platter or cutting board and serve.

✔ **WHY THIS RECIPE WORKS**
When you're hosting Thanksgiving for a crowd, it's best to keep things simple when it comes to appetizers since dinner alone is labor intensive, and this classic cheese board fits the bill.

Make-Ahead Turkey Gravy

Six drumsticks can be substituted for the thighs; however, we found drumsticks to be a bit more unwieldy. Depending on when you make the gravy, you may be able to add the neck (hacked into chunks) and giblets (except the liver) from the turkey to the roasting pan in step 1. For extra flavor, we like to add the defatted roast turkey drippings (from step 5 of the Roast Turkey for a Crowd recipe, page 317) to the gravy; the gravy will still taste great, however, if these drippings are left out.

6 turkey thighs, trimmed, or 9 wings, separated at joints
2 carrots, chopped coarse
2 celery ribs, chopped coarse
2 onions, chopped coarse
1 head garlic, top quarter cut off to expose garlic cloves
   Vegetable oil spray
12 cups low-sodium chicken broth, plus extra as needed
2 cups dry white wine
12 sprigs fresh thyme
   Unsalted butter, as needed
1 cup all-purpose flour
   Salt and pepper
   Defatted drippings from roasted turkey (optional)

1. Adjust oven rack to middle position and heat oven to 450 degrees. Place thighs, carrots, celery, onions, and garlic in roasting pan, spray with vegetable oil, and toss well. Roast, stirring occasionally, until everything is well browned, 1 to 1½ hours.

2. Transfer contents of roasting pan to Dutch oven. Add broth, wine, and thyme, and bring to boil. Reduce heat to low and simmer slowly, stirring occasionally, until broth is brown, flavorful, and measures about 8 cups when strained, about 1½ hours. Strain broth through fine-mesh strainer into large container, pressing on solids to extract as much liquid as possible; discard solids. Let broth sit until fat has risen to top, 15 to 20 minutes. (Broth can be refrigerated for up to 2 days.)

3. Spoon off and reserve ½ cup of fat (add butter as needed if short on turkey fat). Heat fat in Dutch oven over medium-high heat until bubbling. Whisk in flour and cook, stirring constantly, until well browned, 3 to 7 minutes. Slowly whisk in turkey broth and bring to boil. Reduce heat to medium-low and simmer until gravy is very thick, 10 to 15 minutes. (Gravy can be refrigerated for up to 2 days and frozen for up to 1 month. Thaw, if necessary, and reheat in saucepan over medium heat until bubbling.)

4. Before serving, add defatted roast turkey drippings to taste, if desired. Stir in additional chicken broth as needed to adjust gravy consistency, and season with salt and pepper to taste. (Makes about 2 quarts.)

✔ **WHY THIS RECIPE WORKS**
Since this recipe doesn't depend on drippings from the big bird for flavoring, you can make this gravy days before your crowd arrives. Turkey thighs roast with aromatics to caramelize and provide deep flavor and body to the chicken stock and white wine base. Cooking the roux to a dark brown color eliminates unpleasant raw flour flavor and adds richness to the gravy.

Whipped Potatoes

WHY THIS RECIPE WORKS
Conventional wisdom may warn against overmixing potatoes, but we found that whipping potatoes yields a surprisingly light, fluffy texture with no trace of gumminess. Rinsing the potatoes before cooking gets rid of their surface starch, the main culprit behind gummy mashed potatoes, and steaming—rather than boiling—the potatoes keeps them out of the water and less likely to absorb liquid. A quick toss in the pot dries the potatoes further, so that they whip up to maximum fluffiness in the mixer. Since the texture of the potatoes is already creamy, a mixture of melted butter and whole milk, rather than heavy cream, moistens and flavors the potatoes.

Do not attempt to cook the potatoes in a pot smaller than 12 quarts; if you don't have a large enough pot, use two smaller pots and cook the potatoes in two simultaneous batches. If your steamer basket has short legs (under 1¾ inches), the potatoes will sit in water as they cook and get wet. To prevent this, use balls of aluminum foil as steamer basket stilts. A stand mixer fitted with a whisk attachment yields the smoothest potatoes, but you can also use a hand-held mixer and a large bowl.

6   pounds russet potatoes, peeled and cut into 1-inch pieces
2   cups whole milk
12 tablespoons unsalted butter, cut into pieces
2   teaspoons salt
¾   teaspoon pepper

1. Rinse potatoes in colander under cold water until water runs clear, about 1 minute; drain well. Fill 12-quart stockpot with 1 inch water and bring to boil. Place steamer basket in pot, add potatoes, and cover. Reduce heat to medium and cook until potatoes are tender, 25 to 30 minutes.

2. Meanwhile, heat milk, butter, salt, and pepper in small saucepan over medium-low heat, whisking until smooth, about 3 minutes; cover and keep warm.

3. Carefully pour contents of Dutch oven into colander, drain potatoes well, then return potatoes to pot. Cook over low heat, stirring constantly, until potatoes are thoroughly dried, about 1 minute.

4. Using stand mixer fitted with whisk, whip half of potatoes into small pieces on low speed, about 30 seconds. Add half of milk mixture in steady stream until incorporated. Increase speed to high and whip until potatoes are light and fluffy and no lumps remain, about 2 minutes, scraping down bowl as needed. Transfer to large, warm serving bowl and cover to keep warm. Repeat with remaining potatoes and milk mixture. Serve. (Potatoes, covered, can be held at room temperature for up to 20 minutes.)

Cranberry Sauce with Pears and Ginger

WHY THIS RECIPE WORKS
Cooking the cranberries until they just begin to pop gives this sauce appealing whole-fruit texture, a far cry from the homogeneous, jellylike cranberry log that comes from a can. The sweetness of the pears balances the tartness of the cranberries, and fresh ginger adds a warm, spicy kick. Though the sauce is quite loose while hot, it thickens as it cools, achieving the perfect consistency at room temperature.

If you've got frozen cranberries, you don't need to defrost them before using; just pick through them and add about 2 minutes to the simmering time.

I   cup sugar
¾   cup water
I   tablespoon grated fresh ginger
¼   teaspoon ground cinnamon
¼   teaspoon salt
2   pears, peeled, cored, and cut into ½-inch chunks
I   (12-ounce) bag cranberries, picked over

Bring sugar, water, ginger, cinnamon, and salt to boil in large saucepan over high heat, stirring occasionally to dissolve sugar. Stir in pears and cranberries. Return to boil, then reduce to simmer and cook until slightly thickened, about two-thirds of berries have popped open, and pears are soft, about 5 minutes. Transfer to serving bowl and refrigerate until thickened, about 1 hour. Serve. (Sauce can be refrigerated for up to 3 days; bring to room temperature before serving. Makes 2¼ cups.)

Herbed Bread Stuffing

Be sure to use fresh bread for this recipe and do not cut off the crusts. We used one very large baking dish for this recipe (measuring about 4 quarts), but you can portion the stuffing into two smaller dishes if preferred.

3	pounds hearty white sandwich bread, cut into ¾-inch cubes
12	tablespoons unsalted butter
4	celery ribs, chopped fine
2	onions, chopped fine
½	cup minced fresh parsley
3	tablespoons minced fresh sage or 2 teaspoons dried
3	tablespoons minced fresh thyme or 2 teaspoons dried
5	cups low-sodium chicken broth
4	large eggs, lightly beaten
2	teaspoons salt
2	teaspoons pepper

1. Adjust oven racks to upper-middle and lower-middle positions and heat oven to 300 degrees. Spread bread out over 2 rimmed baking sheets and bake, stirring occasionally, until bread is dry, about 1 hour. Let bread cool completely, about 15 minutes.

2. Melt butter in 12-inch nonstick skillet over medium-high heat. Add celery and onions and cook until softened, about 10 minutes. Stir in parsley, sage, and thyme and cook until fragrant, about 1 minute. Transfer to very large bowl.

3. Add cooled bread, broth, eggs, salt, and pepper and toss to combine. Spread mixture evenly into greased 15 by 10-inch baking dish. (Stuffing can be refrigerated for up to 2 days.)

4. As soon as turkey is removed from oven, adjust oven rack to middle position and increase oven temperature to 425 degrees. Cover dish tightly with aluminum foil and bake for 25 minutes. Remove foil and continue to bake until top is golden, 20 to 30 minutes longer. Serve.

WHY THIS RECIPE WORKS
This traditional bread stuffing delivers big flavor without a slew of fussy ingredients. A simple mixture of parsley, sage, and thyme works with an aromatic blend of onions and celery for a stuffing that can stand up to the gravy. Chicken broth, rather than milk or cream, brings a clean taste to moisten the stuffing without overwhelming the herb flavors. Covering the stuffing with foil during cooking steams it, mimicking the moist cooking conditions inside a turkey. For a crisp crust and toasty flavor, we remove the foil for the last 20 minutes of baking.

Buttery Peas with Shallots and Thyme

To make this last-minute side dish a real breeze, prep and measure all the ingredients an hour or two in advance (keep the peas frozen).

4	tablespoons unsalted butter
2	shallots, minced
2	teaspoons minced fresh thyme
2	garlic cloves, minced
1	tablespoon sugar
	Salt and pepper
2	pounds frozen peas (do not thaw)

Melt butter in 12-inch nonstick skillet over medium-high heat. Add shallots, thyme, garlic, sugar, and ½ teaspoon salt and cook until softened, about 2 minutes. Stir in peas and cook, stirring often, until thawed and heated through, 5 to 10 minutes. Season with salt and pepper to taste and serve.

WHY THIS RECIPE WORKS
Since most of the recipes in this menu require the oven, it's nice to have a vegetable dish that can be made on the stovetop in just minutes. In the test kitchen, we have come to depend on frozen peas for their convenience and bright flavor.

Deep-Dish Apple Pie

✔ **WHY THIS RECIPE WORKS**
When raw apples are used in a pie, they shrink to almost nothing, leaving a huge gap between the top crust and filling. Precooking the apples eliminates the shrinking problem and actually helps the apples hold their shape once baked in the pie. Cooling the apples before putting them in the pie crust is essential so that the butter in the crust doesn't melt immediately. Finally, we drain almost all of the juice from the apples (reserving just ¼ cup) to ensure a perfectly juicy and moist, but not soupy, apple pie.

Freezing the butter for 10 to 15 minutes is crucial to the flaky texture of this all-butter crust. If preparing the dough in a very warm kitchen, refrigerate all of the ingredients before making the dough.

PIE DOUGH

⅓ cup ice water, plus extra as needed
3 tablespoons sour cream
2½ cups (12½ ounces) all-purpose flour
1 tablespoon sugar
1 teaspoon salt
16 tablespoons unsalted butter, cut into ¼-inch pieces and frozen for 10 to 15 minutes

FILLING

2½ pounds Granny Smith, Empire, or Cortland apples, peeled, cored, and sliced ¼ inch thick
2½ pounds Golden Delicious, Jonagold, or Braeburn apples, peeled, cored, and sliced ¼ inch thick
½ cup (3½ ounces) plus 1 tablespoon granulated sugar
¼ cup packed (1¾ ounces) light brown sugar
½ teaspoon grated lemon zest plus 2 teaspoons juice
¼ teaspoon salt
⅛ teaspoon ground cinnamon
1 egg white, lightly beaten

1. FOR THE PIE DOUGH: Whisk ice water and sour cream together in bowl. Process flour, sugar, and salt together in food processor until combined. Scatter butter pieces over top and pulse mixture until butter is size of large peas, about 10 pulses. Pour half of sour cream mixture over top and pulse to incorporate, about 3 pulses. Repeat with remaining sour cream mixture.

2. Pinch dough with your fingers; if dough feels dry and does not hold together, sprinkle 1 to 2 tablespoons more ice water over top and pulse until dough forms large clumps and no dry flour remains, 3 to 5 pulses. Divide dough into 2 even pieces.

Place each piece of dough on sheet of plastic wrap and flatten into 4-inch disk. Wrap each disk tightly in plastic and refrigerate for at least 1 hour and up to 2 days.

3. Let chilled dough soften slightly at room temperature, about 10 minutes. Roll 1 piece of dough out to 12-inch circle on lightly floured counter. Fit it into 9-inch pie plate, letting excess dough hang over edge; cover with plastic and refrigerate for 30 minutes. Roll second piece of dough into 12-inch circle on lightly floured counter, then transfer to parchment paper–lined baking sheet; cover with plastic and refrigerate for at least 30 minutes and up to 4 hours.

4. FOR THE FILLING: Toss apples, ½ cup granulated sugar, brown sugar, lemon zest, salt, and cinnamon together in large bowl. Transfer apples to Dutch oven, cover, and cook over medium heat, stirring frequently, until apples are tender when poked with fork but still hold their shape, 15 to 20 minutes. Transfer apples and any accumulated juice to rimmed baking sheet and let cool to room temperature, about 30 minutes.

5. Adjust oven rack to lowest position, place aluminum foil–lined rimmed baking sheet on rack, and heat oven to 425 degrees. Drain cooled apples thoroughly in colander set over bowl, reserving ¼ cup of juice. Stir lemon juice into reserved juice.

6. Spread apples into dough-lined pie plate, mounding them slightly in middle. Drizzle with lemon juice mixture. Loosely roll second piece of dough around rolling pin and gently unroll it over pie. Trim, fold, and crimp edges. (Pie can be frozen until firm, about 3 hours, then wrapped thoroughly in plastic then foil, and frozen for up to 2 weeks; remove from freezer and continue as directed, adding 5 minutes to both baking times.)

7. Using paring knife, poke four 2-inch-long vent holes in top crust. Brush crust with egg white and sprinkle with remaining 1 tablespoon granulated sugar. Place pie on heated baking sheet and bake until crust is golden, about 25 minutes. Reduce oven temperature to 375 degrees, rotate baking sheet, and continue to bake until juices are bubbling and crust is deep golden brown, 25 to 30 minutes longer.

8. Let pie cool on wire rack until filling has set, about 2 hours; serve slightly warm or at room temperature. (Pie can be stored at room temperature for up to 1 day; reheat in a 300-degree oven for 15 minutes before serving.)

MAKING AN APPLE PIE

After piling the apples inside the dough-lined pie plate, loosely roll the second piece of dough around the rolling pin and gently unroll it over the top. Use scissors to trim the overhanging edges of the top and bottom crusts to about ½ inch. For a neat pie edge that stays sealed during baking, fold and press the top and bottom edges of dough together. The folded edge should be flush with the lip of the pie plate. Use your fingers to crimp the folded edge of dough.

Classic Pecan Pie

The crust must still be warm when the filling is added. Serve with vanilla ice cream or lightly sweetened whipped cream.

PIE DOUGH
1¼	cups (6¼ ounces) all-purpose flour
1	tablespoon sugar
½	teaspoon salt
3	tablespoons vegetable shortening, cut into ½-inch pieces and chilled
5	tablespoons unsalted butter, cut into ¼-inch pieces and chilled
4–6	tablespoons ice water

FILLING
6	tablespoons unsalted butter, cut into 6 pieces
1	cup packed (7 ounces) dark brown sugar
½	teaspoon salt
3	large eggs
¾	cup light corn syrup
1	tablespoon vanilla extract
2	cups (8 ounces) pecans, toasted (see page 29) and chopped coarse

1. FOR THE PIE DOUGH: Pulse flour, sugar, and salt together in food processor until combined, about 5 pulses. Scatter shortening over top and process until mixture resembles coarse cornmeal, about 10 seconds. Scatter butter pieces over top and pulse mixture until it resembles coarse crumbs, about 10 pulses. Transfer mixture to medium bowl.

✓ WHY THIS RECIPE WORKS
The biggest problem with pecan pie is that the filling is usually overly sweet and bland. It can also often suffer from a soggy crust. We tackled these problems by reducing the amount of sugar, and partially baking the crust, which helped keep it crisp. We also recommend simulating a double boiler when you're melting the butter and making the filling because it's an easy way to maintain gentle heat, which helps ensure that the filling doesn't curdle and ruin the texture of the pie.

2. Sprinkle 4 tablespoons ice water over mixture. Stir and press dough together, using stiff rubber spatula, until dough sticks together. If dough does not come together, stir in remaining water, 1 tablespoon at a time, until it does. Turn dough onto sheet of plastic wrap and flatten into 4-inch disk. Wrap dough tightly in plastic and refrigerate for at least 1 hour and up to 2 days.

3. Let chilled dough soften slightly at room temperature, about 10 minutes. Roll dough out to 12-inch circle on lightly floured counter. Fit dough into 9-inch pie plate, then trim, fold, and crimp edges. Cover with plastic and freeze for at least 30 minutes and up to 4 hours.

4. Adjust oven rack to middle position and heat oven to 375 degrees. Press double layer of aluminum foil into pie shell and over edges of pan, then fill with pie weights. Bake until crust looks dry and is light in color, 25 to 30 minutes. Transfer pie plate to wire rack and remove weights and foil. Adjust oven rack to lower-middle position and reduce oven temperature to 275 degrees. (Crust must still be warm when filling is added.)

5. FOR THE FILLING: Melt butter in heatproof bowl set in skillet of water maintained at just below simmer. Remove bowl from skillet and stir in sugar and salt until butter is absorbed. Whisk in eggs, then corn syrup and vanilla until smooth. Return bowl to hot water and stir until mixture is shiny, hot to touch, and registers 130 degrees. Off heat, stir in pecans.

6. Pour pecan mixture into warm pie crust. Bake pie until filling looks set but yields like Jell-O when gently pressed with back of spoon, 50 to 60 minutes. Let pie cool until filling has firmed up, about 2 hours. Serve. (Pie can be covered and refrigerated for up to 1 day. Bring to room temperature, or reheat in a 300-degree oven for 15 minutes, before serving.)

MAKING A SINGLE-CRUST PIE

Use scissors to trim the overhanging dough about ½ inch beyond the lip of the pie plate. Fold edge of dough under so that it is even with the lip of the plate. Use the index finger of 1 hand and the thumb and index finger of the other to create an attractive, fluted edge.

CONVERSIONS
& EQUIVALENCIES

Some say cooking is a science and an art. We would say that geography has a hand in it, too. Flour milled in the United Kingdom and elsewhere will feel and taste different from flour milled in the United States. So, while we cannot promise that the loaf of bread you bake in Canada or England will taste the same as a loaf baked in the States, we can offer guidelines for converting weights and measures. We also recommend that you rely on your instincts when making our recipes. Refer to the visual cues provided. If the bread dough hasn't "come together in a ball," as described, you may need to add more flour—even if the recipe doesn't tell you so. You be the judge.

The recipes in this book were developed using standard U.S. measures following U.S. government guidelines. The charts below offer equivalents for U.S., metric, and Imperial (U.K.) measures. All conversions are approximate and have been rounded up or down to the nearest whole number. For example:

1 teaspoon = 4.929 milliliters, rounded up to 5 milliliters
1 ounce = 28.349 grams, rounded down to 28 grams

VOLUME CONVERSIONS

U.S.	METRIC
1 teaspoon	5 milliliters
2 teaspoons	10 milliliters
1 tablespoon	15 milliliters
2 tablespoons	30 milliliters
¼ cup	59 milliliters
⅓ cup	79 milliliters
½ cup	118 milliliters
¾ cup	177 milliliters
1 cup	237 milliliters
1¼ cups	296 milliliters
1½ cups	355 milliliters
2 cups	473 milliliters
2½ cups	592 milliliters
3 cups	710 milliliters
4 cups (1 quart)	0.946 liter
1.06 quarts	1 liter
4 quarts (1 gallon)	3.8 liters

WEIGHT CONVERSIONS

OUNCES	GRAMS
½	14
¾	21
1	28
1½	43
2	57
2½	71
3	85
3½	99
4	113
4½	128
5	142
6	170
7	198
8	227
9	255
10	283
12	340
16 (1 pound)	454

CONVERSIONS FOR INGREDIENTS COMMONLY USED IN BAKING

Baking is an exacting science. Because measuring by weight is far more accurate than measuring by volume, and thus more likely to achieve reliable results, in our recipes we provide ounce measures in addition to cup measures for many ingredients. Refer to the chart below to convert these measures into grams.

INGREDIENT	OUNCES	GRAMS
Flour		
1 cup all-purpose flour *	5	142
1 cup cake flour	4	113
1 cup whole wheat flour	5½	156
Sugar		
1 cup granulated (white) sugar	7	198
1 cup packed brown sugar (light or dark)	7	198
1 cup confectioners' sugar	4	113
Cocoa Powder		
1 cup cocoa powder	3	85
Butter †		
4 tablespoons (½ stick, or ¼ cup)	2	57
8 tablespoons (1 stick, or ½ cup)	4	113
16 tablespoons (2 sticks, or 1 cup)	8	227

* U.S. all-purpose flour, the most frequently used flour in this book, does not contain leaveners, as some European flours do. These leavened flours are called self-rising or self-raising. If you are using self-rising flour, take this into consideration before adding leavening to a recipe.

† In the United States, butter is sold both salted and unsalted. We generally recommend unsalted butter. If you are using salted butter, take this into consideration before adding salt to a recipe.

OVEN TEMPERATURES

FAHRENHEIT	CELSIUS	GAS MARK (IMPERIAL)
225	105	¼
250	120	½
275	130	1
300	150	2
325	165	3
350	180	4
375	190	5
400	200	6
425	220	7
450	230	8
475	245	9

CONVERTING TEMPERATURES FROM AN INSTANT-READ THERMOMETER

We include doneness temperatures in many of our recipes, such as those for poultry, meat, and bread. We recommend an instant-read thermometer for the job. Refer to the table above to convert Fahrenheit degrees to Celsius. Or, for temperatures not represented in the chart, use this simple formula:

Subtract 32 degrees from the Fahrenheit reading, then divide the result by 1.8 to find the Celsius reading.

EXAMPLE:

"Roast until chicken thighs register 175 degrees." To convert:

$$175°\,F \; - \; 32 \; = \; 143°$$
$$143° \; \div \; 1.8 \; = \; 79.44°C, \text{ rounded down to } 79°C$$

INDEX

O

Oats
Apple Crisp, *178*, 179
Oatmeal Fudge Bars, 274, *275*
Raspberry Streusel Tart, 173

Olive(s)
and Baby Mozzarella, Marinated, 140
Beef Stew Provençal, *258*, *259–60*
Caper, and Spicy Garlic Pizza Topping, 153
Chicken Tagine, *264*, 265–66
Easy Mini Chicken Empanadas, 102–3
and Feta, Cherry Tomato Salad with, 284
Green, and Feta, Marinated, *60, 63*
Hearty Vegetable Lasagna, *252*, 253–54
Italian-Style Salad with Fennel and Artichokes, 147
Roasted Cherry Tomatoes, Capers, and Pine Nuts, Spaghetti with, *80, 81*
Sun-Dried Tomato Tapenade with Farmer's Cheese, 15
Tapenade, Crispy Polenta Squares with, 196–97
Tomato, and Basil Skewers, 254

One-Pot Bolognese, *206, 207*

Onion(s)
Caramelized, Blue Cheese, and Prosciutto Tart, 212
Caramelized, Jam, Goat Cheese with, 50
Caramelized, Tart, Rustic, with Goat Cheese, 23, *23*
Carbonnade, *238*, 239–40
chopping finely, 9

Orange(s)
Blood, and Radishes, Spinach Salad with, 173
Citrus Salad with Bitter Greens, 154
cutting, for salad, 127
–Dark Chocolate Mousse, *236*, 237
making strips of zest from, 28
Moroccan Carrot Salad, 127
Sangría, 76
-Sesame Vinaigrette, 17
Vinaigrette, Bibb and Radicchio Salad with, 268

Orzo with Lemon, Basil, and Feta, 109

Oven-Poached Salmon with Lemon-Dill Sauce, *288*, 289–90
Oven-Roasted Salmon Fillets with Almond Vinaigrette, *20*, 21–22
Oven thermometers, ratings of, 7

Oysters
on the Half Shell with Ginger Mignonette Sauce, 311
shucking, 311

P

Paella, *244*, 245–46
Palmiers, Ham and Cheese, 172, *172*
Panini Bites, Cheddar and Apple, 203, *203*
Panna Cotta, Vanilla Bean, with Strawberry Coulis, *34*, 35
Pan-Roasted Halibut with Chermoula, *90*, 91

Parmesan
and Artichoke Hearts, Bruschetta with, 32
Caesar Salad, 256
and Fennel, Farro with, 213
Ham and Cheese Palmiers, 172, *172*
Hearty Vegetable Lasagna, *252*, 253–54
Homemade Cheese Straws, *87, 88*
Pesto Pasta Salad, *282*, 285
Polenta, Creamy, 183
Potato and Fennel Gratin, 51, *51*
Shaved, Arugula and Fennel Salad with, 140
Shaved, Zucchini Ribbons with, 134
shaving slices of, 32
Spinach Salad with Sherry Vinaigrette, 63
Thin-Crust Pizzas, *150*, 151–52
Tomato and Mozzarella Tart, 132, *133*
Vinaigrette, 17
and Walnut–Stuffed Dates, 176
White Bean Gratin, 228–29

Parsley
Boneless Leg of Lamb with Garlic-Herb Crumb Crust, *294*, 295–96
Fresh Mint Relish, 296
Roast Beef Tenderloin with Persillade Relish, *48, 49*
Salsa Verde, 108, *108*

Pasta
Hearty Vegetable Lasagna, *252*, 253–54
Macaroni Salad with Cheddar and Chipotle, 276, 279
One-Pot Bolognese, *206*, 207
Orzo with Lemon, Basil, and Feta, 109
Salad, Pesto, *282*, 285
with Sautéed Wild Mushrooms, *194*, 195
Spaghetti and Meatballs, *144*, 145–46
Spaghetti with Roasted Cherry Tomatoes, Olives, Capers, and Pine Nuts, *80, 81*
Spring Vegetable, *30*, 31–32
see also Couscous; Noodles

Pâté
Chicken Liver, 159
Easy Mushroom, 222

Peach
Shortcakes, 98, *99*
Squares, Easy, *286*, 287

Pear(s)
Crumble, Autumn, 165
and Fennel, Romaine Salad with, 159
and Ginger, Cranberry Sauce with, 320
and Ginger Turnovers, *214*, 215
Skillet-Caramelized, with Blue Cheese, 228

Peas
Buttery, with Shallots and Thyme, 321
Indian-Style Vegetable Curry, *166*, 167
Sautéed Buttery, 16
Spring Vegetable Pasta, *30*, 31–32

Pecan(s)
Apple Crisp, *178*, 179
Butter-Pecan Ice Cream with Maple and Bourbon, 17
Dates Stuffed with Prosciutto and Nuts, 297, *297*
Grapes, Fennel, and Gorgonzola, Arugula Salad with, 183
Pie, Classic, 323–25, *324*
and Radishes, Baked Goat Cheese Salad with, 33, *33*

Pepper(s)
Asparagus and Spinach Salad, 298
Black Bean Chili, 69, *69*
Edamame Succotash with Jalapeños and Cilantro, 96–97
